NEW SHANGHAI

The Rocky Rebirth of China's Legendary City

NEW SHANGHAI

The Rocky Rebirth of China's Legendary City

PAMELA YATSKO

JOHN WILEY & SONS, INC

New York • Chichester • Weinheim • Brisbane • Singapore • Toronto

Other Wiley Editorial Offices

John Wiley & Sons, Inc., 605 Third Avenue, New York, NY 10158-0012, USA
John Wiley & Sons Ltd, Baffins Lane, Chichester, West Sussex PO19 1UD, England
John Wiley & Sons (Canada) Ltd, 22 Worcester Road, Rexdale, Ontario M9W 1L1, Canada
John Wiley & Sons Australia Ltd, 33 Park Road (PO Box 1226), Milton, Queensland 4064, Australia
Wiley-VCH, Pappelallee 3, 69469 Weinheim, Germany

Library of Congress Cataloging-in-Publication Data
ISBN 0-471-47915-2 (paperback)
ISBN 0-471-84352-0 (cased)

Typeset in 11/13 points, Bembo by Cepha Imaging Pvt Ltd, India
Printed in Singapore by Saik Wah Press Pte Ltd
10 9 8 7 6 5 4 3 2 1

Contents

Acknowledgements

I could not have written *New Shanghai* without the help of many people, foremost of whom are the Chinese citizens and foreign professionals in China who shared with me over the course of the last six years their stories, views, and insights on Shanghai. I'm particularly indebted to those friends and acquaintances who went out of their way to introduce me to people who either enlightened my thinking about Shanghai and China or provided a perfect example of an important trend. Juliet Chang, Kika, Kim Wu and Virginia Moore stand tall among them.

I'm also grateful to the *Far Eastern Economic Review*—and in particular Gorden Crovitz and Nayan Chanda—for giving me the opportunity to report on Shanghai at a fascinating time in Chinese history. I did not go to Shanghai thinking that I would write a book. But because of the in-depth reporting that the *Review* expects from its correspondents and the range of topics the magazine covers, I found that I had unearthed a trove of rich material by the time I moved down to Hong Kong in mid-1998. As important, I had a story that needed to be told. And thanks to the news assistants whom I was able to hire to help me—Hui Yi, Kim Wu, and Yan Zhihua,—I did not miss the story even when my Mandarin skills proved insufficient.

I'd also like to thank friends and family who provided encouragement and advice during the project's stop-and-go embryonic stage. Diana Pawlik's contribution—a warm room and conversation after a busy day of interviews in Shanghai—was a godsend, as was Mary Child's knowledge of the publishing industry. Heartfelt thanks also go to Lynne Curry and Mike Chenoy for mentioning the project to publisher Nick Wallwork at John Wiley & Sons. Nick recognized the need for this book, for which I am most grateful.

A number of people were kind enough to take time out of their busy schedules to read chapters and make detailed comments: I tip my hat in particular to Melissa Mowbray D'Arbela, Willie Brent, Norman Givant, Charles Tan and Grethchen Worth. I also salute all those friends and acquaintances who endured dinners that turned into searches for the perfect book title and helped in *New Shanghai*'s marketing.

But the person whom I thank most of all is Brewer Stone, my husband. From my first kernel of ambition to write this book to poring over drafts, Brewer generously offered his knowledge and time despite his many other commitments. His encouragement, advice, humor, and love helped me through long days and tense moments. His support for this project and for me never wavered. For these reasons, I dedicate *New Shanghai* to him.

1

Introduction:
The Allure of Shanghai

What makes one fall in love with a particular city? It's understandable if the object of desire is scenically breathtaking, like Hong Kong, or overflowing with magnificent art works and architecture, like Paris. When the city is none of those things, the allure is more difficult to explain. Before I left the United States in 1994 to take up a position as Shanghai Bureau Chief for the *Far Eastern Economic Review*, I recall telling friends how I had long dreamed about living in Shanghai. Inevitably their chin would sink into their neck, their nose would crinkle up on one side, and they would ask: "Why?" Although they might have some notion of Shanghai in its legendary 1920s heyday, their incredulity was based mostly on vague impressions of China as a poor country and of students being run over by government tanks in Beijing in 1989. They obviously thought I was a little crazy to leave the tree-lined streets and modern comforts of Cambridge, Massachusetts in exchange for that. Well, maybe I was, but all I could tell them was that ever since I had first visited Shanghai in February of 1986, the city had fascinated me.

My recollections of that first weeklong visit to China's largest city are somewhat foggy, obscured by time and the dreary winter drizzle that hung stubbornly over Shanghai's low, interminable skyline. Slate-like sheets of water swirled down the Huangpu River, which my guidebook told me had turned Shanghai into a thriving port well before 1842—the year the British first expropriated large swathes of Shanghai territory from China's declining Manchu rulers. The grand neoclassical buildings along the waterfront, symbolizing the ensuing 100 years of foreign domination, had abandoned their white-washed patina for an egalitarian sootiness more in keeping with the ideology of their current Communist Party occupants. Even the city's residents had an ashen quality as they shuffled slowly past in dull unisex clothing.

My hotel, a dilapidated western architectural relic catering to penny-pinching foreign backpackers like myself, melted seamlessly into this somber skyline, making it barely distinguishable from a distance. The guidebook informed me that before the Chinese Communists kicked the foreigners out of Shanghai in 1949, the building was in fact the elegant Astor House Hotel, a stomping-ground for well-heeled Europeans. I later learned that the famed British ballerina Margot Fonteyn stayed there in 1928. In her autobiography, she wrote:

The Astor House Hotel was the land mark of the white man in the Far East, like Raffles Hotel in Singapore ... Our rooms were big, sparsely furnished with old-fashioned wardrobes and dressing tables and only a small rug or two on the cool stones ... The lobby was furnished with the heavy mahogany chairs and coffee tables of the period. The Chinese 'boys' who served teas and drinks wore white robes, black cotton trousers and black cloth shoes. And always had a fly swat to hand. The place was crowded with jovial Europeans talking loudly and calling 'Boy—Bring another round.'
Outside the busy streets were thronged with rickshaws...[1]

By the time I got to Shanghai in 1986 at the age of twenty-three, the streets were neither thronged with rickshaws nor busy. Cars were scarce, overcrowded buses clunked along, and the ringing of bicycle bells provided the most memorable sound. China had just started opening up to foreigners again after a 30 year hiatus and the few Europeans around town usually made sure not to call hotel waiters anything but "Comrade." As for the Astor House Hotel's spacious rooms, the renamed hotel rented me a cot in one that had been converted into a dorm room fitting probably 30 beds. Having just finished a year studying Mandarin and teaching English in Taiwan, I was backpacking for three weeks around the Chinese mainland and group rooms were the most I could afford. The clerk charged me roughly the equivalent of US$8 a night for the cot. While the price was miniscule by western standards, it was astronomical compared to those I had just encountered in China's southwestern Guangxi and Yunnan provinces.

Perhaps it was the squalor of the accommodation I unwittingly chose in those inland areas, but that dorm room in decaying Shanghai, with its high ceilings, western-style fixtures, and higher price tag, seemed like a palace. I had finally returned to civilization—even if only relatively.

The famous waterfront Bund, where foreign banks had left their magnificent cement signature a century earlier, might have been run-down, but it somehow made me, as an American from the northeastern United States, feel at home. So did the windy tree-lined streets of the former French Concession with their decrepit mansions—so what if eight families' worth of pink and orange long underwear hung to dry from their windows! Then there were the real finds, like elephant-ear cookies—the recipe inherited, I assumed, from a long-defunct French or Russian bakery. It was impossible for me, like most westerners, not to walk past the dilapidated shops selling shoddy goods on the former Avenue Joffre (now Huaihai Road) and fantasize about pre-Revolutionary Shanghai ... Old Shanghai ... the Paris of the East ... the Whore of the Orient ... the Queen of the Pacific. I closed my eyes and tried to picture the Shanghai that Belgian cartoonist Herge so vividly depicted in the *Blue Lotus*. In that story, written in 1946, the young journalist Tintin races through Shanghai's colorful streets, dodging bullets and sneaking into opium dens, to save his new Chinese friends from evil Japanese invaders and corrupt western businessmen.[2] With such a backdrop framing my sub-conscious, I imagined gangsters, singsong girls, and socialites puffing away on flute-like opium pipes. I conjured up images of bespectacled intellectuals and disheveled artists finding refuge from vicious warlords fighting in China's vast interior. And I envisioned powerful foreign *taipans* (big bosses) making outrageous fortunes in the then-commercial and financial capital of the Far East. Images of the grinding poverty, misery, and bigotry endured by the vast majority of the city's Chinese residents did not enter my daydream. All I could think of was what a lively place Shanghai must have been compared with 1986, when getting a meal in a restaurant past 6:30 in the evening was impossible. Shanghai's history as one of the world's greatest cities cloaked it in a romantic aura, which made the reality of its decay in the 1980s all the more poignant.

Then too, despite the gray overlay of 35 years of communism, the exotic Chineseness of Shanghai also allured me. I loved watching white wisps of vapor rise from stacks of bamboo steamers filled with *xiaolongbao* (or little dragon balls, a local specialty). I couldn't get enough of the gray-haired, toothless men sitting on tiny stools along the narrow, disorganized streets of the old Chinese City; or the children, who were so bundled up in layers of clothing that they waddled rather than walked. To me, paradise was whiling away an hour in the five-sided Wuxingting teahouse in the Yuyuan bazaar, where I could envision officials in long flowing robes tugging on long beards and sipping small cups of *longjin* tea centuries ago.

I also found fascinating the egalitarian inefficiency of 1986 Shanghai. Making a long distance telephone call, for instance, meant waiting in line at a grimy post and telecommunications office. To buy a wool sweater, I had to beg a surly saleswoman behind a counter to show me it, a painstaking procedure that either required her to take it down from the wall or pull it from a pile. God forbid it did not fit since there was no telling if she would be willing to repeat the exercise. Paying was another ordeal. Laconic clerks shuffled me from one counter to next where they calculated sums on a wooden abacus, stamped receipts, collected cash, or handed me my purchase. *Meiyou* (I don't have it) was the usual reply to a request, debris littered the floor of the average restaurant, and ordering a meat dish meant picking through a plate of fat. In short, Shanghai had all that the rest of China had to offer but in a setting that made me feel more at ease than anywhere else I visited on the mainland. Beijing, my next stop, seemed less livable, mostly because of the monstrously large soviet-style buildings that lined its wide, dusty avenues. Whatever it was about Shanghai, I liked it.

These feelings were reaffirmed during my next visit to the city nearly three years later. Having caught the China bug during my first China adventure, I had returned to the United States to pursue a master's degree in international relations specializing in China studies. I then decided that the best way to get a job working with China was to first have some experience living there. Based in Nanjing for five months in late 1988 as a post graduate student, I desperately looked forward to weekend escapes to civilization, which for me was Shanghai. In reality, the city still moved slowly in comparison to big cities in the West. But Shanghai with its old western architecture and big city feel had infinitely more spark than sleepy Nanjing, which was my point of comparison. Shanghai by that time had started attracting foreign investment, which encouraged foreign developers to build a few high-rises and five-star hotels. The city's restaurants, though not plentiful, offered fresher and tastier dishes than during my earlier visit. Even better for a student who had been eating Chinese food day-in and -out for months, a little western-style, foreigners-only convenience store called Jessica in the old Jinjiang Hotel complex sold a foregone western delicacy: cheese. But most exciting was the sight of a colorful neon sign glowing from a small building not far from the new Hilton Hotel: It read "Jams." Shanghai in the late 1980s was still very dark in the evenings and this "Jams" in all its eerie luminescence was the first sign of commercialism that I had noticed. It turned out to be a tiny privately run bar patronized by foreigners, mostly guys, and adventurous young Chinese, mostly women. A dank interior and poor furnishings gave it a slightly seedy air, but that did not matter. What did matter was that it existed! If previously the decaying city evoked images of a bygone era, now it was showing slight signs of a pulse.

After I took a journalism job in Hong Kong in early 1989, I used to visit Shanghai now and again, either on reporting trips or just for fun. Hong Kong with its comfortable living standards, English proficiency, frenzied pace and over abundance of westerners did not really feel like China to me. I often found myself needing a China fix and a shot of Shanghai in particular. The city's heartbeat seemed to grow a little stronger each time I visited—and with it, my desire to live there. My chance to live in Shanghai finally came in 1994, when Brewer, my husband, was asked to open an American investment bank's Shanghai branch and the *Far Eastern Economic Review* asked me to open its first bureau in Shanghai. Why was everyone suddenly opening offices in Shanghai? Because China had started booming in the first half of the 1990s and no place more so than Shanghai. After the political unrest of 1989, diminutive paramount leader Deng Xiaoping tapped the city to reassert itself as an international financial, commercial, and manufacturing hub, loading it down with preferential policies. As the "dragon's head," Shanghai's job is to fuel the development of inland provinces along the Yangtze River and to be a showcase for China's reforms. With foreign business clamoring to get their hands on China's 1.2 billion consumers, Shanghai with its relatively skilled workforce, preferential policies, and 14 million-plus population became a highly attractive entry point. The success or failure of its reincarnation thus became an issue of international significance. However, foreign news coverage of Beijing's "anointed son" was sketchy since the Chinese government had only allowed foreign correspondents based in China to live in Beijing. For foreign investors to pump money into Shanghai, they needed more information about it, which is why the central government in the mid-1990s began allowing foreign news agencies to post correspondents there. I was lucky enough to be part of this first wave of reporters.

During those first few months of settling into Shanghai in late 1994 and early 1995, I must admit some unexpected pangs of dismay. I felt conflicted by those feelings—after all, wasn't Shanghai the place I had dreamed of living for almost 10 years? But Shanghai, during the four years I had been away seemed to have turned into a massive construction site, with all the dust, ear-piercing noise, and ugly views that go along with pile drivers and cement mixers. Visits to the suburbs and miles beyond only seemed to bring more factories and more construction. That's of course if you dared venture that far afield since traffic moved at a snail's pace. On top of bicycles and buses, the city's narrow streets also teamed with cabs and imported cars ferrying Chinese officials and foreign business people. Somewhere drivers in Shanghai, and all over China for that matter, had learned that beeping their horn at every car, bicycle and pedestrian in view would speed their way. Maybe it did, but the experience in the back seat frayed nerves. Our newly built "luxury" apartment, which cost a whopping US$6,800 a month to rent, was smaller than what we had left behind in the United States, had far less character, was far more expensive. Paint kept bubbling up from the walls and the heating units released so little warmth in the winter that I sometimes resorted to a hat and mittens inside the house. And to think, this was the best flat available in the price range afforded by our not insignificant housing allowance. I had to chuckle when I related some of these aspects of my new life to a friend in Cambridge, Massachusetts— a friend, mind you, who had heard all about my Shanghai dream—and she replied: "Be careful what you wish for. You might get it."

But those feelings of unease subsided after a few months as my memories of New England faded and my new life in Shanghai took shape. It helped that I stopped comparing Shanghai to Boston and instead focused on how much Shanghai was improving with each passing day. During my three-and-a half year tenure in the city, foreign investment poured in and sky-scrapers, factories, expressways, advertising agencies and stock brokerages sprang up. An entirely new city, called Pudong, emerged out of farmland on the east side of the Huangpu River to spearhead Shanghai's development. Making a phone call became as easy as anywhere in the developed world. The little foreigners-only convenience store in the Jinjiang Hotel gave way to western-style supermarkets, drug stores, and fashion outlets that both Chinese and foreigners could enter. Over the next few years I watched in wonder as Shanghai became a welter of modern Chinese restaurants, Mexican eateries, pizzerias, book cafés, internet cafés, espresso bars, night clubs, bowling alleys, go-cart tracks, amusement parks, department stores, designer shops, western movies and neon, neon, and more neon. Ok, maybe the activity did not yet approach New York, Hong Kong, or Old Shanghai in terms of variety and quality. But Shanghai in the 1990s had started offering things that it hadn't for half a century: choice, ease and opportunity.

Of course, people could not all partake of Shanghai's new fruits equally. Patrons stepping out of those swank new establishments were sometimes accosted by another new phenomenon of a resurgent Shanghai: smudge-faced child beggars. Expatriates, party officials, successful stock speculators, and Shanghai's upwardly-mobile urban professionals had emerged as Shanghai's new elite. For the many laid-off by faltering state-owned companies, living on fixed pensions from state employers, or fleeing the countryside to work on construction sites, the possibilities were far more limited. For them, the prospect of paying the equivalent of US$2.50 for a glass of mint-laced water at the swish Park 97 Café or nibbling on Shark's fin soup costing US$20 per bowl boggled the mind.

Besides offering more trappings of a modern city, Shanghai was an easier place to live in the 1990s because I could socialize openly with local residents. This had been difficult to do when I was a student in Nanjing in 1988. The Chinese I met at that time were usually wary of spending too much time with foreigners, particularly in their own homes, lest the Public Security Bureau question them. The government forbade the average Chinese to enter certain five-star hotels, where foreigners did much of their socializing. And even if they could fraternize freely, the gap of understanding between mainland Chinese and westerners was vast. On top of the differences between Chinese and, let's say, American culture, that might create misunderstandings in Taiwan, friendships on the mainland had to contend with 40 years of Chinese isolation from the west and antithetical political-economic systems. Hence in Nanjing, I found little common ground with the Chinese I met and, despite everyone's good intentions, interaction seemed more forced than fun. The Chinese called me *waiguoren*, which literally translated means "outside country person," and that's exactly how I felt: on the outside.

By the mid-1990s in Shanghai, there was more common ground. For one, Shanghainese, particularly well-educated young ones, had started working in new fields like advertising, computer software, and investment banking. No longer guaranteed assigned jobs out of university, they now faced the same difficult yet exhilarating choices as western graduates. This along with exposure to foreign movies, television, and other media gave them common interests and vocabulary. The fact that more Shanghainese who had gone overseas to study were now returning also helped. I set up a Mandarin conversation class with a "returned student" not long after I arrived and pretty soon my new tutor and I were laughing together, sharing confidences, or catching a movie and dinner outside of our language sessions. Between her experience in North America and mine in China, we could easily cross cultural gaps. And every now and them, I'd run into a person who had never lived abroad and yet somehow had become cosmopolitan.

It was also easier to get to know Chinese because the people I met no longer had to worry much about the political risks of fraternizing with foreigners. During my tenure in Shanghai, I invited roughly five Chinese women and five foreign women to participate in a "book club" that met once a month, usually at my house. Over cookies, tea, and mineral water, we discussed topics ranging from the cloning of Daisy the sheep to extra-marital affairs. I know the Shanghai authorities noticed our little group because one of our middle-aged Chinese participants, who was a Communist Party member, was once called in to report on our activities. After the incident she no longer felt comfortable attending the gathering regularly. Our freedom of congregation was obviously far from perfect. But apart from that one occasion, the authorities never interfered, even though by law all groups are supposed to register with them. I was able to interact with Shanghai society in a natural way— not just as a voyeur.

When I think about how far and from where Shanghai has come in such a short time, its achievements are truly impressive. It is surely one of the greatest examples of infrastructure development that the world has ever seen. And multinationals, which found it an agonizing place to do business in the 1980s, today find it a much better place to operate. After witnessing this dramatic metamorphosis, few visitors leave without expressing awe and contemplating the city's potential for usurping Hong Kong's role as Asia's pre-eminent business center. French President Jacques Chirac, for instance, told Shanghai Mayor Xu Kuangdi in May 1997 during his first visit to the city in six years: "Shanghai is one of the most vigorous cities in the world ... From the airport to the hotel,

I almost could not recognize any old things." Or take the observations of Tungku Ahmad Yahaya, vice chairman of Sime Darby Berhad, Malaysia's largest diversified conglomerate. I interviewed him during a visit of multinational company heads to the city in 1997. "I didn't realize Shanghai was so competitive!" he exclaimed in a crisp British accent, "From everything I've seen and heard here, Shanghai is not planning to come in second." A few years later, *Time* magazine labeled Shanghai a rival to New York City as the "Center of the World" in the 21st century.[3] China's largest city has clearly recaptured the world's imagination.

Its turbo-charged transformation mesmerized me as well. But the more reporting I did on Shanghai, the more I also came to realize that the visible changes that left visitors' jaws agape were often less a testament to the city's underlying reality than to its potential. Shanghai's new skyline is the most obvious case in point. It rose exponentially, but at the time of writing many of those new glass-curtained skyscrapers and high-priced villas stand half empty. The city's glitzy new department stores, unable to attract enough paying customers, are often unprofitable or barely break-even. Their outside tells a story of lightening-speed growth; their inside one of incompetent planning, poor market research, half-baked state enterprise reform, and overzealous investment.

The pace of Shanghai's inner progress does not match its outer renaissance in other striking ways. For instance, the president of the Shanghai Stock Exchange proclaimed in 1993 that "Shanghai will revive its central position in the Far East by 2010," and added that no other city in Asia could rival it as a financial hub.[4] The city then erected a state-of-the-art stock exchange building to symbolize its financial reemergence. Yet Shanghai today has far to go to become the New York of Asia financially. Its underdeveloped capital markets are largely ignored outside of China and are rife with speculation, government intervention, and scandal.

Besides reemerging as an international financial hub, Shanghai is determined to remain a manufacturing powerhouse. However, the city's indigenous consumer product companies, burdened by a highly interventionist municipal government, have been slow to adapt to the market economy and in many cases have lost market share to more aggressive domestic rivals and foreign multinationals. Despite Shanghai's reputation in the West as China's most entrepreneurial city, indigenous private and high-tech firms have not developed as well as in some other parts of the country.

Likewise Shanghai, which drove artistic innovation in China in the decades before 1949, has made little headway in reclaiming that standing. Although the municipal government built a stately performing arts center and modern museum to symbolize Shanghai's cultural rebirth, it still tightly controls the city's cultural pulse. Artists continue to find Shanghai a lonely city, enjoying more opportunity, creative freedom, and artistic ambience in Beijing, the country's political capital.

It also became clear that for all the palpable energy and adaptability of the Shanghainese, streaks of smugness and risk aversion lurk in the recesses of the city's persona, hindering its progress. And as much as Shanghai may want to move ahead faster, the central government keeps its pet city on a short leash. The popular Shanghai saying "when a pin drops in Beijing, Shanghai shudders" continues to resonate loudly. Important financial, business, and personnel decisions that affect the city's fate are still made in the nation's capital.

That Shanghai has a way to go to fulfill its dreams is understandable. After all, it only received Beijing's blessing to reassert its pre-1949 status at the end of the 1980s. Since then it has focused on building the infrastructure of a great metropolis. A great municipality, however, is more than glass and concrete, which is not always easy for Chinese officials schooled on communism, control, and state planning to understand. Shanghai at the dawn of the new millennium faces the daunting task of reviving a great city's soul.

Notes

[1] Margot Fonteyn, *Autobiography*, W.H. Allen, London, 1975. Excerpted from *Shanghai Electric and Lurid City*, Ed. Barbara Baker, Oxford University Press, Hong Kong, 1998.
[2] See Herge, *Le Lotus Bleu: Les Aventures de Tintin*, Casterman, 1946.
[3] *Time*, Dec. 31, 1999, p. 131.
[4] *Asia Inc.*, Dec. 1993, p. 40.

2

Building the New Shanghai

"Shanghai won't be a center just for China—that's too small.
It will be a leader in the world."

Jing Ying, the 34-year-old deputy director of the foreign affairs department at the Shanghai Foreign Economic & Trade Commission, made
that comment to me in 1996. A petite, energetic woman with short
black hair and an easy smile, she was not making an official policy
statement but instead asserting a personal conviction. Had I not heard
Shanghainese express similar sentiments many times before, I might have
been surprised at her brashness. After all, a look outside a window in
Shanghai in the mid-1990s usually revealed half-razed buildings, partially
erected skyscrapers, and deep construction pits. Shanghai was undoubtedly
on the move, but it had only seriously begun to renew itself at the start of
the 1990s.

The confidence that Shanghai residents have in their city's destiny
derives partly from history—a history that did much to shape their
personality through the 20th century. Apart from a depressed period in
the 1980s, Shanghai during the last 100 years has set the pace of change
in China, providing a model for the rest of the country to follow—
whether it be as a capitalist icon before the 1949 revolution or as a
state-planning paragon after the Chinese Communist Party took control.
So once China's central government in 1990 gave Shanghai the nod
to reemerge as an international financial, commercial, and trading
hub, many Shanghainese saw it just as a matter of time before their

city recovered its pre-1949 status. As long as Shanghai's special relationship with Beijing and its favorable policies continue, the reasoning goes, Shanghai will inevitably reclaim its rightful place as Asia's leading city.

What I learned in my job as Shanghai bureau chief for *The Far Eastern Economic Review*, however, leads me to believe that Shanghai's renaissance will not occur quite so easily. For sure, I am impressed with the city's progress in rebuilding its decrepit infrastructure, attracting foreign investors, raising living standards for many residents, and improving service in some quarters. But I have had to dig deeper into Shanghai's renewal—through the layers of chrome, glass, and newly painted concrete that coat much of the city. The sight on the inside is not always as well formed or as modern, exposing a city often stuck in control-oriented, authoritarian ways. Closer examination reveals Shanghai's fixation on building the hardware or physical infrastructure of an international economic hub, while undervaluing the importance of the necessary software, including a fair and effective legal system, access to accurate information, and market-oriented corporate incentives. Unfortunately, nurturing software in some cases takes more than time; it takes difficult reforms that reduce the Communist Party's power. Shanghai in this regard is not so different from other Chinese cities, but then again, other Chinese cities are not vying to be "a leader in the world."

At China's Fore

Ask a Shanghainese when in modern history his city was *not* China's economic pacesetter and he probably will scratch his head.

He definitely will not say the decades prior to the Chinese Communist Revolution in 1949, even though the city was not fully his own. Following the Opium War of 1840, Great Britain forced China's weak Qing Dynasty rulers to open to trade five ports along the country's coast. Shanghai, which was a flourishing market town and an active Chinese port at the time of the foreign assault,[1] was among the cities chosen. Its well-sheltered harbor and strategic location at the mouth of the mighty Yangtze River made it a key waterway into the Chinese interior. The British carved out a large chunk of Shanghai territory for their empire, demanding immunity for British residents from Chinese sovereignty and freedom to conduct affairs as they saw fit. Other foreign powers soon followed suit, with the French creating the French Concession and the British combining forces with the Americans to establish the International Settlement. The foreigners who landed on Shanghai's shores mostly came to make their fortunes, and in the process erected banks, factories, and roads, the likes of which China had never seen. To replicate their lives back home, they built villas, schools, racetracks, clubs, cabarets, and theaters, turning Shanghai into China's most cosmopolitan city.

Shanghai was the city of firsts for China: the first electric trams, the first stock market, the first night clubs, the first movie industry. It was also the city of superlatives, possessing the tallest buildings, the most banks, the cleverest entrepreneurs, the best products, the freest press, the fullest cultural life, the fiercest gangsters, and the grandest gambling dens. Its women, clad in body-hugging *qipao*, were the country's most stylish, and its prostitutes the most numerous. Shanghai grew into China's leading commercial, financial, industrial, and cultural center, thanks to its strategic location, the know-how of its occupiers, and the resourcefulness of its Chinese inhabitants, many of whom had migrated to Shanghai from the provinces. Local residents worked well with foreigners and adopted their ways, sometimes amassing huge fortunes for themselves in the process. To the world, Shanghai became known as the Paris of the East and the greatest city in Asia. To traditional Chinese in the interior, it was a den of iniquity bereft of Chinese virtues. To the Shanghainese and their more open-minded compatriots, it was the definition of Chinese modernity.

After the Chinese Communists marched into Shanghai and hoisted their flag over the whole of China in 1949, the city lost its status as a metropolis of international consequence. Foreigners left and the local elite fled, investing and remaking fortunes in Hong Kong, the United States, and elsewhere. Beijing appointed a string of politically powerful non-Shanghainese officials to Shanghai's top posts to whip the capitalist enclave into socialist shape. Shanghai's new Communist rulers closed markets and nationalized private companies, integrating the city into the country's new centrally planned economy. Cultural life dried up as Communist bureaucrats seized control over arts that might influence people's minds. They also rounded up prostitutes, forbade horse racing, and closed cabarets, relegating Old Shanghai's legendary decadence to history. Political movements aimed at eradicating any vestiges of the city's former bourgeois lifestyle and capitalistic ways cowed the city's population into submission.

But even if Shanghai no longer mattered internationally after the Communist revolution, it mattered to China. A Shanghainese could feel proud that his city, which boasted the country's mightiest industrial base, was powering China's drive toward Communism, and churning out the best-quality goods manufactured in the country. Known for their management and technical skills, hundreds of thousands of Shanghai residents were seconded to other parts of the country to help their less-advanced brethren build a socialist China. The competence, adaptability, and obedience that the Shanghainese had nurtured under foreign occupation served them well under their new Communist masters, helping to turn capitalist Shanghai into a model of state planning.

Certainly the most painful period after the Communists came to power was the Great Proletarian Cultural Revolution from 1966 to 1976. Young people were relocated to the countryside, factories stopped producing, formal education ceased, and youthful Red Guards terrorized alleged counterrevolutionaries, as Mao Zedong called on the masses to make revolution above all else. During the Cultural Revolution, Chairman Mao selected Shanghai as the birthplace of his revolution within a revolution. With the help of his wife, Jiang Qing, and her Shanghai-linked cohorts, he used Shanghai to launch political attacks against his rivals in the capital. But the battles between Red Guard factions usually were not as violent as in cities like Beijing, Wuhan, and Chengdu and the city's residents returned to work more quickly than in many other parts of the country. Qian Xiao, a Shanghainese teenager at the movement's outset, commented:

If you could live in Shanghai during the Cultural Revolution you were lucky. There wasn't a lot of fighting between Red Guard groups. When the central government told everyone in the country to both work and make revolution, Shanghai listened the best. A lot of places didn't listen. Life in Shanghai was relatively stable. There was still food and clothing in the shops. In other places, you couldn't find these things.

So just as Old Shanghai "saw itself in the front ranks of China's march into the modern age," Shanghai under Communism loomed large in the Chinese psyche as a guiding light. It stood for prosperity *(fuyu)*, wealth *(fanhua)*, fashion *(shimao)*, civilization *(wenming)*, modernity *(xiandai)*, and excellence *(youxiu)*. The Shanghainese basked in their superiority.

Wrote noted Chinese journalist-author Yang Dongping:

Anywhere in the country you found Shanghainese, they would strut about and put on airs. No matter where they were, you could hear them speaking Shanghainese in a loud voice as if no one else were around. People from other parts of China showed Shanghainese traditional respect, acted modestly around them, and were jealous of them.[2]

Then came the 1980s and Deng Xiaoping's market reforms.

Decade of Disrepair

Anyone aware of Chinese history would have expected Shanghai to lead China's march toward capitalism in the 1980s. But a Shanghainese would have to admit that during the first decade of reform, Shanghai lost its place at China's forefront. The swagger in the Shanghainese step became a little less sure.

By the mid-1980s, Shanghai resembled an overworked middle-aged woman who had lost her good looks—her deterioration underscored by the appearance of a number of fresh-faced rivals. A quick look at some statistics gives a sense of the city's relative decline. After 1949, Shanghai was a bastion of socialist industry, providing in 1980 one-eighth of China's total industrial output, one-quarter of its exports, and one-sixth of the central government's revenues—more than any other city or province.[3] Its industry grew at an 11.3% average annual clip during the 30 years following the Communist takeover.[4] During the 1980s, however, the city's industry pumped more slowly, and Shanghai, which had always placed first in China's national economic rankings, found other parts of the country surpassing it. Between 1982 and 1986, for instance, Shanghai's industrial growth averaged only 7.5%, compared to the 21% jump enjoyed by neighboring Zhejiang province. By 1991, it accounted for only one-fourteenth of China's total industrial output. In 1986, for the first time in 130 years, exports from Guangdong, whose provincial capital was previously known as Canton, exceeded Shanghai's.[5] Discerning Chinese consumers no longer coveted Shanghai brands, while the Shanghainese, once so proud of their "made in Shanghai" label, found themselves snatching up goods made overseas and in Guangdong. Things Cantonese became the rage among Shanghainese. Wen Hua, a 21-year-old sociology student at Shanghai's prestigious

Fudan University, whose white miniskirt and mod glasses pegged her as a budding fashion plate, commented to me in 1997: "In the 1980s Shanghai girls liked to marry Cantonese men. I liked to watch Cantonese singers on TV. I liked clothing made in Guangdong because Shanghai brands didn't offer much choice." Students at Fudan even signed up in droves for Cantonese language classes in hope of moving south after graduation. This was quite a comedown for the Shanghainese, who had always viewed themselves as more sophisticated, cultured, and clever than their southern brethren.

Shanghainese who fled the mainland in 1949 and returned to Shanghai in the 1980s were struck by how little the city had physically changed in the 30 years since their departure. For famous Taiwanese writer Bai Xianyong, returning to Shanghai in 1987 was like a walk into his past— even the ping pong table he had used as a child was still standing where he left it.[6] The time warp delighted foreign tourists, not to mention film crews looking for an authentic 1930s location. As long as they ignored the city's soot-streaked exteriors, they had before them an almost perfectly preserved city from the first half of the century. They could admire the curved lines of art-deco homes built by French architects in the 1930s, the waterfront Bund's European skyline, and the house-packed lanes that made up the old Chinese quarter.

But what was fascinating for tourists and film crews was dismal for local residents. Much of Shanghai's infrastructure—roads, housing, and sanitation—dated from before 1949, and new construction since then was woefully insufficient to service a population that had increased exponentially. Shanghainese, the supposedly most modern of Chinese people, enjoyed the undignified distinction of existing in some of the country's worst urban conditions. In 1979, they each lived in only 4.3 square meters of space on average and enjoyed less than half a square meter of greenery, roughly the size of a newspaper.[7] In 1986, more than 60% of Shanghai homes did not have toilets,[8] forcing residents to rely on traditional chamber pots. The city's narrow streets were clogged with buses and bicycles, causing traffic to flow at a snail's pace. Qian Xiao, the Shanghainese teenager during the Cultural Revolution, recounted how getting to work by bus every morning in the 1980s took her an hour-and-a-half, even though she only had to travel six kilometers. But worse than the plodding traffic were the crowds vying for space on public transportation. Although 18 times more people rode the city's buses at the end of the 1980s than in 1949, there were only four times more buses.[9] I remember from my student days in the 1980s watching residents jam themselves into those caterpillar-like vehicles only to receive an elbow or a foot in the stomach. I had to keep reminding myself the problem was not inherently rude people, but a system that provided too few resources.

During my years in Shanghai, very few Chinese friends ever invited me to their homes. I believe they were embarrassed. (After all, they did invite me to do other things.) However, I did enter quite a number of Shanghai dwellings while reporting, after which I better understood my friends' lack of reciprocation for their many visits to my own house. An acquaintance, who knew I was doing a story on housing reform, agreed in 1997 to take me to see her mother's place down a lane off of Yanan Road, a coveted location. There before me stood a large French-designed villa dating from before 1949. My friend, who went by the English name of Shirley, informed me that the villa had a garden reaching to the road when she was a child in the 1960s, but that it was torn up to make room for a factory and later an ugly apartment block. From the outside, old villas like these have a romantic allure. Despite their chipped paint, dusty exterior, and laundry-lined windowsills, it is possible to imagine a genteel life taking place inside. Upon stepping through the doorway, however, such illusions disappear. In this case, we squeezed our way past a row of bicycles parked in the foyer and made our way slowly up a dark stairway stacked haphazardly with grime-covered boxes. Wires without destination dangled dangerously from the ceiling. A gray-haired woman no more than five feet tall walked out of her room carrying a chamber pot brimming with the day's refuse. I asked Shirley how many people lived in the house. Twenty-four, she said, adding that the second floor originally housed a dining and living room, the third floor the bedrooms, and the fourth floor an attic—all for one family. It was hard to imagine given the squalor around me. Because most families in the villa only had a single room to their name, they had set up cooking stations in the hallways. Black grease dripped from the walls and ceiling around gas-burning stoves.

Once we entered her family's apartment, however, the scene brightened up. The space was spotless—albeit cramped to an American. In the living room, all of the furniture, including a crib, a table, a television, a bed, chairs, and a medicine chest, had been pushed against the walls to create more room. Still, by Shanghai standards their home was good-sized, totaling 38 square feet for four people, roughly half the size of a basketball court. Originally a bedroom with a bath, the family used wood paneling to divide it into a parlor and bedroom and turned half of the bathroom into a kitchen. Shirley, who held a senior position with an American multinational, gave her mother 20,000 yuan (US$2,410) to install the kitchen. I complimented her on the renovation, after which she replied proudly, "Many people would love to live in this place."

The constancy of Shanghai's appearance during the first 40 years of Communism meant that returning Shanghainese, like Bai Xianyang, the Taiwanese author, could easily find their way around. But instead of comforting, the effect was chilling. Lynn Pan, who wrote a number of books about Old Shanghai, fled to Hong Kong in the early 1950s and visited her hometown for the first time some 30 years later. Pan, an elegant, soft-spoken woman, had spent much of her life in Great Britain. Speaking to me of her feelings about Shanghai in the 1980s, she sighed:

I was depressed about Shanghai because Shanghai wasn't moving at all. Everywhere else was taking off but not Shanghai. Then there was all the breast-beating among the Shanghainese themselves. "Shanghainese have lost the touch. Shanghainese have become narrow-minded," they said. These are self-fulfilling prophecies and then you lose your confidence. I was worried about that self-questioning because Shanghainese are always terribly arrogant: "we're the best; better than everyone else." If you think you're good, you are good.

Indeed, it was much more than just the city's physical deterioration that alarmed observers. The Shanghainese seemed to have lost the spark that made their city arguably the world's most capitalistic before 1949. Commentators like journalist-author Yang Dongping upbraided the city for its leftist thinking, management backwardness, and lack of commercial spirit.[10] Thirty years of state planning and focus on manufacturing seemed to have left Shanghai managers bereft of their former entrepreneurial prowess and dependent on the state, prompting scholar Peter T.Y. Cheung to write, "Unlike businessmen from its main rival Guangdong who were noted for their commercial acumen, Shanghai's managers often first looked at the books and waited for policy guidance before doing anything, even in the 1980s."[11]

What had happened to Shanghai?

For one, the central government had been bleeding the city dry, or as the Chinese would say, "draining the pond to get the fish." Ever since 1949, Beijing had depended on Shanghai's industrial muscle to help finance poorer parts of the country. Of the hundreds of billions of yuan in revenues the city earned during the first 30 years of Communism,

Shanghai remitted most of it to Beijing for redistribution. The money allocated to Shanghai for basic construction under the state plan, however, accounted for a piddling 7.4% of the sum Shanghai sent up north.[12] Of that fraction, the city—like its counterparts all over China—spent the vast majority on manufacturing. It neglected items deemed nonproductive, like housing, culture, health, and education. This underinvestment turned Shanghai from a modern metropolis into an aged industrial town no longer able to lead the country.

Meanwhile, Shanghai's importance to Beijing's budget made Deng Xiaoping, the architect of China's economic reforms, reluctant to include the city in his first wave of market-oriented change. Uncertain whether his policies would succeed, he preferred to experiment with southern China, which could easily attract investment from nearby Hong Kong and was not a heavy industrial base. So when the central government in 1979 decided to set up four special economic zones offering new infrastructure, tax holidays, and other perks to foreign investors, it set them up along China's southeastern coast. It also allowed Guangdong to remit a far lower percentage of its revenues to national coffers than Shanghai.

Not that the central government completely ignored Shanghai. It could ill afford to, considering the importance of the city's contribution to its coffers. In 1984, the central government named Shanghai one of 14 cities open to foreign investment; in 1985, it opened the Yangtze River Delta to foreign investment; and in 1986, it allowed Shanghai to establish three small economic zones. But these were baby steps compared to the bold experiments taking place elsewhere.

So while much of southern China took off, Shanghai, the cash-poor bastion of state enterprise, foundered. Compared to non-state firms popping up elsewhere, Shanghai's government-owned enterprises reacted slowly to market changes and were overwhelmed by the cost of cradle-to-grave care for their larger workforces. Shanghai managers, who for decades had done little more than meet government-set production targets, had lost their entrepreneurial drive and know-how. At the same time, the government was also bleeding the city's small non-state sector, which lumbered under a heavier tax burden than other provinces along China's coast.[13]

There's also a political dimension to Shanghai's decline. After Mao's death in 1976, the Party, led by Mao's handpicked successor Hua Guofeng, immediately arrested Mao's wife and three of her

Shanghai-linked cohorts, delivering them to history as the notorious Gang of Four. It replaced the city's leaders with reliable bureaucrats who could be trusted to toe the new Party line. Shanghai spent the next few years purging its party and administration of "Gang of Four" supporters, leaving the city's economy adrift. Making matters worse, the city's new leaders owed their positions to Hua and traditional Communist orthodoxy. So when Deng Xiaoping started waving the banner of economic reform in 1979, they opposed his policies, making it even more unlikely that Deng would launch his experiments in Shanghai.[14]

Unfortunately, the city's political situation did not improve much after these leaders departed in 1980. Although supportive of Deng's reforms and intent on improving Shanghai's lot, the city's next set of bosses, unlike most of their predecessors since 1949, did not simultaneously hold positions in national decision-making bodies in Beijing or enjoy close connections with central government leaders. Shanghai consequently was poorly positioned in the first half of the 1980s to lobby Beijing for more favorable policies and experienced its most politically anonymous period since the founding of the People's Republic. Shanghai Mayor Wang Daohan pushed for the development of a 520-square-kilometer special economic zone in Pudong—a vast tract of farmland on the east side of the Huangpu River that Chinese leaders had talked about developing since the early twentieth century. Wang wanted to build a new city across from Shanghai's waterfront Bund that, like Shenzhen bordering Hong Kong, would not be burdened by 30 years of state planning, would give Shanghai industry room to expand, and would offer special privileges to foreign investors. However, he found no takers in Beijing.[15]

Shanghai's days as China's greatest city finally seemed to be over.

A Change in Fortune

The depths of Shanghai's decline in the 1980s made its resurgence in the 1990s all the more stunning.

Shanghai's star first showed signs of brightening in the mid-1980s. Starting with Jiang Zemin in 1985 and the Zhu Rongji in 1987, Beijing began transferring officials to Shanghai who were both well-educated technocrats and well-connected—giving Shanghai a voice again in the capital. Shanghai's new leaders used their clout to lobby for Pudong's development and persuade Beijing to let Shanghai retain a greater portion of its revenues and foreign exchange earnings. By 1988, Shanghai had finally negotiated a financial contract system similar to Guangdong's and Fujian's, which allowed it to keep all revenues above an agreed-upon amount.

Then came the student unrest of June 1989.

Ironically, the government's tragic shooting of unarmed students in Beijing on June 4, 1989, probably helped Shanghai's cause.[16] After the military's bloody suppression of pro-democracy demonstrators on Tiananman Square, apolitical Hong Kong suddenly looked political to China's nervous leaders. A million people took to the streets, attended mass rallies denouncing the "butchers of Beijing," and held candlelit vigils in Victoria Park to mourn lives lost. Hadn't Shanghai students hit the streets in huge numbers as well? Yes, they had, but the Shanghai government led by Party Secretary Jiang Zemin and new Mayor Zhu Rongji had kept them well under control. Instead of dispatching the police or military, like leaders did in Beijing, Zhu sent 100,000 workers from the city's state enterprises into the streets to calm the protests. Shanghai's students returned to their classes. In contrast, Hong Kong, which was a British colony until July 1997, could not be similarly restrained. Demonstrators grew more boisterous after the government's show of force in Beijing—an alarming prospect given that Deng had focused the country's reforms in areas just over Hong Kong's border.

Rejuvenating Shanghai, meanwhile, made good economic sense. Located at the mouth of the Yangtze River, Shanghai offered closer access than any other city to both inland provinces along the river and China's northern and southern coasts. It also boasted a strong human resource and technical base, arguably the best in the country. Deng subsequently decided to give the green light to long-neglected Shanghai. Visiting the city during the Chinese New Year in February 1990, he surprised Shanghai leaders by urging them to speed up work on the Pudong project and place the city once again at the forefront of China's economic development.[17] The central government then backed up Deng's words with a slew of preferential policies. Shortly after Deng's visit, Premier Li Peng officially launched the Pudong project in April 1990 and Shanghai Mayor Zhu Rongji announced 10 preferential policies for Shanghai and the zone, including permission to set up new service industries, establish a free trade zone, and attract foreign banks. Beijing also made Shanghai the site of one of China's two experimental stock exchanges, putting it on track to reclaim its crown as a financial hub.

Shanghai's ascendance coincided with Deng's tapping of Shanghai Party Secretary Jiang Zemin at the end of June 1989 to be his heir-apparent after Deng dismissed Premier Zhao Ziyang. Jiang was the first in a long line of Shanghai officials to take up top central government posts in the 1990s, including Zhu Rongji, who made the trip north in 1991, first as vice premier, then as premier in 1998. For Deng, bringing Jiang and Zhu into the inner sanctum had twin advantages. They were not tainted by strong relationships with Zhao, who took the side of the students during the Tiananmen debacle. (Zhao had close ties to Guangdong province.) Moreover, Jiang and Zhu were also technocrats with a track record of achievement. To strengthen their power bases in Beijing, they subsequently promoted a string of former Shanghai officials to national-level slots. During the 1990s, leaders with ties to Shanghai in Beijing came to outnumber those from any other single city or province in China. Although a posting in Shanghai had been a stepping stone for future central government leaders for most of the history of the People's Republic,[18] developments in the 1990s underscored that status and reaffirmed Shanghai's role at the forefront of China's economy.

After Deng promoted Jiang in 1989 and gave Pudong his blessing in 1990, Shanghai did not immediately take off. Why the delay? China's booming economy by the late 1980s was careening out of control, and to quell double-digit inflation, Beijing in 1988 instituted a tight credit policy that eventually smothered economic activity. Only after Deng launched the country's next economic boom in early 1992, inspired in part by the Soviet Union's collapse, did Shanghai's renaissance begin in earnest. For Deng, Shanghai and its Pudong project provided perfect symbols at home and abroad that China was forging ahead with reforms. Moreover, he saw Shanghai's revival as crucial to China's national development strategy. The reforms in Guangdong and Shenzhen in the 1980s were always experimental. There was nothing experimental about his intentions for Shanghai. During his 1992 southern China tour, he said:

Shanghai now entirely has the conditions [to develop] a bit more quickly. In the areas of talented personnel, technology, and administration, Shanghai has obvious superiority, which radiates over a wide area. Looking back, my one major mistake was not to include Shanghai when we set up four special economic zones. Otherwise, the situation of reform and opening to the outside in the Yangtze River Delta, the entire Yangtze River Valley, and even the entire nation would be different.[19]

Central government leaders subsequently put forth big plans for the city. Jiang Zemin told the 14th National Congress of the Chinese Communist Party in October 1992:

> We must take the development and opening of Pudong in Shanghai as the dragon head, advance another step to open cities on the banks of the Yangtze River and establish Shanghai as an international economic, financial, and trading center as soon as possible, in order to induce a new economic leap in the Yangtze River Delta and the entire Yangtze River Valley.[20]

The central government followed up its words of support for Shanghai with a number of deeds. Shortly before the Party's Fifth Central Committee Plenum in September 1995, for instance, it handed down 18 more "super-special" policies to speed up Pudong's development. These included allowing foreign banks that located in Pudong to conduct business in local currency; granting projects in Pudong the status of "priority national projects"; and allocating Pudong government loans of 700 million yuan (US$90 million) annually.[21] While the rest of the country was starting to feel the pinch of the central government's inflation-fighting, tight-money policies in 1995, Pudong continued its meteoric development, seemingly immune from the edict. Central authorities throughout the decade looked first to Pudong when they wanted to experiment with a new market reform, like allowing joint ventures in foreign trade, making Shanghai once again a pacesetter for China.

Although the central government has pegged Shanghai to become an international finance, trade, and services hub, it also has supported the city's desire to remain a manufacturing dynamo by channeling lucrative domestic and foreign-invested projects to the city. In 1998, central leaders awarded the city a US$1.26-billion investment with Germany's Krupp-Thyssen Stainless Steel after planting China's newest and most modern model steel mill, Bao Iron & Steel, in Shanghai in the 1980s. In the 1990s, Beijing boosted the city's telecommunications dreams by locating the country's first state-of-the-art semiconductor foundry, the US$1.2 billion Shanghai Huahong Microelectronics project, in Pudong. State-owned Huahong subsequently partnered up with NEC of Japan. Shanghai also dreams of becoming the Detroit of China and, toward that end, the central government bestowed on it two of its highly coveted automobile manufacturing joint ventures: one with Volkswagen of Germany in the 1980s and the other in 1997 with General Motors.

The situation led Jonathan Woetzel, a Shanghai-based principal at McKinsey & Co., to comment: "These deals are being negotiated in Beijing and Shanghai guys tag along for the ride."

The central authorities have also kept the city well-financed. The Bank of China, for instance, helped fund many of the city's big-ticket construction and investment projects, and in 1998 vowed to "give priority to Shanghai when deciding how to allocate its loans."[22] After all, Shanghai is the model by which the Communist Party hopes to prove to the world that "socialism with Chinese characteristics" works.

The deal between the central government and Shanghai cannot be more mutually beneficial. The central government plies Shanghai with favorable economic policies for its accelerated development in exchange for the unswerving allegiance of the country's most populous city. The statements of former Shanghai Party Secretary Wu Banguo and former Shanghai Mayor Huang Ju regarding the central government's controversial revenue-sharing policies in 1994 are indicative. Wu told the press at the National People's Congress in March of that year that "Shanghai will resolutely carry out anything that has been decided on by the central authorities." Huang explained how Shanghai would benefit: "In deciding the sharing relationship between the central authorities and Shanghai, the central authorities once again assured that the policy of developing and opening Pudong will not change."[23]

The symbiotic nature of Shanghai's relationship with the central authorities suits the personality of the city and its people well. Shanghainese or other mainlanders asked to name the qualities that define the Shanghainese character normally say "adaptable," "detailed-oriented," "competent," and "calculating." "Calculating" means Shanghainese are excellent at numbers, try to get the best of every deal, and eschew emotional involvement in matters that do not offer them personal benefit. It also means they are obedient and politically risk-averse since being otherwise might jeopardize their well-being under China's undemocratic, one-party rule.

The Shanghai personality has been shaped by the city's hundred-year foreign occupation and then hardened by Communist central planning, mass movements, and party discipline. The Party's system of appointing political and business leaders has further bolstered the city's personality traits, as has Shanghai's status after 1949 as a launch pad to a central government post. Ambitious politicians in the city are normally too smart to spoil their careers by not following orders. How else could Shanghai have transformed itself so quickly in the 1950s from a bastion of capitalism into a state-planning juggernaut? According to journalist-author Yang:

Due to one political movement after another, the Shanghainese who had previously formed a nonaggressive personality became ever more nervous, sensitive, and obedient; and Party cadres at different levels became ever more persistent and resolute in implementing the instructions from their leaders and gaining their trust. That was why such a model as Ke Qingshi [Shanghai's Party secretary from 1954–1965 and mayor from 1958–1965], known as "Chairman Mao's good student," was found in no place but Shanghai and leftist thinking also found a perfect environment to flourish in Shanghai.[24]

Likewise, Shanghai politicians in the reform era could be counted on to avoid actions that undermined President Jiang Zemin, the city's most influential patron up north.

Shanghai's reputation in China is therefore hardly surprising: The city is known (along with Shandong) for adhering more closely to Party dictates than any other part of the country. Guangdong, on the other hand, is considered more "innovative" in implementing Beijing's directives.[25] The southern province in the 1990s was like a child who tried to get what he wanted by walking down the road as fast he could until his mother grabbed him. Shanghai achieved its aims by being mother's pet. What it lost in autonomy by staying by mother's side, it gained in preferential treatment. This is not to say that tensions do not sometimes erupt between individual bureaus in Shanghai and the central government, or that Shanghai does not lobby for its interests. But once Beijing lays down the Party line, Shanghai is usually among the first places to implement it.

Shanghai's special relationship with a central government stocked with former Shanghai officials has engendered resentment around the country. The indignation became visible in the mid-1990s. At the time, a national debate was raging across China on the way to close the growing income disparity between coastal areas like Shanghai and inland provinces, which had not benefited nearly as much from the country's reform policies. And yet there seemed to be no end to the central government's support for its pet, as the 18 "super-special policies" that it awarded Pudong in September 1995 indicated. In October 1994, at the Fourth Central Committee Plenum, representatives from inland provinces, for instance, stated their opposition to the promotion at the central government level of Shanghai natives Huang Ju to the

Politburo and Wu Banguo to the Party Secretariat. The festering displeasure caused Shanghai officials and former Shanghai officials in Beijing to go on the defensive. They damped their rhetoric regarding Pudong, stressing the importance of its development for the entire country and taking pains to reiterate that paramount leader Deng Xiaoping—not Jiang Zemin—created the policy of favoring the zone. In late 1995, Jiang stated: "Deng said he regretted not having made Shanghai a special economic zone and the central authorities must make up for lost time by giving Shanghai favorable policies."[26] Provincial disgruntlement, however, has not been enough to make Beijing change its stance toward Shanghai.

The Great Build

Armed with Deng Xiaoping's mandate to make Shanghai great, the city embarked in 1992 on what has to be one of the biggest building sprees the world has ever seen. From the top of the Hilton Hotel, which in 1995 was still one of the tallest buildings in the city, the horizon yielded more tower cranes in every direction than the eye could count. Block after city block had been razed to make way for new development. Laborers from the provinces, numbering close to three million, scurried around the city's estimated 21,000 construction sites,[27] soldering metal, hammering nails, and hauling heavy buckets to make the city grow like a well-tended cornfield. Whether it was two o'clock in the afternoon or two o'clock in the morning, the growl of cement mixers, the thump of pile drivers, or the roar of heavy trucks filled the air. The construction never seemed to stop. In 1997, I asked Allan Edwards, a Shanghai-based World Bank consultant on Shanghai's urban rehabilitation, to compare the pace of rebuilding in Shanghai with what he had seen elsewhere. A British national, he said:

What's happening here [in Shanghai] reminds me of Britain in the 1960s, when we got the economy moving after the war and knocked down everything in sight—only here the scale is far wider. The Shanghai government has decided that by 2010 Shanghai will be equal to any international metropolis in the world in terms of infrastructure services. Lots of cities around China are developing, but Shanghai can outpace all of them.

Investing seven times more in infrastructure between 1992 and 1997 alone than during the whole of the 1980s,[28] Shanghai rebuilt itself more quickly than most observers thought possible. During the decade, the city flattened old neighborhoods and erected elevated highways, extension bridges, roads, and tunnels with lightening speed. A 27-kilometer road ringing Shanghai, for instance, shot up in just two years. The Shanghai municipal government completed two metro lines of a proposed 350-kilometer light rail system. Shanghai also laid down millions of digital telecommunication lines, making once-tedious telephone calls instantaneous. It renovated its existing international airport in Hongqiao and broke ground in 1997 on a new one in Pudong, which received its first passengers in the fall of 1999. On a site once dominated by old warehouses on the eastern edge of the Huangpu River in Pudong's Lujiazui, there soon emerged wide boulevards, towering glass skyscrapers, malls, and park space. On the west side of the river in Puxi (Shanghai proper), there sprouted grand cultural complexes, including a library, a stadium, a museum, and a performing arts center. The city brightened its appearance by planting flower beds and stringing neon lights along major avenues. To make Puxi into a commercial district, the municipal government started shutting down or moving out hundreds of labor-intensive, low-tech, polluting industries lodged in decrepit factories around the city. By 2010, it plans to rid the area within the inner ring road of two-thirds of its factories.

Consider Shanghai Continental Pharmaceutical, a state-owned Western medicine maker, which in 1995 transferred its factory in downtown Shanghai to the far reaches of Pudong. Before then, it sat at the fashionable intersection of Huaihai and Xinhua roads, dumping pollutants on a daily basis. Local officials deemed the site better suited for commercial development and told Shanghai Continental to move. Fortunately for the pharmaceutical company, the relocation made good economic sense. "Otherwise, we wouldn't have moved so quickly," admitted a company manager. The firm's profit had eroded 50% from its 1990 high due to soaring costs and slumping finished goods prices. Expanding production was one way to reverse the trend, but the factory had no space to grow at its small site in the city. Its 15,000-square-meter factory was cramped and its equipment corroded. So the company took advantage of the government's relocation policies and received half of the land transfer fee paid by the site's foreign developer. It then contracted with a Hong Kong firm to codevelop the original site into a 33-story residential-office complex, keeping a 15% stake in the project for itself. With half of the land transfer fee and preferential government loans in its coffers, Shanghai

Continental bought new equipment and built a 26,000-square-meter plant on Pudong grassland.

To finance its dreams in the 1990s, Shanghai relied partly on foreign financing and selling the land-use rights of residential neighborhoods and factories, like Shanghai Continental Pharmaceutical. The city raised roughly 100 billion yuan (US$12 billion) through such sales.[29] As a result, infrastructure was not the only thing to obtain a facelift in Shanghai during the decade. Developers, like the Hong Kong firm that worked with the drug maker, rushed to take advantage of the housing and office shortages thwarting the city's ability to attract foreign investment. There were simply very few acceptable places for foreign managers and their families to live and work. Huaihai and Nanjing roads quickly became a who's who of Hong Kong property developers like the Kerry Group, Shui On, and Hang Lung. By the beginning of 1998, the supply of offices had surged 10 times over end-1994 levels.[30] Millions of square meters of modern office towers soon sequined Shanghai's evening sky. Investors poured money into new luxury apartments and villa complexes. More than 70 big shopping centers and an explosion of new retail outlets and restaurants opened their doors by the end of the decade. Shanghai's Xujiahui district, which in 1990 had just one 5,000-square-meter department store, had turned into a shopper's mecca by the end of 1998, with 10 large shopping malls boasting 150,000 square meters of space. Glimpsing quickly from side to side while driving down certain roads, I could easily mistake my location for a Western city—dazzled for a moment by the numerous boutiques and multistory department stores.

Shanghai was not the only city in China to experience a boom by the end of 1998. Its renaissance coincided with the wave of pell-mell growth hitting the country after Deng's 1992 speech opened wide state bank spigots. Sensing their chance to finally get a piece of China's legendary 1.2-billion-person market, foreign investors poured funds into China's coastal areas, intensifying the explosion of economic activity. In 1993, they pledged a whopping US$111.4 billion in investment, making China one the most popular foreign investment destinations in the world. China's GDP between 1992 and 1997 subsequently grew at an average 10% pace. But thanks to Shanghai's prime location at the mouth of the Yangtze River, its relatively skilled workforce, its 14 million-plus population, and its preferential status, the city was particularly well-placed to benefit from Deng's relaxed credit policies and foreign investor zeal. Its GDP surged at a 13.8% annually between 1992 and

1997—a gargantuan leap from the sluggish growth experienced in the 1980s. Per-capita GDP reached 28,200 yuan (US$3,400) in 1998, four times the national average and high enough to rank Shanghai among the World Bank's medium-income-level countries.[31] Foreign property developers, retailers, manufacturers, and other multinationals through 1998 invested US$34 billion in 17,620 projects in greater Shanghai.[32] One after another, international banks, stock brokerages, insurance companies, accounting firms, advertising agencies, and other capitalist institutions hung their shingles in Shanghai, attesting to the city's new status as a service industry center. If financial institutions hoped to do yuan business in China, the government told them to move to Pudong, boosting the zone's aspirations to become China's Wall Street.

The municipal government channeled much of the city's new foreign manufacturing investment into Pudong, which by end-1998 had signed up more than 5,400 foreign-funded projects.[33] The zone might have attracted more foreign investment had it not demanded such steep prices and been less picky about the types of investments it wanted. Still, the government's efforts to build Pudong, which through the end of 1998 received US$40 billion in infrastructure and fixed asset investments,[34] drew some of the biggest names in international business. Siemens, Hoffman-LaRoche, Intel, IBM, Krupp Steel, Sony, Allied Signal, BASF, GM, and Philips are among the multinationals that erected factories there during the 1990s. Those investors who landed in Jinqiao Export Processing Zone, the most developed industrial district in Pudong, were impressed by how quickly the district's basic infrastructure improved. Thorpe McConville, the American general manager of Diebold Financial Equipment Co., recounted how the main road in front of the district's development company was one lane wide and covered with dust in 1992. He had to walk half a mile to see a potential building site. In 1996, he said:

When we first came to Jinqiao, there was nothing here—Pudong itself had a couple of roads. Jinqiao was all farmland, filled with peasants, old farm houses, and rice paddies. Now the difference is night and day. The infrastructure has come a long way. Then there was no electricity, now there is most of the time. There were no roads, but now the roads are all in place. In 1992 it was difficult to believe what the development company told us. They said it was going to be a good road. And it is a good road.

The strides the city made in the 1990s to rebuild its inadequate hardware are truly impressive. For perspective, contrast the giant elevated highways, underwater tunnels, and suspension bridges that Shanghai erected during the decade with the length of time it is taking the city of Boston in the United States to build one highway system through the city center. Boston began construction on its US$10.8 billion "Big Dig" —an eight- to 10-lane expressway along a 7.5-mile corridor—in 1991. After five years, the city had completed 25% of the project. After seven years, 50%. And only in 2004 is the Big Dig expected to be totally dug.[35] Shanghai's infrastructure feats seem miraculous in comparison.

What was it like for residents to live through their city's physical transformation? Huang Tianmin, a 72-year-old retiree who had also experienced Shanghai's conversion to communism in the 1950s, summed up the experience. He said:

The first time I went to the United States was in 1992 to visit relatives. I went to Los Angeles and San Francisco. That's the first time I visited a mall. Things were clean. There were lots of highways and cars. At the time I thought that Shanghai would never be like that. Even though Shanghai was China's biggest commercial city, I felt that we were really backward in terms of city construction. For 40 years there was not much change in Shanghai. But over the last five years I've seen all these changes taking place so quickly. There is a popular saying in Shanghai now: Every day has new things, every month brings change. When I went to my old work unit in Xujiahui, which I hadn't visited for a month, I did not recognize it. Big buildings had replaced all the houses. The same for where my daughter lives. In 1996 it was all small shops. After several months, it was all big buildings. The changes were hard for me to accept at first. I was worried that we were selling the country like the Nationalist government did before 1949. I did not quite understand the market economy. So at first I opposed it, but now I don't oppose it because I can see that the economy is developing. Now so many places are like Los Angeles and San Francisco. Now I understand that only with economic reform can we be prosperous.

The infrastructure achievements of the 1990s have had a profound effect on the lives of residents like Huang. For one, they are moving again—literally. Besides laying down more than 1,300 kilometers of new roads and a subway line between 1990 and 1997, the city also added hundreds of new public buses, which meant I no longer spied harried commuters pushing fellow travelers off of overcrowded coaches. The city also restricts the number of vehicles allowed on the roads and controls traffic flows more effectively—a difficult feat in a city where millions of bicycles vie with cars, buses, pedestrians, and motorcycles. As a result, Shanghai residents and visitors no longer routinely find themselves stuck in hours of excessive traffic, which is not the case in Asian cities like

Bangkok and Chinese ones like Beijing. Not that traffic tie-ups no longer occur in Shanghai, but for people like Chen Gang, a young executive at Shanghai Volkswagen's plant on the city's outskirts, the difference is striking. It used to take him more than two hours in traffic to get home from work every night. On one particularly harrowing evening, he left the office at 4:15 only to walk in his front door at 8:00. As the result of a new highway, the same trip in 1997 took only 90 minutes to an hour, freeing him up to partake in more interesting pursuits. Likewise, the opening of Shanghai's first subway line in 1995 halved travel time from home and work for residents like Thomas Frater. Instead of spending 90 minutes commuting from Puxi to his packaging plant in the southwestern suburb of Songjiang, he only needed 45 minutes. He cooed:

The traffic situation has improved remarkably. And the commute to the airport, it's unbelievable. It only takes 30 minutes from the Hilton Hotel in the city center to get there. Before it took an hour—or never. In 1993 when I first got here, you'd just sit in traffic.

How long into the 21st century this bucolic situation will endure depends a lot on Shanghai's success in developing its public transportation system and, in a city with more than 14 million people, controlling the number of cars. Although the number of roads in Shanghai grew exponentially during the decade, the number of vehicles plying them grew even faster despite the Shanghai government's efforts to restrict automobile and motorcycle ownership, particularly for private citizens. It auctioned only 500 car license plates annually to individuals and charged an exorbitant 120,000 yuan (US$14,500)[36]—a huge sum considering that urban residents on average earned only 8,439 yuan (US$1,017) in 1997.[37] Taxi companies, foreign enterprises, and Chinese work units subsequently own most of the cars in the city, leaving most Shanghainese to ride bicycles or buses to work. Beijing, which charged private citizens much less for their license plates, had some 400,000 private car owners compared with Shanghai's 4,000 in early 1998, which helps explain the capital's perpetual gridlock. At the end of the decade, however, the Shanghai government relaxed its stance on private car ownership.[38] Apparently, the change of heart came from a need to stimulate private consumption in a slowing economy as well as to boost sales of the city's flagship Santanas made by the Shanghai Volkswagen joint venture.

Thanks to the Great Build and the reforms that accompanied it, many Shanghainese—albeit not all[39]—have seen their standard of living surge. They not only have more money in their pockets than ever before, but also have more things to do with it. By 1999, the average per capita income of urban Shanghai families surpassed 8,700 yuan (US$1,048) per head, more than triple its 1991 level.[40] For the first time, many families can afford to buy things like refrigerators, color television sets, air conditioners, video recorders, washing machines, water heaters, phones, and mopeds. As a result of higher incomes and a five-day (instead of six-day) workweek as of 1997, they are traveling more for fun both inside China and to government-approved destinations overseas, like Thailand, the Philippines, Singapore, Malaysia, and Hong Kong. They now enjoy the convenience of shopping in modern supermarkets, department stores, and western-style boutiques. Fashion-conscious Shanghainese women don bright orange platform shoes or whatever latest style suits them. The image of a poorly dressed Shanghai official is an outdated stereotype. And whereas Shanghai in the 1980s offered a miserly selection of weekend diversions, the city today boasts an array of leisure-time venues: tea houses, coffee shops, restaurants, amusement parks, bowling alleys, karaoke clubs, and an excellent art museum. Take the new public library. Whereas Shanghai's old city library near People's Park was a cramped, ill-frequented place, the new one is packed on Saturday afternoons with people perusing computerized car catalogues, reading English novels, and scanning newspapers. Echoing the remarks of his fellow library-goers, a 30-year-old engineer surnamed Chen sitting on a library bench explained:

I only went to the old library once or twice. It was disappointing. Apart from being old and dimly lit, the service was poor. The normal situation was that the reader had to sort of beg the service staff to find you a magazine or book, which was usually nowhere to be found. If you were lucky enough to obtain the book eventually, you felt like you owed the service staff so much that it would be asking too much to ask them to find you another book or magazine. If you wanted to look at a foreign publication, it was even worse. I once went to the old library to check an English magazine on engineering because my boss asked me to do so. On the first trip, the librarian would not give it to me because I did not have a stamped introduction from my employer. However, when I returned with the stamped document, I wasted my time once again. The librarian told me that I needed a medium- or high-level professional certificate to enter the foreign magazine room. So I never returned.

We like this library. First, it's modern in keeping with Shanghai's status as a metropolis. Second, it's more well-organized than the old one. Readers can easily find where they should go. If they want to have a chat there's also a drinking zone. Also the service has improved. The reader no longer finds himself having to beg, to say pretty words to get something. After all, the new library is an important representative of Shanghai—a cultural Shanghai rather than an entirely commercial Shanghai.

Ultimately, the new library's popularity reflects residents' drive to better themselves and their thirst for information in Shanghai's increasingly market-driven economy. It also demonstrates how the city's improved infrastructure and systems are facilitating those goals.

During the 1990s, Shanghai finally started resolving its dire housing situation. Rising incomes and housing reform policies have helped some residents buy their own flats, while the city government moved more than 85% of families living in less than four square meters per person to larger accommodations. To make way for more than 25 million square meters of highways, skyscrapers, and other new infrastructure (imagine an area almost the size of Belgium), it also relocated nearly 10% of the city's 4.7 million households to new housing developments on the city's outskirts, usually to more modern and spacious apartments. As a result, Shanghai residents occupied 9.6 square meters of space per person by the end of 1998, enjoying three more square meters per capita than in 1990.[41] Some foreigners complain that Shanghai's urban renewal has cost the city much of its color. Gone are many of the cramped old neighborhoods where on hot stifling summer days residents without air conditioners or fans took to the street, playing cards or resting on wicker lounge chairs well past midnight. But for someone like Yang Shifang, who works off and on as a domestic helper after having been laid off from a state-run textile mill in the mid-1990s, relocation has brought relief. Until 1996, the 46-year-old shared an 11.5-square-meter room in a dingy pre-1949 tenement with her husband and teenage daughter. There was no flush toilet, running water, or kitchen. There wasn't even a proper wall to separate her family from the folks next door; the two families coexisted in a room subdivided with makeshift paneling. Yang was therefore thrilled to learn from district officials that her neighborhood was being redeveloped and that the government would provide a 37-square-meter flat, complete with kitchen and bath, in a Shanghai suburb. "It's very good. Now I have five rooms. I have a kitchen and a toilet—before we just used a chamber pot," Yang said, her smile lighting up her face. "It's a little far, but I like it."

The Great Glut

The many achievements of Shanghai's Great Build have not come without costs—costs that highlight the city's focus on the physical infrastructure of a great modern metropolis while often neglecting less-tangible softer components. For instance, despite the one-sided accounts in the state-controlled press, not everyone was as thrilled as Yang Shifang to be relocated to new public housing in the suburbs. A desperate woman rushed into my office in the summer of 1995 to complain that her family's home in Pudong's Lujiazui district was about to be bulldozed against her and her neighbors' will. "They're making us move, but we don't want to," she declared in a quivering voice. Why didn't she and her neighbors want to move? For one, even though the apartments in the government's new housing projects are larger and more modern, they are far from Shanghai's center. This not only makes residents' commutes longer, it makes it more difficult to visit friends and family. These new communities also often lack convenient shops, schools, hospitals, and public transportation. Rushing to get residents out of their old neighborhoods, the government also made people move into new flats before they were fully ready for occupancy. Electricity, gas, telephone lines, or even water were in some cases not yet connected.

In the fall of 1997, I visited an elderly couple at their apartment in a new housing estate in Meilong in the far reaches of Xuhui district. A six-story concrete block built in 1994, it is surrounded by rows of other nondescript concrete blocks sitting beside a six-lane highway and a chemical factory. In 1996, the government made Mr. Wu, a retired doctor of Chinese medicine, move with his wife from their old tenement in downtown Shanghai to make room for a highway. They had some good things to say about their new abode. "There are green plants in the front area of the building. And neighbors can't look into each others' rooms like before. This place is a little bigger. We have more freedom now because we don't need to share a bathroom or a kitchen," explained Wu, his five-foot-tall frame resting against the kitchen table. Overall, however, he was not satisfied. Pointing to the ceiling, he said:

The quality isn't good. There's a leaking pipe in the bedroom and the Housing Bureau says they can't fix it because it's a construction problem and therefore the responsibility of another bureau. The balcony floods because the drain is full of cement. The air is bad because of the chemical factory and it's noisy because of all the trucks on the highway. The commute is very inconvenient. It takes one hour from downtown. No relatives ever visit us here because it's too far. After dinner, there's nothing to do. There's no cinema or theatre. In our old place we could walk along Huaihai Road. I used to go to Peking Opera a lot. But now the opera finishes too late for me to make the last subway train. I preferred it before when people would see each other every day. Now people just shut their doors. We feel lonely. When I go downtown, my wife stays here alone. There's no one to talk to.

Some of Shanghai's residents were so upset about their forced relocation that they took their grievances to the street. One of the biggest outpourings of indignation occurred in March 1995 when 200–300 demonstrators blocked traffic along Huaihai Road, Shanghai's main shopping drag, in a peaceful protest against the demolition of their quiet residential neighborhood. Residents were incensed because their homes were good ones by Shanghai standards—with kitchens and toilets and average per-capita living space far above the minimum. And yet, the district government had sold the site's land-use rights for an undisclosed hefty sum to a developer who planned to turn it into an office block. "Such a commercial office building is not in accord with the city government's construction plans nor is it for the good of the public. We will not move," railed a petition signed by most of the families and sent to the district, municipal, and central government.[42] Such protests, however, did little to change residents' fate, while the Chinese press and the Public Security Bureau (PSB) did their best to cover them up. The PSB, Shanghai's police, harassed foreign news agencies that reported on these events since their stories did not conform to the stable, progressive image that the city wanted to project. In 1995, for instance, the police subjected a Chinese employee at an influential foreign news service to several 24-hour interrogation sessions for talking to protesting families. They also told her to change jobs, which the frightened woman duly did.

Such incidents put the comparison between Shanghai's Great Build and Boston's more modest Big Dig in better perspective. The Boston project is taking so long partly because the elected city government has had to placate diverse constituencies. The Boston authorities, for instance, spent US$1.4 million to soundproof and air condition the apartments of angry artists living near the construction site. They spent another US$1 million on a system to protect fish that might unknowingly be swimming near underwater blasting. And they hired personnel to patrol the city to ensure noise levels did not disturb residents.[43] The follies of a rich country? Perhaps. But Shanghai, with few of the constraints of a democratic society, including powerful labor unions, organized citizen groups, and a free press, could barrel ahead with its plans.

Shanghai's zeal to rebuild itself also led the city into a massive property glut that is taking years to make right. Standing on top of one of Shanghai's many new skyscrapers at night at the end of the 20th century, I could see gaping holes in the cityscape where office blocks without tenants stood as black as the inky sky. Or when I walked into one of the many new blue-tinted glass office towers in Pudong at rush hour, I felt the eeriness of an empty lobby. Along the new elevated expressway from the Hongqiao International Airport and on other highways leading out of the city center stood row after row of empty luxury villas and apartment blocks. Month after month I passed by those developments and still barely a curtain was a hung or an air conditioner installed, although occasionally I spied a naked lightbulb illuminating a migrant worker's drying laundry. Shanghai in early 1999 was expected to have more than 10 million square meters of unsold, empty housing, an area almost the size of Hong Kong.[44] The tenancy rates in the city's shiny new office towers did not edge much past 40%,[45] with Shanghai claiming more than 500,000 square meters of empty Grade A offices in mid-1998, an area almost the size of Singapore. The glut was most severe in the part of town that claimed to house one in five of the world's construction cranes: Pudong. There, occupancy rates for offices and expatriate housing in 1998 hovered below 35%.[46] Although Shanghai was not the only city in China, or Asia for that matter, to struggle at the end of 1990s with too much new real estate, its oversupply problems were particularly serious. Andrew Escott, Shanghai-based commercial director for realtor Colliers Jardine, commented in 1998: "Shanghai's property glut is bigger than anything that has happened in the world before. It's bigger than Houston's oil boom building glut in the 1980s. As for the Southeast Asian gluts [of the late 1990s]—those don't compare to Shanghai."

How did Shanghai's great build turn into a great glut?

A number of factors came into play to turn the office and housing shortage of the early 1990s into massive oversupply, demonstrating vividly how the development of hardware in Shanghai far outpaced the development of a market economy's software. The seeds of the debacle were first sown in the early 1990s when the municipal government decided to decentralize control over land leasing to individual city districts. The districts' directors soon discovered a quick route to revenue and promotion: selling land-use rights for hefty sums to deep-pocketed foreign developers. The more foreign investors they attracted, the more money they earned for infrastructure investment and the better the numbers looked that they sent to their superiors. Bureaucrats and managers were rewarded for quantity and reaching targets rather than quality. The decentralization policy sped up the city's development, but it, and the fact that no central body was put in charge of controlling the overall number of leases sold, set the stage for the ensuing construction free-for-all. As a result, between 1993 and 1997, Shanghai sold leases for 1,334 land parcels covering 78.4 million square meters to developers,[47] an area almost twice the size of Switzerland. Planned supply bore no relation to future demand.

Why were developers so eager to buy the land leases? After Deng Xiaoping called for China's economy to boom in 1992, foreign companies started pouring into Shanghai, but found very few places up to international standards for their expatriate personnel to live and work. Moreover, the Chinese government did not want local residents to fraternize too closely with foreigners and therefore did not allow non-citizens to lease most existing properties in Shanghai, since they were slated specifically for domestic use. Most foreigners living in Shanghai in the 1980s and early 1990s subsequently took out long-term leases on hotels rooms, using them both as offices and homes. The few office blocks available for foreign occupancy in the first half of the 1990s filled up quickly and charged rents of more than US$2.4 per square meter *per day* at their 1995 peak, roughly US$7,200 a month for a small, 100-square-meter office. The Shanghai Centre, the city's first Grade A office-residential complex, charged some clients a whopping daily rate of US$3.2 per square meter, nearly US$9,600 for 100 square meters. When my husband and I signed a lease for our first apartment in Shanghai in the fall of 1994, we were shocked by its US$6,800 per month price tag. For that, we got a 120-square-meter, three-bedroom flat that was nothing special from a Western perspective. The building's four-story exterior was plastered with small green bathroom tiles that had discolored, and the interior, though clean and modern, was nondescript. The living and dining areas shared a single, slim room abutting a terrace that was too narrow to fit more than two very small chairs and a side table. The view was of our neighbors' kitchen windows and drying mops, some 10 meters away. Trying to get the service company to fix problems was a patience-trying experience. And yet, it was the best apartment in Puxi of that size and rent range available. Our situation was typical of the thousands of expatriates moving to Shanghai in the mid-1990s. Developers in those days could throw up buildings without regard for quality or service, charge exhorbitant sums, and still fill their flats.

The shortage of quality homes and offices for expatriates and the city's assignation as China's commercial hub made investing in Shanghai real estate seem like a sure bet to overseas investors, mostly from Hong Kong, Taiwan, and Singapore. Big Hong Kong property developers soon had rights to the choicest sites on Huai Hai and Nanjing Roads, while small-time overseas developers also jumped into the fray. Kennic Lui, the senior partner in his own certified public accounting firm in Hong Kong, for instance, raised US$150 million among his friends in just two months in 1994 to build a 36-story building on Nanjing Road. A consultant at the time estimated a spectacular four-year payback period for the project. Said Lui: "To be able to raise that kind of money in that type of time frame meant that Shanghai must have a certain attractiveness. It's a sexy city for foreign investors." Individual overseas investors were so hungry to get a piece of the booming Shanghai market that developers could sell the vast majority of a building before its construction was even completed. Take Cynthia Poa, a 42-year-old Singaporean health food executive, who bought four offices in Shanghai in 1993 and 1994. "Rosy reports led people to believe they would earn double-digit returns. In Singapore you could only make 6%–7%," she explained in 1996. Indeed, from the big to the small investors, everyone was hoping to replicate the fortunes made in property speculation in Hong Kong in previous decades. What they did not know when they made their investments was how many other new buildings were going up at the same time.

Local developers were not about to miss their chance at some easy money either. And as a result of the loose credit policies launched after Deng Xiaoping's 1992 southern tour, there was no shortage of investment funds for state-owned companies. Roughly 60%–80% of the money invested in Shanghai real estate in the 1990s came from domestic sources.[48] Finding a Chinese enterprise in the 1990s that had not diversified into real estate was a Sisyphean feat—whether the company was Shanghai's Kai Kai Knitwear Co. or Xinmin Evening News Group. Why did garment makers and newspapers companies build real estate? Apart from the belief that they could make a killing in property, Chinese managers in the 1990s operated under the assumption that relying too heavily on one sector made them vulnerable to adverse market or regulatory changes.

Plus, everyone was going into real estate in the early and mid-1990s, which was sufficient reason for many Chinese managers to take the plunge. Real estate, like electrical appliances and pharmaceuticals, were among the decade's "hot" sectors and indeed, many industries—not just property—eventually suffered from severe oversupply in the 1990s. Few Chinese state companies had become sophisticated enough to do market research (and even if they had, the paucity of good market data made doing proper market studies problematic). Finally, there was little reason for state companies not to make a bet on the property market. If they lost money in the venture, they were not accountable for losses and did not have to pay the state funds back.

In 1996, the government announced a moratorium on new land leases for offices and luxury apartments.[49] But the damage was already done. Massive oversupply caused rents to plunge in the second half of the decade. Rates for prime office blocks in Shanghai's central business district, including the swish Shanghai Center, dropped from their US$2.4 per square meter per day peak in 1995 to less than US$1 in 1999, roughly US$3,000 a month for 100 square meters. In mid-1999, the Shanghai Statistical Bureau announced that prices would continue to fall throughout that year due to continued "relatively high" vacancy levels.[50] Developers and small landlords pushed return on investment projections far back into the future. Kennic Lui, the Hong Kong developer whose consultant in 1994 estimated payback in four years, in 1999 did not expect to see returns for 15–20 years. Dai Guoqing, a property expert at Shanghai University of Finance and Economics, in 1997 sighed: "The government had planned to make real estate a backbone industry in Shanghai to solve the problem of unemployment and to make other industries like building materials, construction, and home decoration develop more quickly. But so far things have not worked out very well." There was a silver lining, however. Lower rents made Shanghai a more affordable place to locate an office. And keen competition during the decade's waning years started prompting property developers who previously skimped on service and quality to do a better job.

What's ironic about Shanghai's property glut and the oversupplies wracking major cities around China is that they occurred while many local residents still lived in small, decrepit flats. Almost 80% of the unsold properties in Shanghai at the end of 1997 were residential housing.[51] Shanghai's new skyscrapers and villas, however, were built mostly to house foreign expatriates on company housing allowances who could afford to pay rents that ranked among the fifth or sixth highest in the world.[52] Unfortunately, foreigners did not descend on the city in numbers capable of absorbing so much new space, a situation that was exacerbated by the slowdown of new foreign investment into Shanghai and China during the Asian Financial Crisis of the late 1990s. The Shanghainese, with average annual incomes of a little more than US$1,000, could not afford to take up the slack. (And even if they could afford to pay such hefty prices, Chinese law prevented them from leasing apartments built for foreigners.)

Meanwhile, local residents were also slow to jump on the many new lower-priced apartments built specifically for them, resulting in even more empty housing blocks around the city. The reason: For most of the decade, they had little incentive to buy. Most still lived in state-allocated apartments at low state-subsidized rents. In 1996, for instance, a household only paid a piddling 70 yuan (US$8.40) in monthly rent for a 60-square-meter apartment, and that was after several rate increases under the city's housing reform program.[53] In contrast, new commercially built flats went for 500,000–600,000 yuan (US$60,000–US$72,000).[54] "No one wants to buy," explained Xuan Weiming in 1997, a director at state-owned Shanghai Wool & Jute, which had been trying unsuccessfully to wean workers off of state-subsidized housing. "Rents are too low and purchase prices are too high. The Shanghainese look at it this way: If you put money in the bank, the interest is enough to pay rent, so why buy?" Although it is not exactly true that no one wanted to buy—roughly 800,000 families bought new commercial flats through 1997 and 650,000 households purchased their state-subsidized apartments[55]—sales were still too slow to absorb the enormous amount of surplus stock.

Also hurting sales to local residents were the lack of a well-regulated secondary market for public housing and horror stories circulating by word of mouth and in newspapers of some consumers' disastrous home purchasing experiences. On International Consumers' Day in 1998, Shanghai residents lodged more complaints regarding real estate purchases than on any other subject.[56] Take the experience of Stephanie Yan, a well-educated, white-collar employee for a foreign company. Yan and her new husband purchased a three-bedroom apartment in a 20-story tower for 630,000 yuan (US$75,904) from a local developer in July 1997. She recalled:

I can't say I was intoxicated with the apartment when we bought it. It was a little big and there weren't any trees or greenery in the neighborhood, but it had a good location close to town, which I liked. I thought it was a good investment. We've been living with my parents and had been looking forward to moving into our own place.

The developer, however, had not yet finished construction and promised in the contract that the apartment would be ready by October of that year or he would pay a penalty. In January 1998, three months after the original completion deadline, the developer's agents told her she could collect the keys and move in, even though construction was not yet finished. Besides not paying her any compensation for the delay, they told her she owed the developer an additional 50,000 yuan (US$6,024) because the apartment turned out larger than stipulated in the contract. Other buyers faced the same predicament. The agents told her to go to court if she was not satisfied, which Yan did, expecting redress. She did not get it. She explained:

To my surprise, the court, at the mere sight of my case, refused to accept it. They didn't even give me a chance to present my reasons for launching it. They simply asked, 'Do you want to return the house? If not, why don't you pay for the extra area and get in?' The court even embarrassed me in front of scores of people in the reception room by saying, 'How can you get something for nothing? You don't want to pay money, but you want the house.'

The experience left Yan and other buyers suspecting that either the developer had bought off certain court personnel or had some powerful connections. But the worst was yet to come. In mid-April, Yan learned that the developer had skipped town with the remaining money, leaving her with an unfinished apartment. She fumed:

It's like a big conspiracy. How can he do that? It's also said that the police are seeking him right now. Actually, the district government knows where the developer is. Why not arrest him? Because if they did, the government officials who helped him get certificates illegally would probably also end up in jail. We feel it's very unfair. Justice will not be done through the court system or official legal channels. At times, we have felt desperate. On the positive side, with the government involved, even if our case won't be resolved through normal channels, there's a good chance it will be resolved somehow. The government does not want more than 100 buyers to demonstrate, so it will seek a solution.

Glumly, she added:

To solve these problems I had to spend a lot of time consulting lawyers, seeking legal documents, and having dinner with those who have helped me. More than that, I have made much effort in vain to contact and try to negotiate with the developer. I can now attest to the widespread saying here: nine out of 10 property developers are cheaters.

Yan's story demonstrates both some of the progress and problems of Shanghai's rebirth. On the positive side, Yan went to the market to buy a house instead of asking her employer for a free one. During the decade, the market became the primary provider for a slew of goods and services that the state had previously supplied. Moreover, Yan had avenues to seek redress that would not have been open to her in previous decades. Instead of going to her employer or to the police when she ran into a problem with her developer, she took her grievance to court. During the 1990s, citizens increasingly looked to the legal process to settle disputes, indicating society's growing regard for the rule of law. Besides the courts, they could also call radio talk shows or reveal their story to the press, which might do investigative work on disgruntled consumers' behalf. On the other hand, Yan's problems buying a home underscored the slow development of a world-class city's software, providing an example of how inconsistent regulation, government intervention, and petty corruption have stymied the city's advance. The courts in Shanghai simply are not yet reliable intermediaries. Local governments appoint judges, pay their salaries, and control their promotions, making them anything but independent arbiters of justice. As a result, the market can sometimes be a dangerous place for the unconnected.

Given the keen desire of Shanghai residents to improve their housing situation in the 1990s, the key to resolving the housing glut for local citizens boiled down to offering them the right incentives. Throughout the decade, the Shanghai government took measures to encourage residents to purchase their own homes. It raised rents, set up public housing funds, and provided mortgages for the first time since before 1949, becoming a leader in housing reform in China. But its efforts only really took off in 1998 when the immensity of the glut became apparent and economic growth both in Shanghai and nationwide started to slow, in part due to weak consumer demand. To kick start consumption, the nation looked to the domestic residential property sector and the more than US$600 billion that Chinese citizens held in personal saving accounts in 1998. Premier Zhu Rongji in early 1998 announced the state would no longer distribute new houses starting in July of that year. Shanghai became bolder in offering favorable terms on mortgages and personal income tax deductions of 100% of the price of a new home.[57] The value of home mortgage loans subsequently jumped more than 75% in Shanghai in 1998[58] and property sales, of which the vast majority were to domestic residents, rose 50.4%.[59]

In the meantime, Shanghai's property fiasco was harming the city's economy, tying up an enormous amount of capital and exacerbating the tight credit environment that prevailed in China between 1995 and 1997. To cool the country's growth, which by late 1994 was again resulting in 20%-plus inflation, the central government started to rein in credit in the mid-1990s. It also started getting serious about banking reform, telling state banks to clean up their bad debts and lend only to viable projects in the future. At about the same time, the huge cash infusion from land-lease sales to foreign developers that had helped fund Shanghai's growth during the decade's first half dried up as the city government stemmed new building and foreign developers shied away from the oversupplied market. Investors who had already jumped into the market had no way of getting their money out. I talked to Professor Shen Hanyao, the president of the Shanghai Institute of Economic Development, in 1997 about the city's property situation. He explained:

Both foreign and domestic companies now have capital stuck in these properties. When they invested, they expected to finish construction in three years and then sell, but now no one is buying so their capital is trapped. This is having a big impact on the Shanghai economy. Now most enterprises lack money. When they don't have money, they don't have demand to buy things and then there's no market. Real estate influences the furniture, building materials, and transport industry. It also influences banking. Companies borrow money for their investments but can't pay the bank back. As a result, the banks have had less money to lend to other industries.

Indeed, regulators in 1999 closed down Pudong Lianhe Trust and Investment Corp., the city's second largest trust and investment company, after it defaulted on US$1.3 billion in debts incurred developing property in Shanghai's new Lujiazui financial district. A company official told reporters: "We invested a lot of money in the Pudong property market, but many of the buildings are still empty and we have no way of recovering those loans."[60]

When I interviewed Shen in 1997 he estimated that Shanghai would enjoy double-digit growth for another three years, after which growth would slow to less than 10% a year. "Without the real estate problems, growth would be around 12%–13%," he added. What neither he nor other mainland economists anticipated at the time were the other forces that would soon blunt Shanghai's and the country's growth. For example, most experts did not foresee how much consumer demand would slacken. Holding consumers back were rising unemployment and feelings of job insecurity caused by state sector reform, as well as citizens' growing inclination to save for big future purchases such as education, healthcare, and housing. In 1998's first quarter, per capita consumption in Shanghai declined 3.4% from the same period a year earlier.[61] Most economists also had not anticipated that the country would lose interest in Shanghai's stock market in 1998. A bull market had helped propel the city's 13% GDP growth during the previous year. At the same time, they did not appreciate how much overcapacities in many industries—not just property—would stifle companies' investment plans in the late 1990s. By early 1998, a total 500 billion yuan (US$60.2 billion) in unsold goods sat in warehouses in Shanghai and around China.[62] Finally, few economists predicted Asia's financial meltdown starting in mid-1997 and the ensuing slowdown in foreign investment and trade.

Shanghai's problems in some ways resembled those of the Southeast Asian countries that fell into recession in the late 1990s. During the decade, credit was loose, foreign direct investment flooded in, domestic companies expanded willy-nilly beyond their core businesses, and investors and creditors performed limited due diligence. A saving grace for Shanghai and China in general was that Beijing had not yet liberalized the county's capital account nor opened its capital markets much to foreign portfolio investment in public securities. So when China's economy started looking shaky, there were few short-term foreign investors to withdraw their money, and the Asian contagion stayed largely outside China's borders. Another saving grace for Shanghai was its strong concentration of foreign manufacturers whose export growth remained strong despite the Asian flu. To stimulate flagging growth, the central government in 1998 launched a massive infrastructure spending spree. It also introduced consumer loan programs for cars, housing, and other major purchases; increased incentives for exporters; and tried to reignite the country's stock markets to encourage residents to spend more. Although Shanghai no longer grew at a frantic 12%–13% annual pace, these and other policies helped the city's GDP surge 10.2% in 1999.

Bright Blinding Lights

Shanghai's cityscape of new high-rises, villas, malls, department stores, and neon symbolizes its renaissance into a modern, prosperous metropolis bent on becoming an international economic, financial, and trading center. However, given that so many of those establishments are struggling to find tenants and shoppers, they also symbolize some of the problems with Shanghai's resurgence. Shanghai is not yet as modern nor as prosperous as it looks. The rush of beautification activity that Shanghai underwent in 1997 highlighted the somewhat deceptive nature of Shanghai's progress. Gray, filthy pre-1949 houses that hadn't seen a paintbrush for years suddenly received a fresh coat of ivory, seafoam, or salmon paint. A small park on the corner of Yanan and Jiangsu roads appeared almost overnight. Trees and shrubs moved in; grassy knolls popped up. The sudden concern for aesthetics was welcome, making Shanghai a brighter, more prosperous-looking place. But I was intrigued by the abruptness of the makeover and the fact that the city was suddenly spending so much on beautification. Some research set me straight: Shanghai was hosting the China's Eighth National Games that autumn and was taking the opportunity to show to the rest of China how well Shanghai, the showcase of the country's economic reform efforts, was developing. Given the sums and effort spent on the facelift, I was saddened to watch the city tear down many of the newly painted houses along Yanan Road a year later to make room for a freeway. The paint job around the city, moreover, was only skin deep: Workmen only painted the front side of the buildings abutting the road. Their out-of-view backs and sides, as well as the homes in the second rows or further back, remained their same drab gray. A closer look revealed paint splattered over the ground and on windows. Inside, the same poor living conditions remained. As TV cameras panned Shanghai's new, modern skyline, broadcasters did not mention that Shanghai was experiencing a massive property glut, that many of those new department stores were losing money, or that once well-known Shanghai brands were losing out to more adept domestic and foreign competitors. They did not mention that while Lujiazui was the home of some of China's most spectacular new skyscrapers, the district was barely off the ground as China's Wall Street, despite the government's hardball tactics to get foreign financial institutions to locate there. Shanghai had once again become a pacesetter for other parts of China, but the exaggerated hype surrounding the city was unsettling, reminding me of China's efforts to create model communes in the Mao era.

The same rush to finish projects, beautify the city, and project a government-approved image occurred again in 1999 for the city's hosting of *Fortune* magazine's annual "Fortune Global Forum," which amassed 350 chief executives officers from major multinational companies that September to discuss China's future. The central and Shanghai governments hoped the high-profile bosses would leave the event impressed by Shanghai's progress and ready to reignite flagging foreign investment. The Shanghai government by all accounts did a superb job of hosting the three-day affair, demonstrating its flair for managing big projects. But what was also striking about this celebration of Chinese-style capitalism was just how centrally planned it was: from the 2,000 workers who toiled in continuous shifts for a year to ensure the completion of the city's convention center in time for the forum; to the 200 government-selected Chinese participants who hailed mostly from big state-owned enterprises and government bureaus; to the order for Chinese journalists to report only news items selected by Shanghai's Information Office.[63] The central authority's ban that same week on *Time* magazine's issue commemorating the 50th anniversary of the People's Republic was particularly striking given that *Time* and *Fortune* shared the same parent company, which planned to pass out free copies of the issue at the conference. Also noteworthy was the amount of time and energy *Fortune*'s conference organizers devoted to coordinating the affair with the Shanghai government: John Needham, the president of *Fortune*'s conference division, actually moved to Shanghai for 10 months. Previous international venues for the conference did not require constant on-site oversight, indicating the continuing complexity of dealing with government officials and getting things done in Shanghai relative to developed international cities. The Great Build has put the city on the right track toward modernity and prosperity, but the transformation is not occurring at the breakneck pace suggested by the remarkable changes in the city's infrastructure.

Some of the challenges that Shanghai faces will resolve themselves with time. For instance, while the infrastructure growth that took place in Pudong in the 1990s is remarkable, the zone still has far to go before it satisfies more than investors' basic needs. There still is not a lot to draw foreigners and Shanghainese to live there. Its districts lack a critical mass of restaurants, supermarkets, public transport, and other amenities. The opening of the new airport, a subway line, and an international school have helped, but the oft-heard saying "rather a bed in Puxi than a flat in Pudong" summed up Shanghainese and foreigners' attitudes toward Pudong in the 1990s. Companies cannot hire enough well-educated people in the zone, busing employees in from the other side of the river. Shanghai Vice Mayor Zhao Qizheng, before his promotion in 1998 to Beijing as spokesperson for the State Council, China's cabinet, was in charge of Pudong's development. Discussing the challenges facing the zone in 1997, he commented:

Just like a computer cannot run without software and memory. So Pudong must have software, program, and memory. Otherwise Pudong cannot run. This is Pudong's biggest challenge. Hardware in Pudong means infrastructure, workshops, and buildings. Software means law, banks, and telecommunications as well as hospitals, schools, and other services. Only with both hardware and software will Pudong have its place in the world. The construction of software will probably take a longer time.

Thinking about Vice Mayor Zhao's comments, it is not hard for me to visualize a not-too-distant future when Pudong will have the "software" that he mentioned. But to me, his idea of software is actually hardware. What he did not mention is that laws are only good when enforced consistently, while banks and telecommunications are most useful when all vendors are free to offer the full array of services that customers demand—not just those the government approves in a piecemeal fashion. The city can build more hospitals in Pudong, but if it does not reform the sector, which is largely closed to foreign investment, and significantly upgrade the quality of care provided, foreign residents will continue to seek medical treatment abroad. It takes more than tangible objects to build an international economic, financial, and trading center. A well-enforced legal system, business know-how, decision-making autonomy, access to reliable information, a well-regulated market economy, and vigorous domestic companies are just some of the software items taking longer to develop from the nonmarket, undemocratic foundations laid in Shanghai during 40 years of Communism. Ultimately, the sectors changing most quickly are those that the central government has opened widest to market forces, such as retail, real estate, and consumer products. But Shanghai has little autonomy to go further faster. Given China's political setup and Shanghai's mother–pet relationship with the central government, Shanghai cannot overstep the boundaries of reform and opening set 1,500 kilometers north.

Proud to Be Shanghainese

Whatever Shanghai has yet to achieve, there is no question that the Shanghainese once again feel proud of their city. "The Shanghainese have regained their confidence," commented Hu Shoujin, a sociology professor at Fudan University. "Shanghai has become a leader that other parts of China must follow." They no longer needed to go to Guangdong to find the new and modern in China. "Now Shanghai has its own famous foreign brands," quipped the 21-year-old fashion plate who previously looked south for guidance.

Shanghai's success during the 1990s also fueled the city's rivalry with Hong Kong, which in Shanghainese eyes only replaced Shanghai as Asia's most important commercial hub after Shanghai defaulted on that status in 1949. Many of Shanghai's elites fled to Hong Kong following the communist takeover, using their textile, shipping, and financial expertise to help make Hong Kong Asia's premier international business center in the second half of the 20th century. Shanghainese see their city's return to the top of Asia's hierarchy as their destiny. Shanghai-based sociologist Shen Guanbao explained:

Shanghai people think Hong Kong's economy developed quickly because it had a market economy after 1949. But in the 1930s and 1940s the Shanghai economy was much stronger than Hong Kong's. Today, Shanghai's economic potential is much stronger than Hong Kong's. Because its area is larger, it has more room to expand. Information can easily spread to other places. This is a crucial condition. Shanghainese think they are more clever, capable, and more highly educated. They think if political policies allow, Shanghai will be greater than Hong Kong.

Maybe some day. But at the start of the 21st century, it still has a long way to go to match the software that makes the former British colony an international financial hub for Asia.

Notes

[1] Betty Peh T' I Wei, *Crucible of Modern China*, Oxford University Press, 1987, p. 1.
[2] Yang Dongping, *City Monsoon: The Cultural Spirit of Beijing and Shanghai (Chengshi Jifeng: Beijing he Shanghai de Wenhua Jingshen)*, Oriental Press (Dongfang Chuban Shi), 1994, p. 312.
[3] Ibid. p. 314.
[4] Ibid. p. 315.
[5] Ibid. p. 316.
[6] Ibid. p. 323.
[7] Ibid. p. 314.

[8] Ibid. p. 320.

[9] Lynn T. White III and Li Cheng, "Government and Politics," *Shanghai and the Yangtze Delta: A City Reborn,* ed. Brian Hook, Oxford University Press, Hong Kong, 1998, p. 49.

[10] Yang, op. cit, Chapter 6.3.

[11] *See* Peter T.Y. Cheung, "The Political Context of Shanghai's Economic Development," *Shanghai: Transformation and Modernization under China's Open Policy,* ed. Y.M. Yeung and Sung Yun-Wing, The Chinese University Press, Hong Kong, p. 54.

[12] Yang, op. cit., p. 315.

[13] *See* Cheung, op. cit. "The Political Context of Shanghai's Economic Development,"; White and Li, op. cit. "Government and Politics;" and Yang, op. cit., Chapter 6.

[14] *See* Cheung, op. cit., pp. 66–68.

[15] Ibid. pp. 68, 78.

[16] Ibid. p. 79.

[17] Ibid. p. 78.

[18] Shanghai's status as a training ground for potential central government leaders started long before the reform era. Shanghai's first mayor Chen Yi became vice premier in 1954, a Politburo member in 1956, and foreign minister in 1958. The central government made Ke Qingshi—a Shanghai's party secretary and mayor from the mid-1950s until 1965—a Politburo member in 1958 and a vice premier in 1965. The total number of Shanghai officials appointed to the Central Committee during the Cultural Revolution jumped from two to 10 at the 9th Communist Party Congress in 1969. *See* Cheung, op. cit. pp. 63–65.

[19] *See* Bruce Jacobs and Lijian Hong, "Shanghai and the Lower Yangzi Valley"; p. 1.

[20] *People's Daily,* Oct. 21, 1992.

[21] *South China Morning Post,* Sept. 20, 1995.

[22] *Shanghai Star,* Jun. 30, 1998.

[23] *See* Cheung, op. cit., pp. 74–75.

[24] Yang, op. cit., p. 327.

[25] Cheung, op. cit., p. 81.

[26] *South China Morning Post,* Nov. 20, 1995.

[27] *China Daily,* Nov. 12, 1996.

[28] *People's Daily,* Apr. 7, 1998. Shanghai poured 142.8 billion yuan (roughly US$17 billion) into infrastructure projects in 1992–97, of which US$10 billion came from abroad.

[29] *South China Morning Post,* Jul. 26, 1998.

[30] Ibid., Jul. 9, 1998.

[31] *South China Morning Post,* Jan. 22, 1998.

[32] China Statistics Yearbook 1999.

[33] Ibid., Dec. 4, 1998.

[34] *South China Morning Post,* Apr. 8, 1999.

[35] *See* www.bigdig.com.

[36] *Shanghai Star,* Jul. 3, 1998.

[37] Ibid., Nov. 3, 1998.

[38] The Shanghai government cut license plate prices to 20,000 yuan (US$2,409) for individuals and approved certain local banks to launch installment payment programs and grant automobile loans to private citizens. *See Shanghai Star,* Jul. 3, 1998 and Mar. 26, 1999.

[39] As part of Shanghai's efforts to reform state enterprises, some Shanghai residents lost their jobs and found it harder to make ends meet. Their travails are covered in Chapter 3: The "Haves" and the "Have-Nots."

[40] Ibid., Jan. 7, 2000.

[41] Figures provided by the Shanghai Housing & Land Administration Bureau and the *Shanghai Star*, Dec. 22, 1998.

[42] Reuters, Mar. 11, 1995 and Apr. 29, 1995.

[43] *International Herald Tribune*, Sept. 19, 1997.

[44] *Shanghai Star*, Jan. 29, 1999.

[45] *Asian Wall Street Journal*, Mar. 18, 1999.

[46] *Shanghai Star*, Sept. 8, 1998 and Sept. 15, 1998.

[47] *China Daily*, Jan. 22, 1998 and Jan. 25, 1998.

[48] Roughly 40%–50% of the money invested in Shanghai real estate came from domestic bank loans, 20%–30% came from enterprises' own funds, and another 30% came from overseas sources. Statistics provided by Dai Guoqiang, the associate dean of the School of Finance at the Shanghai University of Finance and Economics.

[49] Ibid., Jan. 22, 1998.

[50] *Xinmin Evening News*, Jun. 1, 1998.

[51] *Shanghai Star*, Mar. 31, 1998.

[52] *South China Morning Post*, Jan. 15, 1998.

[53] Shanghai Housing Authority.

[54] *Shanghai Star*, Nov. 11, 1997.

[55] *China Daily*, Dec. 25, 1997.

[56] *Liberation Daily*, Mar. 16, 1999 and *Xinmin Evening News*, Apr. 12, 1998.

[57] Ibid., Nov. 12, 1998.

[58] Ibid., Oct. 20, 1998.

[59] *South China Morning Post*, Feb. 24, 1999.

[60] Associated Press, Jul. 7, 1999.

[61] *China Daily*, May 20, 1998.

[62] *Shanghai Star*, Feb. 17, 1998. Some 66% of 600 major goods were in oversupply in 1999 according to the *Shanghai Star*, Mar. 5 1999.

[63] *Asian Wall Street Journal*, Sept. 27, 1999.

3

New York of Asia?

atching Shanghai's capital markets in the 1990s was like riding a rollercoaster whose brakes had failed because the ride operator had neglected to install and service them properly. Whenever the car threatened to career out of control, the operator— read authorities—used a sledgehammer to stop it in its tracks. During a period of particular volatility in 1996 and 1997, Chinese traders like Jimmy Zou gave me a good idea of what makes Shanghai's markets tick. Zou worked for the Shanghai branch of a trust and investment bank owned by an inland province. To me, his story suggests how far Shanghai has come since China's Communist policy makers in Beijing reopened the Shanghai Stock Exchange in December 1990 and designated the city to reemerge as an international financial hub. It also shows how far China's largest city has to go.

In January 1997, I asked Zou to meet me for lunch at Pasta Fresca, one of Shanghai's new Italian eateries. Wearing a long wool overcoat against the winter chill, the 30-year-old had the look of a prosperous man. A diamond-studded gold band circled his ring finger and his pocket bulged with a new mobile phone—most Shanghainese at the time still relied on pagers. After we found seats and placed our orders, I asked Zou how he started trading A-shares. (The central government only allows domestic investors to trade these domestic-currency-denominated shares. It limits foreigners to trading foreign-currency-denominated B-shares in China, H-shares in Hong Kong, N-shares in New York, etc.) Exuding confidence, he happily explained: "I first got the bug in 1991 while working at the Shanghai tourism bureau; I had a friend at the Shanghai Stock Exchange who helped me make a lot of money."

"What do you mean you had a friend at the stock exchange who helped you make a lot of money?"

"Oh, she would give me good news."

"What do you mean by 'good news'?"

"She told me inside information early. She would tell me which A-share to buy, and, never fear, within two days it would go up."

Good news, indeed. "How much money did you make that year?"

"Oh, about 200,000 yuan," he chuckled.

Zou had a lot to laugh about. Two hundred thousand yuan was about US$24,100. The average annual income of a mainlander in 1991 was roughly US$280. He quickly quit the tourism bureau in favor of the stock trading business to become a millionaire in yuan terms many times over.

"So how do you pick your stocks now?"

"Oh, there are newspapers that tell you which stocks will go up, maybe because the listed company's earnings were better than the previous year or because some institution is buying the stock. All they want to do is move the market. But sometimes the articles are good and actually analyze the company, telling readers about its financial status or its managers. But really this is not the most important way to get information. We offer our own daily reports about the markets, which tell what happened yesterday and what will happen tomorrow. We also recommend stocks that we think will rise."

The waiter brought our lunches, setting before the trader a piping hot portion of pasta marinara.

"How do you know which stocks will rise?" I asked.

"Typical reasons either have to do with the company's fundamentals, like whether or not it has high earnings per share, or technical issues, like whether its trading volume will be greater tomorrow than yesterday because a big player is buying it. This point is the most critical. These big players buy low and make the stock's price rise. When individual investors see the stock going up, they jump in. Then the big player sells it," he explained as he unsuccessfully tried to wrap the sauce-coated noodles around his fork.

"How do you know that's what is going on?"

"Sometimes we know who is doing the buying because we have an information network. In other cases, we know what is going to happen just from experience."

Zou then proceeded to tell me in some detail the method used by one of China's largest brokerages at the time, state-run J&A Securities in Shenzhen, to ramp up the share price in 1996 of a listed hotel and real estate company in Pudong. In brief, after accumulating for some time the company's stock, which traded originally at seven yuan per share (US$0.84), J&A started selling it when the price hit 27 yuan (US$3.25) in December 1996. "J&A knew from government sources that something bad was going to happen in the market, so they sold their stock," he explained. "They have ties to the People's Liberation Army and the Public Security Bureau, so they can know. Then, we got the news from the boss of J&A, so we also sold the stock." J&A was right. Something bad did happen in December of that year: The government cracked down hard on the overcharged markets.

After finishing his tale, Zou took pains to assure me that he and other Chinese traders do not always rely on inside information to buy and sell. "Sometimes we go to the listed company to do research," he said, his expression growing serious. "For instance, there is a listed company in Wuxi (Jiangsu province) that makes chemical fibers for cigarettes. Trading of its stock was very dull. It was priced at four yuan (US$0.48), but the company had just completed a 17-billion-yuan (US$2.1 billion) project. We noticed this and decided to visit the plant. We learned that it would establish a joint venture with a Dutch chemical company. We thought this was good news because it would give the Wuxi company a lot of cash."

Unfortunately, Zou's big foray into analyzing a company's fundamentals did not have a particularly happy ending. He explained: "The company's half-year results were not good. Its earnings per share were only 0.08 yuan [US$0.01]. But it expected good results for the whole year and its earnings per share to reach 0.25 yuan [US$0.03]. Its stock price was just too low, so we decided to buy. At the same time, we wrote a newspaper article and told everyone that it was a good company. In the beginning no one believed us, but a month later a lot of people started buying. Its stock price went from four yuan [US$0.48] to nine yuan [US$1.08] in three months. Then just two weeks ago, the company said its earnings per share for the year were only 0.18 yuan [US$0.02], but three months earlier, we had predicted they would be 0.25 yuan [US$0.03]. Our prediction was too high. That taught us a lesson."

"What lesson?"

"Fundamental analysis is very difficult," he said earnestly. "We made a careful analysis of the company's profit and loss statement and its balance sheet. You know, Chinese companies had poor results in 1996. They hide some of their profit so that they can transfer it to the next year. Accounting in China is not too strict."

I then asked Zou how long he held a stock before selling it. "Some only one day," he replied. "In the Chinese market, if you keep a stock for more than one month, it's very long. Usually I hold stocks for one to three weeks."

"Do you play B-shares?" I asked, knowing full well that it was against the law for a trader like Zou to participate in the foreigners-only market.

"No, the A-share market has more opportunity. You see, there isn't a uniform law to regulate A-shares. There are lots of acts and regulations, but no one minds them. According to US law, I think many people would be put in jail."

"For what, exactly?"

"Oh, you know, market manipulation and insider trading. If I'm working for a big institution and am buying a stock for my company, I buy it for myself first. Or someone in a listed company knows his firm's earnings per share because he knows the company's profits before they are announced. Then he can tell you. It's like the US market at the beginning of the 20th century. You can make a return of 30% a year. This is average. In China it's easy to make money. Everyone can be George Soros or Warren Buffet!"

By the time the waitress brought our cappucinos, Zou must have been feeling particularly relaxed because he decided to make me an offer. "If you want, I can do something for you," he said, staring me straight in the eye.

"But I'm a foreigner. I'm not allowed to trade A-shares," I replied.

Undeterred, Zou continued: "1997 is going to be a very prosperous year. I'm very confident that more and more opportunities await us. In China, if you want to earn money, all you have to do is buy, buy, buy and the stock market will go up and up! All you have to know is when to sell and when to buy and I'm sure of when to do this. I'm sure this year I can get a 50% return or even more," he grinned.

"How can you be so sure?"

"The A-share market at first will suffer a correction but then it will go up because there's a huge amount of dormant capital in China and few investment opportunities, so the stock market is the only choice ... You know, the richest people in China are only in stocks. Some of them do not have a good education. Their cultural level is low. They don't understand art. But they know how to make money."

The waitress delivered our check. As I was paying the bill, I asked Zou what his family thought of his success. Scrunching up his nose, he replied: "They want me to work in an office as a government official or an engineer. They want me to be white collar."

"But you ARE white collar."

"They think I'm a gambler. But now, more and more Chinese are gambling—from professors to workers to beggars. You know, I doubled my parents' money last year. I earned 40,000 yuan [US$4,819] for them."

Shanghai's Promise

In the fall of 1998, the editor of an influential American business magazine based in New York City asked me to write an article about the ability of the Shanghainese to create the New York of Asia. I paused before replying, thinking of Zou's story and so many others. I also marveled at the topic, given that 10 years earlier Shanghai did not even have a stock market while Hong Kong, the former British colony that is now a Chinese city, has long been a vibrant regional financial hub along with Tokyo and, increasingly, Singapore. The fact that the editor of such an important magazine suggested the subject said something to me about the international community's perceptions of Shanghai at the end of the 20th century and its high expectations for Shanghai to reassert its illustrious pre-1949 status as the New York of Asia.

Why do expectations for Shanghai's future run so high? Partly because in the early 1990s the central government, under the leadership of Deng Xiaoping, blessed Shanghai's rebirth, and in a country as administratively and politically centralized as China, such endorsements count for a great deal. President Jiang Zemin, Deng's chosen successor, and other top leaders subsequently reiterated the benediction. At the 14th Communist Party Congress in October 1992, Jiang told delegates that Shanghai must be established as "an international economic, financial, and trading center as soon as possible," deeming the city's success a key to the entire Yangtze River Valley's future.[1] Such high-level support gave the first president of the Shanghai Stock Exchange, Wei Wenyuan,

the confidence to declare to the international community in 1993:
"Shanghai will revive its central position in the Far East by 2010,"
adding that other cities in Asia cannot rival it as a finance hub.[2] The fact
that the country's two top politicians, President Jiang and Premier Zhu
Rongji, and numerous other central government leaders are former
Shanghai officials reassured foreign investors that Beijing would continue
to support the city's ambitions.

Shanghai's status as Asia's most sophisticated financial center before
the Communists took over China in 1949 further excites the world's
imagination. Back in the 1930s, Shanghai was the region's most
commercially vibrant city thanks to a number of advantages. For one,
the British, who governed a large part of Shanghai territory, let
businessmen run the city for businessmen. Shanghai's strategic location
at the mouth of the Yangtze River made it the chief conduit for trade
to and from China's interior. Under these conditions, the city's Chinese
and foreign inhabitants turned it into a beehive of activity. It developed
vibrant commodity, stock, and foreign exchange markets. Nearly 30 of
the world's most important foreign banks had set up branches there by
1935, and most of China's biggest domestic banks made the city their
headquarters. Besides attracting fortune-hunting foreigners, it lured the
likes of John Wei's ancestors. Wei, a 71-year-old chairman at Prudential-
Bache Securities in Hong Kong, fled China in 1950 and subsequently
spent his career managing the money of the wealthy Shanghai families
who also escaped from the Communists. His grandfather was a Qing
Dynasty official who became a point-man for trading tea with the
British and moved his family from Canton in southern China to
Shanghai, midway up the Pacific coast. After learning English and going
to law school, Wei's father took a job dealing in foreign exchange at
an American bank. He eventually left the bank to start his own foreign
exchange company and earned a fortune. What made Shanghai the
most important financial center in Asia at the time? According to Wei:
"People wanting to do business in this part of the world went there
because of foreign expertise, general acceptance of English as the
language of business, and adherence to British law." Today, anyone
interested in physical proof of Shanghai's significance can visit the
Shanghai Pudong Development Bank's headquarters on the Bund—
the former digs of the Hong Kong & Shanghai Bank before the
Communist takeover. On the ceiling of the neoclassical building's
enormous lobby is a colorful mosaic depicting Shanghai, New York,

London, Calcutta, and Tokyo, which were in those days the world's most important finance and trade hubs. The fact that Shanghai once climbed to such heights makes its current aspirations all the more plausible to many in the international financial services industry. Indeed, because of the city's pre-1949 history, foreign banks setting up operations in Shanghai expect the process of educating new recruits to be less painful than elsewhere in the country. If Guangzhou or Beijing were to announce their intention to become China's and the region's financial capital, their lack of such an illustrious background would prevent them from being taken as seriously.

Then there is the China market's legendary potential, which would make almost any city in China that was anointed the country's financial capital an exceedingly exciting prospect. Unlike most countries in Asia, China has a domestic economy big enough to support its own capital markets and, indeed, at the rate the Chinese economy was growing in the early and mid-1990s, many expected it to become the world's largest some time during the 21st century. There are potentially tens of thousands of companies around China to feed deals to Shanghai's financial services industry, compared with the limited number of companies based in Hong Kong and Singapore. And with a 1.2-billion population, there are millions of potential retail customers. Besides boasting a 14-million-plus population itself, Shanghai offers easy access to the provinces along the Yangtze River Delta, which make up more than 40% of the country's industrial output. Jack Wadsworth, the chairman of Morgan Stanley Asia, pretty much summed up the international financial world's high hopes when he told the Hong Kong-based English-language business magazine *Asia Inc.* in 1993: "I think Shanghai is capable of becoming the financial center [in Asia-Pacific] by the year 2000." At the time, as many as six Chinese companies were going public a month, leading the well-respected investment banker to conclude that the Shanghai exchange's market capitalization in seven years' time could reach US$1–2 trillion, surpassing Tokyo's. "It's a business opportunity unequal to anything we've seen this century," he declared.[3] Given the international community's keen interest, I often revisited the notion of Shanghai as a financial hub for the region. I found plenty of progress—enough to change Shanghai over from a frustrated industrial town into an increasingly sophisticated city for conducting financial transactions—but not enough to make it the financial center for Asia for many years to come.

Shanghai's Progress

Shanghai got off to a quick start in the early 1990s when central leaders supported its ambitions with a number of important deeds. The central government approved the creation of the Pudong New Area out of a vast expanse of farmland on the east side of Shanghai's Huangpu River. The move helped the city expand its manufacturing capabilities and attract foreign investment, swelling the potential pool of local customers for Shanghai-based financial services firms. The central authorities made Pudong's Lujiazui district the country's only financial and trade development zone. They also selected Shanghai as the site of one of the country's two experimental stock exchanges and the base of the country's foreign exchange and interbank markets. They allowed foreign banks and insurance companies with central government approval to set up representative offices, branches, and sub-branches in the city, and they chose Lujiazui as the first place in China where foreign banks could conduct local currency business, albeit in a limited fashion. Foreign banks interested in getting an early foothold in this prized business subsequently had no choice but to settle there.

Government policies like these, combined with a mad rush of foreign investment into the city, a well-educated workforce, and double-digit growth rates for much of the decade convinced domestic and foreign financial institutions to set up shop in Shanghai. One after another, the most important names in international finance announced big plans for the city—companies such as Citibank, Goldman Sachs, and Merrill Lynch. The hullabaloo surrounding the opening of Morgan Stanley's Shanghai office in early 1994, its first bureau in China, gives a sense of the excitement. According to press accounts at the time, top Morgan Stanley officials first met for 40 minutes with Prime Minister Li Peng in Beijing before hopping on a private jet headed for Shanghai. With sirens blaring and lights flashing, a police escort whisked them through the city to the swank foreign-invested Shanghai Center, where the city's government and business glitterati gathered to greet them.[4] The American company had gone to tremendous effort to renovate its new representative office in the Shanghai Center, known at the time for its US$75-per-square-meter monthly rents. With high-quality office space scarce, the Shanghai Center agreed to move the complex's tennis court so that Morgan Stanley could occupy part of the office block's top floor. Morgan Stanley also installed sophisticated hidden wiring systems for a full-service securities trading floor. Such exhibitions of enthusiasm were common in those days and before long Shanghai had attracted more foreign financial institutions than anywhere else in China. By 1996, some 40 foreign commercial banks had established branches, 30% of the country's total, and another 119 foreign financial service firms had set up representative offices. By early 1999, the number of foreign banks with Shanghai branches had climbed to 64. Major commercial banks, including Citibank and Standard Chartered, declared Shanghai their China headquarters and moved senior executives in charge of China business to the city. By the end of the 1990s, Shanghai had become a hive of activity for foreign banks serving multinationals settling in the vibrant Yangtze River Delta.

Shanghai had always boasted one of China's more skilled workforces and the rush of foreign financial institutions to the city in the 1990s helped accelerate this trend, nurturing a budding corps of well-trained, English-speaking financial professionals. While going about my research, I repeatedly ran into young Chinese who were working for foreign brokerages and were not only knowledgeable about their field but also displayed an excellent command of English. Often they had spent some time for school or work overseas, but in some cases they had never gone abroad, making their accomplishments particularly impressive. I'll never forget an interview in 1997 with a personable young analyst at Credit Lyonnais Securities in Shanghai. I contacted the firm, which had earned a reputation for high-quality China research, for background on China's listed electrical appliance companies. The receptionist directed me to white-goods analyst Jason Yin. Dressed in a well-cut dress shirt and tie, he gave me an informative, professional account of the sector's situation in fluent English. After the interview, we started chatting and I asked him if he was from Hong Kong. He told me he was from Shanghai. I then asked him, "But you *have* studied or lived abroad, haven't you?" "No, no," he replied, "I've been in Shanghai." I was flabbergasted. How in just a few short years could he have become so polished? I left his office muttering that people like Yin make Shanghai's future as an international financial center imaginable.

During the 1990s, Shanghai consistently strove to build some of the most sophisticated infrastructure in Asia and the finance area was no different. For instance, the Shanghai exchange by 1996 offered speedy computer-matched stock trading and a paperless central stock registry, leaving little room for processing mistakes. In 1997, the city made the final touches on a 27-story, glass-and-chrome stock exchange tower in Lujiazui—the symbol of Shanghai's reemergence as a financial hub. Reminiscent of an oversized square doughnut with silvery blue frosting, it boasts 21 high-speed elevators, 16 escalators, 10,000 IDD lines, and—last but not least—the region's largest trading floor, some 3,600 square meters worth. Two immense electronic screens displaying split-second trading statistics shine down on hundreds of black-haired, white-collared traders sitting quietly behind rows of computer terminals. It is an amazing sight in a country that still claims its ultimate goal is Communism. Likewise, the city's banks are modernizing their hardware. During my visit to Shanghai Pudong Development Bank, an enthusiastic official named Sun Fuji expounded on the growth of the bank's integrated circuit (or "smart" card) business, which by the end of 1996 had 450,000 customers. He also waxed on about the bank's new client-server computer system that, for the first time, connects its branches in the city so transactions no longer have to pass through the bank's headquarters. As I later walked around the bank's spacious marble lobby, I marveled at its similarity to slick counterparts in modern market economies. No longer was a trip to a Chinese bank necessarily a grim, patience-trying experience involving long waits in a dreary concrete box. Better yet, automatic teller machines started dotting the city, making it no longer necessary to enter the bank at all.

Thanks to the growing concentration of expertise and hardware in Shanghai, the city quickly became one of the most sophisticated places in China to conduct financial transactions. Compared with China's four big state banks, which were notorious for their wobbly financial state in the 1990s, Shanghai-based Bank of Communications was a relative star. The Bank of Communications grew out of the central government's efforts to make banks more commercially oriented in the late 1980s. Although still sometimes pushed by the Shanghai government to extend policy loans, it is more independent in its lending decisions, more professionally managed, and less burdened by surplus staff than China's four suffering state banks in Beijing. When international rating firm Moody Investors Services gave poor marks to China's banking sector overall in a 1998, it lauded Bank of Communications for pursuing "its commercial and business-like strategy with remarkable persistence and considerable success," despite operating in a state-dominated system.[5] The way Shanghai Pudong Development Bank (SPDB) handled its public listing in October 1999 also drew praise from Moody.[6] Chinese banks traditionally have revealed very little information to the public about their operations. SPDP at the time of its listing, however, published in major domestic newspapers five pages of relevant information, which was more detailed and comprehensive than anything seen before, significantly raising the bar for transparency among Chinese banks. That said, Shanghai has not been immune from the problems plaguing Chinese financial institutions. Although the central government did not force Shanghai International Trust and Investment Co. (SITCO) into bankruptcy like it did Guangdong International Trust and Investment Co. (GITIC) in 1998, the Shanghai "ITIC" may well have had problems repaying foreign debts on its own if not for the largesse of the Shanghai government, commented Moody's Charles Tan in early 2000. In 1999, regulators actually did shutter the Pudong Lianhe Trust and Investment Corp., the largest in Shanghai after SITCO, when it defaulted on US$1.3 billion in debts incurred while developing Lujiazui, Shanghai's new financial district.[7] It's also worth noting that regulators in 1998 uncovered 150 cases of foreign exchange fraud worth US$425 million in Shanghai during a nationwide crackdown,[8] indicating that malfeasance was a problem there like anywhere in China.

During the 1990s, Shanghai's capital markets grew into the mainland's largest. The Shanghai exchange's total market capitalization at the start of 1999 reached 1.06 trillion yuan (US$128 billion) compared with 888 billion yuan (US$107 billion) at the country's second bourse in Shenzhen, on the border with Hong Kong. Some 480 companies had listed shares, 53 more than in Shenzhen. Shanghai also handles most of the country's treasury bond trading and trading of bond repurchases. More than 20 million individual investors have their money in its bourse. Indeed, Shanghai's capital markets are doing the job of capital markets around the world—providing funds for Chinese companies, albeit those selected by the government. In terms of number of companies listed and volume of turnover, it seems set to surpass Hong Kong within a handful of years. During the bull markets of 1996 and 1997, the exchange's daily turnover on some days exceeded Hong Kong's.

This is phenomenal growth given that the bourse only opened its doors in 1990 and considering the ideological reservations within the Chinese leadership during the decade about introducing such a quintessential capitalist tool. In 1996, I paid a visit to Huang Yajin, the dean of economics at Shanghai's prestigious Fudan University, to discuss

Shanghai's emergence as an international financial hub. A thoughtful man who studied for a time in the United States, he commented:

The securities market is where Shanghai's progress has been the greatest. Originally the government saw securities markets as a symbol of economic reform. But after watching them generate 50 billion yuan [US$6 billion] in new capital and 10 billion yuan [US$1.2 billion] in tax revenues [by 1995], it now sees them more as a vehicle to raise capital. When I left Shanghai to study in the United States in 1986, no one knew what stocks were. When I returned in 1992, everyone was talking about them. It's hard for stock markets to develop in a country where no one cares about them. In China people care about the stock market. This interest has surpassed expectations—both the government's and the people's.

Rocky Rebirth

Clearly, Shanghai has come a long way from the days when even mentioning the words "stock market" in a favorable light could land a dunce cap on your head. In terms of building the hardware of a financial center—setting up stock markets, promulgating laws, establishing brokerages, listing companies, etc.—it is quickly catching up with its more advanced rivals in the region. Still, from what I saw in the second half of the 1990s, mostly by watching Shanghai's capital markets, I am convinced that Shanghai's rebirth into a world-class financial center capable of competing with Hong Kong and Singapore, not to mention Tokyo, London, and New York, will take a long time and is not in the offing without extensive reform. In 1996, I interviewed Morgan Stanley's Jack Wadsworth about what Shanghai would have to do to become an international financial center. He listed the following criteria: a yuan convertible on the capital account; high-quality listed companies; a national securities law, uniform disclosure, and consistent regulation; a series of reliable intermediaries (i.e., securities companies); and finally, the development of derivative instruments and options. "Then you will have an international financial center of extraordinary proportions," he added. As China enters the 21st century, none of those criteria—except the passage of a national securities law in 1999—is close to being met. While no one expected Shanghai's rise to maturity to occur overnight, the decade's progress fell far short of what the city's new modern financial gadgetry suggested and foreign financial firms anticipated. Indeed, Shanghai is still struggling to emerge as the financial center of China—let alone for Asia and the world. After witnessing repeated scandals, crackdowns, and wildly volatile capital markets, I came to see that the slow introduction of a financial center's "software" is holding the city back.

Bond Futures Fiasco

My first initiation into the wacky world of Shanghai finance came within two months of my arrival in the city in 1995. A major scandal rocked the city's capital markets—one so major, in fact, that for all intents and purposes it destroyed a firm that *Institutional Investor* in 1994 had touted as China's future Merrill Lynch[9] and sentenced founder Guan Jinsheng to 17 years in jail.

Dubbed "the godfather of mainland securities markets," Guan founded Shanghai International Securities Co. (Sisco) with government money and was China's highest-flying financier until his fall in early 1995. Before I arrived in Shanghai at the beginning of that year, I had already read a lot about him—his success and outspokenness made him a darling of the foreign press. Sporting wire-rim glasses and black hair slicked to one side, the short and pudgy Guan did not exactly conform to the image of a high-powered Wall Street investment banker. But that's what he aimed to be for China. And before his fall he seemed to have everything going for him: a reputation as the mastermind behind China's leading securities firm; excellent academic and professional credentials; good connections with the powerful sons and daughters of China's top leaders; and the respect of the foreign investment banking community. Last but not least, Guan had a vision. At a time when few people in China even knew what securities were, he was laying the foundation for a retail brokerage that would bring stocks into the lives of ordinary Chinese— just like Merrill Lynch founder Charles Merrill proclaimed he would do for America in the 1940s.

Guan's rise was particularly impressive given his humble beginnings as a peasant's son in Jiangsu province. He parlayed his smarts at school into a chance to study overseas at the beginning of the 1980s—a rare and much-coveted opportunity for mainlanders, particularly in those early days of economic reform. He returned from Europe as one of

China's leading experts on market-style finance and took a job at Shanghai's closest thing to an investment bank, Shanghai International Trust Co. A few years later, the audacious 39-year-old was ready to make his superiors an offer: invest in a start-up securities firm run by Guan. He convinced them and nine other institutions under the Shanghai government to throw in a total of 10 million yuan (US$1.2 million).[10] It was a bold move. At the time, China did not even have an official stock exchange and, from the government's perspective, anything having to do with securities was purely experimental.

Bold moves defined Guan's career. With Sisco's 10 million yuan in seed capital, Guan sent his minions into China's vast interior in search of residents ready to sell the state bonds they had earlier been forced to buy from the government. Paying the farmers a fraction of the bond's face value, Sisco then sold the bonds for a higher fraction to speculators on the coast. In doing so, Guan had helped initiate a new form of bond arbitrage. Indeed, with the dynamic Guan at the helm, Sisco always seemed to be at the forefront of Chinese finance. To expand Sisco's brokerage and corporate finance businesses outside of the mainland, he teamed up with Hong Kong tycoon Li Ka-shing in 1993 to acquire two Hong Kong-based securities firms. Besides offices around China and in Hong Kong, Sisco set up shop in the most important financial hubs in the world: New York and London. It collaborated with the likes of Merrill Lynch on domestic and international deals and impressed foreign investment bankers with its willingness to adopt Western practices. Always thinking big, Guan in the mid-1990s started construction on a symbol of Sisco's swelling influence: a 35-story granite skyscraper costing nearly US$150 million located near what would be the new Shanghai Stock Exchange in the heart of Shanghai's budding Lujiazui financial district.

From his vaunted perch as the godfather of China's securities market, Guan seemed invulnerable. Apart from the investment arm of the Ministry of Finance, Sisco traded more bonds than any other Chinese entity. Foreign investment banks vying to underwrite new listings on China's red-hot stock markets from 1992 to mid-1994 regularly found themselves knocking on Sisco's door for a piece of the action. In 1994, Sisco turned a profit of 528 million yuan (US$64 million), had a registered capital of one billion yuan (US$121 million), and assets estimated at 8.6 billion yuan (US$1 billion).[11] Foreign investment bankers saw in Sisco's success the makings of a fierce future competitor. In 1994,

Institutional Investor declared: "Guan is laying the foundations of a full-service investment bank that may well give foreign houses a run for their money in domestic and regional markets as the next millennium approaches."[12] Less than a year later Guan was behind bars and Sisco on the verge of bankruptcy.

His downfall was as spectacular as his rise.

It traced back to 1994 when the central government started to dampen fever pitch trading in the country's equity markets. In the summer of that year Beijing also shut down most of nation's currency trading and commodities businesses, which had likewise become favored casinos for Chinese speculators. Chinese investors, including major brokerages, investment companies, state-owned enterprises, and individual citizens, suddenly found themselves without an attractive place to gamble. Luckily for them, the government was about to hand them a new venue.

Beijing desperately needed to develop the country's bond markets. But because inflation was running in the double digits, it feared the bonds it was issuing would not find enough takers. Among other things, Beijing decided to offset inflation's value-eroding effects by attaching each month a new interest rate subsidy, known as a "kicker," to the basic interest coupon offered on selected three- and five-year bonds. Between the interest on the bonds and the kicker, investors could earn a return approaching 20%.

But the real speculative action was not in bonds—it was in bond futures. Persuaded that the hedging benefits of futures contracts would spur public interest in buying more government bonds, the authorities allowed the Shanghai exchange to initiate the trading of futures contracts, which were in good part bets on the future size of the underlying bonds' interest subsidy or "kicker." And like many futures contracts, Shanghai's were highly leveraged and highly volatile—the gutsy speculator's Holy Grail. For a little money down, traders could bet on a number of tantalizing variables: monthly announcements on the amount of the "kickers," the trading strategy of the market's biggest players, the amount of new government bonds that Beijing would issue and declare tradable, and so on. Moreover, the Shanghai exchange did not regulate the market very tightly, encouraging investors' gambling instincts—in part because this trading became a lucrative source of transaction fees. For instance, the exchange let firms borrow from banks to finance their margin payments and it did not place restrictions on the number of contracts that brokerages could play on their own account. That meant that instead of trading for clients, they would trade primarily for themselves, significantly influencing the direction of the market.

Not surprisingly, turnover in bond futures skyrocketed. In 1994 it accounted for a whopping three-quarters of the exchange's total trading volume of 2.6 trillion yuan (US$307 billion). By January 1995, trading of bond futures regularly surpassed 100 billion yuan (US$12 billion) in contracts a day, while trading in the underlying bonds was a small fraction of that amount, around 100 million yuan (US$12 million). China's voracious investors did not see bond futures as a way to hedge the risk of buying the governments bonds—the normal practice in more mature markets; instead, they saw them as a way to make outsized trading profits. Earning two million yuan (US$241,000) in transaction fees on a typical trading day, the Shanghai bourse had little incentive to stop the party.

Had I not been so new to Shanghai's capital markets, I would have known that something bad was about to happen. Experience would teach me that it always does each time a particular market in China becomes the target of the nation's gambling instincts.

The shoe dropped with a thud on Thursday, February 23, 1995.

With China's roaring inflation starting to abate, Sisco believed the government would lower or abandon the monthly kicker on treasury bonds. It also believed the Ministry of Finance's massive 150-billion-yuan bond issue (US$18 billion) in 1995 would prompt investors to sell their old bonds and trigger a price slide. Expecting the futures market to drop, Sisco and a cabal of other companies that included Liaoning International Investment Co. "shorted the market," which meant they sold bond futures contracts without owning them in the hope of buying them more cheaply in the future and pocketing the difference. The market, however, did not drop. On Tuesday, February 21, the government told the public it would not release the entire 150-billion-yuan bond issue after all, kindling speculators' desire to hold old bonds. Then came a treachery that must grate at Guan from his prison cell. Liaoning International abruptly went long on Thursday, February 23, buying contracts in the belief that prices would go up. Why the betrayal? Either Liaoning International simply saw an opportunity to make a lot of money or, more likely, the Ministry of Finance pressured the provincial institutional investor to change camps. The Ministry was unhappy about Sisco's efforts to push the market down on the eve of its big bond issue and its investment arm, China Economic Development Co. had been busy accumulating long positions since the previous day. If all this were not bad enough for Sisco, a local newspaper claimed the monthly kicker on the bonds might actually rise—not fall or disappear—as Sisco had been betting. These events were not lost on rumor-sensitive investors, who quickly starting buying and driving up bond prices. Trading volume on February 23 soared to 854 billion yuan (US$102 billion), a remarkable sum considering that China's gross national product in 1994 totaled 470 billion yuan (US$57 billion). A single bond futures contract named Contract 327, which was based on a 1992 three-year treasury bond maturing in June, accounted for 80% of that activity. Its price, which started out the day at 148 yuan (US$17.83), jumped to a high of 152 yuan (US$18.31), a disaster for anyone like Sisco shorting the contract.

China's Merrill Lynch found itself facing an estimated six billion yuan in losses (US$723 million)—a sum that would probably bankrupt it. With only eight minutes of trading left in the day, a desperate Guan made the boldest move of his life. Sisco shorted a whopping seven million contracts worth 140 billion yuan (US$17 billion) in an effort to drive down Contract 327's price.[13] It succeeded. By the time the closing bell sounded, the contract had fallen below its opening price to 147.5 yuan (US$17.77). In eight minutes' time Sisco had turned its six-billion-yuan loss into a 4.2-billion-yuan (US$506 million) gain.

Local regulators, however, could not overlook a market manipulation of such massive proportions. They quickly announced the temporary suspension of bond futures trading and declared invalid all deals sealed during the final eight minutes. They opened an investigation into the debacle, while Beijing quickly dispatched its own set of sleuths to Shanghai. In the end, Beijing closed the market down for good; forced the head of the Shanghai exchange, Wei Wenyuan, to resign; and threw Guan into prison. China's high-flying experiment with bond futures had crashed to earth.

The bond trading scandal was just the start of Guan's problems. Most Chinese analysts at the time expected regulators to fine and formally censure Sisco and, at most, dismiss the well-connected Guan. "In China business is always associated with personalities and the CEO of Sisco is very influential in China and controversial. He's backed by political VIPs in Beijing. He could get the boot, but his connections could also save him," a Chinese analyst at an American Investment bank said at the time. Guan's situation, however, turned out be much more serious. In 1995, China was in the throes of a huge anti-corruption campaign, launched by none other than Chinese President Jiang Zemin himself. The Chinese government accused Guan of wide-scale graft and leading a decadent lifestyle, including paying the equivalent of US$50,000 to renovate his bathroom, and sentenced him to 17 years in prison. But as much as Guan's incarceration sent chills up speculators' spines, future events would prove it ineffective in deterring other Chinese institutions and investors from reckless speculation. Investors ultimately saw it as a high-profile but isolated corruption case that might not even have occurred had the country not been undergoing an anti-corruption campaign.

As for China's Merrill Lynch, no one at the time expected the government to allow Sisco to go bankrupt, even though it would have been the best way to discourage speculation. "They will get the major parties together to reach an agreement. This is the way they settle problems between state-owned enterprises," commented a Fudan University finance lecturer. She was right—Sisco was not allowed to fail. Its reprieve contrasted with the widely publicized bankruptcy around the same time of British brokerage Baring Securities, which incurred massive losses when Singapore-based trader Nick Leeson tried to cover up a web of poor trades. By not letting Sisco go under and its employees lose their jobs, policy-makers lost a chance to prove to the country's state-owned firms that they would have to pay the consequences of their mistakes. Part of the reason that speculation was so rampant in the 1990s was that state company managers knew they were playing with the state's funds and not their own. When they won their bets, they profited, but when they lost, they knew the government would bail them out.

Instead of bankruptcy, the government merged Sisco with its stodgy rival, Shenyin Securities, which had modeled itself after medium-sized Japanese investment banks rather than a big Wall Street firm. Kan Zhidong, its head, was known as a cautious strategist compared to Guan, the risk-taker. While employees kept their jobs, Sisco ceased to exist as the budding Merrill Lynch of China from that day forward. Ironically, the government dismissed the cautious Kan from his post in mid-1997 on market manipulation charges when speculation in China's stock market once again ran amuck.

For a new initiate to China's capital markets like I was at the time, the bond scandal of 1995 quickly taught me a few lessons that would crop up again and again during my tenure in Shanghai. For one, the scandal dramatically exposed the extent to which trading activity was allowed to get ahead of the software necessary for capital markets to function well. At its peak, Shanghai's bond market was trading billions of dollars of highly leveraged securities a day. However, this activity took place without settled and enforced rules about how these markets should operate. The country's major market participants had not yet set up adequate risk management systems. Analysts did not do meaningful research or analysis of market trends. Newspapers and other state-controlled business media covered the markets poorly. Certain big players were privy before everyone else to confidential information regarding government policy, making the markets inherently unfair. The scandal also highlighted differences between the Shanghai bourse, which favored less-stringent rules to encourage trading activity, and central government regulators, who increasingly sought to bring China's undisciplined capital markets under national-level control. When China first opened its stock markets in Shanghai and Shenzhen in the early 1990s, each city had considerable authority over its respective exchange to regulate, approve public listings, and appoint personnel. Shanghai bureaucrats guarded this turf closely. The bond scandal, however, marked the beginning of the central government's quest during the next few years to centralize regulatory and decision-making power over China's markets in Beijing.

Part of the problem was that China's securities markets operated until 1999 without a national securities law to regulate them. Instead, a hodgepodge of rules guided the markets on an as-needed basis, leaving gaps in regulation and enforcement. The fact that some of the rules were issued by the China's Securities and Regulatory Commission (CSRC), some by the People's Bank of China, and others by the two exchanges themselves complicated matters further. The lack of a single authority to govern the markets with a single body of legislation led to contradictory rules, turf battles, loopholes, and spotty enforcement. During my talk with Morgan Stanley's Jack Wadsworth in 1996, he commented, "I can't think of anything more fundamental [than a national securities law], aside from good basic companies. Investor confidence requires transparency of markets, consistent regulation, and the rule of law. There's nothing more important to the development of a securities market than investor confidence. Period." When I first arrived in Shanghai in 1995, analysts assured me the law would be introduced some time that year. After all, policy-makers in Beijing had already been debating the law since 1993 and the exchanges had been open since 1990. I soon learned to stop holding my breath. Among the chief sources of delay were controversy over what should be included in the law and infighting between different government bodies over who would be the boss—which together postponed enactment until 1999.

The lack of an enforced legal framework ultimately slowed the development of China's domestic securities firms—the key intermediaries in a first-class financial center. Besides taking part in all manners of market misdeeds, China's investment banks were never clear on what new business lines they could enter or what the standard criteria for getting government approval was. Huang Guixian, senior economist at Shenyin Securities, met with me in a conference room at the company's headquarters on the Bund in 1996. A distinguished-looking man dressed in an elegant blue suit and tie, he commented: "We really hope that the law can be promulgated as soon as possible. It affects Shenyin especially because we have no idea what is legal and what is illegal. It limits what products and projects we can do. If we had a guideline we could be more confident. So for now we take a very cautious approach."

Bureaucrats, Bulls and Bears

During the next few years, I watched Shanghai's capital markets implode several times, underscoring the slow development of an international financial capital's software. The 18 months leading up to the British handover of Hong Kong to China in July 1997 were particularly volatile. After spending 1995 in the doldrums, Shanghai's and Shenzhen's equity markets became the casino of choice for Chinese investors. The Shanghai exchange's all-share index ended 1995 down 14% and total capitalization of listed companies dropped 2.5% despite new listings. Why the bear market? Profits of many listed companies had declined as a result of the tight credit policies that the central government started implementing in 1994 to quell spiraling inflation. And foreign investors in particular had grown disenchanted with the quality of the companies listed on China's foreign-currency-denominated B-share markets. Unlike in more market-oriented countries where any company that meets certain specified criteria can list, the Chinese government decided who went public. Regulators normally chose state-owned enterprises, the country's least dynamic companies. Making matters worse was the tendency of Shanghai and Shenzhen regulators to pick candidates from their own regions instead of from around the country, thus narrowing investors' choices even further. When I first arrived in Shanghai in early 1995, the then chief representative for foreign brokerage HG Asia, John Pinkel, lamented: "We've found good companies that we would like to list. They apply but they can't get quota." Foreign investors expressed their disappointment in company quality by selling shares: Shanghai's B-share index tumbled 20% in 1995 and Shenzhen's more than 30%. Liquidity dropped, making it difficult for foreign investors already in the market to dump their holdings. Concerned with the sorry state of the B-share markets, Beijing in mid-1995 took listing approval power away from Shanghai and Shenzhen regulators, allowing each province to nominate their listing candidates directly with regulators in Beijing. Still, as 1996 got underway, analysts like Pinkel expected little improvement: Company profits would decline again and foreign investors would keep their distance.

So you can imagine the foreign investment community's surprise when Chinese players were by spring bidding up the equity markets, particularly in Shenzhen. Their renewed interest was obviously not based on the prospect of improved company performance. Instead, they took their cue from the government, which started out the year talking about accelerating the development of China's capital markets. The government needed healthy stock markets to list its state enterprises, which were reeling from its austerity program. And with the bond futures market dead ever since the 1995 scandal, Chinese speculators were raring for a new place to make money. By the end of June 1996, the Shenzhen A-share index had jumped 70.4%. Even more intriguing was what was happening to Shenzhen's foreign-currency-denominated, foreigner-only B-shares. They started surging too, but not because foreign investors had suddenly become interested in them again. Instead, local investors had started speculating in the foreign-only market, gobbling up new public listings and accounting for 70%–80% of B-share turnover in June and July. This was an amazing development for a currency that was not supposed to be convertible on the capital account. Expecting the government to merge the A and B share markets within a couple of years and make the currency fully convertible, local investors had spied a golden arbitrage opportunity: purchasing a company's B-shares for 56% less than its A-shares. Shenzhen B-shares by the end of June 1996 rallied 43.5%

Why did the rally start in Shenzhen and not in Shanghai? After all, Shanghai was the anointed financial capital and by far the bigger bourse. Still, the markets in Shanghai picked up more slowly. Its A-share index was up 51.3% at the end of June 1996 compared with Shenzhen's 70.4% and Shanghai B-shares rose only 6%. Shenzhen attracted greater interest for a number of reasons. For one, Chinese speculators were convinced that local and central government regulators would not crack down on the southern bourse prior to Hong Kong's return to China in July 1997. The Shenzhen government furthered the frenzy by lending funds to local securities firms, which in turn ratcheted up the market by speculating in shares of government-owned Shenzhen Development Bank, which had a large enough market capitalization for its trading activity to move the market. Speculators also liked Shenzhen's relatively cheap share prices and looser regulation. Plus, the Shenzhen exchange aggressively took steps throughout the year to make itself more appealing to investors and companies, thus making the Shanghai bourse look complacent in comparison. Spurred by fear of irrelevancy after Hong Kong's handover, the Shenzhen exchange made opening new accounts easier, lowered fees, and offered new services like an Internet website. It also started wooing better-quality companies from all over China to list in Shenzhen, promising them quick listing approval. The Shenzhen exchange's biggest coup was convincing Wuxi Little Swan, China's premier washing machine maker located only a few hours by car from Shanghai, to list in Shenzhen. "In China, investors are all discussing competition between the two stock exchanges. Shanghai investors accuse the Shanghai government of not doing enough to compete with Shenzhen. It's facing a lot of pressure from investors," complained Li Hongbo, a portfolio manager with Shenyin & Wanguo Securities, in August 1996. Analysts chalked up the exchange's complacency to arrogance: Local authorities took Shanghai's position as the site of the country's most important exchange as a given.

I decided it was time to find out the Shanghai exchange's perspective. The official who met me was refreshingly frank about some of the problems. For one, he admitted that the quality of the exchange's B-share companies had disappointed foreign investors. "Shanghai's B-share market will be boosted when we list more companies of better quality and bigger size and that use the funds raised for development and not for some side use. In the past, companies have sometimes used listing proceeds to pay off debt or speculate in the property market," he sighed, shaking his head. He also acknowledged that the exchange's management suffered from complacency but insisted the situation was improving. He said:

The Shenzhen exchange has completely upgraded service to clients. This is something we should learn from Shenzhen. And when we see our companies list in Shenzhen, of course this is something we're concerned about. In the past, our former president never went out to talk to listed companies or prospective listing candidates. He just sat in his office waiting for companies to come to him. Now our new vice president and president are taking more trips. The president took at least five this year.

Besides complacency, the official blamed Shanghai's relatively slack performance on Beijing regulators' closer scrutiny of the country's anointed financial hub, which made ignoring central government mandates harder for Shanghai. He also attributed the situation to the Shanghai bourse's poorer relations with national securities regulators than Shenzhen had at the time, despite the Shanghai government's close ties to national leaders who formerly served in Shanghai, like President Jiang Zemin. Highlighting the arbitrary political nature of regulation in China, the Shanghai exchange official commented:

The vice president and president of the Shenzhen Exchange are appointed by the China Securities Regulatory Commission [the national securities regulator located in Beijing]. Our president is appointed by the Shanghai government and the CSRC. He's a compromise figure. He's not the protégé of the CSRC's chairman like the Shenzhen exchange's president. That's why Shenzhen is getting approvals for listings more quickly. Shenzhen can more easily defy the CSRC, while the central government regulates Shanghai more strictly. It controls Shanghai more because Shanghai is supposed to be the financial center.

While no one expected Shenzhen to usurp Shanghai's status, the Shanghai exchange suddenly found itself in the uncomfortable position of playing catch-up with its little brother to the south. Following the Shenzhen government's example, the Shanghai government reacted by driving up investor interest in one of its large listed flagship enterprises—in this case, Pudong property company Lujiazui. The Shanghai exchange also took a variety of other market-boosting measures, like cutting account opening fees, and turned a blind eye to local investor participation in the B-share market. Share prices of companies that foreign investors would not go near in 1996 shot up, indicating that someone else was doing the buying. For instance, Andy Mantel, a Hong Kong-based fund manager with Shanghai International Asset Management, had nothing good to say about Lujiazui. "Lujiazui looked promising when it first listed in 1994 because some people were leasing land, but that has slowed down noticeably over the last two years. It doesn't make sense to me," he commented. And yet Lujiazui's share prices soared 125% in 1996 as local investors gobbled it up.

Brokers explained to me some of the ways local investors got their hands on US$-denominated B-shares. Shanghai brokers, for instance, would make an arrangement with an overseas account holder, normally a friend, who would wire US dollars to Shanghai in exchange for yuan and a 2% commission. Then all domestic investors had to do to receive the B-shares was visit the brokerage's trading counter with their yuan. Li, the portfolio manager at Shenyin & Wanguo Securities, explained:

Of course, there are some limits. If you have 1,000 yuan [US$120] it's easy to turn it into US dollars, but if you want to buy one million yuan [US$120,000] worth, it's probably impossible. This is just common practice. There are no written regulations since it's supposed to be illegal.

However, local investor participation in Shanghai's B-shares, estimated at 40%–50% of daily turnover in August 1996, did not reach the levels of more freewheeling Shenzhen.

What were regulators doing to block this illegal activity? Not much. Shanghai's B-share index, for instance, plunged in September after regulators issued strongly worded warnings to local investors about trading B-shares. But speculators soon decided not to take the admonitions seriously, figuring that regulators would not want to be blamed for the market's collapse. Moreover, many domestic B-share players had already shielded themselves from regulators by arranging nominee accounts with foreign passport holders.

Stock fever gripped the country as the country's bourses battled for supremacy. Punters, often trading illegally on margin, helped spike Shanghai's A-share market 85% and Shenzhen's 250% over January 1996 levels by the end of October. B-shares were their next target, first in Shenzhen, then in Shanghai. Whereas an average daily trading volume of US$3 million had been the norm for Shanghai B-shares for most of the year, in November it surged to US$15 million, with foreign investors finally joining the buying spree. On December 5 alone, total trading volume on the two exchanges hit 35 billion yuan (US$4.2 billion)— more than four times the daily amount reported by the Hong Kong Stock Exchange at the end of November—an astounding sum considering the total value of China's stock markets was less than a third of Hong Kong's market at that time.

Fanning the frenzy were brokerages playing on their own account, wealthy private investors, and state-owned companies with relationships in Beijing that gave them access to bank funds. Explained a Chinese analyst: "They unite and together they can move the market. They don't make long-term investments and they don't want appreciation of capital. They want to double and triple their money by the end of the year. They are trying to get rich."

But it was not just big institutions that had seized the opportunity to prosper in the bull run of 1996. Millions of ordinary citizens had caught stock market fever, often queuing at sunrise at brokerages to place their bets. In October 1996 the number of people in China trading stock swelled at a rate of 10,000 a day to total 21 million investors by mid-December. One in every two Shanghai residents owned stock. A middle-aged doctor surnamed Zhu in Shanghai, who earned about 800 yuan (US$97) a month, explained to me how he lost 6,000 yuan (US$723) when he first started trading. His mistake was buying stocks simply because they were cheap. "I didn't know anything about the companies," he confessed. He subsequently decided only to buy shares of companies enjoying an earnings-per-share ratio of 0.50 yuan (US$0.06). The strategy panned out during the bull run, netting him a return of 30% on the 10,000 yuan (US$1,205) of savings he invested that year. "Next year will be even better," he beamed. "Every family knows that the 15th Party Congress and the Hong Kong handover will take place in 1997. That means our country will be better off—both the politics and the economy."

The government was clearly nervous that so many common people had taken the same optimistic view and had staked their savings in the stock market. If colluding big players decided to drive down prices, inexperienced small investors would suffer. The last thing the government wanted was a repeat, but on a much larger scale, of the riots that occurred in Shenzhen in 1992 when investors could not get access to newly issued shares. Regulators' efforts to dampen market sentiment, however, had so far proved ineffective and Chinese leaders finally decided to intervene forcefully. On December 16, the central government published a scathing front-page editorial in the official *People's Daily*. In it, the authorities warned investors they would not prevent stock prices from tumbling before the Hong Kong handover and blamed the "abnormal and irrational" market surge on irregularities committed by state-owned enterprises, banks, securities firms, and certain newspapers. The government then added muscle to its pronouncements by placing a 10% limit on daily share price movements, enforcing rules prohibiting margin trading, penalizing Shenzhen's *Securities Times* and the *Shanghai Securities News* for inaccurate reporting, and announcing 10 billion yuan (US$1.21 billion) in new share issues for the coming year. The bull run was finally over.

Or so everyone thought. The markets were quiet in January and February until Deng Xiaoping's death on February 19, 1997, sparked rumors that the government was pumping money into the country's largest brokerages to buoy the market. Once again, investors became convinced that the government wanted a rising market before the Hong Kong handover in July and the 15th Party Congress in September. In the ensuing frenzy, Shanghai's A-share index soared 50% over the beginning of the year to more than 1,365 points by the end of April. Its shares were trading at roughly 50 times earnings—at the same time in the United States, S&P 500 stocks were trading at 20 times earnings, which many considered high in relation to historical averages. Shanghai's B-share index, which started in April 1997 at 73 points, had already jumped to almost 100 by early May. Typical of the type of talk I heard from both domestic and foreign analysts in the spring of 1997, Chen Chen, a B-share trader at Shenyin-Wanguo Securities, said to me in mid-May: "I'm very optimistic. I'm looking forward to the Shanghai B-share index hitting 120 before Hong Kong's handover and I'm conservative."

He and many others turned out to be dead wrong. What they did not understand was that the national leadership's preference for a rising market at the time of the handover was not as great as its fear that the country's hyper-charged markets were headed for breakdown. At the beginning of May the central government imposed some mild market-dampening measures. When these did not work, it became more forceful—its pronouncements indicating the types of abuses taking place. First, on May 22, the CSRC, the central bank, and the State Council body in charge of state enterprises issued rules explicitly prohibiting state enterprises from trading stocks or lending money to others for that purpose, closing two of the markets' key sources of liquidity. Two weeks later, the central bank choked off liquidity further when it told the country's banks and brokerages to recall all unauthorized money they had invested in the markets. It explicitly banned brokerages from margin trading and barred commercial banks from "repo" trading; i.e., lending capital for, say, five to seven days to state enterprises in exchange for collateral. But these measures were just the beginning. In its most severe punitive move since the 1995 bond futures scandal, it fired and fined the chiefs of five important banks and brokerages in Shanghai and Shenzhen on charges of gross stock market violations. The revelation of their crimes showed just how far the two cities still had to go in developing reliable market intermediaries. China's regulators also announced plans to fine the firms, suspend them from trading on their own account, and confiscate illegal earnings. More and even higher-level heads rolled over the summer. In July the State Council dismissed the country's chief securities regulator, Zhou Daojiong, the chairman of CSRC, for his inability to rein in the markets. Not long afterward, the CSRC fired Shanghai exchange head Yang Xianghai, the compromise candidate approved by both the Shanghai government and CSRC after Wei Wenyuan's dismissal in 1995. The CSRC appointed Tu Guangshao in his stead, a senior CSRC official in Beijing. This time there would be no compromise between Beijing and Shanghai. The central authorities used the opportunity to tighten their grip on the Shanghai and Shenzhen exchanges and would continue to do so for the remainder of the decade.

Neglected Software

Central government regulators once again sent a message to the investment community that they were capable of taking firm action against market malpractices. However, their behavior also reinforced investors' belief that government actions were more important than company performance, thus encouraging investors' speculative tendencies. Li Hongbo, the portfolio manager with Shenyin & Wanguo Securities, gave me this piece of advice following the December market crackdown: "In China, government policy affects everything. But government policy is not stable. You have to be very careful about the stock market. If the stock market is too high, you should sell because the government could interfere."

Local investors' single-minded focus on anticipating government actions explained some of the volatility roiling China's capital markets. Instead of focusing their investments on companies they believe will prosper in the long term, most individual investors in China buy for short-term gains, concentrating on government policy changes, rumors, and the behavior of big government-backed market participants. At the same time, big institutional investors, like trader Jimmy Zou's company, do not hold stocks in hopes of long-term capital appreciation like in mature markets, but instead act like individual investors. Policy-makers have thus far taken only tentative steps toward developing a corps of long-term investors. Shanghai and Shenzhen, for instance, have listed mutual fund-type firms that take a long-term perspective in mature markets, but management expertise is low and the funds tend to speculate just like everyone else. Moreover, there is not enough good information available about public companies for investors to make informed decisions. The government's unwillingness to promote an independent press, combined with listed companies' poor disclosure habits, make getting an accurate handle on a firm's situation difficult. It is therefore not surprising that local investors prefer to speculate rather than focus on often unknowable company fundamentals. Add to this equation the erratic enforcement of regulations, the paucity of investment vehicles, and the 5.34 trillion yuan (US$644 billion) in individual banks savings accounts at the end of 1998[14]—and the volatility of the Shanghai and Shenzhen exchanges becomes understandable.

To be sure, not all Chinese institutional investors operate solely on speculative sentiment. By the late 1990s some fund managers had started displaying greater professionalism. Foreign analysts pointed me to Li, the portfolio manager, as an example of this trend. A slim, pleasant-looking 27-year-old, he managed a US$50-million fund trading B-shares and H-shares for Shenyin-Wanguo Securities, which along with a small number of other securities firms had been granted government permission to trade hard-currency shares. I visited him couple of times in his small office shared with three coworkers on Ruijin Er Road. Surrounded by computer screens showing graphs and spreadsheets of the latest stock data, he sported the traditional blue pinstripe shirt favored by Western investment banking types. Like many other Chinese in Shanghai during that chilly January, however, he also wore long underwear, which peeked out from under his shirt sleeve. (Buildings south of the Yangtze River traditionally did not enjoy heat during the winter even though temperatures could drop below freezing.) After talking to Li for a while, I came to see his hybrid attire as quite fitting. Yes, he had adopted some of the more sophisticated trading practices of fund managers in more mature markets, as symbolized by his blue pinstripe shirt. He regularly relied on in-house company research to determine which companies to trade and visited companies himself to find out firsthand about their performance, asking them tough questions about turnover, costs, competition, future plans, etc. Li had developed this approach during earlier years as an analyst. "The companies like to cheat researchers by giving them wrong numbers. This is very common in China. But I often visit these companies many times and when they get familiar with you, they tell you the truth. It's very difficult for a person to repeat his lies exactly," he explained. Li also said he tried to hold stocks for three to six months, an eternity for most Chinese traders, but he maintained that finding a good company in China was not easy and he therefore did not want to sell right away. "And frankly," he added, "you can't get a much better performance if you hold things more short term."

Li's prudence impressed me. However, as I pressed him on his trading strategy, he admitted that it only applied to 50% of his investments. He held the other half of his portfolio for two days to two weeks. He explained: "Sometimes we buy a stock and the price goes up sharply, so we sell two days later." Just as Li wore long underwear to compensate for poor heating, he still operated in a business environment that demanded short-term trading to be successful.

The poor performance of listed companies also hurt the Shanghai exchange and the city's bid to become a world-class financial center. Of the 878 companies listed in Shanghai and Shenzhen, more than 77 posted a loss for 1998, compared to 41 in 1997, and one-third saw profits slide.[15] While a slowing economy and the Asian financial crisis partly explained their troubles, so did poor management, which becomes more apparent during the economic downturn. Why are there so many corporate duds listed on the Shanghai exchange? Because instead of viewing stock markets as a way to mobilize capital for the country's most promising firms, the government clings to the notion that they are tools for restructuring the state sector. The government chooses the companies that list, rather than letting the market decide, and normally selects state enterprises. In 1999, the State Development Planning Commission's Investment Research Center issued a scathing report,[16] which commented:

People thought that in most cases, the most important cause of state-owned enterprises' difficulties was that debt burdens were too heavy and that companies were short of capital. However, after many listed companies have raised large amounts of capital that they do not need to repay ... this still has not produced the expected high efficiency. It is easy to understand that a few enterprises have a mixed performance, but it is difficult to understand how listed companies which were selected from the 'excellent' state enterprises have all seen their efficiency decrease.

Disappointed Dreams

The performance of B-share companies and the liquidity of B-share markets so disappointed foreign investors that by the end of the 1990s they pretty much abandoned them altogether. Shanghai's B-market lost 47% of its value in 1998 as foreign investors sold down their shares. Of far more concern is the precipitous drop in daily turnover. In 1998, it averaged US$4 million, compared to turnover of US$10 million in 1994 when foreign investors had high expectations for the market's future.

In September 1998, I had a long talk with Bruce Richardson, ABN Ambro Hoare Govett Asia's chief representative in Shanghai, about foreign investors' disillusionment. I caught him just as he was packing his bags to leave China and take a job in New York City. Abandoning the guarded tones that foreign executives adopt when worried about maintaining their relationships with Chinese officialdom, Richardson blurted:

B-shares continue to fall because there's absolutely no buying interest from foreigners and only limited interest from locals. There's been no foreign interest for about two years except during bull runs sparked by run-ups in the A-share market. The difference is that in 1996 we had people both buying and selling. Now during the last six months, people are only selling. They're saying, 'we've had enough.'

I asked him for his prognosis for the B-share market. He said:

It's dim in the short term and dim in the long term. This is a failed experiment and it failed for three main reasons: regulators did not have any clear goals when they established the B-share market; regulators don't clearly understand what an equities market is; and the management of listed companies is extremely poor.

He did not blame poor investor sentiment solely on the Asian financial crisis, which had driven many foreign portfolio investors away from Asian markets. He explained:

The basic problems are there during good times or bad, although it's fair to say that the Asian financial crisis accelerated the demise. B-share companies perform well when the economy goes up. But when it falters these companies suffer disproportionately because of their poor marketing management. This doesn't just mean sales, it means examining product markets to find products that match consumer demand so that the company can optimize earnings. I spent four years talking to Chinese managers of listed companies. Their idea of marketing management is making as much product as they can, selling it at a cheap price, getting it out of the warehouse, and gaining the highest market share. But if that is all you do, your goods all sit in the warehouse. The demise of B-shares would have happened without the Asian crisis. Eventually investors tire of buying companies with all the same problem: state enterprises in the process of reform. It's not possible for B-share markets to get a new life in their current form as a way for state enterprises to get free money to do what they please. This is no longer a viable setup. Fundamental change will have to occur before foreign investors return.

At the same time, foreign investment bankers complain that unwieldy rules make taking Chinese companies public on the Shanghai exchange highly risky. According to regulations, the time period during which international investment banks bear underwriting risk exposure is significantly longer than in other major markets. When that risk is added to the other challenges of dealing with Chinese companies—mixed performance and lack of transparency—many investment banks hesitate to underwrite firms listing on the exchange.

This state of affairs combined with the belt-tightening brought on by Asia's economic difficulties has led some foreign securities firms to reduce their local and expatriate staffs in Shanghai. Previously, their long-term commitment to China made losing money a necessary evil, saving Chinese and expatriate employees from the downsizing that typically rocks the international securities industry in hard times. In 1998, however, Sassoon Securities Co. laid off more than a dozen employees and closed its Shanghai office, deciding to conduct China B-share research out of Hong Kong. Chris Drake, the firm's Hong Kong-based director, cited a lack of client interest as a critical reason for the move.[17] Jardine Fleming—the foreign brokerage that built the largest operation in the city, with more than 28 employees—let go a third of its staff in 1998, including its expatriate chief representative, whom it did not plan to replace with another expensive foreigner. I talked to the outgoing chief representative, William Hanbury-Tenison, in January 1999 about the changes taking place. He explained:

Companies are downsizing because the B-share market is so small. Before, foreign securities firms had been hoping the B-share and the A-share markets would merge or the foreigners would get access to A-shares. But now no one thinks that is going to happen for at least five years. We're downsizing because we're not making money overall in Asia and we can no longer afford places like China where we can't even break even. Companies know now that China is going to be a drain for a long time. People are very discouraged.

So much for Shanghai offering the business opportunity of the century that some foreign investors expected. The exchange's total capitalization at the beginning of 1999 was roughly US$130 billion; a little more than a third the size of Hong Kong's. And because foreign investment houses in Shanghai are still only allowed to trade B-shares, in 1999 they were dealing in a market with total capitalization of only US$1.2 billion. Even the value of war-torn Sri Lanka's market was more: US$1.7 billion. Nothing reveals better how American investment banks view the size of the opportunity in Shanghai than by how they staff their offices there. Take Morgan Stanley. In 1999, its Shanghai office had only four permanent staff, none of whom were costly expatriates. The director in charge of the office resided in Hong Kong, as did the head of Morgan Stanley's overall China business and the rest of the China execution staff, who traveled up to Shanghai when business warranted. Meanwhile, Morgan Stanley's Hong Kong office had 800 staff, 50 of whom were devoted part or full-time to China work, making Hong Kong the key venue for decision-making for Asia and China business. Explaining the Shanghai office's permanent staff size in 1995, Wadsworth said: "We have always had a view that we will keep our commitment scaled to the size of the immediate opportunity while taking a long-term view." Clearly, the Shanghai exchange at the start of the 21st century is a minor opportunity.

For foreign commercial banks, opportunities were also limited in the 1990s—albeit less so because they at least had an army of foreign manufacturing clients to service. Although Shanghai boasted the largest number of foreign bank branches in the country, the central government did not permit most of them to do yuan business. They instead had to content themselves with conducting import and export settlements, foreign currency loans and deposits, and other plain vanilla, hard-currency transactions. For the 19 foreign banks approved to deal in yuan in 1998,[18] the go-ahead did not amount to much. Policy-makers only permitted banks to provide local currency services to foreign firms located in Shanghai, not to local enterprises or Chinese individuals. As a result, at the end of that year, the combined outstanding yuan loan balance for foreign banks reached only US$128 million—peanuts considering that General Motor's investment to manufacture automobiles in Shanghai alone exceeded US$1 billion.[19] "Yuan banking is not much of an opportunity because of all the restrictions," commented Steve Harner, a commercial banker who arrived in Shanghai from Tokyo in 1993 thinking that Shanghai was where the banking action in Asia would be. Except for business with foreign-invested companies, "the action did not particularly turn out to be in Shanghai," he said. Likewise, the Chinese government granted licenses to conduct business in Shanghai to nine of the 50 foreign insurance companies that set up offices in the city by the end of 1998. They earned a total of one billion yuan (US$121 million) in premium income compared with the mainland's four major state insurers, who together took in roughly nine billion yuan (US$1.1 billion).[20] The exception among foreign insurers was American Insurance Group (AIG), which by 1998 had licenses to sell both life and property casualty insurance in Shanghai and Guangzhou, and had a sales force exceeding 4,000 agents. This progress, however, came after nearly 20 years of patient effort by company chairman Maurice Greenberg. Throughout the 1990s, China's government was only willing to open the country's financial services sector a crack for fear foreign firms would steal business away from less-sophisticated Chinese banks and insurers.

Future Prospects

Asia's financial meltdown of 1997–1999 was a wake-up call to Chinese leaders. The crisis underscored the dangers of a weak financial system, accelerating efforts to clean up and reduce risk in the financial services sector. For instance, the authorities starting letting banks write off bad loans and they set up asset-management companies at the country's four leading banks to absorb at least some of their nonperforming debt. China also seemed to be getting serious about letting major financial players that overextended themselves go bankrupt. As part of efforts to bring the country's hundreds of freewheeling investment and trust companies (ITICS) to heel, the central government in 1997 launched an audit of their activities. This resulted in the highly publicized October 1998 closure of influential Guangdong International Trust & Investment Co. (GITIC) after it could not meet its debt obligations.[21] The securities industry was another central government target after a 1998 audit of the country's major securities firms revealed a multitude of irregularities, including trading in customer assets without their permission and concealing profits. In January 1999, Chinese legislators finally passed a national securities law, putting the CRSC in charge of regulating all market matters. And following the spate of loss announcements by listed companies in early 1999, the CSRC announced its future intention to make profitability and quality the most important criteria for approving a company to go public. It also talked of scrapping the quota system for public listings. Probably the best news of all, however, was China's signing of an agreement with the United States in November 1999 to enter the World Trade Organization. Although the accord did little for foreign investment banks, it granted foreign commercial banks the right to conduct local-currency transactions with domestic companies within two years of China's accession and with individuals after five years. Of course, progress will depend on how well China, with a history of fudging on trade accords, implements its promises. And its market-opening initiatives often come with caveats.[22] But overall, China's WTO entry is expected to accelerate the reform of China's state enter-prises, banking system, and financial services industry, which will only benefit Shanghai.

However, the CSRC's moves in June 1999 to stimulate the country's lifeless stock markets provoked unsettling feelings of deja-vu—making observers question how much the country's leaders had really learned. The rallies started when the central government told domestic securities firms to dive back into stocks and play up their prospects to investors.[23] Following an upbeat market assessment by CSRC vice chairman Chen Yaoxian, the *People's Daily* ran an effusive front-page editorial endorsing the rally. The central government's moves came just as its massive infrastructure spending spree—launched in 1998 to compensate for slowing investment demand, consumer consumption, exports, and foreign investment—showed signs of running out of steam. Prices were still falling. Interest rates hung at their lowest in the history of the People's Republic. Overcapacities plagued most sectors and companies posted disappointing results for 1998. Despite this reality, the commentary concluded that the recent rally reflected "the public's upbeat expectations for a good [economic] picture," and that the Chinese economy was in "good shape" as a result of the government's investment policies. It hoped that consumers, flush with their new stock market winnings, would start spending their mountains of savings and revive the slowing economy. In the process, it once again dashed hopes that it would stop trying to use its muscle to bludgeon the country's markets into submission.

In comparison with Hong Kong, Shanghai ultimately has a long way to go to be an international financial center. Granted, Shanghai has some advantages: a huge domestic market, lower costs, a larger labor pool, an up-and-coming reputation, and Beijing's backing. Although the Shanghai government started publicly downplaying Shanghai's ambitions as an international financial center on par with Hong Kong in a run up to the Southern city's return to Chinese sovereignty in July 1997, Premier Zhu Rongji, made his preference perfectly clear. During a trip to North America in April 1999, he compared Shanghai to New York and Hong Kong to Toronto.[24] Such a comment on the eve of the 21st century was absurd, but it demonstrated Beijing's view of the future.

Unlike Shanghai, Hong Kong today has a corps of senior managers with 15–20 years' experience who understand Asian markets and are trusted by their home office to make decisions for the Asia-Pacific region. There's a lot keeping them in the former British colony. For one, Hong Kong has a fully convertible currency, more high-quality listed companies, good disclosure practices, reliable financial intermediaries, and, perhaps most importantly, a well-enforced legal system based on British tradition. For these reasons, even the Chinese government lists many of the country's biggest companies in Hong Kong rather than Shanghai. Discussing the importance of an independent and dependable judiciary, Tom Preston, the managing director of the SOPEX investment fund in Hong Kong, explained: "If I do a business venture in Shanghai, I want to sign the shareholders' agreement in Hong Kong or Singapore because, then, if I get into a fight, I know that in those two places I could win on the merits of my case. That's not the case in Shanghai." Hong Kong also has a far larger pool of financial talent. Although the availability of high-quality financial staff has improved in Shanghai in the 1990s, it is harder there to find top-notch people with credit analysis, administrative, and other skills important to financial service companies. Hong Kong also offers top executives a better standard of living. It provides proximity to both north and southeast Asia, decent medical care, good schools, easy access to nature, English-speaking housekeepers, spectacular apartments on the Peak, and a slew of other amenities for expatriates. Although improving, Shanghai is not yet as pleasant a place to live as Hong Kong or Singapore—the other avid contender to the "New York of Asia" title. Even if Shanghai were to catch up with Hong Kong in all the ways mentioned, its status as

Asia-Pacific's financial center is by no means assured—thanks ironically to one of Shanghai's advantages. Because of the huge size and complexity of China's market, firms fear that regional executives stationed in Shanghai will inadvertently become so absorbed with China business that they will neglect their responsibilities to the rest of the region.[25]

That said, Hong Kong faces its own set of challenges. These include worsening pollution, middling education quality, declining English skills, deteriorating press freedoms, high costs, and, until the recent Internet craze, myopic focus on the property and banking sectors as a route to wealth. How Hong Kong deals with these issues will help determine Shanghai's future.

In the meantime, Shanghai is still struggling to emerge as China's domestic financial capital. The city, as a result of Beijing's policies, is already the site of the country's most important financial markets, excluding Hong Kong. And Shanghai has again become a hub for foreign commercial banks in China, taking on some tasks previously carried out in Hong Kong. But Shanghai in the 1990s was at best a financial center for China's *Huadong*, or eastern region, and provincial protectionism made even this status somewhat spurious. Because Chinese banks were organized along provincial lines, banks in Shanghai could not lend to non-Shanghai-based firms. Local branches of the State Administration of Foreign Exchange often refused to give local companies permission to open working accounts in Shanghai for no other reason then they wanted them to borrow locally. For most of the decade, each province also had its own central bank branch, which meant that the Shanghai branch of the People's Bank of China did not have regulatory or monetary adjustment power over the *Huadong* region. In 1998, however, the central government started reforming the system, setting up nine new central bank branches to oversee different geographic regions. It gave the Shanghai branch regulatory responsibility over Shanghai, Zhejiang, and Fujian and appointed a high-level central bank official to run the influential area. In another breakthrough, the Bank of China in 1998 agreed to transfer its treasury functions from Beijing down to Shanghai.

Promising as these developments are, the center of power for China's domestic financial systems remains in Beijing. Besides the central bank, the State Planning and Development Commission, the State Administration of Foreign Exchange, the CSRC, and the Ministry of Finance, Beijing is headquarters to a wide assortment of financial institutions. These include four of the country's five national commercial banks, which provide the vast majority of the country's domestic loans. The smaller Bank of Communications is the only one of the five that is headquartered in Shanghai. The four Beijing-based state banks, meanwhile, started reasserting control over local branches at the end of the 1990s, including those in Shanghai. At the same time, Beijing is the headquarters for many of China's largest companies—former government ministries turned into state-run corporations—with subsidiaries all over the country. According to Moody's Charles Tan, "If you look at where people are with the ability to structure big deals with foreign institutions and capital market issues, these activities are mostly done in Beijing." Although Shanghai is the site of China's major financial markets, real power rests with the Beijing-based institutions that make key decisions.

In the securities field, authority has actually migrated north to the capital. Shanghai and Shenzhen regulators used to have the power to approve an allotted number of new listings until Beijing withdrew that privilege in April 1995. The Shanghai municipal government originally had authority over the Shanghai exchange, but during the last years of the decade the CSRC in Beijing usurped that power too. Explained Hanbury-Tenison, the chief representative for securities firm Jardine Fleming: "After I first took the Jardine Fleming job, it took me a few months to realize that what business we needed to do was in Beijing and that power was going up to Beijing." When I asked Morgan Stanley Asia corporate communications head Gerald Kay in 1999 if the Beijing office was the company's most important in China, he immediately replied, "Absolutely. That's where the government is."

So is the New York editor correct in anticipating Shanghai's status as the New York of Asia? Thinking back over conversations and all I had witnessed, I would have to say that the obstacles loom at least as large as the city's progress and potential. In the 1990s the city did a fine job of building the bricks and mortar of an international financial hub—it has a state-of-the-art stock exchange building, modern company headquarters, and plenty of new highways. However, it did not focus enough on building soft infrastructure, including consistently enforced regulations, good companies, reliable intermediaries, transparency, and a strong independent business information network. The importance of these intangible qualities has proved difficult for bureaucrats schooled in control and output-oriented state planning to recognize. Shanghai's progress in developing the software of an international financial center

during the next 20 years will ultimately determine the city's place in the
21st century's financial history.

Do the Shanghainese have it in them to create the New York of Asia?
They certainly have the will and talent potential. Shanghainese see their
city's overshadowing of Hong Kong to become China's most international
city as their destiny. I have met many highly competent Shanghainese,
who with the right incentives work very hard, efficiently, and successfully.
Many learn at home from a very young age the value of money. By all
accounts, that training has created a very number-oriented civic culture.
And if the many Shanghainese who work in finance in New York City
or in Hong Kong ever return to Shanghai, they will accelerate Shanghai's
advance exponentially. Until the city's financial markets become much
more open, however, there's little to draw them back despite the city's
impressive infrastructure advances. In 1999, Pan Ming, a Shanghainese
economist with Prudential-Bache Securities in Hong Kong, explained:
"I'd love to go back. I understand the culture. I understand the system. But
I don't plan to go back anytime soon. The market is just not that open."

Even if Pan and his ilk return to Shanghai, however, the city will
still need more than will and talent to become the New York of Asia.
It needs the right tools, including the power to decide its own destiny,
which Beijing has not yet granted. After all, Washington's tight leash
did not make New York the world's largest securities market. But
Beijing at the start of the 21st century decides how quickly Shanghai's
markets will open, when the currency will become convertible, and
when the big state banks will move their headquarters to the city. If
Shanghai wants to issue a Yankee bond, it needs Beijing's permission.
If Shanghai Industrial, the Shanghai government's flagship firm, wants
to do a backdoor listing, it needs Beijing's permission. If a foreign
securities firm based in Shanghai wants to change the English name of
its company, it again needs Beijing's permission. The Shanghai branch
of the People's Bank of China does not have approval authority over
even that small a matter. Certainly city leaders lobby the center hard for
initiatives to benefit the city, and with so many former Shanghai officials
in the nation's capital they can find sympathetic ears. But Shanghai is
by no means calling its own shots. As Richard Graham, the former
Shanghai-based chief representative for ING Barings, cleverly put it:
"Shanghai proposes, Beijing disposes." Shanghai finance officials and
executives, appointed by their superiors up north, have little incentive
to deviate from the party line if they want their careers to advance,

particularly after watching Beijing ruin a number of their colleagues' careers throughout the decade. Given that national-level policy-makers have such a big influence over the pace of change in Shanghai, the city's fate rests largely in Beijing's hands.

Not that local officials did a very good job of building the city's financial software when they had more control earlier in the decade. The government favored its own state-run companies of questionable quality when it had power over the listing process—a policy that the city is paying for with a dying B-share market. It regulated the markets poorly, allowing widespread abuse and reaffirming the central government's inclination to control.

But Shanghai today is a city dominated by little-reformed state enterprises, a powerful bureaucracy that does not understand the underpinnings of healthy financial markets, and a Communist Party that doles out preferential policies and promotions to those who kowtow to it. Under current conditions, the full abilities of the Shanghainese have yet to be tested. Only when market forces hold sway, the city gets over its state-enterprise bias, and it is free to run itself will the Shanghainese be able to take advantage of their city's myriad advantages to make Shanghai a serious contender.

Notes

[1] *People's Daily*, Oct. 21, 1992.

[2] *Asia Inc.*, Dec. 1993.

[3] Ibid.

[4] *South China Morning Post*, Mar. 3, 1994.

[5] Banking System Outlook: China, Moody's Investors Services, Global Credit Research, June 1998.

[6] Shanghai Pudong Development Bank was the first bank in China to gain approval from central government regulators to list shares. However, the Shenzhen Development Bank, which was approved by local regulators, listed earlier.

[7] *China Weekly Fax Bulletin*, Orbis Publications, Jul. 12, 1999.

[8] Reuters, Sept. 28, 1998.

[9] *Institutional Investor*, Jun. 1994.

[10] *Asian Wall Street Journal*, May 25, 1994.

[11] *South China Morning Post*, Nov. 12, 1998 and the *Hong Kong Standard*, Mar. 3, 1995.

[12] *Institutional Investor*, op. cit.

[13] *South China Morning Post*, Nov. 12, 1998.

[14] *South China Morning Post*, Jan. 26, 1999.

[15] Ibid., May 1, 1999.

[16] *AFX-Asia*, Feb. 10, 1999.

[17] *Asian Wall Street Journal*, Oct. 8, 1998.

[18] As of April 1999. See *South China Morning Post*, Apr. 10, 1999.

[19] *Shanghai Star*, Apr. 13, 1999.

[20] *South China Morning Post*, May 12, 1999.

[21] Political considerations undoubtedly also played a role in GITIC's closure—the central government hoped to rein in freewheeling Guangdong province. At the same time, it sent a chilling message to China's foreign financial community that it could no longer count on provincial loan guarantees, unless explicitly approved in writing by the central government.

[22] For instance, Reuters reported in February 2000 that China's central bank was "considering limiting yuan lending by foreign banks to four times their operating capital." *See South China Morning Post*, Feb. 10, 2000. Also see the *Asian Wall Street Journal*, Mar. 2, 2000.

[23] Ibid., May 25, 1999.

[24] Ibid., Apr. 19, 1999.

[25] *See* Chapter 6, Return of the Foreigners, for a fuller explanation.

4

The "Haves" and the "Have-Nots"

A s Shanghai changes physically so do the Shanghainese. Take Zhou Zheng, also known more recently to the world as Isabella Zhou. When Canadian businessman Assaf Drori interviewed her to be his bilingual secretary in 1993, a timid Zhou spoke poor English, had long stringy hair, and wore a dress that looked like it had been "inherited from her grandmother." So imagine his surprise when he saw her in 1997 for the first time in three years sporting a well-tailored outfit, fashionably cropped hair, and strong English. After working as Droori's assistant for a couple of years, Zhou landed an even better job as a top administrative aide at American computer-maker Hewlett-Packard. The 24-year-old's salary had already more than doubled her parents' earnings at their state-owned work units and the opportunities she enjoyed exceeded their imaginations. For Zhou, and for the many young, well-educated Shanghainese like her hired by one of the multinational corporations flooding the country in the 1990s, the future looked rosy. Over coffee at a new espresso bar in downtown Shanghai, Zhou talked about her situation:

I really like my life now. When I'm working I feel very productive. I can learn more working for a foreign company than for a Chinese company. I'm very impressed with Hewlett-Packard's system, their focus on employees' training and development. There's training in computer skills, business practices, Hewlett-Packard ethics and culture. Some engineers go for training in Singapore or Hong Kong. I have a development plan for myself. I want to work in the Human Resources department.

I don't think I would have changed as much if I had not worked for a foreign company. It's now easier for me to accept new things. And in the future it will be even easier. My way of thinking has changed and so have my values. For instance, before I did not think shopping was very worthy, but now I do. Also, working life is very busy. I need relaxation. And I have money to spend—my salary is higher than my parents ....

I like to visit places like Huangshan or some islands. I also like to read, gather with friends at restaurants, sing karaoke, go bowling, play ping pong, go swimming, or go mountain climbing. When I was little, I never traveled. You need money and time to travel ...

Also, my opinion about marriage has changed a lot. Before I thought that at a suitable age I should marry and have children, but now if I have a baby I want to give him a good life or I won't have him. When I was a child, my family's income was not high. I had a peaceful, normal life. I got lots of love. But that's not good enough. If I'm a parent, I'll give my child training in a specific hobby. I'll take them to parks and exhibitions, and traveling, both outside of Shanghai and outside of China. When I was a child I didn't get these things. To give this, we need money. If I don't have money, I don't want to have children ...

I still live with my parents. Girls like me don't have to worry about a car or a house. We put stress on dressing and eating. In other countries, they have these other concerns. Here we can use our money to have fun. But now I'm starting to think about owning a house. My company offers a housing fund and the bank offers mortgages. Three to five years ago I never would have thought about this.

Unfortunately, not everyone in Shanghai looks forward to such a bright future as Isabella Zhou. When I met Ah Hua one evening in 1996, she had just been laid off from the state-owned textile factory where she had worked for 17 years. I made my way up an unlit, dingy stairwell to the 32-square-meter apartment she shared with her husband, mother, and 13-year-old daughter. Sitting on a bed wearing a night shirt festooned with a sleeping puppy, she looked much younger than her 38 years. She offered me a glass of tea and began explaining her predicament:

I started working at the factory when I was 21. My father had retired early so I was able to take his job. I was eager to work there: It was considered a good job. State factories were stable. I entered that factory as a young, pretty girl. Now I'm middle-aged. I worked on a cloth-measuring machine. My job was to make sure the cloth entered the measuring machine properly. I had to concentrate all the time. It was hard, boring work. They call it light industry but it was really heavy industry ...

I did the same job for 17 years. I'm not very clever. I graduated from high school in 1977, but I really did not have much of an education. I went to school during the Cultural Revolution. I got my diploma, but there was nothing in it ...

My factory altogether had about 10,000 employees. Before the layoffs started, many people had already left the factory—those were the people with connections. Last year about 100 got laid off. I was part of the first group dismissed this year and there are going to be many more. There were rumors that the layoffs would occur, but no one expected it to happen so fast. They only gave us two days advance warning. I was very surprised because I had spent 17 years in that place. I thought the factory would always find a way …

When I still worked I earned 600–700 yuan [US$72–84] a month depending on my bonus. Now the factory pays me 200 yuan [US$24] a month plus medical insurance. I'm not sure how long that will last. But 200 yuan is nothing in Shanghai. Our basic expenses for four people are about 1,000 yuan [US$120] a month. Luckily my husband still has a job at a pharmaceutical factory and earns 1,000 yuan a month …

I tried going to the labor market, but when I looked at the job requirements, I didn't dare fill out the form. It asked for your education level and field of expertise. Today, society requires a kind of level that people like me can't reach. Of course we want to work hard and start another job. Many of my work-mates have been able to find jobs as cleaning ladies in hotels and kitchens. The factory helped them arrange it. The jobs only pay between 200–400 yuan [US$24–48] a month. None of my friends who started a job finished their one-year contract. They either hated it or society didn't think they were good enough. Society looks down on laid-off workers from this industry. These are low-level jobs. At least in the factory we had skills. We had a voice …

The factory provides information on courses offered by the government. I'm interested in taking one, but admission is limited. Only two people from my workshop received permission and other people had been laid off longer than me. Before that course, the factory organized training to become a neighborhood surveillance worker, but the job had high political requirements that I didn't have. You had to be a Communist Party member. It paid 900 yuan [US$108] a month …

I don't feel cheated that I was laid off. After all, the factory promised it would find us jobs. But I do feel a little angry that the jobs are the lowest type with the lowest pay and no status. I'd like to be a shop clerk. If I were 25 I'd just go for it. But the factory promised to find us jobs in a short time. So we're scared that if it calls and finds we're already working, it will stop providing medical insurance and won't help us anymore. If we lose the new job, then what?

Ah Hua and Isabella Zhou exemplify the two faces of modern-day Shanghai. Zhou, the Hewlett-Packard employee, stands for the future: white collar and well-educated. For people like her, Shanghai's renewal signifies new opportunity, greater prosperity, and a more comfortable life. Ah Hua, the laid-off state factory employee, represents Shanghai's blue-collar, low-skilled past. The changes taking place spell uncertainty and hardship. The two women's divergent paths grew out of China's transition away from state planning in the 1990s toward a market economy and competition—a transition that at the start of the 21st century is transforming Shanghai into a society of haves and have-nots.

Overall, incomes in Shanghai soared over the roaring 1990s after Deng Xiaoping gave the city his blessing to reemerge as an international business center. Local residents, for instance, earned 8,700 yuan (US$1,050) per capita in 1999, a more than 80% jump over 1992.[1] They invested their swelling paychecks in clothing, color televisions, refrigerators, furniture, houses, cars, and overseas travel.

But while standards of living rose for many, something else happened during the course of the decade: Some residents got rich much faster than others and still other residents were left behind altogether. Income disparity between the city's top 10% and bottom 10% of citizens with Shanghai residency permits quadrupled from 1,964 yuan (US$237) in 1990 to 11,168 yuan (US$1,345) in 1996, with the wealthiest 10% taking home 14,953 yuan (US$1,801) and the poorest 10% pocketing 3,785 yuan (US$456).[2] And these figures do not include the three million migrant laborers working in the city, mostly on construction sites. According to a Shanghai's Statistics Bureau report, the poorest families among official residents could not meet monthly expenses, forcing them to draw on their savings or even borrow funds to make ends meet, while "unfair competition and policy loopholes allowed others to make fortunes."[3]

Obtaining more up-to-date statistics on the city's and the country's growing income gap in the waning years of the decade was problematic since the state-controlled press stopped reporting on the subject for fear of stoking social tensions. The subject grew increasingly sensitive as worker and rural unrest escalated around the country in the last half of the 1990s. But in 1999, amid a nationwide debate on how to revive China's flagging economy, some revealing data came to light. Chinese central bank official Sun Guofeng divulged in a local newspaper that only 3% of private bank account holders in China accounted for almost half of the country's total private bank savings of 5.9 trillion yuan (US$711 billion) as of June 1999.[4] It was for that reason government officials kept insisting to the public that a new tax they imposed on savings accounts in 1999 would not hurt the poor much.[5] Although income inequality in China and Shanghai in the late 1990s did not approach Latin American extremes, the gap was great and growing compared to the People's Republic's pre-reform past. Managing the expanding gulf between the haves and have-nots in a society weaned on egalitarianism is a key challenge facing China's leaders today. Because of Shanghai's status as the country's most populous city, as a role model for the rest of the country, and as its designated international financial, commercial, and trading hub, the government considers social stability in Shanghai of paramount importance to the country's future.

Old Shanghai's Darker Shade of Inequality

Shanghai has always had "haves" and "have-nots," although the degree of income inequality has fluctuated dramatically. At no time was it more dramatic than before the Communist Revolution in 1949. Prior to the Communist takeover, Shanghai was known throughout the world for its laissez-faire capitalism, the extravagance of its upper classes, and the wretchedness of its poor. What made Old Shanghai a paradise for the rich and a living hell for many others? The city's unusual political setup, for one. In the 1800s, foreign powers, including Great Britain, the United States, and France claimed sovereignty over large tracts of Shanghai territory. China's Qing Dynasty emperors in Beijing could do little to stop them. Foreigners did not have to answer to Chinese law, but instead enforced their own law in their spheres of influence. Businessmen ran the International Settlement for businessmen and fiercely resisted encroachments on their freedom to make money. Tycoon Victor Sassoon, for instance, decided to uproot the headquarters of his family's business empire from Bombay to Shanghai in 1931, partly to flee the more humane factory law under debate in India's parliament. In Old Shanghai, "The International Settlement had rejected calls for even the gentlest Factory Act."[6]

Foreigners in Shanghai, also known as Shanghailanders, led privileged lives. The wealthiest foreign merchants, like the Sassoons, the Hardoons, and the Kadoories, built themselves opulent mansions that made the fabulous villas built by other wealthy businessmen look modest. The Kadoorie home, for instance, boasted a 65-foot-high, 80-foot-long ballroom with 18-foot chandeliers, 43 servants, and a novel luxury for those days: air conditioning. With the help of the surplus servants that cheap labor provided, foreigners threw lavish invitation-only masquerade parties, spent leisurely weekends on their houseboats, or idled away hours over cocktails in their exclusive clubs. Not that all foreigners in Shanghai had money. Russians fleeing the Communist Revolution in 1919, for instance, often arrived in Shanghai with little except their clothes and found low-status jobs as body guards or dollar-a-dance girls.

In general, however, Shanghailanders were owners, bosses, and executives and lived more comfortably than most local residents.[7]

Not that entrepreneurial Chinese in Old Shanghai did not become owners and bosses themselves. Stories abound of quick-witted Chinese who moved to the city and amassed fortunes. Immigrants from Guangdong, known then as Canton, did particularly well in retail. Those from Ningbo in Zhejiang province excelled in banking. Some from Jiangsu province made good in textiles, which became the backbone of the city's wealth. Lynn Pan, who fled Shanghai at age 10 around 1949, recounts in a memoir of her family, *Tracing It Home*, how her grandfather started his life in Shanghai laying sewers in the International Settlement and ended it as a property tycoon.[8] Wealthy merchants, industrialists, bankers, government officials, and a special group known as compradores who worked closely with foreigners, made up Shanghai society's top echelons. Like the new rich everywhere, they liked to show off their wealth. They built expansive villas filled with modern comforts, well-tended gardens, and multiple servants. They sent their children abroad to study or enrolled them in the prestigious foreign schools, providing Shanghai a core of Westernized and cosmopolitan Chinese. They learned English and the foxtrot, wore jewels and chinchilla, listened to jazz and Chinese opera, and played tennis and mahjong. Pan remembers her parents as socialites, flitting from one engagement to the next, and her uncle as a polo-loving playboy. "He was trained as an accountant but I don't think that he ever did much work," she commented during a return trip to Shanghai in 1996.

At the other extreme were the teeming masses streaming in from the countryside to escape natural disaster, poverty, and war in China's interior. Charities popped up to help the less fortunate, but they could by no means satisfy the successive waves of desperate immigrants flooding the city. Poor sanitation and overcrowding turned poorer neighborhoods into breeding grounds for communicable disease like cholera. People frequently starved or died from exposure. They took whatever work they could get, no matter how poorly they were paid or treated. Men broke their backs pulling the wealthy around in rickshaws, building Tudor mansions, and hauling cognacs and French lace off ships. Women peddled vegetables, made shoe soles from old rags, and worked as prostitutes. Misery compelled many to sell their sons and daughters for cash. If they were lucky they found a steady job in a factory where they labored under Dickensian conditions. The city's textile mills regularly employed children, required 12–14-hour days six to seven days a week, and paid piddling wages. Plenty of other wretches were ready to take their place if they complained.[9] To borrow a phrase from English philosopher Thomas Hobbes' description of Europe in the 1600s, the lives of Shanghai's multitudes, though far from "solitary," were "nasty, poor, brutish, and short."

But whether a Shanghainese was upper, middle, or lower class, the political domination and condescending attitudes of foreign residents exacerbated the sense of inequity that pervaded society. Out to enrich themselves, most foreigners had little respect for the culture and people who were enriching them. The idea that certain races could be superior to others made sense to many people in those days and citizens of the occupying powers treated Chinese accordingly. Huang Tianming had just entered his 72nd year when I first met him in the mid-1990s. He moved to Shanghai in the early 1930s and led a privileged life for those days. He lived in the foreign concessions, attended the most prestigious missionary schools, and worked after graduation as a clerk in Shanghai's foreign-controlled customs house. The fluent English speaker earned 600 silver dollars a month, whereas a regular employee at a Chinese company might make 40 silver dollars. Nonetheless, he recalled bitterly some 50 years later the feeling of being a second-class citizen in his own home:

In Shanghai everything had foreign names. You couldn't remember the name because the Chinese characters when put together did not make sense. All the documents in the customs house were in English. It was a humiliation. I did not like foreigners but I wanted a better living. If I studied English I could get a higher salary. But I felt very uncomfortable in the foreign concessions. In the 1930s foreigners walking down the street would walk right over you. Chinese kids would walk to the side of the road when they saw them because they felt scared. Foreigners did not treat us like people.

Birth of the Egalitarian Ethic

After the Revolution in 1949, much changed. Foreigners who had not fled the Japanese invasion during World War II packed their bags with the news of the Communists' victory. Under the leadership of Mao Zedong, the Party pledged to wipe out the inequalities that plagued Chinese society, raising the low status of workers and peasants while ending the privileges enjoyed by the country's capitalist and intellectual classes. It rejected the market, private property, and material incentives in favor of state ownership and planning, which allowed the Party to control and redistribute resources. Huang, the clerk at the Shanghai Customs House who had been earning 600 silver dollars a month before the revolution, worked at his state-run work unit after the revolution for 100 yuan (US$12) a month. Or take the experience of our landlord, Mr. Shen. At the end of 1996, my husband and I moved into a spacious three-story, English-style house built in the 1920s and owned by the elderly retiree. We were his first tenants since before 1949, when as a young man he had regularly rented to foreigners. In those days he owned a number of properties in the city, all of which the authorities confiscated after 1949. They subsequently allowed him to squeeze into one as a renter, along with a handful of other families who also paid rent to the state. Only with reform in the 1980s did the authorities let Shen resume ownership of one of the houses. His gait little more than a shuffle, he showed us, with great excitement, a small room on the third floor where his last foreign tenant before 1949 used to develop photos. But as prospective tenants at the time, we were more focused on the townhouse's decrepit condition: bathroom floors soiled with decades of dirt, broken fixtures, grime-covered kitchen counters, a bricked-in terrace to make room for another family, an overgrown, untended garden. Everyone shared the same squalor.

As a result of Mao's egalitarian policies, which intensified in the 1960s, intellectuals and capitalists in Shanghai and other cities could be found doing the same jobs as workers, no matter their skills. They earned roughly the same wages and owned the same things. Citizens were supposed to "eat from the same big pot." To control their consumption, the government allocated ration coupons for food and other commodities. It determined which schools people attended and which fields they studied. It then distributed jobs to them no matter what their preferences. Once assigned a work unit, directors, technical personnel, and administrative staff only earned a little more than workers. No matter how well citizens worked, they were unlikely to get a raise, a bonus, or a promotion. No matter how poorly they worked, they did not have to worry about losing their job: The state promised workers cradle-to-grave security. In Mao's workers' paradise, health care, housing, schooling, and other benefits were free. In exchange, the work unit controlled people's lives. Residents needed their employer's permission to change enterprises, travel, move house, relocate to another city, marry, and divorce.

Mao ultimately succeeded in stifling large-scale income inequality in China's cities, but he never fully achieved his egalitarian goals. Top Party officials drove around in limousines, shopped at stores selling imported goods that were off-limits to regular folk, and enjoyed myriad privileges that raised their standard of living above everyone else's. Their children went to the best schools and obtained the best jobs. Unbeknownst to the masses, Mao himself lived like an emperor. And if a person hailed from a family deemed by the Party to belong to the wrong political category, he was no longer financially or socially equal. Qian Xiao, who was 14 in 1966 when the Cultural Revolution started, remembered wishing she came from a working-class family, which Mao had proclaimed the pillar of Chinese society. Her grandfather, however, came from a family of large landowners. Worse, the Party in 1957 had labeled her banker father a rightist in the aftermath of the Hundred Flowers Movement, during which Mao asked intellectuals to voice their opinions and criticize the Party's mistakes. For pointing out problems caused by his Party-appointed superior's lack of banking knowledge, Qian's father not only received the rightist label but also saw his salary cut from more than 100 yuan (US$12) a month to less than 70 yuan (US$8.40) a month. During the Cultural Revolution, his work unit punished him further by assigning him to clean the toilets and cutting his monthly wage to 30 yuan (US$3.60). He had five children. "We were very poor. On Children's Day in elementary school when my classmates wore new red outfits, I wore hand-me-downs. My mother had to borrow money from her work unit near the end of every month so that we'd have enough to eat," Qian recalled. During the Cultural Revolution, she was afraid to walk the street because "working class" schoolmates would call her a *gouzaizi,* a son of a dog. She didn't dare make a fuss, she said, because they would claim she opposed the working class and, therefore, must oppose Mao. In society's eyes, she was inferior.

Mao's obsessive stress on egalitarianism and ideological incentives rather than material ones did not achieve Communism's objectives in many other ways. The average wage dropped, housing conditions deteriorated, and educational standards fell. Universities closed during the Cultural Revolution, setting back an entire generation. By the late 1970s, the economy could not create enough industrial jobs to match the supply of young people needing jobs. This phenomenon and the state's determination to place people in jobs led to serious unemployment, underemployment, and unsuitable employment, causing that same generation to waste more productive years. By the end of that decade, the central government simply could no longer afford to bankroll the generous benefits it granted urban workers.[10]

Recognizing that China under the Communist Party would not survive if these policies continued, Deng Xiaoping launched market-oriented reforms starting in 1979 that spelled the beginning of the end of China's "egalitarian" way of life. Deng no longer claimed that being "red" was more important than being "expert" for advancement in Chinese society. Instead, he told the nation to seek truth from facts and reinstituted material incentive schemes, private enterprise, and foreign investment. He insisted that some groups would have to get rich before others, whether it be the coastal provinces over the hinterland; or the capable, well-educated, and well-connected over everyone else. Those who got rich first were to pave the way for others. The Communist Party slowly loosened the state's grip over economic life, forcing the country to put greater faith in the market and themselves than in the plan and the government. By the mid-1990s, for instance, the state no longer assigned college graduates to jobs. And when China's President Jiang Zemin told delegates at the country's 15th Communist Party Congress in September 1997 that "workers should change their ideas about employment," his meaning was clear: China's state-enterprise workers officially could no longer count on the Communist Party to fulfill its former pledges of womb-to-tomb care. Commented Fudan University sociology professor Hu Shoujun:

Now students can choose the companies they want to work for. They can transfer jobs. Every district has a labor market where jobs are listed. People depend on their work units less and less. This is a revolutionary change. Young people, people with skills, intellectuals like this kind of change. People without skills who don't have this new concept are afraid of change. But change is going to happen anyway. There's no way to turn back.

The Haves

The people benefiting from Shanghai's renewal take many forms. And just as in pre-1949 days, some of them are foreign.

The vast majority of foreigners living in Shanghai enjoy a standard of living far above most Shanghainese—in the same way that foreigners do in other cities in China and developing countries around the world. To entice employees to move to Shanghai, a city still considered a hardship post, multinationals offer them generous housing packages that allow them live in "luxury" condominiums and apartments whose rents at their peak in the mid-1990s ranged from US$3,000 to US$20,000 per month. Although these homes would not be considered luxurious by Western standards, they are by Shanghai standards since they offer amenities far beyond what most Shanghai residents enjoy. Whereas Shanghainese on average lived in less than 10 square meters of space per person during the 1990s, a foreign couple could easily share 120 square meters or more. Thanks to their astronomically high salaries by Shanghai standards, foreigners generally can afford to hire full-time help, take taxis everywhere, eat and drink regularly in chic new foreign-invested establishments, and play 18 holes of golf for 400–1,000 yuan (US$48–120). They can leave China whenever they want, vacationing at palm tree-lined resorts around Asia or destinations farther afield. The majority of Shanghainese can only dream of leading such a lifestyle.

That said, the disparity between foreign and local residents today is less than before the second World War. Although foreigners live privileged lives, they do not claim sovereignty over Shanghai territory as they did in pre-1949 days. They live in Shanghai as China's guests under China's laws. Western multinational corporations do not fill their factories with underpaid, overworked labor. On the contrary, they usually go out of their way to be good corporate citizens. Expatriate tycoons do not erect magnificent mansions for themselves from the spoils of their China business, like the Sassoons and the Kadoories in Old Shanghai. Today more intermingling between Chinese and foreigners occurs even if different income levels, taste, and language inadvertently separate the two groups.

Just as in pre-1949 days, the Shanghainese able to attach themselves to foreign companies, particularly in white-collar positions, have emerged as one of society's new set of haves. When multinationals started investing heavily in Shanghai after 1992, they created a huge demand for English-speaking graduates with a technical skill. Consumer product companies needed marketers, securities firms needed company analysts, advertising agencies needed creative personnel, and consulting firms needed consultants. Everyone needed qualified secretaries and accountants. But due to state planning and the city's focus on manufacturing after 1949, many of these fields did not exist. Foreign companies subsequently set their hiring sights on the city's college-educated young people, who could learn easily and would not be as tainted as their elders by years of motivation-draining state planning. Multinationals offered modern methods, training, and higher salaries than domestic companies, and young college graduates subsequently flocked to them. Nonetheless, the supply of talented young people was too small to meet all their needs and foreign investors soon found themselves locked in an intense competition to hire and retain personnel. In finance, recruits with a little experience can easily start at 10,000 yuan (US$1,204) a month at a Western bank and work their way in a year or two to 18,000 yuan (US$2,169). Alexander Yu, a smart, open-minded physics graduate of Shanghai's prestigious Fudan University, for instance, started in finance in 1993 at a local securities firm where he earned a monthly wage of 2,000 yuan (US$240). Five years later, the 30-year-old pulled in 14 times that amount as the chief Shanghai representative for an American investment bank. In less well-heeled industries, college graduates with a few years of work experience at a foreign firm can make well over 4,000 yuan (US$482) a month, a hefty sum considering that their parents working at state enterprises were lucky to together make half that. The general manager at an American building materials company found himself raising wages 25%–40% annually in the middle of the decade just to keep up with competitors. Still, that was not enough to satisfy highly sought-after managerial and technical personnel who were quitting the firm at a 15% annual rate. Turnover in some sectors, like five-star hotels, well exceeded 60% a year in the mid-1990s. Li Yi, an attractive 25-year-old graduate from Shanghai Normal University, in three years had worked at a British bank, an international school, and a Hong Kong real estate agency before deciding to set up a video conferencing company with her new American husband in 1997. She and her friends could afford to be both picky and demanding, although the economic slowdown of the late 1990s helped mitigate job-hopping and huge annual salary increases. Capturing the spirit of the decade for the young and well-educated, she sipped on her Coca-Cola and said, "I have a lot of confidence for the future."

Even more well-placed to prosper are the Chinese who went abroad to study and then found work in their field overseas before returning home. Throughout China, the Shanghainese are known for sending their children abroad to study. A popular saying summed up the

trend: *Beijing ren ai guo, Guangdong ren mai guo,* and *Shanghairen chu guo,*
which literally translates as: Beijingers love the country, Cantonese sell
the country, and Shanghainese leave the country. Indeed, it is hard to
meet a well-educated, middle-aged Shanghainese with a respectable
position who has not sent a child overseas to study. By the second half
of the decade, a small but growing number of these prodigal sons and
daughters had returned to Shanghai. Most find jobs at foreign
multinationals where they enjoy better compensation packages and
higher-status positions than their compatriots who never went abroad.
Small and medium-sized European and American companies with little
knowledge of China sometimes pay "returned students" US$5,000 per
month plus housing—an extremely generous sum compared with the
market rate—to set up their representative offices in the city. The
Shanghai government also desperately wants to tap into their talent, and,
in 1997, unveiled a slew of preferential policies, including higher salaries,
housing, and research grants, to entice overseas students back to Shanghai
to help develop its industry. Xiao-lin Yang is one of the many returnees
who chose to work for a foreign company. She went to the United States
to study business in 1984 and eventually found a job at AT&T, which
sent her to Beijing, and then later with General Electric, which posted
her to Shanghai in a top executive slot. Like many of her fellow overseas
students, she secured a foreign passport while abroad. This gives her
the ability to enter and leave China freely, a luxury unknown to most
Chinese. Dressed in collegiate khakis and a pullover over a striped shirt
on GE's weekly "dress-down day," she said:

Headhunters are calling me all the time. There is definitely more opportunity
here in China because things are just starting here. China is at the beginning of
capitalism. In the US, so many people are well-educated and speak English. It's
hard to differentiate yourself. Unless you do a job with China, you have no
advantage over them.

But one does not just have to work for a foreign company or have
studied abroad to be a "have." Residents who attach themselves to up-
and-coming Chinese companies, particularly in the city's new services
industries, also reap the rewards of economic reform and Shanghai's
favored status. Consider someone like Quan Dansong, who worked for
Ping An Insurance Co., the fiercest domestic competitor in the city's
nascent individual life insurance market. Shenzhen-headquartered Ping
An recruited 200 agents in Shanghai in 1994, its first year of operation

in the city. One of them was the then 23-year-old Quan, whose knack for sales—a new skill in Shanghai's socialist market economy—quickly became obvious. During his first three months on the job, he amassed 500,000 yuan (US$60,240) worth of premium income for Ping An and pocketed 100,000 yuan (US$12,048) in commissions. During the next two years he continued to prove himself, earning as much as US$6,000 in commissions a month. By the time I met him in mid-1996, Ping An had already promoted him seven times. "At some Chinese companies, the tradition is to be jealous. Here the attitude is: You should be brave. You can achieve whatever you want to," said Quan. He had already bought two apartments: one for his parents and one for his wife and himself in swish parts of town.

Another source of wealth has been Shanghai's stock market, which roared back to life in 1991 after the Communists banned it as a capitalist tool following the 1949 takeover. Consider Li Qi, who started dabbling in stocks while working in a state-owned textile equipment company as a department manager. Dressed in a black-and-white striped shirt, gray tie, and black windbreaker, the middle-aged Li explained how at least a dozen people in his factory played the market in the early 1990s. "So a lot of people in our factory got rich. I made a lot of money," he beamed. He later gave his notice to the factory where he had worked for 12 years, pouring his earnings into two restaurants and an auto repair shop. Many of these new *da kuan* or millionaires make their fortunes with the help of insider trading, market manipulation, and poor regulation. A mobile phone in one hand and a diamond ring on the other, 30-year-old stock trader Jimmy Zou unabashedly recounted how he had a friend at the stock exchange in 1991 who regularly fed him confidential information. When he made 200,000 yuan (about US$24,100) speculating on stocks that year, he quit his job at the Shanghai tourism bureau to work for the fledgling securities firm. "I thought it could be a good opportunity to become a millionaire," he quipped. Although he did not want to divulge his earnings for tax reasons, he conceded in 1997 that he was more than a millionaire in yuan terms. "Actually, a yuan millionaire is quite common. I know a person who is a billionaire!" he exclaimed.

Many "haves" earn their money by using their connections within the state sector and the city government. They use them not only to play the stock market, like Zou, but also to take part in lucrative business ventures financed with state money. In Shanghai, as elsewhere in China, having the right personal ties or *guanxi* is a key to getting government approvals for projects and state-sector customers. High-ranking Party members and their children normally have the best relationships of all. At the end of 1999, I had dinner with a "princeling entrepreneur" in Shanghai whose grandfather and father had both been soldiers in the People's Liberation Army. His father, a long-time Communist Party member, helped a senior official in the Shanghai government join the Party years ago. I met the princeling, who asked that I not print his name, just after he, his wife, and son returned from a two-week, four-country vacation in Europe—a luxury for most Shanghainese. He owns at least three factories and four businesses in industries ranging from advertising and printing to lighting fixtures. His three homes, two cars, and expanding middriff further attest to his affluence. When I asked him the secret to his success, he said matter-of-factly, "In Shanghai, if you want to do well you need two things. You need good friends and a good wife. It all depends on friends and relationships." He went on to recount how, with the help of friends, he was able to get into the advertising business and open up distribution channels that otherwise would have been closed. He was also able to use his connections to start a printing factory in Pudong, even though the sector was normally off-limits to nonstate-owned companies. "My wife just made a few phone calls and then got all the special approvals needed. Without friends this would never have happened," he said. The princeling is so well-connected that he does not employ any salespeople. He and his wife work out of their home with a fax, computer, and constantly ringing phone. While we were eating dinner, a call came through on his mobile. "That was a friend who needed uniforms for his workers. So I will arrange that," he said after hanging up. "Now I don't need salesmen. All I need is friends." Sucking on the shell of a hairy crab, he later added: "For me, Shanghai is a good place to do business."

An untold number of Shanghai's "haves" have also made their fortunes by ripping off the government. Corruption in China's state sector runs rampant partly as a result of reforms that granted managers more autonomy without monitoring their behavior. Unable to become a "have" on a low state enterprise or civil servant salary, they use their posts to enrich themselves. Take the behavior of a general manager at a small state-owned plastic flower manufacturer in Shanghai. He transferred equipment and a significant portion of sales orders to a factory in the same line of business started by his son. While the family grew rich, the state firm racked up heavy losses and unpaid debts, putting its workers steadily closer to the unemployment line. The only reason the fraud came to light, said a lawyer involved in the case, is that a disgruntled foreign supplier decided to sue the state company. Even during efforts in 1998 to reform small state enterprises by selling shares to employees, some managers used the opportunity to pad their pockets. In the spring of 1998, I visited a state-owned shirt-maker that was supposed to be a model for employee shareholding reforms. By sheer coincidence, the wife of the cab driver who drove me to the interview worked for the company. When I asked him what he thought of the reforms, he immediately replied: "Shareholding reform is cheating. There are a lot of corrupt cadres. Managers at the company asked employees to pay 5,000 yuan (US$602) for 5,000 shares. They, however, paid 20,000 yuan (US$2,410) and got 40,000 shares." Sure enough, when I later asked a company official how much managers at the firm had paid for their 40,000 shares, he first said 20,000 yuan, then, realizing his error, quickly changed his response to 40,000 yuan (US$4,819).

Not everyone who becomes a "have" enjoys the benefits of a fine education, well-placed connections, access to poorly monitored state assets, or a lax regulatory environment. Some manage to seize opportunities in the country's reforming economy through innate smarts, ability, and drive. But it has not been easy. Private entrepreneurs have faced greater difficulties in Shanghai than in southern China and some other parts of the country because the city implements the central government's discriminatory policies against private enterprise more strictly. Chen Rong, the son of a peasant and a worker, is a prime example of a resident who overcame great odds to make good in Shanghai. I met him in mid-1998 at his company headquarters about 40 minutes outside of Shanghai proper in an area that 20 years ago had been little more than farmland. Although Shanghainese living in Puxi would undoubtedly consider him a country bumpkin for having been born and continuing to live in the city's Nanhui suburb, he looked surprisingly sophisticated in his white-collared blue dress shirt and speckled red tie. The 39-year-old started in private business in the 1980s for lack of better options. When he applied to join the army at the age of 18, recruiters rejected him because the Party had convicted his parents of counterrevolutionary crimes during the Cultural Revolution. He decided to take advantage of Deng Xioaping's economic reform policies and invest in a clothing shop the 2,000 yuan (US$240) he had saved raising fowl, even though private entrepreneurs enjoyed roughly the same low social status as karaoke club managers and ex-convicts. He earned 10,000 yuan (US$1,204) that first year and dreamed of reinvesting it in a garment factory. Unfortunately, the government imposed unbearably high tax rates on private firms and prohibited them from hiring more than 10 employees. To make the investment worth his while, therefore, Chen did something that many private businessmen did in those days: he illegally changed his company's status from private to "collective." After the June 1989 massacre of pro-democracy demonstrators in Tiananmen Square in Beijing, the authorities started investigating "pseudo-collectives" like Chen's, sentencing one of his fellow entrepreneurs to 1½ years in jail. Investigators let Chen off—he had diligently paid a large sum of money at the collective enterprise tax rate—but they warned that less-understanding government officials might investigate him in the future. "I was not a brave man. I did not open a shop to go to prison," said Chen. "I closed down my shops and my factory. It was a great hurt. I had already paid a whole year of rent and decoration fees. I still had a lot of garments in inventory."

However, he also still had 200,000–300,000 yuan (US$24,096) in profits—a relatively huge sum—and when Shanghai reopened its stock exchange at the end of 1990, Chen discovered his new calling. He did not have Jimmy Zou's insider connections nor a technical knowledge of stock trading theory. "Instead I studied the psychology of regulators and common folk to judge what was going to happen to certain stocks," he explained. His strategy paid off. By 1994, he made more than enough to invest 100 million yuan (US$12 million) of his own money in his next entrepreneurial project. Sensing correctly that bowling would become the next entertainment fad, he began manufacturing bowling alley equipment to compete with expensive imports. In 1998, his company did 400 million yuan (US$48 million) in sales and earned a profit of 130 million yuan (US$16 million). His next dream, which he told me about as we sped into the city in his chauffeured black sedan, was to set up a stock brokerage—a business that the central government at the time reserved for state-owned entities. In the meantime, Chen was enjoying the improved status for entrepreneurs that came out of the 15th Party Congress in Beijing in September 1997. In 1998, Shanghai Mayor Xu Kuangdi invited Chen and other entrepreneurs to share views on private business. For Chen, becoming a "have" meant more than becoming rich—it meant obtaining the social status previously denied to him.

The Good Life

Money and things to spend it on have opened up a whole new world for Chen Rong and his fellow "haves." Shanghai's young professional women working at foreign multinationals, like Hewlett-Packard employee Isabella Zhou for instance, discovered a passion for shopping. "There are so many modern shopping centers in Shanghai now. Before I'd just look, but now I like to buy," the 24-year-old laughed. The "haves" have also discovered the joys of eating at restaurants, going bowling, singing songs at karoke lounges, taking taxis, and filling their homes with modern appliances. If they are married, they save their money to move out of the cramped quarters they share with their parents into more modern, spacious digs. For millionaires like Chen, that meant building a 2,000-square-meter villa with an indoor swimming pool for 10 million yuan (US$1.2 million). For the average "have," however, it means spending 200,000–700,000 yuan (US$24,000–US$84,000) to buy a flat in one of the many new apartment blocks built for domestic residents during the decade.

Xiao-lin Yang, the returned student, for instance, bought a 129-square-meter apartment boasting three bedrooms, two baths, and a large living room. Like most of these apartments, it came completely unfinished, so Yang spent 140,000 yuan (US$16,800) to fit it out. She took me to visit some friends who had just finished renovating their new home. The wife worked for a foreign multinational and the husband, who was home that day, worked for a state trading company officially, but actually made his money doing his own trading on the side. "If I only received a salary from a state-owned company, it's unimaginable that I could live here," he said as he proudly showed us around the two bedroom, 98-square-meter flat. The 30-year-old homeowner pointed to his many renovation choices: his- and-her closets in the bedroom, black marble tiles in the bathroom, and beechwood paneling in the living room. The sleek black Sony television, VCR, and Kenwood speakers nicely matched the simple Scandinavian-style furniture. The couple also had an air conditioner, washing machine, and a few other appliances. Seated on his new sofa, the husband explained how he took out one of the government's mortgage loans to help pay for the 400,000-yuan (US$48,000) flat and had to make monthly repayments of 4,100 yuan (US$494) over five years—a small fortune considering that many couples working at state-owned enterprises were lucky together to bring home 2,000 yuan (US$241) a month. He was in no mood to feel guilty about his good fortune, however, saying: "We work hard on the outside, so we want to be comfortable at home."

Besides creating comfortable nests for their families, Shanghai's "haves" are also traveling for fun—both within China and to certain government-sanctioned foreign locations such as Hong Kong, Singapore, the Philippines, Thailand, Malaysia, and Australia. For Joan Dong, who worked as an account executive at a foreign advertising agency, travel provided a chance "to leave the dull routine of daily life." During the spring festival break in 1997, for instance, the 25-year-old embarked on a two-week Southeast Asian tour that took her to Singapore, Malaysia, and Hong Kong. "I like Singapore the best. It's a very beautiful and elegant city. The city's neatness and tidiness impressed me, as well as its high level of civilization," she cooed, her hair pulled back in a neat and tidy chignon. She liked Malaysia the least, apparently because of problems with her tour guide. "She always took us to jewelry shops because she could get paid according to sales. She asked us for tips!" Dong spewed. The problem was not that Dong and her fellow travelers did not like to shop while on their foreign excursions. Shopping was, in fact, an important pastime. On top of the 12,000 yuan (US$1,445) Dong paid for the two-week package tour, she spent 3,000 yuan (US$361). "I like to buy jewelry and clothes," she said.

To travel, live in modern apartments, wear fashionable clothes, eat at restaurants, dance at discos, and afford good schools all take money and the city's residents are intent on making it. Whereas Communism stressed equality and the group, the religion for the young and upwardly mobile is material well-being and self-fulfillment. Money, which played a minor role in their parents' lives, has become not only a route to comfort but a proof of a person's ability. This does not mean that Shanghai's "haves" are high rollers: Shanghainese parents traditionally teach their children from an early age to economize and get the best of every deal. Instead of spending freely, many white-collar Shanghainese sock their earnings away in bank accounts. They are saving for the items that the state, as part of economic reform, has stopped supplying for free: an apartment for their family, a university education for their child, medical care, and maybe even a car. In the meantime, ambitious young professionals, motivated by a desire to improve their earning power and themselves, do all they can to get ahead. They attend lectures or enroll themselves in night schools to learn computers, finance, accounting, and management. They go abroad for study or live in a different Chinese city than their spouse for extended periods, if the process will benefit their future. They enroll their toddler-age children in boarding schools, picking them up on the weekends. That way they can devote themselves to earning a living and giving their children a head start.

In the spring of 1998, I decided to visit some of Shanghai's new boarding kindergartens to learn more about the trend. At the Bai Yulan kindergarten (No.1), colorfully clad tikes screamed with excitement as they scampered around a miniature playground while matronly women supervised their play. Lin Ling, a school director who had been teaching children for 50 years, showed me around, explaining that the parents of the children were mostly private business owners, company bosses, or white-collar workers. "These people are in the upper income brackets. After all, our tuition is quite high: 2,500 yuan (US$301) for the year plus 700 yuan (US$84) per month for food and accommodation," she explained. Besides playing games that taught basic skills, the 141 students—aged between two and six—could also take optional courses in things like piano, computers, and drawing. According to Lin, the most common reason for enrolling children in boarding kindergartens is to accommodate parents' busy work schedules. Demand was so great that by 1998 the group had opened three branches in the city.

Sophy Chen, a 25-year-old advertising executive who often worked overtime, was about to put her three-year-old son into a boarding kindergarten in 1998. She explained her motivations:

First of all, no one here can take care of him if we do not send him there. Both my husband and I are working, my parents-in-law live in Guangdong, my father is old and weak, and my mother has passed away. We thought about hiring a nanny, but we don't have a spare room so we gave up the idea. We're not able to look after him carefully after a whole day's work. If we have to wake up several times a night to take care of him, then how can we concentrate at work the next day? And we don't want our son to have irregular meals and sleep because of his parents' busy lifestyle. Also, if my son goes to a boarding kindergarten, he will hopefully be able to live more independently and to learn some skills like English and the computer.

Neither she nor her husband dreamed of quitting their job or cutting back on work hours. She, like many of her peers, demonstrated her love and devotion by providing her child financial security and opportunity.

Looking every bit the professional in a gray suit, she said:

First of all, if one of us had to quit, it would definitely not be my husband, because his job is more stable than mine and he would not abandon it easily. As for me, I am not willing to quit my work. I am not a housewife type of person or a family-oriented woman. I have career pursuits. Even if I stay home to look after my son, I would not do a good job because it would waste my professional resources. I won't be able to fulfill myself. Secondly, it's just not economical for one of us to quit. If one of us gives up working, it'll be a 3,000-yuan (US$361) loss. Why would we want to do that? As a matter of fact, we need to work as hard as possible to earn as much money as possible. Because, you know, we need money for several things. We need money to purchase our own house. Most of our savings were used for our marriage expenses. My son will also need a lot of money for his education. He will eventually enter a society where competition is fierce, so he needs a good education. He won't receive a good education staying at home. Therefore, if possible I will send him to private boarding schools. I always think that if he is unable to excel among his peers because of his own lack of abilities and intelligence, it is his problem. But if he cannot excel just because I am not able to finance a good education for him, then I will feel very sorry. So we have to make as much money as we can.

Chen is a typical Shanghai parent in her determination to give her son her idea of the most conducive environment for his future success. Indeed, thanks to higher incomes under economic reform as well as the central government's policy of restricting couples to one child, children have become a class of "haves" unto themselves. These single children, or little emperors as they are known, normally bask in the attention of their parents and two sets of grandparents. Adults give their tots music lessons, buy them computers and cute little outfits, take them to amusement parks, and treat them to McDonald's "Happy Meals." The upside of all this parental doting is that children belonging to white-collar families enjoy comfortable lives filled with new opportunities. Growing up during a period of peace, prosperity, and opening to the outside world, they know nothing of the hardships and international isolation that their parents experienced. Their world is filled with music videos, the Internet, and exciting future prospects. Having lived their formative years under reform, they are better prepared than their parents for the challenges posed by a market economy.

Unfortunately, all the attention lavished on Shanghai's only children has had some downsides. Many are turning into self-centered brats unable to take care of themselves or perform mundane chores, a topic that drew considerable media attention during the decade. This is another reason why Sophy Chen wanted to send her son to boarding kindergarten. She said:

It's certain that such a school will benefit my son. First, he will learn to be more independent since, at home, parents or the people who look after him usually prepare everything for him, including dressing him, brushing his teeth, and washing his face. But in a boarding kindergarten he has to learn such things on his own. In addition, nowadays, each family only has one child, so inevitably the child is spoiled or has a bad temper—if someone does not behave as the child wishes or something doesn't happen the way he wishes, the child might cry or shout, or refuse to eat, sleep, etc., until his wish is realized. But in boarding kindergarten it's different. The child is part of a team, surrounded by children who are all the same age. No one will spoil him. It is good for him to develop a healthy temperament and learn how to deal with teammates.

Not that children in Shanghai and other urban centers enjoy a carefree life. Part the reason that parents and grandparents exempt their "little emperor" from household chores is that they prefer he spend his free time studying or taking an extracurricular lesson. After all, these only children are families' one great hope for the future. Whereas parents were assigned a job after graduation, their kids live under a market economy where competition with their peers decides their high school, their university, and their future income. The opportunity that parents provide their children subsequently comes with considerable pressure to succeed. School provides no relief. Children are thrust into a world where students compare grades, teachers publicly announce exam results, and getting into a "key" high school (and subsequently a prestigious university) means doing better than most everyone else.

Some children crack under the pressure. Doctors in Shanghai, and around the country, are diagnosing a growing number of young patients with nervous tics, obsessive-compulsive behavior disorders, and other mild mental health problems. In the early 1980s, Du Yasong, a child psychiatrist at the Shanghai Institute of Mental Health Institute, saw a child with a nervous tic once every half year but by the late 1990s saw 10 a day. He recounted a typical case involving a seven-year-old boy in first grade whose parents were successful university professors:

After the child got home from school, his parents would tell him about competition, to study well, and to get a high score. After school he studied computer, painting, and a musical instrument: the accordion. He had no free time. The child now has problems when he writes. He has to write absolutely perfectly. He takes two to three hours to write 10–15 characters. This is obsessive behavior.

Relief may be on the way. After a 17-year-old boy in Zhejiang province killed his mother with a hammer in January 2000, China's Ministry of Education issued regulations banning schools from holding mandatory classes on weekends, vacations, and evenings and from giving written homework to first and second graders.[11]

Of course, children are not the only ones to experience mental health problems. Psychiatrists in Shanghai and around China also report a growing incidence of anxiety, depression, and other mild mental illnesses among adults, although the numbers for both adults and children are still low compared with developed country standards. While improved diagnosis accounts partly for the trend, mental health professionals believe the competitive pressures and lightning-speed changes buffeting Shanghai are causing more people to lose emotional balance. According to statistics from Shanghai's Psychotherapy and Counseling Center, the number of people seeking help for mental health problems grew 20.7% a year from 1996 through 1998.[12] Whether they are "haves" striving for their next promotion or "have-nots" fighting for their next job, no one is immune from pressure and change and, like in all societies, some people are not psychologically equipped to cope as well as others.

The "Have-Nots"

But whereas the "haves" look forward to a future filled with opportunity and material comfort, the "have-nots" live in a world of dimmer prospects. The unemployed, workers at faltering state enterprises, retirees on low fixed pensions, and migrant laborers are some of the groups emerging as Shanghai's new urban underclass.

In the 1990s, the city's once-coddled factory workers started paying a heavy price for years of inefficient central planning. Under the planned economy, the government subsidized China's state firms, whose mandate under Mao was as much to take care of workers as it was to provide goods. Providing workers cradle-to-coffin security subsequently was not a problem, which at big enterprises included running a school and hospital as well as providing free medical, housing, and a lifetime job. But after those subsidies dried up under reform and more efficient competitors entered the market, over-staffed and poorly managed state companies started to founder, with more than half of them in Shanghai losing money by 1997. They had little choice but to retreat from providing such generous benefits. Profitable state enterprises hoping to survive had to do the same, which was why President Jiang Zemin announced at the China's 15th Communist Party Congress in September 1997 that "workers should change their ideas about employment."

That meant massive layoffs in a city like Shanghai, where state enterprises accounted for 80% of the city's workforce in 1992 and roughly 60% of the city's jobs in 1997.[13] From 1990 through 1998, Shanghai laid off more than one million workers, according to the Shanghai Economic Commission.[14] Xie Yonghua is one of those workers. The 42-year-old lost his job in 1993 and has led a humble existence ever since. Sitting in a leafy park on a sunny June day in 1997, he recounted:

Before getting laid off in 1993, I worked in the storeroom at the Shanghai Textile Machinery factory. I started there in 1975 after graduating from high school. At the time I thought I'd work there for the rest of my life. I felt lucky to get to work in a factory. I started as a machine operator, then was transferred to the storeroom as a stock keeper. I did not make much—just 500 yuan (US$60) a month, plus a 10% bonus. I had full medical coverage. Everything was taken care of. Unfortunately, the factory could not sell the products—so many just piled up in the storeroom. Now the factory is in the process of going bankrupt. It had probably 2,000 workers. Now probably all of them have been laid off. The factory gave me less than 200 yuan (US$24) a month when it laid me off. That was it. Now it gives me 230 yuan a month (US$27).

Also, at the time, the government had not yet set up reemployment service centers to help laid-off workers find jobs. So after I left the factory, I started selling cookies with some friends for a Shandong company. It wasn't easy to find a job. A friend introduced me. I was paid a percentage of sales but didn't earn much. But for the last half year, business has basically stopped because the quality isn't good and the factory can't compete. There's lots of competition for cookies in Shanghai. I've had almost nothing to do for the last six months. I definitely need to find a job. Living on this little money makes life very tiring.

Friends who know I have difficulties help me. If they buy some food and have something good to eat they give whatever they can spare. Without friends, life would be harder.

Before I go to bed at night I wonder what kind of work I will do in the future, what kind of life I will have. I'm taking a government-sponsored training course in computers. The software we're learning is very old, but computers are the most basic skill and it's not too difficult. So now I have confidence to look for a job, but until I find one I'm worried.

At first, Shanghai's unprofitable textile mills did most of the laying off. Shanghai's textile industry went from 550,000 workers at its peak in the early 1990s to an estimated 250,000 in 2000.[15] But by the second half of the decade a slew of the city's labor-intensive industries, from watch-makers to machinery manufacturers to chemical producers, were also cutting their workforces. Also, most of those laid-off initially were women. That was partly coincidence: the textile industry counted more women than men among its ranks. And it was also partly by design. The government estimated that laid-off women would be less of a security threat than jobless men. By 1998, however, many factories had no choice but to start giving more men the heave-ho as well.

The state sector's problems also mean that the many workers still "officially" working at their struggling enterprise do so for reduced wages. Many state-owned enterprises in Shanghai and China that should go bankrupt do not because they have not yet received government approval. Worried about the instability that could arise from massive unemployment, the authorities limit the number of bankruptcies. While companies wait in line, they sell land, lease equipment, and do whatever they can to keep things going a little longer. The 52-year-old father of Li Yi, the young Shanghainese "have," for instance, was in 1997 an electrical engineer for a state-run television manufacturer. He had watched his salary drop from more than 1,000 yuan (US$120) a month early in the decade to around 500 yuan (US$60). While he was lucky not to have been laid off and put on a government subsidy of 230 yuan (US$27) a month like so many of his colleagues, surviving on 500 yuan a month in Shanghai was still difficult. Li, the father, ended up asking his 25-year-old daughter to help him find work, but given that most companies were looking for young people with English speaking skills, the younger Li was not terribly optimistic for him. That said, at least he has a successful child to help tide him over, which is not the case for everyone.

The Shanghai government does not leave laid-off workers completely to the mercy of the marketplace. On top of offering them a basic living allowance for two years, which in 1998 was 230 yuan a month, factories try to find new jobs for workers, and the government has set up reemployment training centers and job markets. According to official statistics, some 583,000 of the more than one million people laid off between 1990 and 1998 signed up at the city's 308 reemployment centers and 420,000 of them found jobs.[16] The Shanghai government also implemented preferential policies to encourage laid-off workers to start their own businesses to employ laid-off workers—policies that were subsequently copied by other cities. But in general, the work found for laid-off workers or that they find on their own is low-paying. Many end up cleaning hotels rooms, waiting tables, minding someone else's children, driving cabs, hocking wares on the street, or staying at home. As the Chinese economy slowed in the late 1990s and the number of laid-off increased, finding decent work became even more difficult. Xie, the 42-year-old who sold cookies for a time, explained:

It's easy to find a low-paying job at 500 yuan (US$60) a month, but finding something better is harder. The white-collar jobs available have a lot of requirements, like a university degree and several years' work experience. So there's lots of opportunity for university students. They're young and educated. They are much luckier. When I look around at friends and colleagues who have found work, most of them are food vendors at a wholesale market. They can earn some money, but it's very hard work, from early in the morning until late in the evening.

A fundamental problem for people like Xie is that they are at the short end not only of China's efforts to transform itself from a state-planned into a market economy but also of Shanghai's plans to become an international business hub. Traditionally China's major industrial center, Shanghai in the 1990s started focusing on services like finance, trade, and retail. While it will continue to do manufacturing, it is dismantling low-tech, labor-intensive state-owned factories that can no longer compete. Instead, it is emphasizing higher-tech industries like automobiles and pharmaceuticals that require fewer workers. Shanghai's industries of the future demand well-educated, adaptable staff—not poorly schooled, middle-aged factory workers with bad work habits. As a result, the laid-off often have no choice but to take menial, low-paying jobs just to survive—jobs that they complain lack the status they enjoyed as factory workers.

Many of these people are not capable of doing much more than menial work. In secondary school during the Cultural Revolution, they learned more about Maoist sloganeering than reading, writing, and arithmetic. Having learned little when their minds were supple, they have trouble retaining new knowledge as adults. And because the government assigned them jobs after high school, they have never had to look for work before or improve themselves. They often did the same low-skilled job their entire working life. Wang Hua, a 21-year-old sociology student, summed up the plight of her parent's generation—also known as the *laosanjie*:

My parents have no concept of competition. After they were laid off, they had no concept about learning new skills or getting a new job. They were like a fish after the tide leaves the beach: the fish gets stuck on the rocks. My generation grew up with competition. In school we compete for high marks. Competition is always there, whether to get into school or to get a job.

Most people who find jobs do so through relatives and friends, often in Shanghai's private small business sector. Ah Hua, the laid-off textile worker, for instance, eventually stopped waiting for her state enterprise to find her a job after it laid her off in 1996 and a year later was working in her brother's restaurant. That reality is the reason why the Communist Party finally recognized the private sector as an "integral part" of the Chinese economy in 1998—private businesses grew much more quickly in the 1990s than the struggling state sector. Between 1994 and 1997, private firms in Shanghai hired roughly 102,000 workers who had been laid off by state-owned and collective enterprises.[17]

Those numbers underestimate how many laid-off workers actually find some source of income beyond the unemployment subsidy provided by their state firm. The laid-off workers that I spoke with in the late 1990s usually estimated that half their former colleagues had found new work and half had not. Workers who find new jobs in the private sector normally do not tell their state employer and live in constant fear that it will find out. Xiao Han, a laid-off textile mill employee who found work as a housekeeper for a foreign family, explained:

Now we are so nervous all the time. Before everything was so stable. We had a job, we had a regular monthly wage. Now we don't know what's going to happen from one month to the next. Even if I have a job now, I don't know if my employers will leave Shanghai in three years. Then I have to hope that they'll help me find a new job. Naturally, there's no pension with this job. This is why everyone tries to stay attached to their old work unit, so that they'll have a pension when retirement age comes and get the 230 yuan (US$27) in monthly laid-off workers benefits. If our work unit finds out we're working somewhere else, they'll stop giving us the monthly stipend plus they'll ask us to give them 100 yuan (US$12) for managing our pension funds. You have to sign a contract with them for this and it's not just a short-term contract but may be four to five years. If during that time you lose your new job, you still have to pay the work unit 100 yuan a month. How can you pay if you don't have a job any more?

Part of the reason that workers cling to their old state employers so fiercely is that Shanghai, like the rest of the country, is still in the process of setting up a modern welfare safety net. Based on pension, unemployment insurance, and medical coverage plans used in the United States and other developed countries, these schemes seek to provide citizens a buffer should misfortune or retirement befall them, but without impoverishing the government and employers like the old system did. Shanghai is a leader in the country in implementing these much-needed reforms, setting up, for instance, the country's first municipal social pension system in 1993. According to government statistics, four million workers in Shanghai had unemployment insurance as of early 1998, which had been doled out to 500,000 people. Some 98% of workers had joined the city's new pension system and 97% had basic medical coverage.[18] To help the city's most needy residents, the city has also established charities and has allowed some private citizens to establish their own non-profit organizations. Xu Chongren, an official at the government-backed Shanghai Charity Foundation, commented in mid-1998:

Our purpose is to help solve new problems that have arisen during the economy's transition period. More and more poor families have appeared with the increase in laid-off workers. For instance, we've given eight million yuan (US$963,855) to 14,000 households. They include families which can't afford medical costs for a severely sick member. These are the people in Shanghai experiencing the greatest difficulty. Before the Lunar New Year this year we gave 200 yuan to another 10,000 families. It's the most important holiday of the year and people feel a lot better if they have money to celebrate. Admittedly, most problems are still up to the government to solve, but we're here to fill the gap. The government can no longer cover everything. More and more charity organizations will appear.

Despite these efforts, it is clear that the new welfare system has holes through which the less-fortunate sometimes fall. Profitable firms have no problem taking part in the new welfare schemes, which generally ask employers and employees to contribute a certain percentage of each worker's salary into a fund. But chronic loss-making enterprises cannot participate fully. In late 1998, for instance, Shanghai's Labor and Social Security Bureau inspected 37 local firms and found that almost 40% of them had not contributed their fair share to the city's pension fund, with some of them complaining that to do so would put them in the red.[19] In the worst cases, bankrupted and faltering firms delay pension payments or stop paying retirees their pensions altogether, a situation that the Shanghai government sought to redress in September 1998 by taking responsibility for distributing pensions away from employers and putting it into the hands of a specialized government agency. Zhu Junyi, the director of the Shanghai Labour and Social Security Bureau, told the press at the time that it would probably take three years to ensure that all retirees received their pensions without delays.[20]

Erecting a well-functioning pension system is critical given the speed at which Shanghai society is aging and the changes taking place in Shanghainese family life. In a traditional Chinese family, grandparents depend on their multiple children to take care of them. Extended families live under one roof. As a result of China's family planning programs, however, families only have one child, leading Shanghai's population growth to decline for most of the 1990s. That leaves one adult child and spouse to take care of two sets of parents, putting a huge financial burden on the younger couple. Moreover, adult children in the reform era are far busier making a living than in the past and are moving into their own flats, making it harder for them to care for aging and sick parents. With roughly 17% of Shanghai residents more than 60 years old in 1999 and their numbers expected to reach 37% by 2030, ensuring all retirees a pension that allows them to survive without undue hardship is a key challenge. In the meantime, retirees with prosperous children may not have to worry about making ends meet, but those whose children have lost their jobs or work at struggling state enterprises are having a harder time.

Another challenge is ensuring the "have-nots" have the health care they require. Chronic loss-making firms often take years—if ever—to reimburse workers and retirees for legitimate medical expenses, while profitable companies cover 80%–90% of expenses and reimburse employees right away. The problem is exacerbated by the fact that for much of the 1990s medical costs surged 20%–30% a year. As a result, many laid-off and retired people either borrow from friends and family to cover their healthcare expenses or delay dealing with medical problems. Da Han, who worked in a faltering sock factory employing 1,400 people until she took early retirement at age 42, explained how well workers fared under the old system and the difficulties some family members now face getting reimbursed for medical expenses. Her situation is typical. She said:

Five years ago, we didn't have to pay for any medical expenses at all. I had a card from my factory, which I'd show to the hospital, which would seek reimbursement directly from the factory. Now for a cold I can still go to the factory clinic and they'll give me some cheap medicine for free but if the problem is at all more serious, they'll tell you to go to the hospital. The factory is supposed to reimburse us for 80% of the hospital charges. But we don't dare go to the hospital or see a doctor because it takes so long to get reimbursed.

You see, if I have an illness that costs 1,000 yuan (US$120) to treat, I don't get reimbursed all at once. Instead I can only register each month to receive 200 yuan (US$24) of the expenses, which I pick up at the factory a year later. The next month I can only claim another 200 yuan and then the next month another 200 yuan and so on. It can take one to two years to get fully reimbursed and each time you register and pick up your money you have to stand in line. Now if I have a serious illness like cancer and it costs 10,000 yuan (US$1,205) for an operation, the factory will give maybe 2,000 yuan (US$240) after which I have to do the 200 yuan monthly registration thing. Also, not all medical problems are reimbursable. If I break my arm, for instance, I have to pay the medical charges on my own. Also, you can get your 200 yuan a month if you make a stink, but if you don't make a stink, they'll forget about you. My husband's work unit has some money so he only has to pay 10% of the expenses if he goes to the hospital. But my 68-year-old mother, who retired 13 years ago, was told by her factory that it does not have any money to give her for a gall bladder operation that the doctor says she needs. She used to have pains once a year, then a few times a year, then once a month. Now it's once a week and it's been like this for two months. If it hurts, she can't eat. The doctor wants 10,000 yuan for the operation, but she decided not to have it because it's too expensive.

The "have-nots" are also less likely to benefit from Shanghai's housing reforms that encourage residents to buy either their state-allocated apartments or one of the many new apartments shooting up in and around the city. The government offers long-term mortgages, tax breaks, and price discounts to home-buyers. It also is raising the miniscule rents traditionally charged on state-subsidized apartments. But despite these policies, the prospect of buying a home seems a remote dream for Shanghai's new underclass. Zhang Baoli, a 49-year-old night watchman at a state-owned toy factory, for instance, lives with five family members including a paralyzed grandmother in a 60-square-meter apartment in Spanish-style housing built in the 1930s in the old French Concession. Together, he and his wife bring home a monthly income of roughly 1,500 yuan (US$180). Waving his rent invoices in my face, he fumed:

In June 1996 the rent was 85.50 yuan (US$10.30) a month and a year later it went up to 128.30 yuan (US$15.45). The rent keeps going up. We don't know what we'll do. Everything has gone up: the water fee, every fee!

I asked him if he planned to take advantage of government policies to make it easier for people to buy their own homes. He quickly replied: "We have no money to buy a house. Most common people can't afford it." Adding to his difficulties is a system stacked against the common man. The government offers discounts to people who purchase their state-allocated apartment, the amount of which depends on things like one's level in the enterprise's hierarchy, length of service, and the apartment's age. As result, a factory laborer who has worked for 10 years will not get as much of a discount as a senior staffer who has put in 20 years of service. That makes the price of buying an apartment relatively more expensive for the small-fry, who normally have less money for the purchase anyway. Unable to buy a home that they can one day resell, they subsequently take a step deeper into lower-class status. The good news is that during the 1990s the Shanghai government moved many of the city's most poorly housed residents—those living in state housing smaller than four square meters per person—into larger, more modern flats. So even if they cannot afford to buy a home, their living situation has improved.

The city's three million migrant workers, meanwhile, do not enjoy medical insurance, pensions, unemployment subsidies, or any other benefits. Fleeing poverty, joblessness, or poor prospects in the countryside, most migrant workers descend on Shanghai and other big cities in China to make money for their families back home or to save enough to start their own business one day. The city, like others in China, only allows migrants to do certain low-status jobs, barring them from better jobs and kicking them out of the city if they cannot prove they are employed. Migrants mix little with the Shanghainese, who hold their country cousins in contempt and automatically blame them first when a crime is committed in the city. The majority of migrant workers are men who find work on the city's omnipresent construction sites. They sleep at night in makeshift barracks on the site, rent cheap accommodation on the city's outskirts, or grab a slab of pavement if they have not yet found a job. Migrant women sometimes work as maids for Shanghai families or in decrepit barbershops in bad parts of town, washing hair for 10 yuan (US$1.20) a head and, in some cases, providing sexual services for a bit more. Smudge-faced migrant waifs in rags, with or without their mothers, regularly beg for spare change outside popular watering holes, particularly those frequented by foreigners. According to a 1999 survey by the Shanghai Academy of Social Sciences, roughly 36% of migrant children between the ages of seven and 15 in Shanghai do not attend school,[21] even though education is compulsory in China. Many migrant families simply cannot afford to pay public school fees.

They earn on average 700 yuan (US\$84) a month, two-thirds the average of permanent Shanghai residents.[22]

Zhao Liping is typical migrant worker in Shanghai. When I met the 31-year-old from impoverished Anhui province, he had already been hauling steel beams and mixing cement in Shanghai for seven years and was used to putting in 10-hour-plus days. His deeply tanned skin, tousled hair, and soiled baggy pants pegged him immediately for a migrant. When I asked him if he had medical insurance or other benefits, he laughed and said:

Of course I don't have insurance, I have to pay myself for everything. If I have a fever or a cold, there's no reason to go to the doctor. If I get really sick, then I'll go back to Anhui. In Anhui we pay for everything ourselves. We can't afford to go to the hospital for little things, but if we have a more severe illness, we just borrow money from family and friends. I don't think about whether it's fair or unfair. It's hard to have things be fair if you're a peasant.

Zhao's comments indicate just how low most peasants' expectations are for a comfortable, equitable life—an irony given that the 1949 Communist Revolution was made in their name. Indeed, migrant workers generally view a chance to work in Shanghai or other big cities as a great opportunity compared to eking out an existence as a peasant. They do not writhe in anger over their poor conditions compared with the Shanghainese around them. Thirty-five-year-old Wang Haishen, for instance, is simply grateful to be making far more money working construction in Shanghai than as a farmer in his hometown in Northern Jiangsu province. His chief concerns are: not finding new work after his current job ends and government moves to further limit the types of jobs available to migrants. He explained:

I came here with 20 other guys from Lianyungang more than 10 years ago. My income is unstable because I myself can't get work—I can only rely on subcontractors. I do low-level jobs like laying bricks. My wife and father can handle the fields back home. Agricultural prices are going lower and lower. Before the price of oranges was one to 1.5 yuan (US\$0.18) per half kilo. Now it's less than 10 mao (US\$0.012) so many farmers don't bother to pick oranges. Same with watermelons. At least I make 1,000 yuan (US\$120) a month here in Shanghai, which is much better than at home. Also for migrants, it's harder and harder to get work in cities. My wife used to operate an elevator for a real estate management company in Shanghai, but because so many workers are being laid off, the government says that migrants can't do many kinds of work, so my wife had to go home. Luckily, Shanghainese are not willing to do the hard work that I do.

Life in Shanghai for the "have-nots" is clearly tough. Instead of eating at restaurants, planning vacations, and shopping in the city's many new department stores, they enjoy few of the fruits of Shanghai's new prosperity. Qiang Shuangyin, a skinny, loquacious 49-year-old woman, is a case in point. Laid off in 1996, she found a job as a substitute sales clerk in a department store only to lose it when management discontinued her department. Her 54-year-old husband, who lost his job at end of 1997, found a new position buying wood in Burma for a private company. It paid 1,000 yuan a month (US$120)—a decent sum for a laid-off worker—but now he travels most of time, leaving Qiang at home by herself. Their son just entered Shanghai Normal University, which all-in costs the family 6,800 yuan (US$819) a year—almost half their annual income. Qiang's goal in life is to save every penny possible. To save on gas, for instance, she only boils one pot of water a day. She does not watch television because she fears running up her electricity bill. She only showers once a week to save on water. Just that day, she had gone to the store to buy shampoo only to learn that the price of her brand had increased five yuan (US$0.60) to 35 yuan (US$4.2). She didn't buy it. "My God. I don't even dare wash my hair," she said. She doesn't dare eat out, even at a noodle shop. "If I go to eat outside, one bowl of noodles will cost me three yuan (US$0.36), but I can buy half a kilo of noodles in the market for 1.2 yuan (US$0.14), which I can eat for several days." She would like to visit some friends across town but by the time she changes buses and takes a subway, she will have spent five yuan (US$0.60) and three hours just to get there. After reeling off a long list of her monthly expenses, she sighed and said:

Life is so hard. I'm wasting my life. It's so boring. I want to read some newspapers, but it's so expensive. I want to visit people, but it's so expensive. So all I do is sit at home and do nothing. I'm bored to death. I will take any work, even if it means being a cleaning lady for 400 yuan (US$48) a month. At least you have people to talk to and the company probably subscribes to newspapers. But it's even difficult for me to find that kind of job because of my age.

Many of the laid-off workers and workers at troubled or bankrupt factories with whom I spoke resent their reversal of fortune. After all, they did not choose their state-run employer or their profession, but instead were assigned them long ago by the government. If the authorities happened to place them in an enterprise in a sunset industry with corrupt managers or uninspired leadership, they are now suffering disproportionately since the reality in Shanghai is that profitable enterprises provide decent wages, benefits, and prospects, but unprofitable ones do not. Their bitterness is most severe when they suspect their factory's leaders of padding their own pockets with state funds. According a survey conducted by the Shanghai Federation of Trade Unions in 1998, more than 90% of the 6,100 workers queried ranked the issue of officials using their power for personal profit as the major source of discontent among workers.[23] In workers' eyes the Communist Party made a lot of promises to obtain their support before and after the Revolution in 1949, but reneged on those commitments. "We're angry!" exclaimed Da Han, whose retired mother could not afford the much needed gall-bladder operation. "Now so many illnesses are not reimbursable." Many pine for a return of state-planning days and life under Mao Zedong. Take 40-year-old Xiao Xu, who lost his assigned job in the mid-1990s and found work driving a taxi. He said:

Yeah, I get the 230 yuan a month in unemployment benefits, but I don't get reimbursed for medical expenses. I think Jiang Zemin is very bad. If we get sick now, they just let us die. And if we say anything about it, they think we oppose them. We're very angry. Life was better under Mao Zedong. He cared about us.

But for all the ranting of "have-nots" like Xiao Xu in Shanghai, they are far better off than their compatriots in other old industrial centers, particularly those in the Northeast and in country's western provinces. Shanghai, and other big cities in richer parts of the country like Beijing, Zhuhai, Shenzhen, Guangzhou, and Dalian have an easier time taking care of their "have-nots." Shanghai's advantages are many. The central government, for one, has designated it as the country's commercial and financial hub and periodically bestows on it special policies and special projects like the US$1.57-billion car manufacturing joint venture with GM in 1997. Shanghai can also count on a steady stream of central government funding. In 1998, for instance, the Bank of China, one of the country's largest state banks, entered a cooperation agreement with the city in which it pledged it would give Shanghai priority when deciding how to allocate its loans.[24] Shanghai's special status, in addition to its large indigenous market and relatively well-educated workforce, subsequently make the city popular with foreign investors. Such advantages not only spell more jobs for the "haves," they also spell more jobs for the "have-nots"—even if those jobs are relatively poorly paid.

Thanks to the city's growing population of expatriates and urban professionals, demand for hotels, restaurants, entertainment, and other services is greater than in most other cities. While most laid-off workers do not have enough savings to open a restaurant, they have a better chance of finding a job in one than in the country's other cradles of state-owned industry. Xiao Xu found a job driving a cab. Ah Hua found work in her brother's restaurant. Xiao Han earns money cleaning for a foreign couple. The jobs might not be good ones but they bring in income. A 72-year-old retired mid-level cadre in a state company who teaches English and Chinese to supplement his 700 yuan (US$84) a month pension explained:

My son-in-law, who is a massage doctor, makes ends meet by giving massages outside of work. My daughter-in-law, who is an accountant at a state-owned firm that is in bad shape, moonlights on weekends for a private businessman. My wife has a broken hip and I've hired a laid-off textile worker to take care of our home. Our housekeeper's work unit has no money. It can't pay workers' salaries and told her to wait a year to get reimbursed for medical expenses. So now she earns money by being a maid and delivering milk. There's a saying in Chinese: Shrimps and crabs have their own ways to make money. There are opportunities. Even migrant workers—three million of them—come to Shanghai to do the work that Shanghainese won't do.

Indeed, Xie, the laid-off textile worker who sold cookies, knows he can find a job if he takes a job paying less than 500 yuan (US$60) a month. But like many urban workers in China, he refuses to do certain types of work, creating opportunity for migrants.

Moreover, Shanghai and other relatively well-off cities have made more progress weaving together a modern social security net than other old industrial areas, like China's Northeast. Shanghai has more money to finance new welfare systems as a result of its substantial pool of foreign enterprises, large government-supported projects, and increasingly service-oriented economy. Loss-making factories, often located on prime real estate, can sell off land parcels for huge sums to investors and use the proceeds to help workers. Although not without problems,[25] Shanghai also manages its welfare funds better than less-sophisticated and less-scrutinized parts of the country. According to Zhou Lukuan, a director at the Labor and Personnel Institute at People's University in Beijing, "In some place like Shanghai, they systematically deposit funds in the bank at favorable rate. In other places they do nothing with the funds, just let it sit in the labor department and in a small percentage of cases misappropriate the funds."

In the fall of 1997 I took a couple of trips to northeastern Liaoning province—one of China's industrial hubs. There, the holes in the welfare net are wider. Two-thirds of the province's 1,000 medium- to large-sized state firms at the time lumbered under heavy debts. If they were not losing money, they were barely squeaking by.[26] When I visited Shenyang Internal Combustion, a loss-making tractor maker in Liaoning's capital, it had not paid salaries to its more than 3,000 workers for 10 months, leaving them to survive in the market. With only 30 million yuan (US$3.6 million) in fixed assets but 100 million yuan (US$12 million) in debt, state banks, also under reform pressure, would no longer lend to it. It applied for bankruptcy but the authorities told it to wait in line. In the meantime, it did not take part in social security schemes because it had no money to contribute. I talked to a company official about how workers were faring. Sitting in a dingy office with paint chipping from the walls, he said:

Today more than 20 retired old ladies gathered outside the factory gates demanding their pensions, which had not been paid for two months. The factory decided to give them 150 yuan (US$18) each, though they're supposed to get 270 yuan (US$32.50). We haven't paid workers for 10 months. Our clinic here used to have a budget of 70,000 yuan (US$8,434) a month. Now our monthly budget is 5,000 to 7,000 yuan (US$602–US$843). That's not enough to treat even one seriously ill patient. Cancer patients get at most 200 yuan (US$24) a month. It's almost nothing. Those people go home and wait to die. Fifty yuan to 500 yuan (US$6–US$60)—that's the most that anyone gets and that's for people who make a stink. This money is to keep factory workers stable. Otherwise people break windows or complain to the head of the factory or the head of the bureau that controls the factory. Some people have tried to rip out telephones and break down doors at the hospital and at the factory head's office ... We no longer distribute free housing and no one can afford to buy their apartment because they don't earn a salary. No one pays rent either because rent is supposed to be deducted from their salary. As a result, the factory no longer bothers maintaining the apartments. Rain started leaking through the ceiling of my neighbor's apartment. He lives on the top floor. When the factory's maintenance people came to check it, they told him to buy the repair materials himself and deduct the cost from the rent. Since he doesn't pay rent in the first place, the problem is totally his responsibility. Only if people can't bear the problem will they pay to fix it. The water leaking from my neighbor's ceiling is not that severe so he won't bother. I feel very sad. I've worked here for more than 20 years. I don't understand why this is happening.

In Benxi, a coal and steel town nestled among Liaoning's rolling hills, scores of men in blue jackets and pea-green army pants gather on the sidewalks each day holding cardboard signs offering house painting, floor polishing, and other services. One of the men—a tall, thin 50-year-old—told me how he left his state-owned construction company four years earlier, not because he was laid off, but because he was not getting paid. "Now I don't get any kind of allowance from anyone," he said. In Shanghai, I did not come across laid-off state workers who received no government assistance of any kind. Another man, who was trying to find work installing water heaters, explained further: "It all depends on the profitability of the factory. If they have money they give it to you, and if they don't, well … Some people haven't been paid anything for two to three years. It's not easy to find a new job." According to local labor official Lu Wenhai, 10,000 workers in the city, whose population is only 900,000, do not receive any money either from the city's welfare funds or from their ailing state-owned employers. They are expected to fend for themselves, although people making less than 85 yuan (US$10) a month can apply for government handouts. The biggest challenge for cities like Benxi is creating jobs—unlike Shanghai, it attracts few foreign investors and the central government does not ply it with preferential policies. The city also lacks a significant base of young professionals and expatriates to spend money on services. So while Benxi's jobless, like jobless around China, can turn to the gray market for work and income, it offers them fewer opportunities. As one of the men holding a placard in downtown Benxi said: "You can open a restaurant but there's no guarantee you'll have customers." Although the same holds true in Shanghai, it holds more true in a place like Benxi.

Workers Unite?

During the student demonstrations that rocked China in the spring of 1989, the Shanghai government, under then Shanghai Mayor Zhu Rongji's leadership, used an innovative strategy to quell protests in the city. Instead of sending the army to put down the uprising, the authorities turned to the city's state enterprise workers to help maintain public order. Recalling those chaotic days, Shanghainese often comment on how good a job the workers' militias did pacifying protestors. Roughly 100,000 workers took to the streets on the government's behalf to entreat protesting students in Shanghai to return to their dormitories. While some workers joined the protestors, the vast majority were not about to throw away their guarantee of an iron rice bowl for the abstract political reforms that students were spouting.

What a difference a decade can make: Students in Shanghai and in major cities around China today appear far more interested in pursuing careers than fighting for political change. They have been co-opted by a system that after 1989 fed them a steady diet of patriotic propaganda and provided material well-being and opportunity. Workers during the same period watched their iron rice bowl turn into a rusty sieve and their guaranteed lifetime security into a broken promise. So instead of students hitting the streets in protest of the system today,[27] the far greater risk comes from laid-off state enterprise workers who, along with farmers in the countryside, no longer feel the benefits of China's economic reforms.

China's official urban unemployment rate was 3.5% in 1998, although real unemployment is much higher. Zhou, the labor expert at People's University in Beijing, explained:

The government avoids registering people as unemployed mostly for ideological reasons. It's not appropriate for a socialist country to have lots of unemployed people. Also, if you make them all unemployed, it's the government's responsibility to pay their benefits. The government's unemployment insurance funds do not have enough money.

The Communist Party performs semantic acrobatics to depress the official rate, which Zhou estimated to be 15%–20%. The official figure does not include the country's 10 million laid-off workers, since they officially are still connected to their work unit, or the 20 million redundant workers who have not yet been laid off but have no real work to do. It also does not count the 70 million peasants who migrated to China's cities, of which maybe 20% have found permanent or temporary jobs.

This hidden unemployment helps explain why reports of worker and peasant agitation increasingly make headlines in the foreign press. Unpaid wages and benefits, unfair taxes, and corruption are protestors' most common complaints. In Hubei province in 1996, for example, more than 500 unemployed workers demanding jobs and benefits often amassed at city halls around the province.[28] In Sichuan province in March 1997, 20,000 disgruntled workers held a 30-hour sit-in in front of government offices in the remote city of Nanchong.[29] In Beijing the same month, a group called the Laid-off Workers' Committee planted two bombs in buildings in the capital.[30] In the first 10 months of 1998, laid-off people in Changsha, Hunan province, blocked traffic more than 60 times.[31] In Daolin, in the same province on January 8, 1999, some 3,000 farmers marched on the seat of government. Ten days later more than 500 workers at a state-run cotton mill in the city of Changde blocked a bridge to protest unpaid wages and corruption. The encore came the next day when a bomb exploded on a crowded bus in the provincial capital of Changsha, wounding 37 people. In November 1999, roughly 1,000 laid-off workers at a defunct textile factory protested corruption and bad management for four days in Shaanxi province before police in riot gear quelled the demonstration.[32] And these are just the incidents that get reported. The most surprising show of defiance in the 1990s came in April 1999 when 10,000 adherents of the Falungong Spiritual Movement held a peaceful vigil outside Zhongnanhai, the central government's leadership compound in Beijing. The movement, which mixes traditional Chinese breathing exercise, Buddhism, Taoism, and mysticism, was estimated at the time to have two million to tens of millions of followers, many of whom were laid-off workers, state enterprise employees, and retirees. China's leaders see Falungong, with it ability to organize thousands of people without the government's knowledge, as a direct confrontation to Communist Party power and launched a nationwide crackdown. Likewise, the Party deals mercilessly with anyone attempting to form an opposition party or organize workers or farmers independently.

Compared to other parts of the country, unrest in Shanghai seems less serious, less violent, and more well-controlled. I attribute this situation to the city's more plentiful job opportunities, the local government's greater success in implementing welfare reforms, and the Shanghai authorities' tough stance on dissent. Shanghai is better managed than most big cities in China and its security forces are always on alert to head off problems. Not that there is no unrest. In May 1999, for instance, some 700 workers blocked the main gate of the Shanghai No. 3 Steel Plant for two days and knocked around a factory Communist Party official to protest the closing of a furnace.[33] But the intensity and scale of outbreaks in Shanghai seem relatively subdued compared to provinces like Hunan and Sichuan.

Shanghai's less-volatile climate can also be attributed to the Shanghainese personality. While the Shanghainese have a reputation as radicals in the West—largely because the Communist Party was founded in Shanghai, students and workers often protested there in the 1920s, and the city was a stronghold of radical political forces during the Cultural Revolution—they do not have the same reputation in China. Whenever I broached the subject of the Shanghainese as radicals with Chinese interviewees, they would look at me as though I were crazy. They liked to point out that few of the Communist Party's founding members were from Shanghai and that Shanghai became the founding venue only because it had the country's largest industrial workforce and the foreign concessions at the time offered less political repression. And even then Shanghai workers did not drive the revolution in 1949: Instead, peasants under the Communist Party's leadership did. They also pointed out that while the initial salvo in the 1966 Cultural Revolution was launched from Shanghai and the Gang of Four controlled Shanghai and used it as their base, Mao directed the movement from Beijing. They consider members of the Gang of Four to be political opportunists who used the Cultural Revolution to advance their careers rather than committed radicals. They also noted that although Red Guards terrorized the city, the most brutal Red Guard activity did not take place in Shanghai but instead in Beijing, Wuhan, and Chengdu. Shanghai residents, meanwhile, obeyed leaders' calls to return to work more quickly than other cities. In more recent times, although pro-democracy demonstrators were active in Shanghai in 1989, the movement's brains and heart were in the nation's capital. Furthermore, neither anti-NATO protests nor Falungong activities in 1999 were as lively in Shanghai as in some other cities.

What's the explanation? Both Shanghainese and non-Shanghainese contend that the Shanghainese in general are less passionate, more practical, and more money-focused. They mind their own business more and concentrate on improving their personal well-being. They eschew politics unless they can derive personal benefit. They feel they have something to lose, namely permanent residency status in China's greatest metropolis, and do not want to lose it. They subsequently are more likely to obey authority and avoid risks that might jeopardize their future. They are good implementers but not visionary leaders.

Central and municipal government leaders are particularly concerned with maintaining order in Shanghai given the size of its population, its role as a model, its importance to the economy, and its international high profile. So far they have done a good job keeping Shanghai stable. They have less to fear from their most populous city than from more desperate parts of the country whose residents have less to lose and hotter heads. The economic situation will have to deteriorate dramatically for Shanghai in coming years to become a driver of political agitation in China. Indeed, if the Chinese Communist Party cannot keep a lid on unrest in Shanghai, it stands little chance of maintaining stability around the country.

Notes

[1] *Shanghai Star*, Jan. 7, 2000 and *Shanghai Star*, Jun. 6, 1998.

[2] Ibid., Jun. 6, 1997.

[3] Ibid., Jun. 6, 1997 and *China Daily*, Jun. 15, 1997.

[4] *South China Morning Post*, Jul. 16, 1999. Central bank official Sun Guofeng quoted the figures first in an article he wrote for the financial daily, *Caijin Ribao*.

[5] *Shanghai Star*, Sept. 3, 1999.

[6] See Harriet Sergeant, *Shanghai*, Jonathan Cape, London, 1991 p. 131 and Betty Peh-T'I Wei, *Shanghai: Crucible of Modern China*, Oxford University Press, Hong Kong, 1987, p. 218.

[7] See Sargeant, ibid., Chapter 4 for a detailed discussion of how foreigners lived in Old Shanghai.

[8] See Lynn Pan, *Tracing It Home*, Martin Secker & Warburg Ltd, 1992.

[9] See Betty Peh-T'I Wei, ibid., pp. 129–134.

[10] Carl Riskin, op. cit., Chapter 11.

[11] *South China Morning Post*, Feb. 20, 2000.

[12] Ibid., Feb. 9, 1999.

[13] Ibid., Oct. 14, 1997.

[14] Ibid., Jun. 1, 1999.

[15] *China Daily*, Apr. 21, 1997.

[16] *Shanghai Star*, Jun. 1, 1999.

[17] *Xinmin Evening News*, Sept. 28, 1997.

[18] *Shanghai Star*, Jun. 30, 1998.

[19] Ibid., Nov. 24, 1998.

[20] Ibid., Sept. 22, 1998.

[21] Ibid., Dec. 14, 1999.

[22] Op. cit.

[23] Ibid., Nov. 10, 1998.

[24] Ibid., Jun. 30, 1998.

[25] The central government, which often let Shanghai launch experiments with economic reform first, allowed Shanghai's Pudong Development Bank to invest pension funds in the stock market rather than just in government bonds and bank deposits. It lost those rights in 1999 when it lost money in the markets. See *The Asian Wall Street Journal*, Nov. 19–20, 1999.

[26] *China Daily Business Weekly*, Sept. 7–13, 1997.

[27] The 10th anniversary of the Tiananmen massacre (June 4, 1989) went by almost unnoticed. The only time students as a group showed a significant taste for political activism in the 1990s was after the United States bombed China's embassy in Yugoslavia during the war in Kosovo in the spring of 1999. The sometimes-virulent demonstrations had the Communist Party's strong support and some claim instigation. In Shanghai, the protests dissipated more quickly than elsewhere. Though the Shanghai government, like

its counterparts around China, supported and directed the ire of student protestors, it was particularly concerned that anti-Western sentiment not get out of hand and scare away foreign investors.

[28] *South China Morning Post*, Jan. 3, 1997.

[29] *Far Eastern Economic Review*, Jun. 26, 1997.

[30] *South China Morning Post*, Apr. 4, 1997.

[31] *International Herald Tribune*, Jan. 19, 1999.

[32] *South China Morning Post*, Nov. 6, 1999.

[33] *The Asian Wall Street Journal*, Jun. 8, 1999.

5

Search for a Soul

In August 1996 an unsolicited resume arrived over my fax machine. Although it was completely unprofessional-looking compared to the resumes I normally received, it intrigued me more than any other. It was not just that the applicant, who went by the English name of Kim, had done plenty of freelance work for other foreign news agencies. She had also had experiences that were highly uncharacteristic of other young Shanghainese I had met. For one, she had left university without obtaining her degree. Studying law in the southern city of Xiamen, she quit school after the central government's violent suppression of student demonstrators in 1989. "There did not seem to be much point in studying law," she later explained. She also had backpacked on her own around China, picking up odd jobs and visiting gritty parts of the country that most Shanghainese disdained for their backwardness. Doing something so unstructured, so off the traditional career path, and so potentially dangerous was unusual for a young Shanghainese—let alone for a Shanghainese woman. Even if I did not hire her, I wanted to meet her. I called her immediately to set up a job interview.

Kim's appearance was as radical as her behavior—at least for Shanghai. Whereas in Beijing, young people on society's fringe sometimes adopt the spiked collars, green hair, and other anti-establishment accoutrements of alienated Western youth, it is exceedingly rare in Shanghai. Just as Shanghai youth prefer sweet pop songs to the hard-edged rock music that draws rabid fans in Beijing, they also favor clean-cut styles. Young Shanghainese women—whether attempting a dainty, classic, sexy, or trendy look—pay tremendous attention to their appearance. Kim, however, did not. Work boots and baggy clothes appealed to her most. She wore her hair cropped close to her Buddha-like face, occasionally shaving her head all together.

133

Although she had never been abroad, she spoke colloquial English with casual fluency rather than the stilted variety that Chinese learned at school. Unlike other applicants, she suggested thoughtful story ideas and understood a foreign journalist's needs. She was switched on to what was going on around her. She was conscientious. She did not mind unconventional hours or travel. She did not turn up her nose at the salary I offered. I hired her immediately.

In her free time, Kim liked to hang out with painters, poets, writers, and other artists. She liked to stay out late, drinking, dancing, and discussing. Shanghai ostensibly should have been the perfect place in China for someone with her energy. The incredible urban renewal taking place in the city brought job opportunities, nightclubs, cafes, museums, theaters, and cultural festivals. Still, Kim became increasingly restless. All she could talk about was moving to Beijing, which in her eyes was a cultural mecca where all things were possible. After working with me for a year, she packed her few belongings and took a train north.

A year later in September 1998, we had dinner together in Beijing. We talked about her decision to leave Shanghai. Sitting around a table at a sidewalk restaurant, she explained: "I was simply bored in Shanghai. After I finished work, there was hardly anywhere to go. I had several interesting friends but that's all. When I came here to attend an international documentary conference, I watched some good documentaries, met some documentary makers, and thought it was very interesting."

"Couldn't you pursue your interest in documentaries in Shanghai?" I asked.

"No, because first of all, there are almost no independent documentary makers in Shanghai. In Shanghai, they all belong to Shanghai TV. In Shanghai, it's difficult to do. At Shanghai TV, it's really mostly all Shanghainese who work there and they are not open at all. It's not like CCTV or Beijing TV, where you have people from all over China. It did not even occur to me to try to break into the field in Shanghai. Shanghai TV rarely does good documentaries. I heard about one good one that they did while I've been in Beijing. CCTV and Beijing TV do interesting ones— definitely. I've met people involved in them. They're young and open to making new stuff. I never met any of these kinds of people in Shanghai."

"But the Shanghainese say they're the most open-minded people in China?"

"In one way, the Shanghainese are open-minded in that they accept Western culture. But in another way they seem brainwashed into thinking that Shanghai is the best and that the Shanghainese are the most modern. While they may be open to the West, they're not open to their own country. I have a Shanghainese friend who came to Beijing after studying media at Harvard University. She says that all you can do in Shanghai is make a lot of money and spend it. So she chose to work at Beijing TV as an executive producer. In Shanghai the whole atmosphere was so boring. If I wanted to talk about art or culture, the only place to go was to my poor poet friend's house who lives in a far corner of Shanghai."

"Maybe you just didn't find the right people. How hard did you look?"

"I know quite a lot of artists in Shanghai. In Shanghai, everywhere you go, you meet the same crowd of artists. In Beijing, everywhere you go, you meet some new interesting people. It's like: 'Wow, wow, wow, wow.' I meet artists from all over China in Beijing. In Shanghai, most of them are from Shanghai or studied in Shanghai and became 'Shanghai-ized.' "

For every possible excuse I could think of for Shanghai's cultural malaise, Kim seemed to come up with a reason why I was wrong. For instance, when I asked her if artists from around China flocked to Beijing rather than Shanghai because they could more easily obtain a government permit to live in the capital, she replied:

Most of my friends here don't have a residency permit and don't care about it. I did not meet one artist while in Shanghai that moved there without a residency permit or a job. In Beijing there are tons of artists like that.

Kim then told me about some of her projects. Besides supporting herself by working for a foreign radio station part-time, she was exploring the possibility of setting up a film club with a foreign friend to show underground and alternative works. "Here I know a bunch of film directors who are making new, interesting, low-cost films. Also, I'm quite confident that there's an audience of young people in Beijing who are interested in alternative Chinese movies. But in Shanghai, there's no audience[1] and there are no directors. I have one director from Shanghai and his film is not that alternative." She was also hoping to work on an innovative new Beijing TV program that seemed willing to hire creative—albeit inexperienced—young people. At the same time, she and a friend were putting together a radio talk show program for a station broadcasting around the country. She said:

In Shanghai, I never would have done any of these things. The idea would never have occurred to me. The atmosphere wasn't right, the people weren't right, and the audience wasn't right. Even the foreigners weren't right. In Shanghai, they're mostly businesspeople. That's very different from here. In Beijing I'm a lot busier meeting friends and discussing projects. Now I go out to clubs much less because I find more interesting things to do here. In Shanghai, what else can you do but go bar-hopping.

Kim's pessimism about Shanghai is shared by many other intellectuals and artists. When I first heard their views, I was perplexed. After all, hadn't capitalist Shanghai been a center of artistic innovation in China before 1949, making it inevitable that Shanghai would recapture that status in a reforming China? Wasn't the Shanghai government erecting the country's most modern museum and performing arts center? As the country's anointed financial hub, wouldn't Chinese artists start flocking to China's richest city in the same way that they gathered in New York in the United States? Wasn't Shanghai the most open-minded place in China?

The reality today is quite different. Despite progress building cultural infrastructure and becoming a more culturally active city, Shanghai is not the center of artistic innovation in China. Counterintuitively, Beijing, the stodgy political capital known best for its intolerance of dissenting voices, holds that moniker. Most of the country's artists continue to congregate in Beijing and this plethora of talent ultimately makes it the country's artistic heart. Shanghai can barely compete. Over time, I have come to understand why.

Old Shanghai's Buzz

Old Shanghai, on the other hand, had no shortage of talent, which by the late 1920s helped it replace Beijing as China's most active and influential artistic hub. In the first half of the 20th century, Shanghai attracted established and aspiring writers, composers, directors, actors, painters, and musicians from around China, giving it the highest concentration of artists in the country. Noted Chinese journalist-author Yang Dongping gave a taste of Old Shanghai's cultural dynamism in his book *City Monsoon: The Cultural Spirit of Beijing and Shanghai*. He wrote:

While it gave birth to the 'Butterfly School' and the 'New Saturday School' of authors, Shanghai also cultivated various types of literary works, opinions, and groups dealing with society, life, revolution, politics, art, beauty, left-wing, right-wing, nationalism, socialism, anarchism, and so on. A great number of elites excelled here: [Yang reels off 35 names of literary luminaries including Lu Xun,

Mao Dun, and Ba Jin] ... If we look beyond literature, the situation was equally dizzying. Despite the city's youth, it had the greatest variety of national operas and the greatest number of theatrical troupes, actors, and actresses ... Any opera, troupe, or artist that wanted to win nationwide recognition and fame had to be well accepted first in Shanghai. Shanghai became a new base for all kinds of art ranging from oil painting, watercolor painting, and sculpture to plate painting. Development of popular art was especially great ... Shanghai became the most influential base for orchestra, movies, and dramas in China ...[2]

What attracted artists and intellectuals to a city that had been little more than a thriving market town before the British usurped part of its territory in 1840? Despite the humiliation that most Chinese felt at foreign domination, Old Shanghai's foreign concessions in the first half of the 20th century offered artists and intellectuals conditions conducive to creativity that did not exist elsewhere in China. For one, compared with the war-ravaged and warlord-controlled Chinese interior, the concessions offered greater political stability and freedom. Artists and intellectuals experienced relatively minimal censorship and government interference and therefore could go where their imagination and political beliefs took them. For instance, the only place that Lu Xun, the era's most influential writer, could publish his writings after 1927 was in the International Settlement.[3] Artists also liked the fact that they could partake in social behavior in the foreign concessions that traditional Chinese society prohibited, like living with their lovers.

At the same time, Old Shanghai offered artists the most stimulating environment in China to pursue their work. Most of the country was isolated from foreign influences, while Shanghai attracted more foreigners than anywhere else. Multiple cultures intermingled, including Chinese, British, French, Japanese, Russian, and American. Foreigners brought with them the latest technologies and cultural forms. Movie making, music recording, radio broadcasting, jazz, the tango, and Asia's first symphony orchestra found their Chinese home in the city. If an artist was seriously interested in making films in China, there was nowhere to go but Shanghai. Because many Chinese in Shanghai were immigrants uprooted from their homes in search of a better life or returned overseas students known in China as fake foreign devils, they were more accepting of the myriad foreign phenomena bombarding them.

The laissez-faire capitalism introduced into the concessions from abroad also created conditions for Shanghai's cultural takeoff. Business-minded folk sniffed out ways to make money from art, turning it into a commercially operated affair for the first time in Chinese history. Artists were no longer limited to producing for society's elites, but instead found a lucrative market in the common man. Romance novels and other pop art genres took Old Shanghai by storm while traditional art forms received a new twist. For instance, Peking Opera in China had traditionally been performed on a small stage for a small audience composed of officials and nobles, but Shanghai troupes started performing in theaters for the man on the street and borrowing theatrical elements from the West to boost appeal. Shanghai used its commercial savoir faire, access to Western technology, and innovative thinking to become China's Hollywood, churning out movies and movie stars that captured critical acclaim and audience attention.

The confluence of art and commerce in combination with the introduction of new art forms not only provided new creative outlets for Chinese artists and intellectuals, it also created jobs. In the prosperous and market-driven concessions, artists could make a living independent of the government-subsidized schools and salons that traditionally nurtured them. Composers could work part-time for record companies or write music for movies. Writers toiling at a novel could pay their rent by working for one of the city's many newspapers or periodicals. Once finished with their opus, authors stood a far better chance of getting it printed in Shanghai than elsewhere, thanks to the city's more developed book publishing industry and relatively lax censors.

Ultimately, Old Shanghai provided artists and intellectuals opportunity and fertile soil for innovation. Whereas Beijing's "*jingpai*" culture, which connoted tradition and elitism, had grown uninspired, Shanghai culture, known as "*haipai*," stood for tolerance, adaptability, popularity, and modernity. Shanghai attracted the country's most culturally gifted, who gave the city an artistic buzz to match its moneymaking energy. Old Shanghai in the 1920s became China's mecca both culturally and commercially.

Revolutionary Shanghai's Stagnation

Shanghai's days as a crossroads of artistic innovation proved short-lived. After the revolution in 1949, the Communist Party cut Shanghai off from the international influences, the free-flowing migration of talent, and the capitalism that had nurtured its creativity. The Party viewed art as a tool to serve the revolution, and as a result, education and propaganda became art's primary function rather than entertainment, profit, or creative expression. China's new leaders put anything having to do with the arts and culture—including movie studios, broadcasting stations, performing arts troupes, and universities—firmly under the Party's control. It located the country's most important cultural agencies in Beijing—the central symphony, the writer's association of China, the national news agency— and transferred the country's most talented people to the capital, recruiting the best graduates from schools around the country. The government appointed bureaucrats to run Shanghai's arts institutions and distributed jobs to artists and intellectuals, putting them to work for the state, controlling their promotions and demotions, and co-opting them into the Party. Those who did not conform to the Party's orthodoxy were, one way or another, forced into submission. The state cemented its control by becoming the only source of funds for artistic endeavors. But because the government had more pressing concerns, the arts were severely underfunded, particularly in Shanghai, which the central government squeezed financially to develop the rest of the country. Spending on cultural activities in Shanghai, which included education, science and technology, and sanitation as well as culture, accounted for 1.8% to 4.4% of the total amount invested annually in Shanghai between 1971 and 1984, compared with 16.6% just after the revolution.[4] Under such conditions, it was difficult for creativity to blossom in Shanghai or anywhere in China, although Beijing, by recruiting the best students from around China, at least received a steady stream of talent.

Despite the Communist Party's attempt to reel in Shanghai's cultural dynamism, the city still influenced China's intellectual life. After the Communist victory, it produced revolutionary movies, movie stars, plays, symphonies, and novels that, within the constraints of politically motivated art, proved popular at the time. By the 1980s, however, its efforts more often than not fell flat. Given Old Shanghai's role as China's most innovative and commercially oriented artistic hub before 1949, one might have expected the city to lead the country's cultural life after Deng Xiaoping first launched his market reforms and open door policies in the 1980s. But Deng initially focused those reforms on southern China. Moreover, the legacy of the Gang of Four, who via the arts used Shanghai as a base for sending thinly veiled political messages during the Cultural Revolution (1966–76), still hung over the city's bureaucracy. Overtaxed, underfunded, uninspired, and old-fashioned, Shanghai did not take off economically or artistically. Observers regularly described Shanghai art works as "prolific but mediocre." Yang, the noted writer, explained:

Admittedly, cultural development in Shanghai resumed in the 1980s and achieved
new progress ... However, in the modernization of humanities, novels, poetry,
movies, theater, fine arts, photography, music, and dance, etc., it seemed that
Shanghai failed to make hits any more in China, nor did it stand out with its
special style or make milestone works—like *haipai* culture once did. Generally
speaking, it was beyond doubt that Shanghai culture had lost its dynamic power,
splendid charisma, and leadership status. The source of creativity and center for
modern China's culture historically shifted back to Beijing.[5]

Building the Hardware of Culture

Deng Xiaoping's decision to shift the focus of China's development
strategy to Shanghai and the Yangtze River Basin in the 1990s gave the
city a new lease on life. But its renaissance meant foremost rebuilding
Shanghai as a commercial and financial hub. That sat well with most
Shanghai residents, who ranked art and culture low on their priority list.

The Shanghainese, like the vast majority of mainland Chinese, have
been hell-bent on making money and improving their living standards
materially. Adults often say they are too preoccupied with earning a living
to partake in cultural events. But while the need to work hard to get ahead
in Shanghai's new competitive environment cannot be denied, it is at best
a partial explanation. In some ways, Shanghai residents now enjoy more
free time than in previous decades since the central government reduced
the legal workweek in China from six to five days in 1997. They also
have more disposable income. When pressed, most adults admit that they
have better things to do with their free time and spare change.
Karaoke, bowling, and browsing in one of the city's many new malls are
far more popular pastimes.

A poor education in the arts and uninspired productions performed by
cash-strapped, state-run troupes are also part of the problem. For instance,
adults I spoke with recalled their school field trip to the old Shanghai
museum as a dull affair at best. At worst, they were taught during the
Cultural Revolution to disdain the products of China's pre-1949 civilization,
and as Red Guards, some purposefully sought to destroy them. Young
people today are not much more enlightened. Take Wu Qunhua, an
attractive 24-year-old Chinese teacher who majored in Chinese literature
at Shanghai's teachers' college in the early 1990s. Not once during her
years at university did she visit the Shanghai Museum, which seemed a

natural offshoot of her studies. She explained:

The teachers never suggested it. So we never went. For young people like me, our understanding of Chinese culture is more and more superficial. People like to study foreign trade, finance, and foreign languages. You need to study things that will help you get a better job or salary. If you study ancient things you'll probably be poor. People like to make money. They like more relaxed forms of entertainment. Culture is not something they pay attention to.

Despite the cultural ambivalence of most residents, the city's leaders recognize that Shanghai cannot restore its former greatness nor be the model of "socialism with Chinese characteristics" if it focuses on commerce alone. So far, they have reacted to that challenge the way Chinese bureaucrats with a state-planning background often do: by building big buildings and organizing big projects. The city spent hundreds of millions of dollars in the 1990s on erecting China's first modern museum, performing arts center, and library—and deserves praise for the results of those efforts. The US$157-million Grand Theater—a futuristic marvel of white steel and glass offering state-of-the-art theaters and sound systems—sits elegantly next to the Shanghai government's new headquarters. Across the way, the new museum, a pink urn-shaped structure, dominates People's Square. Once a cold, concrete site suitable mainly for mass political rallies, the square is now an inviting public space boasting flowerbeds and fountains. Shanghai Mayor Xu Kuangdi, just prior to the museum's opening in October 1996, talked proudly of Shanghai's cultural plans, revealing the administration's focus on big symbolic projects:

We not only want to improve our economy. Even more important is to raise the city's cultural level. We can't become an economically great city, but a cultural desert. Our city took the most expensive plot of land—its most golden treasure— and built a museum there. We also want to build an opera house [a.k.a., the Grand Theater], the greatest in Asia. Also, the equipment and acoustics will be the best in Asia. We want to make People's Square into a place of leisure, culture, and entertainment for our citizens. Shanghai's People's Square used to be exactly like Tiananmen Square in Beijing—it was all concrete. It was a center for political activities. We want to transform it into an auspicious place with flowers, trees, and full of vitality ... We hope it's not just a museum. Have you seen the TV tower? We want to leave something for our descendents. Our predecessors left the Great Wall to us ...[6]

The crowning glory of these infrastructure achievements is the new Shanghai Museum. Housing the treasures of ancient China in eye-catching exhibits, it is China's first modern museum. Around the time of the museum's opening, I talked to James Watt, senior curator of Asian art at New York's Metropolitan Museum of Art. Echoing the reviews I heard from other international observers, he said: "No one can compare the Shanghai museum to any other museum in China. It's the finest museum of Chinese art in the world. Every major branch of Chinese art is shown with style and clarity and in great strength. I can't praise the Shanghai museum enough."

Shanghai, it seemed, had not just managed to build a museum, it had built a world-class museum to kick off the city's cultural renaissance. How did Shanghai create a museum of such high standard? The municipal government's acknowledgement that culture had a role to play in Shanghai and its subsequent support for the museum were key—no project of that size could ever occur without government backing in China. However, the credit for the museum's excellence goes to two determined art historians nearing the end of their careers. Without Ma Chenyuan, the museum's director, and Wang Qingzheng, its vice director, the new museum might not have been built at all. Or if built, it might have looked modern on the outside, but languished under the dull displays and ineffectual management that typify Chinese museums. The two sexagenarians did not just want the Shanghai museum to be the best in China, they understood how to make it the best, demonstrating the *haipai* spirit for which Shanghai had been so well known before 1949.

The story of how the pair made their dream a reality is one of the most inspiring that I encountered during my tenure in Shanghai. It is a case of culture succeeding in Shanghai, initially giving me hope that Shanghai was well on its way toward recapturing its pre-1949 artistic dynamism. It shows both what talented people can do in the city when given a chance, and demonstrates the complexities of achieving excellence in a society where government and ideology still regularly intervene. Ma and Wang created an outstanding museum despite the system, not because of it. Indeed, the remarks of Shanghai Party Secretary Huang Ju, the city's highest ranking official, at the museum's opening ceremony, give a sense of how the government still views culture as a tool of the Communist Party. Huang said:

The establishment and opening of the new Shanghai Museum is another achievement of construction of socialist spiritual civilization of Shanghai. It promotes the development of Shanghai's cultural affairs as well as Shanghai's whole spiritual civilization drive. During the Ninth Five-Year Plan, Shanghai will build more cultural facilities that will symbolize Shanghai's image. These cultural facilities will become the base of spreading cultural knowledge and promoting patriotic education. I do believe that under the guidance of the spirit of the Sixth plenum of the 14th Central Committee of the Chinese Communist Party, Shanghai people are paying close attention to the progress of culture, science, and civilization as a result of boosted socialist spiritual civilization.

The Birth of a Museum

Together Ma and Wang formed a potent partnership that overcame many challenges. Wang, sporting straight silver locks that dip to his chin, is urbane and cultivated—qualities that came in handy when the museum broke new ground in China by raising funds from foreign donors. Ma, who looks more like a stereotypical Chinese official, has the artistic eye that turned the museum's galleries into works of art in their own right. Both men understand how to work China's bureaucracy. And unlike most museum directors in the country, both men are not mere functionaries. They are also respected scholars and well-versed in museum management.

The seeds of their aestheticism were planted in pre-1949 days before Chinese society began vilifying such pursuits as "bourgeois" and "feudal." As a boy, Ma liked to carve Chinese characters into name chops—the stone slabs that Chinese traditionally used to stamp their names on documents. He would also spend hours flipping though his family's books on bronze relics and calligraphy. Wang comes from a family of collectors dating back to his great-great-grandfather and developed a taste for antiquities at a young age.

Their backgrounds in ancient arts eventually brought the pair together at the Shanghai museum, where the city's new Communist leaders assigned Ma in the 1950s and Wang in the early 1960s. At the time, the museum was housed in a former bank building owned before 1949 by Shanghai's most famous mobster, Du Yuesheng. Its cramped rooms and poor lighting made it unsuitable for exhibiting works of art, but for many years there was little to do about that. Indeed, Ma was preoccupied with simply protecting the city's precious artifacts from radical Red Guards during the 1966–76 Cultural Revolution.[7] It was therefore not until Deng Xiaoping launched economic reforms in the late 1970s that the idea for a modern museum began to fester. In 1980, Ma attended a bronze exhibit at the Metropolitan Museum of Art in New York City, where he saw a modern museum for the first time. Laughing at his own audacity, he recalled: "That's when it all started. I asked a lot of questions. The museum staff thought my behavior strange. Then I told them we wanted to build a museum like theirs."

Not that there was money available for a new museum in the 1980s—Shanghai was still remitting the lion's share of its revenues to the central government. Instead, Ma and Wang, who started collaborating seriously in the mid-1980s, began to sow the seeds that would make their dream reality. Having worked for years in Shanghai's cultural bureaucracy, they understood how to achieve their goals. First, they worked hard to create the best museum in China within the confines of the old bank building. They did this by combining their artistic sensibilities with the Western display, lighting, and pedagogical techniques they absorbed during foreign travel and international exchanges. Their efforts paid off by gaining them credibility and access to certain high-ranking Chinese officials, who later supported them in their fight to build a high-quality museum. For instance, the director of the State Bureau for Preservation of Cultural Relics in Beijing, Zhang Deqin, became one of their supporters. Just prior to the new museum's opening, he explained:

Although I went to university in Shanghai during the 1950s, I did not pay attention to the museum while I was there. It only came to my attention when I became head of the cultural relics bureau.[8] In 1991 and 1992, the museum held three exhibitions which I came to see. I was very surprised to see the museum in such a dilapidated building, but with such good displays. At that time I never thought a museum could reach that level. So in May 1991, I decided to call a meeting for all museums and chose Shanghai as the venue because I wanted museums from China to learn from Shanghai. After that, my relationship with the museum grew closer and closer. Ma told me that he had never met a cultural relics bureau head that had shown as much interest in the Shanghai museum as me. After the meeting I understood that Ma and Wang wanted to build a new museum. My role was to help the baby be born.

Similarly, Shanghai's leaders kept hearing about the Shanghai Museum's fine-quality exhibits and how the museum had become a leader among Chinese museums, conforming to their own vision of the city's future. "It drew their attention to the museum," said Zhang, who later interceded on Ma and Wang's behalf with the central government when the museum's construction ran into financial problems.

Second, Ma and Wang assiduously nurtured ties to international art circles, who later proved critical to the duo's plans. Besides proving themselves internationally as professionals by renovating the old museum so well, Ma and Wang opened the museum and themselves up to the international art world in a way that no Chinese museum had ever done before. In the mid-1980s, for instance, they started holding international seminars on Chinese painting and porcelains, drawing the attention of art patrons and scholars overseas. Unlike other Chinese museum directors who tended to be protective of their treasures, Ma and Wang let foreigners see precious artworks buried deep in the museum's storerooms. They further endeared themselves to new foreign friends with their graciousness. Take the comments of Susan Valenstein, the research curator in the Asian Art department at the Metropolitan Museum of Art, who in 1989 was invited by Ma and Wang to participate in a three-day tour of the former imperial kilns in Jingdezhen. Her voice oozing delight, she recalled:

I had the time of my life. They invited 40 of us from around the world. They treated us like visiting royalty. We took a train to Jingdezhen to see the recently excavated Ming Dynasty kilns. I was running barefoot through them. I was never treated so beautifully.

Ma and Wang also found an energetic and committed group of fans in the wealthy overseas Shanghainese families who fled China around the 1949 Revolution. Motivated by their confidence in Ma and Wang as well as a desire to see Shanghai reassert its former glory, they proved indispensable in helping the pair reach out to the international community. George Fan, an overseas Shanghainese businessman and art collector, for instance, financed the Jingdezhen extravaganza. Some of the people on the trip who previously had had little contact with the Shanghai museum, like Hong Kong businessman and philanthropist T.T.Tsui and entrepreneur S.C. Ko, later became financial donors. According to Fan:

For the first time, many collectors and the curators got to spend three nights on a train together. They became friends. Ma and Wang are outstanding people to deal with. When you give them money you feel that something is going to happen. They impressed people on that trip.

Ma and Wang's chance to make their dream come true finally arrived in the early 1990s when Deng Xiaoping turned the focus of China's development strategy to Shanghai, unleashing a cavalcade of urban renewal projects. The pair subsequently took their case to then Shanghai Mayor Huang Ju. The cornerstone of their strategy was to convince the leadership that the project would cost the city very little money—just 30 million yuan (US$3.6 million) in start-up expenses, plus a piece of property in the center of Shanghai. They planned to cover most of the new museum's construction budget themselves with US$25 million earned from selling the old museum building. They proposed to raise another US$10 million for decorating the museum's 14 galleries by taking donations from overseas sources. Wang figured that if the museum could offset some its construction costs with foreign money, the project would be more palatable to city leaders already overloaded by demands for cash. "There was no money for a new museum because it was not allocated under the national plan. If we had donors, we could take less money from the government and relieve its burden," Wang explained.

The plan made sense to Mayor Huang, but approval still took almost two years. A major sticking point was the site on People's Square that Ma and Wang requested. "Everyone wanted it," said Wang. "Some wanted to build an entertainment center, others wanted office blocks, others wanted a park." According to Zhang, the cultural relics bureau director:

The fact that Ma and Wang did not require a lot of money for the project helped Shanghai leaders give the go-ahead. However, the Shanghai government originally wanted to give them the space next to the Shanghai government's headquarters, but Ma and Wang thought the site was too small. Huang Ju finally made the decision to give them People's Square, which is very good for Shanghai.

Wang then spent much of the next two years raising funds from overseas donors. Given the quality of the relationships the pair had developed earlier, he did not have to look very far. "It was more about returning the generosity they had extended in the 1980s," donor Lillian Chin explained in a clipped British accent. Chin, a collector of Chinese porcelain and the Shanghai representative for British Auction House Christie's, was another wealthy overseas Shanghainese who helped smooth Ma and Wang's path to their goal. In 1993, she and her husband made the first foreign donation to the museum—£150,000 to decorate the Chinese seal gallery—affirming for the Shanghai government that Ma and Wang could make good on their plan to raise US$10 million overseas. Diane Woo, an overseas Shanghainese in New York, was also instrumental in attracting donations from the Hotung family—prominent Eurasian industrialists in pre-1949 Shanghai—and the American C.V. Starr Foundation, which also had Old Shanghai ties. Hong Kong tycoon T.T. Tsui, who got to know Ma and Wang on the Jingdezhen trip, kicked in US$1 million, and then recruited other Hong Kong donors. In the end, overseas Shanghainese,

Hong Kong Chinese, and families with historical links to the city accounted for most of the foreign donations.

The far bigger challenge for Ma and Wang came when the museum's construction went 50% over budget. I had heard rumors that the museum had run into funding problems, but could not get anyone credible to confirm it or fill in the details. Little did I know that my luck was about to change when I met Zhang, who had just retired as head of the China's cultural relics bureau and was visiting Shanghai for the museum opening. Sitting in an apartment filled with dark mahogany furniture, he told me the story of the museum's funding woes with the gusto of a man at the end of his career and proud of his personal contribution. He said:

According to the original budget, the museum was supposed to cost 400 million yuan (US$48 million) but ended up costing 600 million yuan (US$72 million). There were two reasons why it went over budget. One was inflation. Prices during the period kept going up. Second, after Ma and Wang broke ground on the museum, they insisted that everything should be done to a very high standard. For instance, they used Spanish marble cut in Italy for both the north and south entrances. People were asking: Why did you import it from Italy when we have marble in Fujian? The answer is that the marble in Fujian province is not buried as deep as Spanish marble and so the quality is not as good. To install the marble, they then used workers from Japan who had a special technique that prevented the marble from discoloring. Ma and Wang understood this problem. This museum was like a magnificent beauty in Ma and Wang's hearts. Once they started to draw the painting they had to make the eyes, nose, and mouth all the best looking. Their attitude was: If I need to spend it, I'll spend it. I mean they already had half the horse in the house. They understood that there was no way the government was going to stop the project halfway through. I think they played a little trick.

Indeed, Ma later commented to me that after the first pile for the museum was driven into the ground in September 1993, he never doubted that museum would be completed.

He was right—the city's leaders were not going to let the museum stand half finished in an ugly construction site in front of city hall. The museum, after all, was one of the high-profile projects heralding Shanghai's reemergence as a modern city. But the additional money did not come without considerable nail-biting. Although the Shanghai government and the state-owned Shanghai Antiques and Curio Store agreed to inject the majority of the needed funds, Ma and Wang were still short 30 million yuan (US$3.6 million). They subsequently had no choice but to ask the central government for help. This was problematic. For one, in 1994

Beijing had launched a nationwide austerity campaign to curb runaway inflation, and had been trying to control the explosion of property development projects taking place around the country. Moreover, Ma and Wang had broken the rules by not asking for approval from the State Planning Commission (SPC) in Beijing to build the museum in the first place. It was at that point that Zhang's friendship came in particularly handy. Zhang said:

According to regulations, big construction projects needed SPC approval. But Ma and Wang thought they could get away with not obtaining the approval since they planned to finance the museum without much government funding. Plus they did not think that they were going to have to spend so much money. So I invited officials from the State Planning Commission to inspect the museum during the construction. I told them that after it was finished, the museum would be the best in China, but if the state did not invest any money, then it could not succeed. But the SPC officials were angry. 'They didn't ask us for approval,' they said. The history museum in Xian had asked for approval and the SPC gave them half of the funds needed. Ma and Wang, however, had not prepared the SPC. This was a problem. The SPC did not want to give them the money, so I explained to the officials the reasons that the museum went over budget. I tried to convince them that the additional money was worth it. Ma and Wang spent a lot of time talking to them. Finally the SPC officials felt moved by the museum's plight. In fact, the museum had originally asked for 30 million yuan (US$3.6 million) and in the end the SPC gave them 50 million yuan (US$6 million).

Ma and Wang's derring-do inspired awe among other Chinese museum officials who, like typical bureaucrats in China, normally spend their lives trying to stay out of trouble. Yang Xin, the deputy director of China's most-visited museum, the Palace Museum in Beijing, commented:

Even though they did not have all the money, they still went ahead with their plan. Construction easily could have been stuck in the middle. Besides their talent and sense of responsibility, Ma and Wang had a lot of guts. If Ma hadn't done this, he could have gone peacefully into retirement—a lot of leaders have this idea. If Ma had retired, he'd have had no responsibility for doing anything wrong. He wouldn't have to worry.

Luckily for Shanghai, Ma and Wang did not fade peacefully into retirement, but instead built a museum that did justice to the city's cultural aspirations. While some Western observers criticized its urn-like exterior design and domed interior atrium as architecturally banal, I did not hear anyone disparage the quality of the museum work inside. The exhibits are artistically laid out and make consummate use of state-of-the-art technology. Take the darkened jade room, where miniature fiber optic lights spotlight the beauty of 1,000-year-old jade ornaments. Or the sculpture gallery on the ground floor. There, ancient stone statues stand in an innovative and easy-to-view pattern against a striking black and red background. The museum also broke new ground in China with its effort to educate viewers in a fun and effective manner. For a quick summary of the development of ancient ceramic styles, for instance, visitors have to look no further than the well-illustrated collection of pottery shards conveniently organized along one of the porcelain gallery's walls. Nearby, real craftsmen practice their art in a life-size model of an ancient ceramics factory.

Such efforts go far in helping the museum fulfill its pedagogical purpose. From my interviews with the man on the street, it is apparent that few people are interested in the museum except as a symbol of Shanghai's growing prosperity and modernity. Although they say the museum will raise the city's "cultural level," adults repeatedly also say they are too busy to visit, the admission fee is too steep, or they just are not interested. Wu Qunhua, the attractive 24-year-old teacher with a Chinese literature degree, said she would go if someone gave her a ticket. When I asked about the museum's purpose, she and others talked about its role in helping Chinese understand their history. Rarely did people appreciate the objects in the museum as art. Their attitudes are reflected in the museum's attendance numbers, which according to the museum averaged only 2,000 to 3,000 a day in 1998 in a city of more than 14 million people.

Given the population's seeming indifference to the museum, I could not help but wonder for whom it had been built. I asked Wang. First, he said, it was for foreigners. "Shanghai is an international city. We have many foreign visitors. Shanghai is a window into China." Second, he said, the museum was for all Chinese people, but especially young people. He explained:

These middle school and college students know even less about Chinese history and tradition. So we will have an education department. We plan to publish books and magazines. There'll be a lecture room where students can attend talks. And we will offer free transport for students. Between 5 p.m. and 8 p.m. on Saturdays, students get in free. Children pay half-price. Most people who visit the museum are parents with their child. Previously parents and children did not visit the museum together. Schools organized visits. Even though parents are not well-educated, they hope their child will have a better future. I think this shows progress.

Recalling the army of pint-sized school kids I had just seen scampering around the museum, I too was hopeful in 1996. My thoughts drifted to some newly middle-class parents I knew who were pushing their only child to take piano lessons. I started to foresee a future for Shanghai when university graduates viewed a knowledge of the arts as an important part of being an educated, successful individual rather than simply judging each other by the thickness of their billfolds. I wondered at the time if I might be witnessing the advent of a genuine cultural revolution in Shanghai—one that had nothing to do with politics like in the 1960s, but that focused on art and rejuvenating the spirit that made Shanghai an innovative artistic hub in the 1920s and 1930s.

Where's the Soul?

More research into the city's artistic and cultural life, however, has made me less optimistic. As impressive as Ma and Wang's achievement is, the Shanghai Museum ultimately represents the hardware of a cultural hub. Schooled in state planning, Shanghai bureaucrats understand the need for bricks and mortar, even if Ma and Wang had to manipulate the system to create a museum of such high caliber. Where Shanghai has fallen short is in creating the software necessary for art and culture to thrive. As a result, the city is still far away from reasserting its pre-1949 cultural status.

This is not to say that cultural life in Shanghai has not improved and will not continue to improve. Although the number of cultural events going on around town during any given week remains woefully small for a metropolis with a 14-million-plus population—not even enough to fill a page of a newspaper—more activities are on offer than in previous years. That's in part thanks to the opening of the state-of-the-art Grand Theater in the fall of 1998, which the Shanghai government built to showcase classical Western performing arts and to symbolize the reemergence of Shanghai's open *haipai* culture. Previously, major international symphony orchestras, ballets, and operas on tour in China and Asia often skipped Shanghai for lack of an adequate performance venue. The city's two major theaters, though charming buildings constructed before 1949 in the art deco style, were too small to accommodate large international ensembles. The troupes that deigned to visit, like the Cleveland Orchestra in May 1998, found themselves performing in a sports stadium. I recall attending a concert by violinist Isaac Stern at the Shanghai Concert Hall only to

The Old and the New: Shanghai residents, who historically endured some of the worst living conditions in urban China, are moving into more modern, spacious digs. But high prices and government restrictions during the last decade made many new high-rises off-limits to Chinese citizens, intensifying a glut in luxury housing.

© 2000 Jiang Ren / Imaginechina.com

Neon, Neon and More Neon: For many years, the streets of Shanghai went dark after dusk. In the 1990s, the city's economy took off and major thoroughfares in the evenings became a rainbow of color and activity.

© 2000 Sun Wei Zhong / Imaginechina.com

Chrome, Glass and Glitz: Modern shopping malls, department stores, and supermarkets have sprung up by the hundreds in Shanghai to cater to the city's new white-collar class. Competition in the city's retail sector is fierce and earning an attractive return on investment is more challenging than many retailers expected.

Lingering Traditions: A vendor serves a customer at a traditional wet market in Shanghai. Some people, like these fishmongers and laid-off state enterprise workers, have not benefited as much from the city's rebirth as more educated or well-connected residents.

hear a thumping disco beat from a nearby karaoke joint in the background. No longer. The Grand Theater has put Shanghai on the international cultural map, making it more likely that world-class troupes will choose to perform there. Residents who can afford the theater's 100-yuan-plus ticket prices or with access to free tickets have had an opportunity to see, for instance, the Hamburg Ballet dance "A Midsummer Night's Dream," the Florence and Shanghai opera houses perform Verdi's "Aida," and the Swedish National Symphony Orchestra play Sibelius's "Symphony No. 2 in D-major." Cultural circles in Shanghai hope the Grand Theater's existence will inspire local troupes to do better work and local audiences to behave more politely during performances. Chen Guangxian, the vice general manager of the Shanghai Symphony Orchestra, commented:

Because the Grand Theater is a very good facility, the performers should be equally good. Shabby and low-quality acts will not be allowed to perform there. So I think the Grand Theater will motivate artists in Shanghai to work harder. From another perspective, we hope the Grand Theater will help train the best audiences. In the past audiences proved less than satisfactory—they made noise, ate food, walked back and forth during performances. So the construction of the Grand Theater is only a first step. There's still a long way to go to achieve the best-quality performance, audiences, and management.

Besides erecting the Grand Theater, the Shanghai government in the 1990s also organized at least one international cultural festival for a few weeks a year, spotlighting painting, performing arts, movies, fashion, or television, which helps raise local cultural awareness and increase overseas contact. In November 1999, for instance, it organized an international arts fair that exhibited both domestic and foreign paintings and that is to date the most professional and well-organized arts fair in China. The Shanghai Symphony, which was established before 1949, also performs more frequently than in the past and makes more effort than other troupes to reach out to its audience, giving it the biggest following of any Western classical art form in Shanghai. Also, avant-garde artists who often skipped exhibiting their works in Shanghai early in the decade now put it on their itinerary.

Foreign and domestic entrepreneurs have helped enliven the city's cultural scene as well. They set up art galleries, trendy city papers, intimate performance venues, media-consulting firms, and other innovations. Switzerland-born Lorenz Helbling, for instance, established the ShanghART gallery in the mid-1990s, which has created a market mostly among foreigners for the paintings of avant-garde artists based primarily in Shanghai.

Although the city's gallery scene is still nascent, by the end of the decade Chinese entrepreneurs also started opening modern art galleries that cater to the city's burgeoning middle class—putting it a step ahead of other Chinese cities, including Beijing.

Not all these entrepreneurial endeavors have been successful—bureaucratic hassles, restrictive Chinese laws, or poor market response has made some of them fold or reinvent themselves. Take the theater subscription series organized by the American-run Shanghai Center Theater in 1997, which brought artists like Deborah Harry, Todd Rundgren, and Luther Johnson to the city. Promoters ended up canceling the loss-making series midway through the year when the central government decreed that only Chinese promoters could import foreign troupes. In 1999, a German and two Chinese artists set up an innovative art exhibit called Art-for-Sale. Featuring video, installations, photography, and painting, the event was supposed to run for 15 days but the Public Security Bureau cancelled it after three. Still, such attempts, even when short-lived, bring much-needed variety and new levels of sophistication to the city's cultural life.

Given the Communist Party's efforts to control the arts in China, it did not surprise me that so few artistic events took place in such a large city and that those that did tended to be mainstream and safe rather than innovative or unexpected. In general, the central authorities' insistence on using art as a propaganda tool, along with slow-moving reform among artistic troupes, has stifled artistic creativity and quality in the country, particularly in the performing arts. What did surprise me was that relative to Shanghai, much more seemed to be going on art-wise in Beijing, the nation's capital. Besides being the center of China's film industry and the home of the country's best symphony and ballet, it also leads China in alternative, edgy arts like avant-garde painting, abstract modern dance, underground cinema, experimental theater, rebellious punk rock, and unconventional performance and installation art. Whereas in Beijing, radical artists might decide to express themselves and provoke the public by creating an installation featuring a dead baby embracing the head of a deceased old man, such limit-pushing activities are not a part of Shanghai's artistic fabric. "Shanghai has a very good reputation for abstract painting," commented Brian Wallace, the director of the Beijing-based Red Gate Gallery, while taking a break from the Shanghai International Art Fair in November 1999. "But Beijing has that too, plus a good reputation in all mediums, including performance art, mixed media, installation—the things that are the cutting edge of the arts scene."

What explains Beijing's relatively greater artistic vitality than Shanghai's? The overarching answer is talent. Beijing simply has much more of it. Very little national-level talent lives in Shanghai except in the fine arts field. Unless they go abroad, many of the best artists in China continue to flock to Beijing. In interviews with honchos at Shanghai's film studio, the Shanghai Ballet, and the Shanghai Symphony as well as at less mainstream operations, they all lamented the shortage of talent in the city. Sawyer Lee, an independent music producer based in Shanghai, spoke particularly passionately about the dearth of artistic genius in the city. I met him in March 1999 at a birthday dinner for Coco, a 22-year-old crooner who sang stirring renditions of "Summertime" and other jazz standards in local clubs and was something of a musical sensation among foreign expatriates in Shanghai. Coco wanted to cut an album of his own compositions and was talking to Lee about producing it. A couple of years earlier, Lee had produced the album "Sister Drum," which was composed by an artist from Chengdu and sung by Guangzhou native Dadawa. Incorporating Tibetan elements, Sister Drum was one of the only contemporary Chinese albums in the 1990s that garnered a modicum of international popularity.[9] A few days after Coco's birthday party, I met Lee in his office in the Shanghai Music Conservatory where he sat on a mod purple couch surrounded by abstract paintings. Lee had studied Italian opera at the conservatory before becoming an independent producer in the late 1980s. He went independent, he said, to find a way to make Chinese culture known outside of China. Wearing his hair below his ears, the fortyish Lee bluntly declared:

I think Shanghai almost has no culture. Even if you have some people like Coco, it's a question of scale. Now there is culture in Beijing. There are lots of events and outstanding artists—not like in Shanghai. In Beijing underground culture is very developed—modern dance, contemporary art exhibits, novelists. There are lots of underground bands and underground films in Beijing. I've never seen an underground film in Shanghai and there's really no underground music scene. Shanghai doesn't have its own modern dance company. You'd think jazz would be most developed here given its pre-1949 history in the city, but it isn't. Beijing held a jazz festival for three years, whereas Shanghai only had its first one last year. I think the key to a city having culture is how many geniuses the city has and how many works they produce. I don't think there are really any geniuses in recent years here. If there were, I would definitely know it because genius will always show itself. Now Coco has a gift, but until recently he was not very serious about writing his own music. If he's a genius, his record will demonstrate it.

Coco, I pointed out, was not originally from Shanghai, but came to the city as a music student from Hunan before launching his singing career in the city. Did he think young artists from around China were starting to see Shanghai as their mecca instead of Beijing? "The trend of artists coming from other parts of China to Shanghai hasn't really started yet. Now when people come to Shanghai, they generally don't stay," he said glumly.

Mianmian, an avant-garde Shanghainese writer whose stories delve into drug abuse, suicide, and ill-fated love affairs, talked to me about life as an artist in Shanghai. A fixture in Shanghai's small alternative scene, she favored silver-toned makeup, black leather pants, and slinky black shirts. After inhaling deeply on her cigarette, the 28-year-old commented:

Shanghai is a lonely city for artists. Artists come, then they go. There are not a lot of new writers but there are some painters. The number of artists is low because the environment is not very good—artists normally want to bump into other artists. A lot of people from Shanghai have left to go to Beijing or overseas. In Beijing there are so many artists—too many. It seems like everyone's an artist. It's very heavy.

That was partly the reason why Mianmian chose to stay in Shanghai rather than head for the capital. "I feel too much pressure in Beijing. I only go there when I have to for my work. Besides, I like Shanghai. It's my home. I feel good here," she explained.

In the fall of 1998, I spent some time in Beijing talking about these issues to people in art circles there. One of my most thoughtful exchanges was with film director Huang Jianxin, who is best known for his direction of the critically acclaimed "Black Cannon Incident." The 44-year-old Huang had just moved permanently to Beijing from Xian, where he had been affiliated with the Xian Film Studio. Dressed in black and drinking a cup of coffee, he explained:

There's been a self-initiated movement of Xian Film Studio people to Beijing. With China's reforms, people are much more mobile. Before it was the government that arranged everything. Film studios were distributed equally around the country. Before Xian was very famous for films, now it's not easy to have a circle of filmmakers there. Everyone left. There are more than 200 of us [from Xian] in Beijing now. I got my work unit transferred here, but a lot of people from Xian or wherever come here without a job, without a residency permit, without knowing people. They rent a house and then look for a job. Everyone goes to Beijing. If you want to break a new path, you go to Beijing. I hear there are 30,000 actors here. What are they doing here? They want to make a film. These actors are not from Beijing but from other provinces. Beijing has a great attractiveness to us.

I asked him if he had considered moving to Shanghai instead. The thought had not crossed his mind. "Shanghai doesn't attract us," he said. "From an artist's point of view Shanghai does not have artistic charm."

The question is why. Why doesn't the city have "artistic charm?" Why do Chinese artists who do not go overseas often seek greener pastures in Beijing?

Shanghai's lag behind Beijing in attracting a critical mass of talent is partly historical. After 1949, the Communist Party put the nation's most important cultural institutions in Beijing. They had the power to transfer talent to Beijing from all over China, and artists were generally thrilled to have a chance to leave their provincial backwaters for potential national glory. Since these institutions were national, they had more money at their disposal than local ones. In the reform era, Beijing opened up to the West earlier than Shanghai, and as a result the opportunities for international cultural exchange were greater. High-ranking intellectuals in the Party in Beijing, unlike their colleagues elsewhere in the country, had access to Western literature and philosophy by the late 1960s, which in turn stimulated new ways of thinking.[10] Foreigners with business to do in China in the 1970s, whether diplomats or executives, settled in Beijing. By the end of the 1980s, Beijing already had a sizable foreign community whereas Shanghai's was just getting started. International troupes touring China might skip Shanghai, but they did not skip the nation's capital. At the same time, painters—encouraged by the looser political environment of the 1980s—left their academies to form artist colonies in Beijing. The city's increasingly lively creative ambiance, a cheap cost of living, and a market among foreign buyers soon attracted other artists. Compared with other parts of the country, opportunities to work in the arts soon abounded, not just in officially sponsored arts but in underground activities. All this has helped create a virtuous circle, with a stimulating environment for artists attracting even more artists. Those arriving from the provinces hook up with others from their province already in the city, easing the newcomer's entry.

Also, the Chinese government still seeks to control cultural activities, and for those who need central government approval, Beijing is simply a more convenient place to be. Take the film industry. Because all films have to pass before the eyes of government censors and government censors are located in Beijing, it is easier for someone like Huang Jianxin to do post-production work on his films in Beijing rather than traveling back and forth to Xian. This does not make it impossible for Xian Film Studio to make good films. In the late 1980s Xian Film Studio produced some of China's finest while Shanghai films generally did poorly. But it does mean that as labor mobility increases under reform, Beijing has had just one more advantage over Shanghai and other parts of the country in attracting artists. According to Huang:

You have a lot more choice in Beijing today to find work, so where would you go? There's a lot more opportunity in Beijing. And this is decided by China's total social structure. The most important officials are in Beijing. Anything you want to do in China, you need to get their approval. When international investors in artistic fields come to China to invest, where do they go to negotiate? They go to Beijing. Beijing is the most suitable place for them to do something because there are so many conveniences. Then you add to that Beijing's cultural atmosphere. Beijing University, Qinghua University are all in Beijing. The newest thought comes out of Beijing. Things happen in Beijing first and art seeks this new feeling. All these factors put together attract artists to Beijing. The feeling is very strong, so everyone goes there.

Artists in Shanghai meanwhile place a large part of the blame for their city's lack of artistic dynamism on the heavy-handedness of Shanghai's cultural bureaucracy. Of course, bureaucrats in Beijing regularly scupper projects too. But artistic circles up North seem to get away with more. Ironically, artists enjoy more freedom to create in the nation's political capital than in its anointed commercial hub.

The problem in Shanghai stems partly from one of the city's strengths: A more well-managed city than Beijing, its culture czars do a better job of keeping tabs on artists and stifling creativity. Arts circles in Shanghai describe the situation by analogy to a mountainscape. If a government department is a mountain, then Beijing has many mountains. These include central government bureaus, municipal government bureaus, and different military branches headquartered in Beijing. They all have cultural departments with approval authority over certain spheres. The confusion over jurisdictions and the sheer number of artists and projects provide valleys between the mountains where overlooked artists can discreetly create without approval. When bureaucratic jurisdictions overlap, artists and arts entrepreneurs seeking formal approval for a project have multiple avenues open to them. If denied approval by one bureaucracy, they can seek support at another. At the same time, Beijing is crawling with the offspring of current or former high government officials who can help pull bureaucratic strings for their artist friends. For instance, the antique art auction business is not an easy one to break into in China and so it is not surprising that in the

1990s two of China's most prominent auction houses, Guardian and Sungari in Beijing, employed "princelings" in their upper ranks.[11] Kim, my former assistant who moved to Beijing, bragged to me about how she had recently met the daughter-in-law of a top military leader. "In Beijing, you regularly run into princelings. It makes everything more possible," she said.

Unfortunately for artists in Shanghai, their city has fewer mountains and, subsequently, fewer valleys. The Bureau of Broadcasting, Film, and Television approves all documentaries and other film-related activities. The Shanghai Bureau of Culture lords over the performing arts, making sure to attend all dress rehearsals, which is an easier feat in Shanghai than in Beijing since there are not nearly as many events or artists to track. China's bureaucracy, bred in the Stalinist state-planning tradition, is control-oriented by nature and Shanghai, with its longtime status as a backbone of state enterprise in China, is even more so. While this benefits the city when it comes to erecting a new theater or organizing international arts fairs, it hinders independent attempts at creativity. The city's culture czars are simply better able to implement their mandate to control the city's cultural pulse. Interestingly, the area that is developing most quickly in Shanghai is avant-garde painting and installation—the radical artistic medium that officials in China interfere in least because of its inability to influence large audiences. Albeit a much smaller population than in Beijing, a new generation of avant-garde artists from Shanghai and its environs today work permanently out of the city.

Moreover, Shanghai bureaucrats, like all bureaucrats in China, are cautious. They avoid making decisions displeasing to local and national-level superiors who control their promotions. The Ministry of Propaganda in Beijing, for instance, picks the head of the Shanghai Propaganda Bureau and enunciates broad policy guidelines. The Shanghai Propaganda Bureau, also responsible to the Shanghai Communist Party, then appoints personnel at the Bureau of Broadcasting, Film, and Television and the Shanghai Bureau of Culture. Adding to Shanghai bureaucrats' caution is the city's unspoken status as a training ground for central government leaders and its assignation as China's premier business hub. The central government simply scrutinizes Shanghai more closely than other cities. Officials who stay out of trouble and do well in Shanghai have a better shot than bureaucrats elsewhere at becoming players on the national stage. They, therefore, have more to lose. Also, bureaucrats in their forties and fifties today often started their careers during the Cultural Revolution, when a wrong decision could lead to exile to a remote inland province or worse. Speaking about his experience with Shanghai's cultural bureaucracy, Hua Jian, a professor at the Shanghai Academy of Social Sciences, said: "They're afraid to be criticized. So they just say they won't approve it. They'd rather you get approval from Beijing."

Hua's efforts to make a mainstream documentary in the port city are typical. Hardly a radical, this distinguished academic wanted in the mid-1990s to film a documentary about the Long March, the legendary 1935 trek of more than 100,000 communists into China's inhospitable Northwest. The middle-aged Hua hoped to mention in the documentary an American journalist's contribution to scholarship on the topic—an innocuous-enough aspiration but one that still needed government approval in China. So he submitted his proposal to the authorities in Shanghai. Unfortunately for Hua, they flatly rejected it, saying they didn't understand the foreign journalist's background despite the pile of supporting material Hua had supplied. Hua, however, suspected they were scared to make a decision that might get them into trouble. Disappointed but not deterred, he decided to take his proposal to Beijing, first to an army-related department with jurisdiction over documentaries and then to the Ministry of Culture. They gave Hua the approvals he needed, after which the Shanghai bureaucrats finally acquiesced.

The Peony Pavilion versus the Bureaucrats

The saddest example of his cultural conservatism is the Shanghai Bureau of Culture's decision in the late 1990s to block the performance at the Lincoln Center Festival in New Yok City of an innovative production of a classic Chinese opera.

The saga began in the fall of 1996 when John Rockwell, the director of the Lincoln Center Festival, began exploring the possibility of staging the Peony Pavilion, a Ming Dynasty masterpiece, for the festival in 1998. Written by the great master Tian Xianzu, whom scholars consider the William Shakespeare of China, the opera was celebrating its 400th anniversary that year. It was an ambitious—even audacious—project. Rockwell wanted to re-create the Peony Pavilion in its full three-day, 55-scene regalia, the idea for which grew out of a movement in the United States during the last quarter of the 20th century to reconstruct works as they were originally performed. The opera, which was written in the Kunju style favored by 16th century literati in Suzhou, had not been staged in its entirety since

Tang died in 1616. No classic version existed, just adaptations of adaptations, and the scores of some scenes were missing all together. Opera troupes in modern-day China performed only seven of the 55 scenes, to an ever-shrinking audience. Now Rockwell envisioned introducing the 20-hour-plus epic to Western audiences whom, if they were acquainted with Chinese opera at all, generally equated it with heavily eye-shadowed actors making stylized gestures to a cacophony of gongs, cymbals, and piercing arias.

Rockwell turned for help to Chen Shizheng, a then 32-year-old Chinese transplant to New York with a background in both Chinese opera and Western performing arts. He initially hired the Hunan native to scout out opera troupes in China and eventually asked him to direct the opera. More than a month prior to the opera's scheduled New York debut, Rockwell commented:

As we went along, Shizheng was the obvious best person. He could work with both the Western and Eastern worlds. Because Shizheng has a Chinese opera background, he is comfortable with the general images and aesthetic of Chinese opera, but not bound to the traditions of Kunju. This gives him enough closeness to the idioms, but also enough distance to re-create something done 400 years ago when there is no record of how it was exactly done. The idea is for Shizheng to re-create the spirit of the opera, not to be utterly authentic because that would obviously be impossible.

In May 1998 I interviewed Chen in Shanghai during a last frantic bout of rehearsals before the production was to head for New York in early July and then on to Paris, Sydney, and Hong Kong. Sitting with Chen in the Old China Hand Bookstore cafe on Shanghai's leafy Shaoxing Road, I pieced together the elements that made him Rockwell's "obvious best person." It started with a tragedy early in Chen's life. After his school-teacher mother was killed during the Cultural Revolution and his father, an intellectual, was sent to the countryside for 20 years of reeducation, the then seven-year-old Chen started following around funeral processions, finding himself attracted both by the spectacle and the folk music. Pushing his straight black, chin-length hair behind his ear, he explained:

Because traditional opera had been banned, all the great musicians just did funeral services, and during the Cultural Revolution there were lots of funerals. The ceremony lasted three days and three nights. The musicians would make up stories about the dead person. Seeing an old man impersonating a woman was incredible to me. It was great entertainment. They made the family laugh and cry.

The musicians eventually adopted him and taught him the local opera. Chen turned out to have a beautiful tenor voice and by the time the Cultural Revolution was officially over in 1976, the musicians encouraged him to go to Hunan art school to study opera formally. During those five years of study, he traveled around China both as a performer and on his own and spent much of his free time reading. He said:

Since I didn't have a family I was always alone. I read every book on liberal Western philosophy. I think that because I lacked a family, I've always opposed having things imposed on me. When you face death at an early age, it puts life in a different perspective. I knew when I was very young that I wanted to be unique.

In 1983, Chen was invited to go to the United States as an opera actor. The experience saddened him. "I was shocked and depressed that China could fall so low for all those years. When you really saw the difference for yourself, China was so far behind." It was around this time that Chen decided to leave traditional Chinese opera. He went to Beijing and did some pop and folk music and tried to get into contemporary music theater. "At the time there was a renaissance going on in Beijing in poetry, film, painting, music, but it did not touch the Chinese opera world. I couldn't find the freedom to do what I wanted to do," he said. With those thoughts in mind, he managed to leave China in 1987 and make his way to New York City, where he pursued a masters in performing arts at New York University and delved into the avant garde. "Part of the reason I went to the United States was so that I could determine my own life. As an artist I wanted to experience freedom," he said. The move eventually led to numerous projects culminating in his well-received direction in 1996 of the Chinese National Beijing Opera Co.'s first performance ever of a non-Peking opera, The Bacchae. Not long afterward Rockwell asked Chen to direct the Peony Pavilion for the high-profile Lincoln Center Festival. By returning to the Peony Pavilion's roots using the sensibility of a modern artist, Chen planned to take Chinese opera where it had never gone before. "I want to give a different understanding to how Chinese opera can and should be done," he said.

In June 1998, I attended the opera's only full dress rehearsal before the production headed for New York in July. It was clear that Chen's years in the United States had given him an appreciation for spectacle. He went far beyond the simple props and sets normally used in Kunju performances to turn the Peony Pavilion into a feast for the eyes and the imagination. For instance, he re-created the intimate theater atmosphere of bygone centuries by making the stage into an elegant Suzhou garden surrounded by real water, chirping birds, and swimming ducks. He judiciously used colorfully dressed acrobats, stilt-walkers, clowns, and clever props to make scenes from ancient Chinese life come alive—a market town, the underworld, a traditional Taoist temple. Chen wanted to give his audience a taste of ancient China and keep them spellbound. As one of the few Westerners in attendance, I felt he succeeded.

Chen also resurrected the many scenes from the opera that had not been performed in modern times. That was no easy task given that so few excerpts were regularly performed in China. And with no classic version to refer to and no record of how scenes were originally performed, Chen had to spend months in China ferreting through centuries of adaptations to get as close to the spirit of the original as possible. He also restored scenes axed by government censors after 1949 for containing "feudal thinking." These included critical parts of the story, like when the young heroine goes to hell only to return to earth as a ghost to seduce her lover, as well as bawdier scenes. In one, character Sister Stone graphically describes in classical Chinese how her "stone door" of a hymen ruined her marriage. With comic timing she told the audience: "He kept displaying clouds to make rain on the love terrace, but no flowers blossomed," and "He had to do it from behind. One opening is better than none."

Chen also staged regularly performed excerpts in innovative ways. Take his interpretation of the Peony Pavilion's most famous scene: The Interrupted Dream. Silk-clad heroine Du Liniang falls asleep in a beautiful garden on a balmy spring afternoon and dreams that a dashing young scholar appears before her. The handsome young man, Liu Mengmei, provocatively traces a willow tree sprig up her arm and across her back. "Since you are so well read, why don't you compose a poem about my willow branch," he sings (which can be interpreted as another one of the great master Tang's risqué allusions—this time to the young scholar's sexual organ). He then starts to disrobe the delighted Du, gingerly separating her from her exquisite pale yellow silk robe. Wrapped only in a white gown, Du allows Liu to lead her to the Peony Pavilion to make passionate love. They disappear behind a traditional Chinese lacquered screen, while a clown vaguely imitates for the audience what is happening behind it. Given that in modern-day adaptations in China Du and the young scholar normally reveal their desire by holding hands and posing in a prim embrace, I was not surprised when a Chinese friend commented after the dress rehearsal: "I never knew Chinese opera could be so sexy."

Chen and festival organizers hoped that their rendering of the picturesque epic would help revivify interest in Kunju, which, though considered the most refined and melodic of the many Chinese opera styles, had become a dead art. Like most Chinese opera, Kunju cannot match the lure of television, karaoke bars, and new Western art forms. Chinese opera companies in general have been scrambling to spruce up their productions' appeal. Their innovations, however, tend to focus on hardware—i.e., introducing big special effects like laser lights and smoke or making more use of acrobats—instead of more subtle issues like updating scripts or making characters more interesting.

But even among Chinese opera buffs, Kunju has a decreasing audience. Shanghai opera circles joke that in a city with a population of more than 14 million, Kunju's audience totals about 200 people who only attend performances when given free tickets. "In the China market, Kunju does very badly," explained Zhang Jun, a member of the Shanghai Kunju Opera Co, whom I spoke with during a rehearsal break in May 1998. Zhang was to play young scholar Liu Mengmei, the male lead. Kunju troupes like his cannot make ends meet and only a handful of them are still performing. Few young people are interested in studying the genre, which is why middle-aged women often end up playing the 16-year-old Du. That's one reason why Chen chose to employ the Shanghai Kunju troupe over the country's five others: it had young actors who would not only be more open to his novel ideas, they would look the part. With his attractive, delicately sculpted face, the 24-year-old Zhang made a convincing young lover on appearances alone.

The poor prognosis for Kunju's future in China helps explain Zhang's enthusiasm for Chen's adaptation. "I hope that by doing this, we can make more people understand Kunju and like Kunju. I hope that it will make more Chinese people see it," he said. Chen's production was not yet slated to be performed in China. But if it received good reviews abroad, Chen and Zhang believed it might be invited since it would them have an international aura that would pique Chinese audiences' interest. Even some of the older actors, like 47-year-old Zhang Mingrong, who had practiced Kunju since age 12, looked forward to Kunju's revival:

Maybe certain changes will arouse controversies in domestic art circles. They might say that it is no longer pure and real Kunju anymore. But for an ordinary domestic audience, most of whom are laymen when it comes to Kunju, these changes will help them understand this masterpiece better. Controversy is no bad thing. We should have a 'Make One Hundred Flowers Bloom' policy[12] so that people have a greater interest in the opera than before. In Britain there was a modern 'Shakespeare' with the characters wearing suits and ties. Though it was controversial, it made people know more about Shakespeare.

Little did I realize at the time how his comments went to the core of a tempest brewing in Shanghai's tradition-bound opera community over Chen's Peony Pavilion. A day before full dress rehearsals started in Shanghai in early June 1998, however, I felt some of the ire firsthand. I had arranged a meeting with the head of another Chinese opera company in Shanghai to talk about the troupe's reform efforts. In his fifties, the artistic director had a kind face and his rolled-up sleeves and blue jeans suggested a relaxed demeanor. After he served me the customary cup of tea, I mentioned, as a way of breaking the ice, that I planned to attend the Peony Pavilion dress rehearsals. Suddenly he was seething:

That production has taken all the good things out of the Peony Pavilion. It's cheating you Americans. Kunju is one of the oldest, best, and most perfect Chinese opera styles. It is the mother of all Chinese opera styles. It is elegant. It combines singing and dancing together. But in that Peony Pavilion you cannot see these best things. Its essence has been replaced by the modern. You know, I formerly worked at the Shanghai Kunju Opera Co. When I heard what that director was doing over there, I was angry. That director doesn't know anything about Kunju. How can he direct it? In the end he's abandoned the essence of Kunju and put in non-Kunju things. The director is an unknown artist who came from Hunan who went to America. After he came back, he just put rubbish into Chinese traditional opera. Kunju belongs to our ancestors. Even Kunju artists are reluctant to see this version. I definitely won't go. If the actors in the troupe are excited about it, it's because they get to go to the United States. If they were performing in Anhui, they would not be excited to do this. The more that the director does things his way, the closer Kunju moves towards its death. He did not do research. In China, he is well-known nowhere. I say this because I like Kunju too much. I devoted a long period of my life to it. Kunju is so beautiful. Its original beauty should be protected. It shouldn't be destroyed. It's like adding Coca-Cola to tea. Of course there are things that we need to do to revive Kunju, but like a body that is sick, if you give it the wrong medicine, it will get worse!

Some voices in China, however, applauded Chen's efforts. After the week of full dress rehearsals in Shanghai, the Beijing-based *People's Daily*, the Communist Party's official paper, ran a glowing review that stated: "The director follows the spirit of Tang Xianzu's work," and "Chinese people the world over can feel proud that this classic of our national culture is at last moving out into the world."[13] And despite the artistic director's comments, Chen's innovations thrilled the young actors in the Shanghai

Kunju Opera Co. Zhang, the male lead, for instance, was delighted to finally have a chance to stretch himself as an artist during eight exhausting months of rehearsals with Chen. Having practiced Kunju for 12 years, the 24-year-old explained:

No one has ever acted the whole Peony Pavilion. They just did excerpts. My character, Liu Mengmei, is multifaceted, but before I only acted one simple facet. Now I can give everyone a chance to see the whole person. I also feel that we've brought the opera up a notch technically. Now it's not just a matter of sounding beautiful or making a beautiful movement, which is the usual standard for judging Chinese opera. We used to just follow tradition. I would do what my teacher did, who did what his teacher did. Now we need to develop our characters. The director is not getting rid of anything, but just building on tradition to reach a higher level. The director's ways are new. We never saw this before. It's opera for the 21st century!

Unfortunately, the Shanghai Bureau of Culture did not think so and, as a result, Zhang never got to show the world his interpretation of the dashing Liu Mengmei. After attending the dress rehearsals in early June, culture bureau head Ma Bomin, a former opera actress, insisted that Chen revise the show extensively before she would allow him to take it overseas. It did not matter that the government had signed off on Chen's script. Nor did it matter that the contract signed by the Lincoln Center Festival and the Shanghai Kunju Opera Co. and approved by Ma did not give the bureau censorship rights, but instead granted the director free rein to stage the production as he saw fit. "We agreed to the contract, and we thought the production was a good idea. But now we find that it includes elements that cannot be allowed, unhealthy elements that violate China's cultural exchange regulations," Ma later said in an interview with the *New York Times*.[14] Chen refused to make some of the vague changes requested and asked Ma to clarify point by point her problems with the script. Falling back on communist censorship customs in China that expect the artist to prove his ideological correctness, she declined the request. "I told him: You're the director. You have to make the changes, and then let us see the rehearsal as it is performed. Then we will decide," she explained.[15] She accused Chen of "lacking knowledge" and "stubbornness" and defended her bureau's right to define Chinese tradition. "We have the power to decide how an opera is performed. You must understand, our standards for Kunju opera and Peking opera are not the same as for other arts. I am an artist and have a responsibility to see it done properly," she railed.[16] In mid-June, just three weeks before the curtin at Lincoln Center was to lift, the Shanghai culture bureau took the drastic step of blocking the shipment from Shanghai to New York of six tons of costumes, props, and sets belonging to the Lincoln Center Festival and coproducers in Paris, Sydney, and Hong Kong. In an official statement following the shipment's seizure, the bureau argued that Chen's version did not "accurately reflect Tang Xianzu's original spirit" and contained "feudal superstitions, stupidity, and pornography." It did not matter that Tang himself wrote the scenes containing ghosts, hell, the bawdy Sister Stone, and other so-called feudal elements; that Chen's version contained no nudity; and that the props were not the culture bureau's property. Shanghai newspapers, which kept silent on the production until the city's culture czars gave their verdict, subsequently published scathing critiques. Nigel Redden, the Lincoln Festival's director, arrived in China on June 22 to try to salvage a US$500,000 show for which tickets had already been sold. He agreed to make some adjustments, but they were not enough to satisfy bureau officials, who insisted on seeing a fully staged revised version before giving the final sign-off. Given that the premiere was scheduled for July 7 in New York and that there was no guarantee Ma and her cohorts would approve the revamped opera, Redden left China in defeat. "They have effectively cancelled the project," he told the *New York Times*. "This is a tremendous loss to us, but it's even worse for the people in the company, who worked day and night for so long to pull this together."[17]

In the end, the city's cultural authorities agreed to release the shipment of props, sets, and costumes, but did not allow the Shanghai Kunju Opera Co. to leave the country for the New York premier. During the brouhaha, the bureau shuttered the artists in an out-of-town safehouse to make sure they did not talk to foreign reporters. When time neared for the tour's second leg in Paris in November 1998, French festival organizers rejected the bureau's offer of an abridged version. In a letter to the Chinese embassy in Paris in September, they wrote: "Supporting the principle of freedom of expression, and asserting solidarity with the artists, we maintain our determination to present the production rehearsed over recent months in Shanghai."[18]

The world may never know exactly why the path-breaking project went so terribly awry, but a couple of themes stand out. For one, Shanghai culture bureau chief Ma was able to scupper a high-profile cultural exchange between the United States and China on the eve of an American president's visit and still have her job a year later. That indicates she has powerful friends in the Shanghai and central governments. Second, few people with experience in the Chinese art world believe she blocked the project purely for ideological or artistic reasons. Bureaucrats in such cases often have a personal gripe with the artist. A well-known Shanghai-based arts critic, who requested anonymity, explained:

> Let's say I have a project that I want to do, but the bureaucrat does not like me or is uncomfortable with me. He won't say publicly that I'm not any good but he will say that my art can't be produced. It's often not because of the art. It's usually because of some kind of authority problem or a bad personal relationship.

Ma and others in the Shanghai opera community were predisposed to dislike Chen, who was an outsider—a Hunan native who had become an American citizen. He had no ties to Shanghai or to Kunju, and yet managed to arrive on their turf with a huge American budget to produce the crown jewel of Chinese opera for an international audience. They had devoted their lives to Chinese opera and yet had never had such an opportunity. Once working in Shanghai, Chen did not ingratiate himself enough with Ma or the tightly knit local opera community, even though the young director insisted to me after the fiasco that he had tried to invite Ma to dinner but that her staff always said she was too busy. Finally, Chen had the audacity to introduce changes to the opera without consulting local experts—changes that reviewers in the Chinese press actually praised. If that were not bad enough, Chen did not obsequiously agree to Ma's request for revisions. Instead, he defied her. It was too much and Ma subsequently showed him who was boss. Although she couched her decision in ideological terms, it clearly had a personal element, hence her comments that Chen "has his own ideas and is very stubborn."[19]

Chen, for his part, seemed to have forgotten that he was dealing with a country where the rule of men still supercedes the rule of law. Despite Chen's American citizenship and Lincoln Center backing, Shanghai's culture czars had no qualms about meddling in the project, even if it meant breaking a contract with the Lincoln Center Festival and scotching the international producers' US$500,000 investment. And as cogs in China's Communist dictatorship, they had the means at their disposal to do it: They did not give the Shanghai Kunju troupe's actors the required permission to leave China. Perhaps if Chen had eschewed the press and dress rehearsals in Shanghai, the censors would not have paid so much attention to him. But Chen hoped that his adaptation would revive interest in the Peony Pavilion in China and all the media attention surrounding the production seemed to be having some effect. It was also far cheaper and more practical to rehearse in Shanghai than in New York. Moreover, Chen had been lulled into a false sense of security two years earlier when he directed "The Bacchae" in Beijing, in which he employed China's National Peking Opera Co. to perform a Greek tragedy. He mused:

The troupe was trained in Peking opera but they performed a non-Peking opera. This was hugely controversial, but no one stopped the show. The Shanghai authorities will allow the Shanghai Peking Opera Co. to do a production with laser lights and smoke. Is that protecting national treasures? What's the standard?

The disaster soured Chen on Shanghai. While he had always considered Shanghai more of a commercial center like Chicago than a cultural center like New York, he had heard that Shanghai was *haipai*—famous for innovation and change in China. He said:

Underneath, it's made up of a more conservative group of people. People told me that if I had done the show in Beijing, Nanjing, or any other city but Shanghai, I would have been able to get it out of China. My previous experience in Beijing was fine. In Beijing, there's a lot more freedom for artists. That's my experience and all my friends live in Beijing, so I know.

Although the Peony Pavilion's cancellation in 1998 was devastating for Chen, he ultimately had the last laugh. Through connections, he managed to spirit Qian Yi, the actress who played beautiful Du in Shanghai, out of the country without the knowledge of the Shanghai culture bureau. He then put together a new cast, made up mostly of Chinese actors based in the New York area. After four months of rehearsals, he put on his Peony Pavilion in a 1,000-seat theater before a consistently packed house at the Lincoln Center Festival in July 1999. During three weekends that month, Americans watched Du Liniang and Liu Mengmei fall in love, Mongol warriors invade southern China, and Sister Stone work her spells. I was lucky enough to attend three acts of the last cycle. At the end of each act, the audience gave the cast a standing ovation—their shouts of "Bravo" intermittently rising above their resounding applause.

Watching the New York audience's overwhelmingly positive reaction, I could not help but think about how the Peony Pavilion's victory in New York could have been Shanghai's; how it would have left an impression on the world that Shanghai was throwing off its creative shackles and reemerging as an innovative Chinese cultural force. Sadly, the city had instead sullied its reputation and become the subject of international ridicule. Sitting in a cafe across from Lincoln Center in 1999, I asked Chen about the show's success. Between hurried bites of a salad, he said:

This production of the Peony Pavilion moved American audiences in a way I never expected. It was a great introduction into Chinese culture for them. In China, the experts said that Americans would only be interested in the acrobats. I think their comments showed a shortage of confidence in their own culture.

What did Chen think of Shanghai's prospects for reemerging as China's artistic hub? "If the Shanghai authorities prevent artists from creating, Shanghai can never be a cultural center," he somberly predicted.[20]

Unconducive Creative Climate

The high-handedness of Shanghai's culture czars ultimately dampens the climate for artistic creativity not just in traditional fields like Chinese opera, but also in more progressive arts. Take experimental theater. Although the medium is not well-developed anywhere in China, the little interesting work done comes out of Beijing—not Shanghai. I talked about Shanghai's theater scene with an aspiring director who worked at the Shanghai Theater Academy. After requesting anonymity, she explained:

Look at the newspapers! There's not much going on in theater here, experimental or otherwise. There have been attempts to do plays by controversial foreign playwrights, as well as by Chinese writers who take on controversial subjects. Sometimes, the Shanghai government approves their work, but with certain limitations, like they can't have any publicity. Everyone is terrified of the culture bureau in Shanghai. Almost no story idea can pass that brick wall.

Although the Shanghai Theater Academy, with the help of a returned student, organized an international experimental theater festival in the fall of 1998, replete with kissing lesbians from Japan, the director viewed the event as at best a partial breakthrough. She pointed out that approval for it came from the Ministry of Culture in Beijing rather than the Shanghai culture bureau. Most of her theater colleagues in Shanghai react to the bureau's iron grip by self-censoring their work. The director said:

Shanghai is always less politically active than Beijing. And controversial is always political in China today. Troupes in Shanghai tend to do things that are very safe. They do what is politically correct. What Shanghai is good at is toeing the party line. The Central Experimental Theater [in Beijing] is much more daring and creative and has done some really terrific plays.

Her comments allude to another reason why Shanghai does not hold much luster for non-Shanghai artists and why little innovative art takes place: the Shanghainese personality. Both Shanghainese and non-Shanghainese contend that Shanghainese in general like to lead well-ordered lives and tend to avoid taking risks that may jeopardize their well-being. They are calculating, detailed-oriented, conscientious, and obedient—qualities that make them good at implementing other people's ideas, but they are not adventurous creators of art. And there are not yet enough artists moving to Shanghai from other parts of the country to change the city's zeitgeist. Part of the reason that artists get away with more in Beijing is simply because they try to. Huang, the director who moved to Beijing from Xian in 1998, explained:

Shanghainese are used to doing things by the rules. But artists can't do things according to the rules. Art needs to break through old things. The most important thing is that artists have courage to create and not fear criticism. My belief is that artists scare themselves. It's not other people. Now in the world, Iranian films are very good. How is this possible? Political and religious limits in Iran are very strict, but Iranian films are really well done. I believe Shanghai Film Studio's courage is small. It's not willing to get involved in sensitive social problems. Shanghainese don't do films that will not be approved and carry too much risk. Other film studios in China have won awards around the world. Why don't films produced and directed by the Shanghai Film Studio? They're afraid something bad will happen. This is a psychological problem of the Shanghainese.

I few weeks later, I spoke with a 29-year-old Shanghainese director at the Shanghai Film Studio about filmmaking in Shanghai. He confirmed Huang's analysis. A handsome man whose hair fell to his shoulders, he said:

When I was studying at Beijing Film Academy, every time we watched movies made at the Shanghai Film Studio, the audience started to boo and hoot. Students knew that if the film was made in Shanghai, it must be conservative and have no new ideas at all. Since Liberation, Shanghai Film Studio has tried to be stable and safe rather than make any mistakes. They prefer to walk on the ground step by step rather than fly as they are afraid of falling down and getting hurt. So when Shanghai directors choose screenplays, they always choose stories of good people and good deeds.

After many conversations like these and observing Shanghai's art scene, I began to see the daring of museum curators Ma and Wang more as an aberration than as a pattern. Or was it that the risk that the duo took was just the type of risk that Shanghainese today are comfortable with—lots of potential upside and little downside? Ma and Wang, with their long involvement in the official culture system, had calculated the government would not let a piece of architecture meant to symbolize Shanghai's renaissance stand half-built in front of Shanghai's new city hall. They were sure they would ultimately get the extra money they needed. So while they were driven and took a risk, it was a well-calculated risk.

Artists also complain that artwork in Shanghai is provincial, suited to local rather than national tastes. They grumble that Shanghainese do not like to discuss art, but instead are consumed with moneymaking and other issues. And they fret that the Shanghainese do not welcome non-Shanghainese. The Shanghai Film Studio director explained:

Shanghainese sometimes don't like people from other cities. They think highly of themselves because Shanghai is a big city. Non-Shanghainese have to show how capable they are for Shanghainese to accept them. Shanghainese think foreign countries are advanced and other places in China are backward.

Little wonder that Shanghai is not more of a magnet for artists in China or a center for artistic innovation. Perhaps more surprising, China's leading commercial center is not yet leading the way in pop arts either.

This is not to say that art in Shanghai is not commercial or that some artists are not successful. "Because Shanghai is a commercial center, artists aim for the market. There is a pure artistic circle, but it's rather small," explained Hua Jian, the professor at the Shanghai Academy of Social Sciences. The quintessential Shanghai artist is the hugely successful painter-businessman Chen Yifei, who lived in the United States for more than 10 years before returning to Shanghai in the 1990s. His oil paintings of 1930s Shanghai, women playing instruments, and Tibetan nomads have fetched hundreds of thousands of dollars overseas and in China. When I interviewed him in 1997, the 51-year-old had just launched, or was about to launch, a number of business ventures, including his own fashion label and modeling company. He drove around Shanghai in a Mercedes Benz, enjoyed showing off his US$2,000 Zegna suits, owned real estate around the city, and prided himself on partying at Shanghai nightspots into the wee hours.

Shanghai has also been successful in producing television dramas. Unlike hugely risky filmmaking, TV dramas generally are money-earners in China. The city's production companies are as successful as those in Guangzhou and Beijing at making popular but uninspired shows, even if most of the actors, directors, and other talent still live in the capital. Its marketing and distribution companies, meanwhile, do a good job delivering works made elsewhere to the public.

But in general, Shanghai itself in the 1990s did not produce bands, singers, or other pop icons that captured the country's imagination.

For instance, the few critically acclaimed films that were profitable domestically in China at the end of the decade were not made in Shanghai. The top two commercially successful films were "Be There or Be Square" and "Party A, Party B,"[21] which were both produced by Forbidden City Film in Beijing. "Shanghai has not had a good idea of mass appeal," said Willie Brent, the Shanghai-based president of China Entertainment Network, who has lived in China since the 1980s. "In film, it has not produced anything commercially successful, let alone artistically successful in years."

That said, Shanghai's assignation as China's financial and commercial center bodes well for the funding of artistic endeavors, particularly commercial ones, and the greater independence of those endeavors in the future. Corporations and philanthropists will have more money to donate to the arts and Shanghai residents will have more to spend particularly once they satisfy their basic material pursuits. The Yangtze River Delta region in general has a long tradition of collecting art and already Shanghainese are starting to buy modern art to decorate their new homes—a first for China. This, in turn, should lead to more exhibitions and more galleries in the city. Also boding well is the city's recognition of its talent problems and efforts to attract new blood. The Shanghai Film Studio, for instance, started to recruit young directors, actors, and actresses from universities in Beijing and around the country in 1997. It gave a number of young directors, including non-Shanghainese, the opportunity to make films. It also set up a new state-of-the-art post-production facility in 1999, and in 2000 released "Crash Landing," China's first Hollywood-style live action film replete with computer-generated special effects. According to China Entertainment Network's Brent:

The film gets away from the Shanghai problem of being for Shanghai. The story has more universal appeal. Shanghai has the idea in its head to make films that are commercially appealing and I believe they will make more of them in the future. If it can do that well, Shanghai will have a decent film industry, which it doesn't have now.

Also promising are Shanghai's efforts to host cultural festivals and attract big-name foreign acts. It attracts more foreigners in cultural fields than other cities, except for Beijing, and they, along with Chinese returning from abroad, will continue to stimulate new ways of doing things.

But this progress does not mean that Shanghai is on its way to becoming a thriving arts center. Some of the foreigners I interviewed in Shanghai see the city's replacement of Beijing as China's cultural hub as inevitable.

According to this view, Shanghai, as the country's financial and business center, will be the richest city in China and artists will follow the money. Isn't New York both the financial and artistic center of the Unites States, they observe. But art and artists do not necessarily follow money in a major way, as the unexciting cultural situation in Hong Kong and Shenzhen demonstrates. In the 1980s and early 1990s, many mainland artists migrated to Shenzhen, the booming development zone in southern China, but few stayed since the city did not develop that elusive intangible: artistic charm.

Under China's current political setup, no place, including Beijing, can fulfill its artistic potential to become China's cultural equivalent of New York in the United States. New York does not have a cultural bureaucracy that regularly uses its power to allow, disallow, and change artistic works and events. Without political reform that diminishes the constraints on—and risks of—creativity, progress will clearly be limited all over China. But Shanghai, because of its bureaucracy's effective grip on the city's cultural life, its risk-averse personality, and its difficulties retaining artistic talent, seems more fettered than the country's capital. And while Shanghai is veering toward more commercial artistic endeavors, even those require creativity and risk-taking to be successful—neither of which has emerged as a strong suit of the city's residents. The Shanghai government made a start in the 1990s by building an infrastructure for culture that in many ways has surpassed Beijing's. But as Huang, the film director, pointed out: "It's not because you build a lot of good-looking buildings that artists will be attracted. Artists don't fear bitterness or discomfort. They seek what they want to do and they go to the place where they can best do it." Shanghai has erected a skeleton of a cultural center, but is still searching for a soul.

Notes

[1] Actually Shanghai did have a homegrown film club, called Film 101, in the second half of the 1990s, but it mostly organized screenings of lesser-known foreign films.

[2] Yang Dongping, *City Monsoon: The Cultural Spirit of Beijing and Shanghai (Chengshi Jifeng: Beijing he Shanghai de Wenhua Jingshen)*, Oriental Press, 1994, pp. 127–128. Also see Marie-Claire Bergere; "Shanghai or the other China;" in *Shanghai: Revolution & Development in an Asian Metropolis*; ed. Christopher Howe; Cambridge University Press, 1981, pp. 12–13.

[3] Harriet Sergeant, *Shanghai*, London: Jonathan Cape, 1991, p. 233.

[4] Statistics from interview with Prof. Hua Jian, Shanghai Academy of Social Sciences.

[5] Yang, Ibid., p. 353.

[6] Comments from interview with *New York Times* correspondent Seth Faison on Oct. 25, 1996.

[7] Had Ma not been at the museum during the Cultural Revolution (1966–76), there would not be much to see in the museum today. Like many people who suffered during that period, he turned his memories into words somewhat reluctantly. He began: "When the Cultural Revolution started in 1966, the museum stopped opening to the public. But the Red Guards felt that they should criticize the museum. When we knew they were going to force their way into the museum, we decided to let them in. They were Red Guards from Beijing—young girls wearing straw shoes like the People's Liberation Army wore during the Long March. The Red Guards wanted to get into the storeroom, but we refused. We said that the museum already had Red Guards and that we could take care of it ourselves." Ma was later imprisoned in the museum for his efforts. He explained: "Before I was interned, I was the chief of the museum's preservation department. After the Red Guards went into a collector's house, they'd call me up and say, 'You'd better come around and see if there are any relics. Otherwise we're going to destroy everything.' We then went to the houses to check. We made an inventory list of the items confiscated by the Red Guards so that we could give them back to their owners. This showed that we would only take care of the items, not keep them. Because the Red Guards used to search people's homes at night, we slept in the museum for two to three months waiting for their calls. Because I was the one in charge of relics preservation in Shanghai, I was interned in the museum for 49 days alone and then for six to seven months with others." Ma fervently believed that China needed to protect its cultural heritage for future generations and paid a price for those beliefs.

[8] Zhang's comments spoke volumes about the lack of expertise often found among the country's cultural bureaucrats. How could the man named the head of the Cultural Relics Bureau in China, who went to university in Shanghai, never have visited or had an interest in the Shanghai museum before being appointed to that job?

[9] *Sister Drum* was distributed internationally by Warner Music.

[10] *See* Yang, Ibid., ch. 8.

[11] The daughter of former Chinese premier Zhao Ziyang was vice president of Guardian and the daughter of former Chinese president Liu Shaoqi was the president of Sungari. When the central government in 1996 issued regulations stating that only six auction companies in the country could deal in cultural relics in China, both Guardian and Sungari made the cut.

[12] The "hundreds of flowers bloom" policy refers to a political campaign initiated by Mao Zedong in 1957 to encourage intellectuals to criticize the Communist Party.

[13] *People's Daily*, Jun. 11, 1998.

[14] *New York Times*, Jul. 24, 1998.

[15] Ibid.

[16] Ibid.

[17] Ibid.

[18] Reuters, Sept. 25, 1998.

[19] *New York Times*, op. cit.

[20] Unfortunately, we will never know if Chen would have had better luck rehearsing in Beijing or some other Chinese city. A few months later, renowned filmmaker Zhang Yimou did successfully stage, albeit with some bureaucratic difficulty, a controversial production of the Puccini's Turandot at the Forbidden City. But comparing the two events is a little like comparing apples and oranges. Turandot was a Western opera, not a Chinese one about which China's cultural authorities could feel ownership. Beijing bureaucrats were far less concerned with the content of Zhang Yimou's adaptation than his choice of venue.

[21] "Party A, Party B" is also known as "Dreams Come True."

6

Return of the Vices

"If you want to see people on Ecstasy, go to a new club called CD at the intersection of Shaanxi South Road and Zhaojiabang Road," Little Wang told me over dinner in March 1999. "That's where the real 'head-shakers' go. It's very dark inside—you can't see anything except kids shaking their heads until eight o'clock in the morning. But don't go before two. It only really picks up after the Miss Ks get out of work."

For the uninitiated, a "Miss K" is a girl paid to provide company to men firing up their vocal chords and sexual desire in Shanghai's many new karaoke clubs. Ecstasy, known in China as *yaotou wan* or the "shake head" drug, is a new form of recreation for some members of the city's young nightclub set. "They're the people shaking their head like this," said Little Wang, turning his head to the right, sweeping his chin across his chest to the left, then repeating the motion in the opposite direction.

Given that Little Wang (a pseudonym) worked nights as an undercover cop in Shanghai nightclubs, I figured he knew what he was talking about and decided to check out CD with two Chinese friends on the following Saturday night. We arrived after 2:30 in the morning. Disheveled security guards sipping on jars of green tea ushered us into an elevator. While we waited for the doors to close, three young women chomping on sticks of gum ran in from the rain just in time to catch the lift. They hastily smoothed their hands over their metallic makeup and tight-fitting tops before disappearing into the club's blackness.

Little Wang was right about CD's dim atmospherics—the bar near the entrance and the dance floor's flashing lasers provided the long, slim room's only light. Groups of young Chinese lounged on black leather sofas, sipping on bottles of BacardiCoke, Corona beer, or mineral water. On the small dance floor, bodies shimmied to throbbing techno beats.

175

My eyes drifted to a girl with long hair sitting on a stool at the dance floor's edge. Holding onto a railing, she swung her upper torso in a circle over and over and over again, causing her black hair to spin like a pinwheel. "Ecstasy," my friends and I nodded in agreement.

Lo and behold, there were Little Wang and his "coworkers" on a couch at the far end of the club, looking the part for their undercover assignment. Instead of the army fatigues he wore the first day I met him, he sported a black short-lapel suit on top of a black shirt and tie. He insisted we sit with him, saying, "This must be fate." I bought the group a round of BacardiCokes, which seemed expected, and sat down. Over the music's deafening pulse, Little Wang screamed: "It's not very crowded now, but just wait, it'll pick up soon." I looked at my watch: after three o'clock in the morning. Sure enough, young Chinese continued to float in, filling the remaining seats and space on the dance floor. In the section of black leather chairs across from me, the women with the pinwheel hair sat on her boyfriend's lap, their bodies facing with her legs hanging behind his back. In perfect unison, they swayed in a circle to the music's thumping rhythm. The smell of marijuana wafted through the room and before long I noticed that one of the Chinese women I came with was lighting up a joint.

"Wait here, and I'll go find a *yazi* for you to talk to," Little Wang said, putting down his cigar. A *yazi*, which in English means duck, is a slang term in Shanghai for a male prostitute. Before long, Little Wang returned with a young man who looked to be in his mid-twenties. Well groomed, he wore a silvery-blue suit over an ivory turtleneck that suggested a playboy rather than the *liumang*, or petty gangster, that Little Wang resembled. Little Wang informed me that the man was the manager or "daddy" for a group of ducks that had until recently worked Shanghai's most popular disco, Real Love. He sat daddy duck down between one of my friends and me. "How much for one of your ducks?" I asked.

"Five hundred yuan (US$60) to talk and 3,000 yuan (US$362) to sleep."

"What do we get for the 3,000 yuan?"

"Anything you want."

"What if we're not satisfied?"

"Then you only have to pay 500 yuan."

We laughed and asked if we could meet a duck. Daddy duck disappeared into the dance floor only to return a couple of minutes later to tell us that his busy boys had already left for the night. "Another time then," we agreed.

The next time I looked at my watch, the little hand was edging toward five o'clock. The place was still hopping, but having scheduled an interview for early Sunday afternoon, I needed to go home and get some sleep. As I entered the elevator, out piled another load of girls with metallic makeup. They scurried into the club, raring for a bit more fun before the sun rose.

The Whore of the Orient, Circa. 1930

China's largest metropolis looms large in the Western imagination as the "Whore of the Orient"—the city where people partied into the wee hours and partook in all manners of debauchery before the Communist revolution in 1949. Just hearing the name "Shanghai" conjures up images of 24-hour nightclubs, pockmarked gangsters, sweetly pungent opium dens, and powdery-skinned courtesans. In a colorful tome describing Old Shanghai, Harriet Sargeant captures the city's prerevolution reputation:

In the twenties and thirties Shanghai became legend. No world cruise was complete without a stop in the city. Its name evoked mystery, adventure, and license of every form. In ships sailing to the Far East, residents enthralled passengers with stories of the "Whore of the Orient." They described Chinese gangsters, nightclubs that never closed, and hotels that supplied heroin on room service. They talked familiarly of warlords, spy rings, international arms dealers, and the particular delights on offer at Shanghai brothels. Long before landing, wives dreamed of fabulous shops; husbands of half an hour in the exquisite grip of a Eurasian girl."[1]

Old Shanghai was a city of nightlife, unlike China had ever seen, thanks in part to the steady stream of foreigners who settled in the sections of town under foreign occupation.[2] Some 70,000 expatriates from all over the world resided in the three-million-strong city by 1932. With them, they brought new forms of entertainment, like movies, symphonies, balls, and horse racing. But foremost among Shanghai's highlights was the nightclub—a fact that an excerpt from a 1935 guidebook makes clear:

Dog races and cabarets, formal tea, and dinner dances and cabarets, the sophisticated and cosmopolitan French Club and cabarets, the dignified and formal Country Club and cabarets, prize fights and cabarets, theatres and cabarets, movies and cabarets, and cabarets—everywhere in both extremities of French Town, uptown and downtown in the International Settlement, in Hongkew, and out of bounds in Chinese territory, are cabarets.[3]

The city's brothels or "singsong houses" were equally ubiquitous and provided the venue for many a wild night in Old Shanghai. The International Settlement alone was home to more than 700 of them[4] and prostitutes, both Chinese and foreign, provided the main entertainment. Sergeant tells a bittersweet tale of an American madam named Gracie Gale who did a booming business, "specializing in demure-looking Americans," until White Russians overran Shanghai following the 1917 Russian Revolution and priced her girls out of the market.[5] The city offered prostitutes to suit every palate—from alluring high-priced courtesans who entertained wealthy businessmen to the *yeji* or wild chickens wearing dresses slit to the waist who solicited men on street corners.[6] Brothel managers would promenade their wares past leering potential customers on Fuzhou Road—Old Shanghai's red light district notorious for its opium dens, gambling holes, and bordellos.[7] Shanghai was also infamous for its part-time prostitutes—women who worked as taxi dancers, masseuses, waitresses, tour guides, etc., and exchanged sex for money either to augment meager incomes or because sex had become an expected extracurricular service in their profession.[8] Besides female hookers, Old Shanghai had its fair share of the male variety. By some estimates, this all added up to more prostitutes than any other city in the world at the time.[9]

Besides singsong houses and courtesans, widespread recreational drug use also helped Old Shanghai earn its reputation as a den of iniquity. Stories of makeshift drug factories near Suzhou Creek, hostesses serving cocaine to their dinner guests, and hotels delivering heroin on order all became part of Old Shanghai lore.[10] But the narcotic of choice by all accounts was opium. Some of it was produced domestically, but the bulk came from abroad: British and American merchants made fortunes pumping opium into China from India after the Opium War in 1840.[11] By the early part of the 20th century, some 40 million Chinese dollars worth of opium annually entered China via Shanghai. A sizable quantity stayed in the city, which boasted more than 1,500 opium dens.[12] Organized crime, led by Huang Jinrong and Du Yuesheng of the notorious Green Gang, eventually controlled the drug's distribution, as well as prostitution and gambling in the city.[13] One of the most colorful foreigners living in Shanghai during the 1930s was an American named Emily Hahn, who became an opium addict in Shanghai and later wrote about the experience. She commented:

> As a newcomer, I couldn't have known that a lot of the drug was being used here, there, and everywhere in town. I had no way of recognizing the smell, though it pervaded the poorer districts. I assumed the odor, something like burning caramel or those herbal cigarettes smoked by asthmatics, was just part of the mysterious effluvia produced in Chinese cookhouses. Walking happily through side streets and alleys, pausing here and there to let a rickshaw or a cart trundle by, I would sniff and move on, unaware that someone close at hand was indulging in what the books called that vile, accursed drug.[14]

What made Old Shanghai in its heyday the "Sin City" described by both Chinese and foreigners? A number of forces came together to create an atmosphere highly conducive to nightlife, vice, and decadence. For one, the colonial powers that divided up the city saw Shanghai as a base to plunder China's wealth, not as the home of future generations of French, British, and American children. Indeed, the whole premise behind the British seizure of Shanghai territory after the Opium War was to sell opium to China in exchange for its tea and silk—hardly a solid foundation for an abstaining society. The British did not even bother to post government bureaucrats to administer their new territory as they usually did in occupied lands, leaving the job of running the International Settlement to a Municipal Council consisting of businessmen. The council's objective was to create a city where businessmen could go about their affairs with the least possible interference. With China's central government in decay, there was no one to tell them otherwise.

The noninterference policy extended to vice. When the Chinese government asked the International Settlement's leaders to take opium addicts to court, the Municipal Council regarded the concept as "incompatible with the principles of individual liberty in the Western sense of the word."[15] The Shanghai-based Opium Combine, made up mainly of Iraqi Jews and Parses, actually cornered the country's opium market in 1916 with the help of local banks and corrupt Chinese officials.[16] Foreign traders sold their drugs for local purchase to underworld bosses like Huang and Du, whose tentacles reached the highest levels of the city's different governments.

The line between business, government, and gangsters in Old Shanghai was blurred beyond recognition. Huang himself headed up the French

Concession's police force. Warlords, including Generalissimo Chiang Kai-shek, used the opium trade to finance their armies. The notorious Du eventually became a member of the French Municipal Council, the president of two banks, and the chairman of a middle school, earning himself a mention in Shanghai's Who's Who as a "well-known public welfare worker."[17] Unlike Al Capone in the gangster-ridden Chicago of the 1920s, there was no Eliot Ness of the U.S. Federal Investigation Bureau to bring Du down. How could there be since there was no viable central government?

The city's peculiar multi-government setup favored vice well. French authorities were especially known for their relaxed approach to law enforcement,[18] but even when police wanted to catch criminals, their efforts were often stymied. Because the French Concession, the International Settlement, and the Chinese city had jurisdiction only over their specific areas, a lawbreaker wanted in the International Settlement could simply flee to the French Concession or disappear into the Chinese city.

If these conditions were not enough to seduce depraved minds, the fact that foreigners did not need a passport or visa to visit the city also helped Old Shanghai earn its notorious reputation. It lured people with pasts to hide and fortunes to make—a reputation that fed on itself, inviting an uninterrupted flow of adventurers. The city also attracted foreigners without a country to call home. Certainly some of the credit for the vibrancy of Old Shanghai's after-hours scene in the 1920s and 1930s goes to Shanghai's large Russian community. Following the Bolshevik victory, they flocked to the city to become one of the largest foreign ethnic groups. Often working as musicians or taxi dancers in the cabarets, "Their glamour and wildness created the mood which overtook Shanghai at night," wrote Sergeant.[19]

Likewise, Old Shanghai enticed Chinese from around China. Most of its population was not native to the city, but instead had been uprooted from their traditions in the Chinese interior by poverty, rampaging warlords, or a personal quest for opportunity. Shanghai's foreign concessions provided a safe haven compared with the instability swallowing the rest of China at the time. But when these migrants arrived, they found a city that was more Western than Chinese to them. There was much they hadn't ever seen before, like Tudor villas, cars, gas lamps, and movies; there was so much that did not conform to traditional norms, whether it be Chinese men wearing pinstripe suits or Chinese girls sporting bobbed hairstyles. New arrivals spent their time trying to survive or move up the ladder rather than bemoaning the loss of traditional Chinese values. Moreover, to survive, people did things they would not need to do under less desperate circumstances, nor dare do under the watchful eye of their clan, like working as an opium dealer's henchman, offering sex for hire, or living unmarried with their lover. Adding sophistication to the whole scene were the sons and daughters of wealthy Shanghainese families, who dressed in tuxedos and mink and frittered away their families' fortunes on pleasure.

The march of Communist soldiers into Shanghai in 1949 sounded the death knell for Old Shanghai and its decadent ways. The foreigners fled, the wealthy Shanghainese fled, the gangsters also fled. Those who didn't depart were forced to adjust to the country's new Communist prudery during repeated campaigns against vice. Although the Communists never eliminated the oldest profession in the world all together,[20] prostitution in China and Shanghai was no longer visible. Brothel-keepers were executed, prostitutes sent to labor reform camp, and drug addicts forced into rehabilitation. No more nightclubs, no more singsong houses, no more opium, no more neon.

No more Old Shanghai.

Nightlife's Comeback

Fast-forward 40 years to the nightclub CD, with its Ecstasy-popping young people, male prostitutes, and packed dance floor at five in the morning. Old Shanghai might be dead, but a new Shanghai is rising from its ashes.

Nightlife and vice only really started making a comeback in Shanghai after 1992. Not that laser-flashing discos and women soliciting themselves in bars did not exist before then. After China started on the path of market-oriented economic reform in 1979, these phenomena began to appear in Shanghai and other Chinese cities, particularly in southern China, which was the first region to embrace economic change. In Shanghai in the 1980s, the action mostly took place in and around new foreign-invested hotels catering to foreign business executives. But the city was still dead for the most part. Its state-run restaurants closed early. Once night fell, the city went dark—it had not yet rediscovered its mania for neon. At the end of the 1980s, there were only a few private bars operating outside of hotels. With high-backed booths and space for 20 if people squeezed, they were at best quaint and at worst sleazy. Foreign expatriates putting together an amateur rock band or the Australian Consulate's Friday evening happy hours provided the high point of the weekend for the small foreign community. Otherwise, there were always the acrobats at the Lyceum Theatre and the out-of-tune octogenarian jazz band at the Peace Hotel, but these activities got old even faster than the first options. Shanghainese, meanwhile, rediscovered the joys of ballroom dancing, usually at functions arranged by their state-owned employer. Resembling toy soldiers, couples practiced the fox trot and waltz with at least an arm's length of space between them. Young people listened to music, saw movies, and had barbecues. Those with a burning desire for more headed for Beijing, which opened up to the West earlier, or Shenzhen, the booming special economic zone bordering Hong Kong. The central government in Beijing did not allow Shanghai to experiment much with market-oriented reforms in those days and its economy was anything but booming.

Deng Xiaoping's call in the 1990s to rebuild Shanghai with foreign and domestic investment changed all that. Particularly since 1995, the number of discos, restaurants, bars, karaoke joints, bowling alleys, massage parlors, and other nighttime venues has ballooned. I'll never forget the buzz in the foreign community in late 1994 when some Canadians opened Malone's American Restaurant, a spacious sports bar, which was one of the first places outside a hotel where people could drink beer, eat a hamburger or pasta, and listen to a band. A fellow journalist later confided that he ate there every night the first week it opened. Today, however, Malone's is simply one of numerous possibilities offering different international cuisines and ambiance. The main thoroughfares are a kaleidoscope of pink, green, yellow, blue, red, and orange neon, flashing late into the night. Young people pack the most popular discos. At Yang Yang's on Yan An Road on a Friday night, for instance, merrymakers wave their arms above their head to their favorite pop songs. Every now and then dance girls dressed in glittering hot pants and cropped tops jump onto a stage and churn their hips in unison. For the older and richer set, there are marble-laden clubs like the Golden Age. There, gloved and tuxedoed waiters serve patrons who pay a cover charge exceeding 200 yuan (US$24) to watch Frank Sinatra-esque crooners. On the nights I visited, the variety show then moved to classical ballet performed by Russian ballerinas and ended after midnight with Chinese

China's Wall Street: Little more than rice paddies and warehouses in the 1980s, the Lujiazui financial district in Pudong is the symbol of Shanghai's renaissance into a modern cosmopolitan city. But as an international financial center, the city still has far to go.

The Return of Nightlife: Shanghai's once-notorious nightlife is booming once again with a welter of new bars, discos, and restaurants. Here, young club-goers watch a model cavort at one of Shanghai's many night-time hangouts.

dancing girls wearing pointy silver cones over their breasts. Shanghai at the end of the 20th century offered Goya's for martinis, the Old China Hand Reading Room for coffee, the Cotton Club for folksy American rock, and the Ying Yang Club for techno dancing in an intimate atmosphere. There were many others: By the end of 1998, Shanghai had a whopping 1,472 discos and 2,106 karaoke bars.[21]

Not that Shanghai's nightlife has yet reached international standards in terms of variety and quality. Particularly where the arts intersect with nightlife, the pickings are still slim. Shanghai does not offer much in the way of live music, theater, or other cultural activities, although the situation improved somewhat during the last half of the 1990s.

For young Shanghainese who are experiencing discos, bars, and foreign cuisines for the first time, however, Shanghai is an exhilarating place to party. They commonly describe Shanghai nightlife as *hen fengfu* or "very abundant." For 22-year-old Jing and 19-year-old Bei, typical young Shanghainese women, the fun on Saturday normally starts at around one o'clock in the afternoon and ends after midnight. The two girls and a posse of former classmates usually first meet for several hours of karaoke at Cash Box, a successful chain offering room after room of karaoke at different locations around the city. There, they take turns singing saccharin Canto-pop love songs and watching the sappy videos that accompany each tune. Between five and six o'clock they go for dinner at a popular noodle shop. Then they head to a teahouse or a bar, preferably foreign-invested ones boasting Western decors, and maybe later a disco.

When I met Jin and Bei, they and their girlfriends were playing a Chinese card game and reading each others' fortunes from tarot cards at a new Taiwanese-invested restaurant-bar on Hengshan Road, Shanghai's emerging trendy entertainment strip. So far that evening, each had spent about 100 yuan (US$12). Given that they earned no more than 1,500 yuan (US$181) a month, keeping costs down was very much on their minds. Between 10 and 11 o'clock, they planned to hit the city's hottest new disco, Real Love, also on Hengshan Road. They were not going there to meet guys, they insisted, but planned to dance with each other for a few hours before sharing a taxi home—like most unmarried Shanghainese in their twenties, they still live with their parents. Jing, who like Bei is reasonably attractive, explained:

Boys only approach outstanding girls in discos anyway. You see, there are two kinds of girls. One kind always goes to discos and wears shiny clothes and makeup. Then there are girls like us who like to have fun, but only go to discos sometimes. We're more obedient. My mother would beat me to death if I went to a disco every week, because I don't get home until at least three o'clock in the morning and it's very bad for my health.

Also typical of new Shanghai youth are the three 22-year-olds guys I met waiting in a 20-person-deep line at midnight at Real Love. Quintessential representatives of the new Shanghai male, these immaculately groomed young men could easily be mistaken for Hong Kong Chinese. Gone were the tacky perms and suits with labels sewn on sleeves that defined male chic in the 1980s. All three donned short, greased-up coifs, which showed off their clean-cut, handsome faces. Dawei, a flight attendant with China Eastern Airlines, wore a tan leather jacket, black jeans, and a gold chain around his neck. Tommy, a clerk in a government bureau, and, Lesley, a hairdresser, looked similarly ready to rock. They told me they normally go out at least one night a weekend and spend 500 yuan (US$60) a shot, sometimes starting at a computer game arcade, but usually at a disco. There, they dance until two a.m. before heading for a karaoke club. Their goal for the evening, they said, was to relax, dance, and meet girls.

Sure enough, when I remet the trio at three a.m. inside the crowded club, Dawei and Lesley had scored with two attractive young women and were off to the ever-popular Cash Box for an early morning karaoke fest. My Chinese assistant and I boldly asked if we could join them and to my surprise, they agreed. I had expected a polite refusal: Three 22-year-old Americans who had just picked up two good-looking young women at three in the morning would definitely not want a nosy foreign journalist and her sidekick around.

At Cash Box, we rented a KTV room for a fraction of the peak hour rate, which is why Dawei, Tommy, and Lesley always arrived after 2:00 a.m. Late-night revelers filled a number of the rooms around us. Ordering tea, milk, and soft drinks, Dawei flipped through the inch-thick book of song titles and started passing the microphone. It became clear as the night wore on, and one song led to another, that the night's objective was to win the girls' hearts with their singing. The two young women were not the shiny makeup type, although they exuded more confidence than Jing and Bei at the restaurant. (After all, I suppose, they were the type of girls who boys did ask to dance.) One of the women mentioned that the evening was the latest she had ever stayed out—she had told her parents she was attending a student gathering. At 6:30 a.m., the gang was still going strong, sometimes performing a duet, but usually showing off with a solo. By the time they were ready to leave at 7:30 a.m., they had gone through more than 50 Hong Kong, Taiwanese, and mainland pop hits—songs with lyrics like "Don't look at me that way. My face is turning into a red apple." I overheard Dawei asking the girls if they might like to play tennis or go horseback riding in the future. They smiled and said yes before heading their separate ways.

Young Shanghainese like Jin, Bei, and Dawei are taking advantage of their youth in ways that their parents never dreamed possible. Thanks to Deng Xiaoping's reforms, young people have many interesting new entertainment venues to discover and money to spend on leisure activities. They also have free time to stay out late and sleep into the afternoon: China instituted a five-day workweek in 1997, which means that young people do not have to work on Saturday and do chores on Sunday like their parents did when they were young. With the relaxation of social mores that has accompanied reform, they also can enjoy the company of the opposite sex prior to marriage without fear of being labeled *fuhua*, or degenerate. In the process, they are helping to bring nightlife back to Shanghai.

Sex, Drugs, and Other Vices

But for all the good clean fun and freedom that nightclubs, bars, and KTV joints offer Shanghai youth, they often have a seamier side focused on money, sex, and drugs.

"You know we don't like to do this, but Shanghai society is practical. We need money because everything in Shanghai costs money," blurted a Miss K who was seated in one the karaoke rooms of MGM, a popular Shanghai nightclub, and was obviously embarrassed about the nature of her work. It was a Monday night around 11 o'clock and although the downstairs bar and dance floor were crowded, the karaoke rooms upstairs had yet to fill up. She and another Miss K were fiddling with their red and yellow mobile phones while waiting for customers. They were young, between 22 and 24, and beautiful, especially the one who had just spoken. Her long black locks waved delicately around her finely sculptured face. A light and tasteful hand had applied her makeup. She wore a nicely cut short black silk cocktail dress that revealed most of her back—the effect of which was more sexy than sleazy. Sheer stockings of a quality rarely seen in Shanghai just a few years earlier covered her long thin legs. Such accoutrements, which the girls can only find at Printemps, Isetan, or other high-priced, foreign-invested department stores, do not come cheap in Shanghai. So they earn their money by providing company from nine in the evening until two in the morning to men. They sit next to them, chat with them, sing for them, and dance with them in exchange for a tip. Many of the girls do not sleep with customers for money—the duty is not part of their job description—but according to men who frequent such establishments, an equal number will agree to an after-work encounter for the right price. While I was talking to the two Miss Ks, five more trickled into the room. They came in a variety of shapes, sizes, and levels of sleaze—a mixture that was obviously aimed at appealing to the club's diverse clientele of overseas Chinese, foreign, and local men. Suddenly, a drunk Swedish businessman entered the room, shouting, "I need four girls." It was Swedish week in Shanghai and the club was full of light-haired, blue-eyed men after a taste of the local culture. Off the girls went, some of them later to be seen working hard for their tips on the dance floor below.

Miss Ks often hope to graduate into *jinseniao* or "canaries"—so named because of a canary's beauty and life in a cage. To become a canary, Miss Ks need to find themselves a *da kuan*—or "millionaire"—often an older businessman from Hong Kong, Taiwan, or Singapore, who is willing to set them up with a house, clothes, and plenty of cash. According to a fiftyish overseas Chinese friend of mine who keeps two "canaries," one in Shanghai and one in Hong Kong, the girls earn 10,000 to 20,000 yuan (US$1,204–US$2,410) a month—more than the average Shanghainese earns in a year—making them definite "haves" in Shanghai's new economic hierarchy. Although every situation is unique, a Miss K normally meets her sugar daddy while working at a nightclub. On return visits, he asks management for her to sit with him. The pair eventually become lovers, after which he plies her with gifts, culminating with an apartment and sometimes even a small business. Some apartment and villa compounds are known as *niaolong*—or "bird cages"—due to the large number of kept women who live there. In return, a canary is expected to service her sugar daddy's needs when he comes through town on business. While some canaries are just in it for the money, others are emotionally involved. Even if her sugar daddy already has a wife and children back home, she can always hope that he will one day dump them and marry her.

Not that Shanghai's canaries sit by the telephone waiting for their sugar daddy's call. On the contrary, both Miss Ks and canaries can often be seen dancing in discos into the wee hours with handsome young men. These men are not boyfriends in the traditional sense. Instead, just as middle-aged businessmen push money at Miss Ks and canaries, the girls push money at their *xiaolanggou*—or "little wolf dogs"—as these boys are known. The women dress up their little wolf dogs in the latest fashions, take them out on the town, and sometimes even buy them an apartment, all in exchange for companionship and sex. Indeed, instead of just "bird cages," one also hears of *langwo*—or "wolf dens." The little wolf dog phenomenon apparently is not common elsewhere in China. A Shanghainese woman, who used to work as a manager in a nightclub in southern China, explained:

Sichuan girls send money home, girls in the Northeast spend it on clothes, and Shanghai girls spend it on little wolf dogs. This is Shanghai girls' style. They always get money from some old, stupid businessman. They don't feel good about themselves, and so they need to do the same thing to these boys. They need to control them.

Miss Ks, canaries, and little wolf dogs are an integral part of Shanghai's new nightlife scene. Clubs often let these pretty boys and girls in for free since they help attract business. Flush with a night's tips and raring to meet up with their little wolf dogs, Miss Ks start pouring into the most popular discos after one o'clock in the morning.

Also integral to Shanghai nightlife are *sanpei xiaojie*—or bar girls. Young women wearing body-hugging clothing can regularly be seen hustling customers for drinks in certain bars. They are not prostitutes per se—it depends on the girl. Often all they want is for a man to hand them money for drinks that cost a fraction of that amount in exchange for sitting next to him, chatting a bit, and maybe some dancing. But many of these women also sleep with their client for the right price. The scene at a five-star foreign-invested hotel in Shanghai's budding financial district, is typical. An acquaintance in Shanghai who knew I was investigating Shanghai nightlife invited me for a drink with two friends visiting from Beijing. All three were foreign businessmen working for multinationals in China for most of the 1990s. After talking about the tribulations of doing business in China, the conversation turned to prostitution. I finally asked them if we could check out a bar together and they agreed—as long as the bar was on the way to their hotel,

I paid for everything, and I did not use their names. I will call the two Americans Bob and Sam, and the British-educated Hong Kong Chinese, T.T.

Since Bob and T.T. were staying at the Pudong Shangrila, we decided to head there. We arrived at the basement bar at 10:30 p.m. on a Wednesday night to find it packed with men—Westerners and overseas Chinese between the ages of 35 and 60—and Chinese women in their twenties, often dressed in tight-fitting clothing. T.T. and I hung back while Bob and Sam planted themselves closer to the bar. Some of the girls not chatting up a man swayed their bodies to the beat of the music. Bob and Sam had not stood at the bar for 15 seconds before a skinny woman in a powder blue ensemble sashayed up to them. After turning her away, Bob, rushed over to me, saying, "What should I ask?" I reeled off a list of questions, reminding him that he had to report their conversation in detail. Again he had not returned to his post for another 15 seconds when a buxom young woman in a body-caressing black and yellow sweater zoned in—the girl in powder blue had since started whispering to another man. Smiling amiably, the new girl quickly wrapped her hand through Bob's arm and around his waist. Two minutes later she was dragging him by the hand to a booth at the far corner of the bar. "You've got to come sit over here so that I can touch you," she said." Can I get a friend for your friend?"

"No," said Bob.

"I'm calling a friend for your friend," she insisted, as she slid next to Bob in the dimly lit booth. T.T. and I changed tables to get a better look.

"Is this place expensive?" Bob asked in Mandarin.

"I want to touch you," she said, caressing his neck, arms, and legs.

'I'm expensive. How much do you pay for me?" he teased. She laughed, by which time her girlfriend had squiggled up to Sam. The first girl introduced herself as Lily and said she'd been working as a bar girl since giving up a career as a beautician. Sam's new date, a prettier version of Lily, called herself Miss Li and said she had been laid off two weeks earlier from an interior design company.

"So what do you girls do here?" asked Bob.

"I can give you a massage for 300 yuan (US$36)," said Lily. "If I massage you in the bar, it's only 150 yuan (US$18), but it's 300 yuan if I go to your room because the police could catch me at the elevator."

"What does a massage include?"

"A massage is a massage, making love is making love, and chatting is chatting," she answered cryptically.

"How much to make love?"

"Two hundred American money." Then, changing tacks, she asked, "Could you buy me a drink? I need 120 yuan (US$14)." She returned shortly with one soft drink, which at most cost 25 yuan (US$3).

"Excuse me, I would also like to drink," purred the second girl. Sam handed Miss Li a 100-yuan note (US$12) and off she went.

By the time she returned with her drink, Bob and Sam were itching to extricate themselves and told the girls they wanted to join their friends, pointing to T.T. and me. Assuming T.T and I were romantically linked, Lily cooed, "They're talking about love. Why don't we talk about love?" The more the girls insisted the guys not leave, the more desperate Bob and Sam became, finally telling the girls they were gay. Lily and Miss Li then asked for a *zuotaifei*—a charge for sitting with them. Handing them 100 yuan (US$12), Bob and Sam scurried back to our table to recount their conversation.

Not long afterward—it was by now 12:15 a.m.—I noticed a group of seven women sitting and standing near the bar, but not pouncing on men like many of the other girls. T.T. waved over the first who caught his eye—a tastefully attired, waif-like woman with a delicate heart-shaped face. In a sweet, high-pitched voice, she told us a little about herself. She had arrived that very day from Chongqing in western China at the request of a Shanghainese woman whom she had met there. The woman planned to set up a bar in Shanghai and asked the 25-year-old to work for her. "Tonight she's just taking us out to have a look around. We're visiting different bars and she wanted us to see this one," the girl explained. She had worked as a salesgirl at home, but business was bad. "So many people are out of work," she said. Her parents had both been laid off, earning only 400 yuan (US$48) per month in welfare subsidies, hardly enough to support her two siblings who were still in high school. Never finishing high school herself, she was expected to send home 300 yuan (US$36) a month. When I asked her where her friend's bar was and what job she would do there, she said it was somewhere in Pudong and that she would serve drinks. She'd much prefer a good factory job earning 800 yuan (US$96) a month, she insisted. When I mentioned that 800 yuan did not get one very far in Shanghai, she said it seemed like a lot of money to her and that someone with her low "cultural level" could not expect much better. In the meantime, she planned to work at her friend's bar.

The bar, however, turned out not to be in Pudong, but instead on the other side of town in the old French Concession on Jule Road, near a new strip of bar-girl joints catering to foreign males. T.T and I found this out by inviting over another girl from the same group, who had also arrived that very day from Wuhan at the request of the same Shanghai "friend." Compared with the girl from Chongqing, this one was less refined. Her hair was frizzier, her outfit less feminine, and her speech more gruff. When we asked them if they would be hustling men for drinks at their friend's bar, the woman from Chongqing replied in a timid voice that she didn't know. The second, however, retorted that she most certainly would, adding that she did not particularly appreciate foreigners asking her questions about it. Fair enough, so we chatted about more banal topics before parting ways. I later asked T.T. if he thought the girl from Chongqing was unaware of the nature of her new job, but he insisted she knew all too well. Several days later at 2:00 a.m. on a Tuesday, I spied the girl from Wuhan at one of the Jule Road bars, honing her hustling skills on a British sailor.

Besides bar girls, Shanghai also has its fair share of bar boys, although they are not nearly as ubiquitous. Like the girls, some are prostitutes and some are not. At a club called Passion on Fanyu Road at 3:30 in the morning, my assistant and I asked a waiter if we could meet one of their "ducks" or male bar boys. Soon enough, a 20-year-old surnamed Tan approached us. He did not look nearly as polished as the "daddy duck" I met at the club CD a few nights earlier. His hair hung limply below his ears and his black suit swam around his body. Finding a table for us away from the dance floor, he told me that the club had hired him to entertain guests, which he insisted meant chatting and dancing. He did not moonlight by having sex after work for a fee. For his efforts, he earned a salary of 1,000 yuan (US\$120) a month plus a 300-yuan (US\$36) table-sitting fee from each client. "Little wolf dogs do much better than me," he lamented, adding that he hoped to eventually become a boss of a food or clothing business. Unlike Tan, many of these bar boys are more than willing to have sex for money, as my conversation with the "daddy duck" at CD well illustrated. The daddy duck said his customers are often women from Taiwan and Hong Kong, although "canaries" in Shanghai are also infamous for hiring "ducks." According to Little Wang, the undercover cop, the police cracked down on a number of *yadian*—or "duck shops"—in Shanghai in the last half of the 1990s, including one opened by a male body builder who had his well-built waiters serve the club's women-only clientele wearing underpants. It operated for roughly a month before the police closed it down, Wang said.

Although bar girls and boys do not necessarily intend to go further than talking and dancing for tips, it is easy for them to fall into contract sex. According to statistics from the all-China Women's Federation, half of prostitution cases in China are tied to nightclubs, prompting the official women's group at the 1999 National People's Congress in Beijing to call for a ban on bar girls.[22] I discussed the phenomenon with a professor at the Shanghai Academy of Social Sciences (SASS). In 1996 and 1997, Xia Guomei had done extensive interviewing of women prostitutes serving time at the city's labor education prisons, where police sent people caught soliciting themselves. She shared with me some of the fruits of her work, including the story of a bar girl turned prostitute.

Meili, a pseudonym, was 19 years old when she first started working at a Korean restaurant as a bar girl. Her parents were officials and her sister a high-ranking member of the Communist youth league, making Meili an unlikely candidate to become a prostitute. But after she failed the exam to enter senior high school, she found herself with nothing to do—her parents did not approve of her attending a technical school. They gave her pocket money to entertain herself and, while idling away the time one day, she noticed some girls her own age wearing expensive clothing and spending lots of cash. She envied them a lot, she later told Xia. When she finally got to know them, the girls explained they worked at a Korean restaurant that paid them to talk and dance with clients. It seemed simple enough. And because Meili was attractive (all the girls Xia interviewed in labor education prisons were good-looking), her new friends did not hesitate to introduce her to their boss. Eventually one of the clients asked her to have sex. She felt ashamed while doing it, she said, but the money—US$200 per encounter—proved too tempting. She could make 20,00–30,000 yuan (US$2,409–US$3,614) a month, astronomical sums for China. Suddenly she could shop at the finest shops and wear designer clothes. The good times lasted until the police arrested her and sent her to labor education prison for a year. Although she vowed not to return to the same life upon her release, she needed money to support her expensive habits, which included a boyfriend who had quit his 1,000 yuan (US$120)-a-month job at a shipping company to live off of her. When the police caught her a second time, she had just finished servicing a regular client—a Korean man who would page her when he came through Shanghai once every two months. The security guard at the Huating Hotel grabbed her as she walked out the door. Taken by surprise, she had no time to get rid of the telltale wad of cash in her bag and ended up with a two-year sentence at labor reform prison. She vowed to Xia that the next time around she would be more careful.

The most notorious venues for prostitution in Shanghai are hotels and barber shops, although men also report receiving sexual services at some of the city's massage parlors. My overseas Chinese friend who keeps the two "canaries," reported that for a 50–100 yuan (US$6–US$12) tip, the masseuse is often willing to massage a man's groin. "At these massage parlors, there are maybe 20 girls," he recounted. "Because they have to wait in line to get a customer and often must wait a long time, they get mad when you don't want the hand job because it means their tip will not be as good." Fishing for information while getting a massage at a fancy Hong Kong-invested "health and entertainment club," I learned that the masseuses working on the men-only floor were in their twenties, while older women were relegated to the women's section. Indeed, the two women working on the women-only floor were neither attractive nor young. When asked if girls wore clothes on the men's floor, one masseuse obliquely answered: "Yes, when they enter the room."

"Do they provide extra service for men?"

"Yes, it seems so."

One American friend of mine was actually getting what he insisted was a *zhengguide anmo*—or standard massage without sex—when the police raided the club. The girls herded their clients out of the individual little massage rooms and into a lounge before three policemen arrived. Unable to find anything illegal, the officers sneered at the crowd and left.

The real action, however, usually occurs in hotels. Prostitutes do not just look for clients in hotel bars and lobbies, but also solicit them directly in their rooms. Few male travelers who regularly visit Shanghai or anywhere in China have not received a phone call during the middle of the night asking if they would like a massage or a woman—even in five-star establishments. I personally received these calls from women believing I was Mr. Yatsko or not realizing that my husband was traveling with his wife. Hotel management is not necessarily in on the scam. The girls sometimes bribe a hotel staffer to get their hands on the guest list. A group of girls also sometimes rents a room in the hotel and calls potential clients from there. This method allows them to bypass the hotel receptionist, who in five-star hotels normally asks callers for the guest's name. Still, given how common prostitution is in many hotels, management, by not stopping it, passively condones it.

Another place men go to pay for sex in Shanghai are barbershops. In the course of my research, I learned about a website that provides information about the sex scene in cities around the world, including Shanghai. Users were asked to write in with their own experiences. One submitted the following excerpt on Shanghai's barbershops on March 26, 1998:

I felt compelled to contact you because there was a conspicuous absence in your article of the MANY, MANY beauty salons ALL OVER the city which provide certain sexual services. You touched upon this at the end of the article with mention of the salons and streetwalkers behind the Longmen hotel near the train station. Here's my contribution. Do with it as you wish but please honor your pledge to keep the source confidential:

The rule for Shanghai's ubiquitous beauty salons is this: the farther away they are from the city center, the more likely the possibility they offer more than just a shave and a haircut. There are COUNTLESS barber shops and beauty salons throughout the city where you can get a massage and a handjob for as little as 100 yuan [US$12] and, if you're lucky, a blowjob for around 300 yuan [US$36] and sex for about 500 yuan [US$60]. These beauty salons are usually owned and managed/operated by a Shanghainese woman or couple. They hire a couple of girls from Wenzhou, Fujian, or some other backwater place to work there. These girls are usually not beautiful in the conventional sense, but since they come in literally all shapes, sizes, personalities, styles, and flavors, you're bound to find one that turns you on. When you enter, ask if they "Qiao Bei" (literally "knock/strike/beat the back"), or give massages. If the answer is yes, they'll either ask you to sit in the barber's chair or to go into a back room or partitioned space with a bed. If they ask you to sit, persist a bit and request the full-body, lay-down massage. If they resist further give up and try another place. Once in the back room or partitioned area, ask the price. It should be around 50 or 60 yuan [US$6–US$7]. That's the "*tai fei*," or fee just to get on the table. On top of that you're expected to give a tip. One hundred yuan, all inclusive, for a massage and a handjob is ENOUGH. Pay them AFTER they finish the job, not before. If they bitch and moan that 100 [yuan] isn't enough, tell them to "*jiao yige pengyou*" (make a friend) and that you'll come back again and again if they accommodate you this time, nine out of 10 times they buy it ...[23]

What the author left out was that these *falang mei*—or barbershop girls—normally have little more than a primary school education and live and work under poor conditions. The barbershops are often small, dirty concrete blocks catering to migrant workers who are in Shanghai to work primarily on the city's construction sites. The shops, said Xia Guomei, the researcher at SASS, are havens for sexually transmitted diseases and a link to the city's growing AIDS population. The girls normally have to hand a third of their profits over to the shop's owner and live in a hovel with some other migrant girls on the edge of the city for 300 to 400 yuan (US$36–US$48) a month. Often their objective is to save enough money to return home and start a business. The alternative—staying in Shanghai—is usually far less appealing. Many of the prostitutes who solicit sex on the streets on the edge of the city or around the old train station are former barbershop girls who either lost their looks with age or never had any. Xia explained:

All they have is that they are women. Sometimes they have no money to eat, accepting a *hefan* [a styrofoam box usually filled with rice, greens, and some kind of meat] in payment. They earn as little as five to 10 yuan per client (US$0.60–US$1.20) and normally can't get more than 30 yuan (US$3.60). They're the worst off of all the different types of prostitutes in Shanghai.

Most of the "working girls" I met in Shanghai were not the hard-edged women in platform boots and hot pants one sees on Avenue Foche in Paris or on 42nd Street in New York. Instead, they often seemed like sweet girls. But it was obvious that they were willing to overlook morality questions for the comforts derived from cold hard cash. Most of Shanghai's new prostitutes did not make it into university or even out of high school, but because they are pretty, they are able to find legitimate work in hotels and other entertainment establishments. "There, they get a taste of the good life, which is vastly different from what their own income can get them. They want to make money to change their status, but because they don't have any real skills, they go for a shortcut," Little Wang, the undercover cop, explained.

In 1999, China as a whole had an estimated 800,000–2.5 million prostitutes, including Miss Ks, canaries, bar girls, barbershop girls, and hotel hustlers.[24] Their proliferation spoke volumes about the moral vacuum engulfing Shanghai and China on the eve of the 21st century. Up until the reform era, Communism forced its strict moral guidelines on society. The Cultural Revolution, however, shattered many believers' faith in the righteousness of that ideology, while the onslaught of market-oriented reforms in the 1980s and 1990s destroyed any lingering credibility. At the same time, the old Confucian and Buddhist ethics that provided guidelines before 1949 were totally discredited during the Communist era. So some people today turn to organized religion and underground spiritual movements. Others find solace in a new god: money. Like the beautiful Miss K said to explain her behavior, "Shanghai society is practical." Indeed, anecdotal evidence suggests that the moral position of these women is ambiguous in society's eyes. Although some people condemn them, others take their behavior in stride. A Shanghainese acquaintance, for instance, commented: "Like everyone else, they can use their special asset—in this case their prettiness—to make money." Even the government's opposition to prostitution is not quite as firm as official rhetoric suggests. While prostitution is illegal and local governments launch campaigns against it, the trade flourishes in both big and small cities in China. The reason: Local governments consider it necessary to develop the local economy and therefore keep one eye closed when monitoring it. Indeed, there's a saying in China: *fanrong changsheng*, which has two meanings depending on which Chinese character one selects to depict the sound "chang." It can either mean "thriving and prosperous" or "thriving and prostitution."

If prostitutes are once again making their mark on Shanghai, so is another long-foregone vice: illegal drugs. Apart from the drug busts one learns about in the press (especially during the Chinese government's intermittent antidrug campaigns), the phenomenon is most obvious in certain nightclubs, where the smell of pot mingles with cigarette smoke and young people on dance floors swing their heads back and forth for hours in an Ecstasy-induced bliss. "The head shakers come in after 12:30 a.m.," commented an employee of Shanghai Night Owl Cafe, a Shanghai nightspot known to locals as *Yemaozi*—or Night Cat. "We were the first big bar frequented by kids on Ecstasy," he continued. "Shenzhen studied it from Hong Kong and Shanghai studied from Shenzhen [in southern China]." For those who cannot afford to pay 200–300 yuan (US$24–US$36) a hit for the drug, a favored alternative is a German cough medicine that sells for only 23 yuan (US$3) a bottle. Many other young people, in an effort to be cool, simply shake their head while dancing, even though they have not swallowed any illicit substances. A 22-year-old Chinese artist who has experimented with a number of different drugs explained Ecstasy's appeal: "One time I felt the earth and sky separate. The sky rose higher and higher and the earth lower and lower. I felt like I was floating—as if I had jumped off a building and was just hanging there. I felt music going around my body. It was really good."

In 1996, Shanghai had an estimated 20,000 drug users.[25] The vast majority of them used heroin, which made its way to Shanghai from Yunnan and Xinjiang. According SASS's Xia, who researched the link between prostitution, drugs, and sexually transmitted diseases in Shanghai, anecdotal evidence suggests that the numbers of users has grown rapidly, both for heroin users and for those enjoying other substances like marijuana and Ecstasy. In the first five months of 1997, for instance, the number of drug trafficking cases in Shanghai rose 105% over the same period a year earlier. Heroin seizures jumped nearly four times as well.[26] In June 1998, police arrested 19 members of two organized gangs from Xinjiang and Gansu provinces and confiscated 83 kilograms of heroin— the biggest drug bust since before 1949.[27] Shanghai's drug rehabilitation centers were so full by the late 1990s that the centers had to ask the police to stop forcing people into rehabilitation. (The first time the Public Security Bureau, China's police, catches a citizen taking drugs, it normally throws him or her into a rehab center for 15 days to three months and ask the offender to pay 5,000 yuan [US$602]. The authorities send repeat offenders to labor education prisons.) Xia commented:

There were no more beds available [at the rehabilitation center], but the police did not stop sending new patients. So the doctors put six beds in a room originally meant for three beds—or they took away the beds all together and let patients sleep on the floor. When a new volunteer center was recently established, it was fully booked as soon as it opened and had to start a waiting list. They've even started sending the surplus patients to Hangzhou and Wuxi, where the authorities have built new rehab centers. The doctors in the centers work very hard and are very tired.

Whereas the vast majority of patients before 1996 were men between 30 and 40 years old who had made money in business, a growing number of them are between 18 and 25, according to Xia's 1997 study. Females accounted for an increasing portion, some 25%–30% of all patients. Like prostitutes, Xia found that most of the women undergoing rehabilitation are pretty, but poorly educated. Apparently their good looks allow them to hook rich boyfriends, who in return hook them on drugs. "They consider taking drugs a symbol of being rich," Xia added. Often they turn to selling their bodies when the money runs out—some 80% of the women in the study had resorted to prostitution at one time or another. In other cases the women already work as prostitutes and are turned on to drugs by one of their regular clients.

Consider the experience of a young, good-looking American-Chinese businessman. Out on the town in Shanghai with a group of "canaries" in early 1998, he drove with them down a series of dark back alleys until they reached an unmarked building. There were no multi-colored neon lights or signboards to indicate the nature of the establishment, but when he walked through the door he realized he had entered an underground nightclub—a full three floors worth. Around him, well-dressed beautiful women fluttered around equally slick-looking men whom he pegged as "ducks." His friends led him to a little back room with seven tables. "Everyone was sitting around. Then suddenly they cleared one of the tables and out poured the drugs—Ecstasy, marijuana, hash, and what seemed like either cocaine or heroin," he recounted. "There were no needles though. They were smoking it."

Unmarked nightclubs filled with gorgeous women, male prostitutes, and drugs? After the businessman told me his tale, I asked Little Wang, the undercover cop, if he knew anything about it. "Oh, that place," he said. "It was an old labor education prison. You had to go in through the back door. It was open half a month before it got shut down."

The Shanghai press announced the closure of another unmarked club in January 1999, only this time the vice was gambling. In July 1998, three Taiwanese started a secret mahjong parlor in Shanghai's Minhang district where players made bets involving hundreds and thousands of yuan. The police eventually raided the joint, arresting the ringleaders and gamblers and confiscating the evening's proceeds.[28]

Little Wang reeled off the names of a host of clubs that the police had closed down for good or temporarily for a variety of offenses, including male prostitution, underage Miss Ks, fighting between rival gangs, gambling, and Ecstasy. Still, it was clear that many were still getting away with their vice activity. Thinking of a number of nightclubs where I saw people smoking pot and shaking their heads wildly, I asked Little Wang if he thought they would get closed down. Speaking about one in particular, he said:

"It may get closed down, but it has good connections."

"What do you mean?"

"It belongs to an industrial bureau underneath the Shanghai municipal government. One owner used to be a *liumang* (petty gangster). Another has a family background relating to the Public Security Bureau (PSB).

The general manager of the industrial bureau is a very modest man. He's nice to everyone even if from the smallest police station. So unless heroin is found there or there's serious fighting on the premises, it won't get closed down," he explained, adding: "But what you have to understand is these places are not protected by the government as an institution but by someone in the government. In China, the relationship network is very developed. Since there's been history, there have been relatives of the emperor."

He then went on to emphasize how important it is for these nightclubs to cultivate ties with district-level police—not just high-level bureaucrats. Speaking about one that had to shut its doors for more than three months after police caught someone selling Ecstasy there, he said: "The place has connections with someone in the central government and in the municipal public security bureau. But they made the mistake of not respecting the neighborhood police. The owner is a Taiwanese guy who didn't develop good relations locally in the neighborhood. Drug dealers selling Ecstasy were not only there, but also in quite a few places for quite a long time. So it's quite obvious. The neighborhood PSB purposefully went there to make the Ecstasy bust because they wanted to shut it down. When there's a crackdown, the police go everywhere. But after the crackdown, your connections determine how long you're closed down." His comments made me recall how solicitous club managers were to Little Wang and his supposedly undercover colleagues during our two evenings out together. There were lots of handshakes and pleasantries as well as free bottles of beer or cups of tea to go around. The managers obviously understood the importance of showing hospitality to the small fry.

Little Wang's comments also alluded to one of the most interesting features of Shanghai's nightlife scene. In Shanghai, like all over China, certain clubs, karaoke joints, and hotels have been either owned or had connections to government bureaus or parts of China's security apparatus, like the PSB, the People's Liberation Army (PLA), and the People's Armed Police (PAP). They got into the entertainment business as part of the central government's drive in the reform era to ease state outlays to the armed forces by encouraging them to diversify into business. In 1998, President Jiang Zemin reversed this policy and publicly ordered the armed forces to divest from their commercial undertakings. "Of course, everyone tries to delay pulling out, but it's starting to be implemented," said Little Wang in 1999. International security experts at Pinkerton and Renful Associates whom I interviewed expected the groups simply to transfer ownership to a relative or some other front man. Taiwanese, Japanese, and Hong Kong mafia have also invested in Shanghai nightspots, sometimes in partnership with different branches of the armed forces.[29] Shanghai's own indigenous mafia has not yet made much of a mark on vice in the city, largely because of the involvement of China's law enforcement agencies in the sector.

There is no question that vice is once again part of Shanghai public life. However, the city is not becoming the "sink of iniquity" that it was before 1949. Old Shanghai was a freak of nature—its wildness born of a unique combination of conditions never to be repeated. These included a weak central government in China; a huge foreign population that did not have to worry about Chinese law; foreign settlements managed by businessmen of the most laissez-faire mindset; a position as China's major opium transshipment point; and an immigration policy that did not require passports. Modern-day Shanghai exhibits certain conditions conducive to an exhilarating nightlife and decadence—lots of foreign investment and new wealth, newly arrived migrants, a moral vacuum, corruptible officials, and the involvement of law enforcement authorities in vice. But it is missing others, and the scale of those it does display is not as great as before 1949. Moreover, relative to the vice found in other cities in Asia— such as Bangkok, where bar girls publicly perform unusual feats with genitalia and transvestites are a dime a dozen—Shanghai is downright tame. A contributor to the Internet sex guide, for instance, wrote: "Shanghai may once have been the 'Pearl of the Orient' and the 'Whore of the East,' but unfortunately for those of us who believed all the hype, those days are long gone. That's not to say there aren't some interesting highlights, there are; it's just that Shanghai is not the Asian hotspot that many of us were expecting." Even in China, anecdotal evidence suggests that vice is not as abundant in Shanghai as in some other cities, particularly in southern China, which borders Hong Kong, Macao, and parts of the Golden Triangle. By all accounts, Hainan Island, China's southernmost point, wins the title of China's prostitution mecca, with visitors either complaining or waxing lyrical that prostitutes are "everywhere." A Shanghai-based foreign businessman who worked in Hainan for a month, for instance, reported how he resorted to keeping the phone in his hotel room off the hook at night to avoid a constant barrage of phone calls from girls asking to pay him a visit. According to Xia, the SASS researcher, "In the South, the situation is definitely the most severe. Shenzhen is a lot worse than Shanghai and Hainan is the worst of all." Likewise, drugs are not as readily available in Shanghai as in cities near China's borders. Kika, an avant-garde Shanghai-based writer who spent three years in Shenzhen as a heroin addict and regularly parties in Shanghai until the sun comes up, commented, "Drugs are here but in other places there are more. I've gone to a lot of cities and think this place is the safest. Guangzhou, Shenzhen, and Beijing are all crazier."

What accounted for Shanghai's cleaner reputation? People in Shanghai contend that because of the city's importance to China's economic development strategy, the central and municipal government monitor it more closely than other places. "Shanghai used to be the wildest place in China [before 1949], now it's the most controlled," said SASS's Xia. "Shanghai is the 'head of the dragon,' so it's important for it to have a good image." According to Little Wang, the undercover cop, "Shanghai is more strict than Beijing, Shenzhen, or other places because it's critical to the Chinese economy and must provide a clean environment to attract investment." Given the steady growth of prostitution and drug use in Shanghai in the second half of the 1990s, it is clear that the city's control efforts are not totally effective. Still, there are regular crackdowns, as my own efforts to find vice near the old and new train station in March 1999 attest. In the 1990s, these neighborhoods in the northern half of the city were the most notorious places in Shanghai for prostitution, drugs, and other illicit pleasures because of their large migrant population and slum-like housing. I jumped in a cab with my assistant on a Monday night around eleven o'clock and asked the driver to head toward that part of town. Eventually we told the driver—a middle-aged man surnamed Chen—our real intentions. In a low gravelly voice suggesting too many cigarettes, he regaled us with his knowledge of the vice scene in the area: Uighur drug dealers from Xinjiang pushing heroin, barbershops asking 30 yuan (US$4) for a half-hour session with their "beautician," and interconnected dwellings along windy, narrow alleys that frustrated police efforts to catch criminals. But he also warned us that the police had cleaned up the area during U.S. President Bill Clinton's visit to Shanghai in July 1998, causing most of the activity to flee to the edge of town. We wanted to see for ourselves and had him drive us around the district. Many of the ramshackle dwellings along the narrow streets were dark, showing no sign of life. The character for hair, *fa*, painted with big red strokes on outer walls, no longer lured customers. Some sections of these neighborhoods were nothing but rubble—the city had started razing them in October 1998. "Before, all these were barbershops and private hotels with prostitutes," said Chen as we drove all around Panjiawan Road and Chang An Road. "There were lots of drugs. Two years ago I handled a lot of traffic in and out of here, but not any more. The government had to do something about it because the train station is the window of Shanghai to the rest of China. I guess the best way for the government handle this place is to bulldoze it."

A Freer Society

The return of nightlife and vice represents a broader trend sweeping Shanghai and other Chinese cities. The country's economic reforms have unleashed a slew of social change that has allowed average citizens to lead their personal lives increasingly as they see fit. So besides singing karaoke until dawn and dallying in illicit pleasures, Shanghai's residents are also partaking in a host of other liberal social activities found in more-developed countries.

Divorce is one of them. Whereas few married couples living in big cities like Shanghai divorced in 1978, 13,000 couples split up in 1998, a 21% surge over 1997. The city's divorce rate reached 2.1 couples per 1,000 people, higher than the national average and approximating levels found in Western countries in the early 1990s, according to a SASS survey.[30] What explains the growing number of divorces? Citizens in the 1990s started paying much more attention to their own individual happiness and fulfillment.

Shu Xin, a short man with puffy blow-dried hair and an indefatigable smile, is the director of Shanghai Matchmaking Co., one of the hundreds of service companies that have popped up since the 1980s to introduce lonely hearts to each other.[31] A significant portion of his company's 8,200-person-strong client base divorced their former spouses. Many of the couples split because either the husband or wife had an extramarital fling—an activity that in prereform days would have landed practitioners in labor reform prison. Some 23% of the couples in the SASS survey cited adultery as the cause of divorce. Although women are increasingly finding paramours, men are the most flagrant philanderers. Shu explained:

When a man is poor he gets along with his wife. They fight to get rich together. Once he gets rich and has all this money, a lot of women come after him, including his female colleagues. Plus men have more opportunities to meet Miss Ks. Some men are quite nice, but they just can't resist the temptation.

Reforms are straining marriages in other ways. Shu sees a lot of women file for divorce because their husbands are working too much and cannot satisfy them emotionally. Or sometimes they do not think their husbands are capable enough. "They see other men getting rich, but not their own," Shu explained. Young people aged 26–33 are also heading for divorce court in greater numbers. Xiao Chen, a 32-year-old accountant at a government agency in Shanghai, is typical. A petite women sporting fashionably short hair, a touch of makeup, and a gray wool sweater, she recounted her story in a McDonald's near her home. During the six months that Xiao Chen, who was 25 years old at the time, dated her first boyfriend, he was the perfect courtier. After he became her husband and they moved in with his parents, conflicts erupted, particularly between her and her mother-in-law. Moreover, he liked going out with his friends and she, more than anything, wanted to continue her studies. The passion in their relationship quickly cooled and after three years they decided to call it quits. "Before marriage we really did not spend much time together, and when we did we only showed each other our best sides," Xiao Chen said, sipping tea from a cardboard McDonald's cup. In the old days, she and her husband would have stayed together despite their differences due to societal pressure. "Now people are becoming more and more tolerant. They can increasingly accept divorce," she said.

Marriages consummated before reforms are often the most troubled. A divorced Shanghainese girlfriend of mine, for instance, got along well with her husband during state-planning days when the Party supplied everything. They lived in a two-room flat without a bathroom with his parents. After Deng Xiaoping launched reforms in the 1980s, however, she wanted to make the most of the new situation, whereas he resisted change, lamenting his lost security. She eventually divorced him. Reform-induced tensions are compounded by the fact that during the first 30 years of Communist rule, most people had very little experience with the opposite sex prior to marriage. Young people in school were not allowed to date, let alone have sexual relations. Yang Xiong, a professor studying youth culture at SASS recalled, for instance, how teachers drew a red line down the middle of each desk to separate boys from girls. "You couldn't cross over the line," he said. "Women and men could only date after they finished three years of training in the factory and started working. You could only really start talking about love with someone once you reached age 23–25 or older." A woman generally married her first boyfriend and only after marriage did she have sex with him. Both partners entered the marriage inexperienced emotionally and sexually.

Concern about rising divorce rates in the city has caused academics like Liu Dalian, director of the Shanghai Sex Sociology Research Center at Shanghai University, to research the influence of sexual problems between couples. "People in the past lacked knowledge about sex. Husbands only cared about satisfying their own sexual life, while wives did not dare express their feelings," he explained. He estimated that 40% of divorces in Shanghai are related to sexual problems, which is why he and his peers strongly support the proliferation of sex shops selling sex tonics and toys in the city and around the country. I found it hard not to get a kick out of the scene at the state-run Huaguang Sex Shop in downtown Shanghai in early 1999. There, matronly middle-aged women in white doctors' jackets helped customers as they browsed the store's desire-enhancing potions, ribbed dildos, and plastic vaginas.

The reasons couples got married in prereform days also did not provide a solid base for a happy marriage. In the 1960s and 1970s, the most important criteria when choosing a mate were access to an apartment, political background, and parental pressure. Intellectuals sometimes married workers for the sake of political security. Alternatively, a girl sharing a small home with her family might be pressured to find a husband with an apartment to make space for her brother's new wife. Even though these couples today do not always get divorced, they often lead separate lives, with one spouse sometimes finding a lover.

Today's young people have replaced the old criteria for choosing spouses with qualifications that reflect Shanghai's new economic situation. According to Shu, people now consider their potential spouse's salary (*piaozi*); ability to buy a house (*fangzi*); position (*weizi*); appearance (*yangzi*); and family status (*duzi*). He commented:

It's better not to have brothers and sisters and best to live without parents. People these days don't want their mate to have too many relationships, which they consider troublesome. They don't want parents interfering in their lives. The want space and freedom.

Changes in attitudes and behavior toward marriage, divorce, and sex are greatest for the generation of Shanghainese in their early twenties and younger. They have many more opportunities to meet and get to know people of the opposite sex. Dawei, Tommy, and Lesley, the three 22-year-old men at Real Love disco, and the two women they met were far more relaxed with each other than adults just 10 years older. Today's young people are also far less inclined to guard their virginity until marriage. According to a 1998 SASS survey, 30%–40% of university students have already had sexual intercourse.[32] "It's very common for young couples to have sex before marriage whether they're going to get married or not. Guys usually have a few girlfriends before they get married now," said Tommy. Reflecting society's loosening mores, many engaged couples are buying apartments and living together before marriage, although cohabiting without intention to marry is not yet common.

The sexual and social revolutions hitting big cities like Shanghai do not only apply to heterosexuals. Homosexuals are also increasingly willing to act on their desires. Gay men looking to meet like-minded individuals in Shanghai could pop over to Eddy's Bar on Nanjing Road or one of the city's three other gay bars. There they find men sitting around tables, sipping drinks, and chatting in a cozy, laid-back, dimly lit atmosphere. If they want, they can dance, although on the nights I went there only a few couples took advantage of the dance floor. If they are lucky, the bar might hold an event aimed at appealing to a gay audience. Eddy, who started Eddy's bar with his boyfriend, packed the place one weekend in 1999 by holding a male fashion show. Young men with stylishly cropped hair sauntered down makeshift runways for two hours, striking suggestive poses and occasionally revealing silky smooth chests. Waiters kept adding new chairs to accommodate the growing male audience, which at its peak exceeded 75. Spectators ranging in age from late teens to mid-forties commented on the models' physiques to each other. "He's too skinny," said one about the show's only foreign model. "He moves well," whispered another. As patrons departed, Eddy stood at the door tempting them with the phrase: "Tomorrow, it's underwear." Although models only showed off their skimpy briefs in four of the 50 passes the next evening, the crowd erupted in applause and howls with each unveiling.

Gays in the past led an unhappy, solitary existence in Shanghai and the rest of China. People denounced as homosexuals risked losing their jobs and arrest. Most homosexuals, whether male or female, kept their desires buried deep in their heart. Economic liberalization and greater communication in the 1980s and 1990s started chipping away at old prejudices and inhibitions and, as a result, life for gays in Shanghai and other major cities has become less risky and less lonely. China's Supreme Court repealed most legal prohibitions against homosexuality during the 1980s and police attitudes toward gays have relaxed. Whereas men caught in Shanghai with a raunchy gay magazine in the first half of the 1990s could land in jail for two weeks, the police now usually just confiscate the publication. Men gathering in public places known to attract gays worry far less about being arrested for disturbing public order. And they no longer have to relegate themselves to shady liaisons in parks, toilets, or bathhouses, but can meet at house parties and bars like Eddy's. Eddy got the idea to open his bar in 1994 after a Korean restaurant that he and his boyfriend had opened earlier inadvertently turned into a gathering ground for gays. Another couple enlivened gay nightlife during the decade by putting on drag shows, which for several years moved from restaurant to restaurant with the police in hot pursuit. "They'd be in one place maybe for one to two months, moving seven times a year. And wherever they went we [the gay community] would follow," recalled Eddy, laughing at the memory on a quiet evening at his bar. The 36 year-old, who combed his inch-long gelled hair fashionably forward, added:

In recent years, the situation for gays has improved. The environment has become more accepting. Sometimes the Public Security Bureau does give us trouble, but because we're careful not to exceed the limits, government policy is getting more tolerant. The policy seems to be one eye open, one eye closed. Also, China's opening to the world has helped change some people's way of thinking about homosexuals. Some Shanghai girls even like to spend time with gays because we're smart, kind, and know how to dress.

But despite improvement, gay men and women in Shanghai complained that gay life was not active enough in the city or even as active as in some other places in China. They attributed the phenomenon mostly to the Shanghainese personality. Eddy commented:

You know, Shanghainese do not like to get into trouble. They fear risk. Whereas northerners are straightforward and will do anything for their friends, Shanghainese are more weak and tender. They know how to take care of their bodies and the importance of going to sleep early. What Shanghai gays do best is buy makeup, wear famous-brand clothes, and make themselves more beautiful.

According to a gay American who lived in both Shanghai and Beijing in the late 1990s:

In Beijing they're much more open and passionate about it. They go with the flow and then pay the consequences. Here, in typical Shanghai style, everyone is always calculating. They're always thinking of the consequences of their actions. If you go to a disco in Dalian [in northeastern Liaoning province], when the hip music goes on, everyone heads for the dance floor. In Beijing, half the people do and in Shanghai no one does, then finally someone saunters up there.

If Shanghainese homosexuals feel a need to be careful, it is because the freedom to enjoy gay activities—for all the progress—is still far from complete. Police regularly visit bars like Eddy's in search of foul play, ready to pounce at the merest hint of drugs, pornography, or prostitution. The central government also takes a hard line on anything that smacks of advocacy of gay rights. And while the central government no longer makes anal sex between men illegal, it denied for most of the 1990s that homosexuals existed in China in any number, viewing homosexuality as a mental disorder. To prove the point that China does not have homosexuals, Shanghai police closed down the city's gay hangouts during U.S. President Clinton's visit to the city in July 1998. The comments of radio talk show host Ling Yu were indicative of official attitudes. During the show, called Secret Words, she answers audience questions about sexual issues, but if a man asks her about his homosexuality, she tells him to visit a doctor. "It [homosexuality] is not a common phenomenon here so it's not necessary to talk about it on the air," she told me.

Though open with other homosexuals, few gays dare tell others about their sexual preference. Jackie, a middle-aged man who frequented Eddy's, said he would never let straight friends, business associates, and family know he was gay for fear that they would no longer associate with him. Some men who visit Eddy's refuse to give their name to other patrons, replying "*shoubuding*," or "can't say for sure," when asked. And for all of Eddy's openness about his homosexuality—he's one of the few homosexuals in Shanghai who dared start a gay bar and live with his lover—he still does not dream of telling colleagues at his day job about his sexual orientation.

The trend, however, is toward greater openness. Like their heterosexual counterparts, gays born during the reform era are more liberated than previous generations and find their non-gay friends more tolerant.

Among the city's small bohemian circle, being gay or experimenting with a same-sex partner has even become trendy. Still, few young people are as willing to cross boundaries as Coco, a 22-year-old musician from Hunan. One of the only openly gay mainlanders in Shanghai, he is not afraid to show off his pierced ears, nose, and tongue or don a dress in a non-gay setting. "I'm able to be open about my homosexuality because I trust myself and I like myself. I believe that if you show people you're a strong person, then they will respect your sexuality," he said in perfect English, his body resting against his Dutch boyfriend. Still, as Coco tries to expand his musical audience beyond a mostly foreign crowd in Shanghai, he finds himself in a quandary: The candor that has defined his public persona could jeopardize his leap into the big time in China. He and potential producers worry that neither the police nor Chinese audiences are ready to accept a new music star whom they know is gay.

The Roots of Openess

Even if China is not yet ready for its version of British pop star Boy George, the fact that the question is broached indicates how much looser Shanghai society is today than at any other time in post-1949 history. What accounts this growing openness? The answer boils down to the fact that the Communist Party no longer constantly peers over Chinese citizens' shoulders to punish them for deviating from social norms. In the prereform era, politics and "collective will" took precedence over everything else, particularly individual happiness. The Party's Communist ideals and totalitarian tentacles reached deep into people's lives, limiting even the most basic freedoms. For instance, without state-provided ration coupons, families could not buy their monthly quota of eggs or other staples. The only way for a person living in a particular city to obtain ration coupons—not to mention a job, home, and medical care—was for the Party to give him *hukou*, or permanent residency, in that city. This policy severely restricted citizens' freedom to move from one city to another. The state assigned everyone a job in a *danwei*—or work unit—whether they wanted that job or not. The work unit then had approval authority over such personal matters as marriage and divorce. If, for instance, the work unit did not approve of a match, the couple did not get married. Work units did not allow couples to wed before the age of 23 and strongly encouraged the generation who returned from the countryside following the 1966–76 Cultural revolution to marry at age 27 or 28. Anyone caught having sexual relations outside of marriage could be arrested, lose his or her job, and be sent to a labor reform prison. For fear of being labeled bourgeois during the Cultural Revolution, citizens had to repress their most mundane desires, like beautifying one's self or gathering a bouquet of fresh flowers.

Getting away with unorthodox behavior was extremely difficult. When not under their work unit's glare, residents had to contend with neighborhood committees, which were responsible for knowing everything that occurred in their jurisdiction. Neighbors were expected to report on each others' behavior, which they could easily discover since families in Shanghai normally lived in sardine-like proximity. Eight families or more might share a single house—in the worst cases separated by no more than a piece of thin plywood. Family members, meanwhile, often lived together in a single room, making individual privacy an unknown luxury, and knocking before entering, an unused politesse. Under such conditions, intimacy as well as unconventional or illegal social activities had little chance to blossom.

During the 1980s and 1990s, much changed. Market-oriented reforms have weakened old systems for controlling lives. Now residents socialize more, they job-hop, and they travel frequently for both business and pleasure, making it easier, for instance, for people to meet and conduct clandestine trysts. Many families have moved out of cramped quarters in Shanghai's *longtang*—or lanes—into larger, modern single family apartments where they do not know or see their neighbors. Couples and single children who have moved into new digs often enjoy a room all to themselves. "Now kids with their own room hang signs on the door: 'Don't enter without invitation,' so you don't know what the kid is doing inside," said, Yang, the SASS professor who studies youth culture. His own son makes him knock upon entering his room and will not let him open his school bag. "He says it's private. I can understand in theory, but it's difficult to carry out in reality. I feel very confused," Yang lamented over lunch near his office.

The state is also no longer able to exert the same control on people as before reform because it no longer satisfies citizens' every material need. Many people now work for nonstate-owned work units and are both emotionally and physically less dependent on the Party. Even for the many who still work at state enterprises, the level of government handouts has dwindled dramatically, leaving them, like the rest of the country, to go to the market for food, homes, jobs, and healthcare. This greater independence makes it unnecessary for people to bend to every Party directive, particularly ones calling for "spiritual civilization." And owing to the abuses of the Cultural Revolution as well as widespread corruption among officials during the reform era, the Party's example no longer encourages people to restrain their behavior.

The Party, for its part, no longer wants to control society so tightly. Unlike Mao Zedong, who required citizens to take his word as truth, Deng Xiaoping told them that practice was the sole criterion for testing theory, making it easier to try new ways. As the Party strives to build "market socialism," it has had to relax its demands over the types of behavior that society will tolerate. It no longer requires citizens to forego simple "bourgeois" pleasures like wearing makeup and buying attractive clothes, but instead views these pursuits as desirable domestic consumption. In fact, China's leadership at the end of the 1990s was doing all it could to encourage people to consume more to boost economic growth.

As the same time, market reforms have helped satisfy many citizens' basic needs for food and shelter, leaving them time and money to pursue new interests. Growing access to information through movies, media, travel, and foreigners during the 1980s and 1990s has made Shanghainese and urbanites throughout the country acutely aware of the possibilities. People expect more out of life, especially young Chinese, who never experienced the social repression of prereform days. The result: Chinese are doing things today that they would not have dreamed of doing 20 or even 10 years ago.

That said, there is still a long way to go before mainlanders can be called a free people, particularly when it comes to political liberty. Although the press prints stories about social issues like divorce and adultery, the Party still strictly controls and censors the media, setting guidelines for the stories covered and messages conveyed. The Party does not tolerate activities that in any way smell of opposition to its rule. Dissidents, labor union activists, underground religious leaders and their practitioners are as harassed as ever. Shanghainese and their fellow citizens face far more difficulty obtaining political freedoms since they require the Party to give up its monopoly on power.

But as China enters the 21st century, Shanghainese in general seem to revel in their newfound freedoms rather than risk demanding those they do not have. For them, the contrast in their lives after 20 years of reform is already as stark as spring after winter.

Notes

[1] Harriet Sergeant, *Shanghai*, Jonathan Cape, London, 1991 p. 3.

[2] After the Opium War of 1840, the British seized a large section of the city that later became known as the International Settlement and the French hoisted their flag over the French Concession.

[3] This excerpt from "All about Shanghai" a standard guidebook 1935 was found in *A Last Look: Western Architecture in Old Shanghai*, Ed. Tess Johnston and Deke Erh; Old China Hand Press, Hong Kong, 1993.

[4] Sergeant, op. cit., p. 73.

[5] Ibid., pp. 116, 118.

[6] Ibid., p. 116.

[7] Betty Peh-T'I Wei, *Shanghai: Crucible of Modern China Hong Kong*, Oxford University Press, 1987, p. 89.

[8] Gail Hershatter, *Dangerous Pleasures: Prostitution and Modernity in Twentieth Century Shanghai*, University of California Press, 1997, p. 39.

[9] Lynn Pan, *Tracing It Home*, Martin Secker & Warburg Ltd., 1992. Excerpted in *Shanghai: Electric and Lurid City*, Ed. Barbara Baker, Oxford University Press, 1998, p. 209.

[10] Sergeant, op. cit., p. 116.

[11] Wei, op. cit., p. 113.

[12] Sergeant, op. cit, p. 174.

[13] Wei, op. cit., p. 102.

[14] Excerpt from Emily Hahn, *Times and Places*, W.H. Allen, London, 1937, found in Barbara Baker, op. cit., p. 156.

[15] Sergeant, op cit. p. 174.

[16] Ibid., p. 174.

[17] Ibid., p. 81.

[18] Ibid., p. 63.

[19] Ibid., p. 31.

[20] Hershatter, op. cit., p. 332.

[21] *Shanghai Star*, Mar. 19, 1999.

[22] *China Daily*, Mar. 3, 1999.

[23] This excerpt was edited slightly to conform to the style of the rest of the book. For example, I've replaced the abbreviation "RMB" that the author used to denote the Chinese currency with "yuan."

[24] *South China Morning Post*, Sept. 28, 1999.

[25] Statistic was provided by Xia Guomei, the researcher at the Shanghai Academy of Social Sciences.

[26] *Shanghai Star*, Jun. 6, 1997.

[27] *Shanghai Star*, Sept. 29, 1998.

[28] *Liberation Daily*, Jan. 26, 1999.

[29] Ibid.

[30] *Shanghai Star*, Jul. 20, 1999.

[31] The company was one of the 130 matchmaking services in Shanghai founded by neighborhood committees, which demonstrated how even the most basic Communist organizations jumped into business in China.

[32] Statistics provided by Yang Xiong, a professor studying youth culture at SASS.

7

Return of the Foreigners

We chose Shanghai over Beijing and Guangzhou for our China headquarters because we look at Shanghai as China's fashion capital. If you want to lead the market, you have to be where the market leader is. So you need to be in Shanghai. Our product is a fashion glamor product. Beijing is very formal and grand, but not glamorous. We need to be in a place that projects glamor. Initially Guangzhou was more open-minded and had more disposable income. Now things are changing very fast. I'm extremely impressed with the speed of improvement in infrastructure here. When I first came here in 1994, I had to rent a mobile phone because waiting for a regular phone line or to buy a mobile phone took six months. Now you don't have to wait for a phone line and it's no problem to buy a mobile phone. It used to take me an hour and a half to get to the Hongqiao Airport from the Hilton Hotel. Now it takes me half an hour at most. We feel well-supported here in terms of infrastructure. Also, in Shanghai, there are mounds of talent. Many applicants come in with foreign company experience already. It has not been that hard for people to accept new ways. People are very receptive. You can mold them.

> —Cecilia Yang, vice president of sales and marketing at Mary Kay Cosmetics in Shanghai, about Shanghai as a site for a China headquarters (1997).

The American market research firm we hired told us we'd be operating at 50% capacity in a year. In reality, we did less than 4% of capacity during that first year. The research firm identified all the state enterprises that used our piece of equipment. It looked huge. To this day we may have 2% of them. Why? Because these customers do not care about quality, they don't have any money, and they don't care about value-added services. Our competitors are state enterprises that have a 50-year history with our potential customers. The joint venture lost

US$2 million during the first year. What is really funny is that before I came to China in 1993, my CEO said to me: 'Jack, it's going to be like post-war Germany over there. Customers are going to be knocking down your doors.' Well, no one knocked on our doors.

> —The American general manager of a European toolmaker's Shanghai manufacturing venture, about difficulties of making money selling to China (1997).[1]

These two quotes pretty much sum up for me the general experience of foreign companies in Shanghai. On the one hand, Shanghai has once again become a magnet for foreign investors. Executives, like Mary Kay's marketing manager Cecelia Yang, like what the city offers, starting with a population exceeding 14 million people[2] and one of the highest per-capita household incomes in China. Located at the mouth of the Yangtze River, it is also a natural gateway to the Chinese interior and, in particular, to the adjacent provinces of Jiangsu, Zhejiang, and Anhui. Multinationals setting up in Shanghai subsequently have roughly 17% of China's population within close proximity. As a traditional manufacturing base with some of the best universities in the country, moreover, Shanghai offers a relatively large pool of skilled labor. Foreign companies also like the Chinese leadership's support for the city's reemergence as an international commercial center. That means, for instance, that market-oriented experiments, such as allowing foreigners to participate in sectors like retail, trading, insurance, and finance, often take place in Shanghai before being implemented elsewhere. And like Cecelia Yang, foreign managers are impressed by the city's extensive efforts to improve its infrastructure and its more sophisticated business environment than most other Chinese cities.

But if Shanghai has become an important base for foreign multinationals in China, conversations with foreign executives, like the general manager at the toolmaking venture, make clear another equally important trend. Shanghai, and China in general, has not turned out to be as easy a place to make money as many foreign investors expected. The mad investment rush of the first half of the decade evolved in the second half into a period of reassessment, restructuring, and cost-cutting. The experiences of foreign investors in Shanghai demonstrate the progress the city has made and the challenges it faces in building on its bricks-and-mortar accomplishments to become an easy and attractive place to do business in all respects.

Shanghai's Comeback

Nearly 50% of total foreign investment in China was concentrated in Shanghai before the Communist Revolution.[3] But despite the city's pre-1949 history as the primary hub for foreign business in China, Shanghai got off to a slow start attracting overseas investors in the reform era. After Deng Xiaoping opened China's doors to foreign investment in the late 1970s and early 1980s, Guangdong province was by far the more popular investment site, absorbing some US$12.2 billion in contracted investment between 1983 and 1989, compared with Shanghai's US$2.66 billion.[4] Deng chose the southern province bordering on Hong Kong for most of his initial experiments with economic reform, including the establishment of three of the country's five special economic zones offering special privileges to foreign investors. Shanghai, meanwhile, was hampered by aging infrastructure and a left-leaning bureaucracy with a reputation within China for making investors' lives difficult. Companies hoping to do a project in the city reported needing to get stamps of approval or "chops" from more than 100 local government bureaus. It was not until the central government appointed Zhu Rongji, a hard-headed, practical technocrat originally from Hunan province, as Shanghai's mayor in 1988, that multinationals felt the city move in the right direction. Zhu set up a "one-chop stop," which put the Shanghai Foreign Investment Commission in charge of coordinating the project approval process for foreign firms. Before heading up to Beijing in 1991 to become the country's vice premier, Zhu also established a mayor's advisory council that asked the heads of major foreign multinational companies to meet with Shanghai's mayor once a year to discuss a specific topic relevant to the city's development. According to Norman Givant, co-head of the China practice for British law firm Freshfields and president of Shanghai's American Chamber of Commerce for five years, the meetings brought a ray of reality into government deliberations. "Even if the suggestions were not adopted wholesale, the ideas were at least presented for discussion and that was a big improvement," he said.

In early 1992, after Deng Xiaoping restarted China on the road to fast-paced growth, foreign investors poured into China like never before. Many of them have placed their bets for the future on Shanghai, which in 1990 became the focus of the country's development strategy and the recipient of a slew of preferential policies, including a huge special economic zone in Pudong. Through the end of 1998, foreign investors injected a cumulative

US$34 billion in actual investment capital into 17,622 projects.[5] Hong Kong and other overseas Chinese have led the charge, throwing their money mostly into property development and other service-related projects. Multinationals from the United States, Japan, and Europe have set up marketing and sales offices, retail operations, and manufacturing facilities. Shanghai has benefited greatly from the central government's decision to channel key foreign manufacturing projects to the city, including General Motor's US$1.52 billion venture in 1997 to make Buicks and steel-maker Krupps' US$1.3 billion investment in 1998. By 1999, the city could boast that 59 of the world's leading companies had a presence there, including GM, NEC, Philips, and GE. The greatest spurt of foreign interest came in the middle years of the decade, before difficulties making money and the Asian Financial Crisis of 1997–1999 damped investors' ardor for China in general.

Shanghai's popularity among foreign investors and central government directives have led local officials to be picky about the types of investment and kinds of companies the city approves to invest. Shanghai, with its close relationship to Beijing, tends to implement central government policies more thoroughly than many other parts of the country and the central government's moves starting in the mid-1990s to tighten entry terms for foreign firms are no different. Flush with foreign investment dollars and a belief that China's vast potential market was enough to attract foreign companies, the central leadership began withdrawing foreign investment incentives and aggressively channeling funds toward specific sectors. It also launched a campaign to protect domestic brands and reform state enterprises. The Shanghai authorities were subsequently less inclined to approve wholly foreign-owned projects than parts of the country hungrier for foreign investment, although that bias has abated as a result of the slide in foreign investment inflows in the late 1990s. Shanghai bureaucrats also take a less-flexible approach when approving contracts like technical licensing agreements. "Shanghai's behavior reflects an increasingly conservative policy at the national level," said Givant, the Freshfields lawyer, in January 2000. "Let us not forget that Shanghai is run directly by Beijing. Major officials are appointees under Beijing's direct leadership and are therefore sensitive to shifts in Beijing's policies. Also, Shanghai, as the premier commercial center of China, feels it can be more selective and demanding."

The city wants to attract big multinationals in clean, efficient, high-value-added industries like bio-tech, automotive, and microelectronics—not labor-intensive, low-value-added businesses. Local authorities tend to snub their noses at projects worth less than US$20–US$30 million and prefer to deal with Fortune 500 companies. Shanghai's Pudong New Area, particularly its Jinqiao Export Processing Zone, has developed a reputation with investors for arrogance and charging high prices. Smaller companies and companies making relatively minor investments often find less-privileged cities in Jiangsu and Zhejiang more welcoming, more flexible, and less expensive in terms of labor and land. As a result, Shanghai has lost some manufacturing investment that otherwise might have found a home there. When US-based AMD Group, for instance, was searching China in the mid-1990s to find a location to set up a facility for assembling and testing integrated circuits, it considered 12 Chinese cities. For various reasons, it chose the city of Suzhou—an hour's drive from Shanghai. Discussing the attitude of Shanghai's investment authorities, Don Brettner, AMD vice president, commented: "Companies like Intel and Motorola make a big splash in Shanghai. Now we got the attention we needed there, but no one made an attempt to make sure you invested. In Xiamen, Tianjin, and Suzhou, we were romanced. In Shanghai we were not romanced."

That said, foreign firms that set up some or all of their China operations in Shanghai generally seem pleased with their choice. Foreigners who work in Shanghai or often travel there for business regularly mention how officials in Shanghai are more sophisticated than their counterparts in inland provinces—a situation they attribute to the quality of the personnel appointed and their greater exposure to foreign investors. According to Freshfields' Givant, "There's been an attempt to bring qualified, well-educated, technically savvy people into the bureaucracy—not just at the mayor and vice mayor level, but we're also seeing a gradual shift in the bureaucracy and state-owned enterprises." This sophistication is apparent when it comes to negotiating deals. Howard Chao, a Shanghai-based partner with American law firm O'Melveny & Myers, commented at the end of 1999:

Shanghai is China's most developed city in many senses. It has sophisticated people in government and business who have done lots of deals with foreigners, especially compared to the hinterlands. It's not uncommon for your Chinese partners here to have already done 10 deals with foreigners, so you don't run into people who don't understand how international-style contracts work. In smaller places, it may be their first international contract so they're afraid to make mistakes. In Guangdong, where they've done a lot of joint ventures with Hong Kong Chinese, they have less patience with real multinational corporations who do things by the books.

Not that negotiating a deal with the Shanghainese is easy. The Shanghainese take negotiating contracts seriously, responding to an initial draft with maybe 60 comments, said Chao. In other parts of the country, particularly the North, people are more likely to try to agree on a basic framework and leave the details for later. Talks might finish in a day or two, but issues not considered during those talks crop up in the implementation phase. Negotiations in Shanghai are also arduous because the Shanghainese are sticklers on price. They use Shanghai's status as China's anointed commercial capital and multinational firms' desire to be based there to their full advantage in contract talks. William Hanbury Tenison, who moved to Shanghai in the early 1990s as Jardine Matheison's chief representative, commented in 1999: "The Shanghainese do count. They know the numbers. They know what you're making out of it. They know that you want a deal in Shanghai, so they try to get more. In the 1990s, the Shanghainese could depend on foreigners wanting a reference project in Shanghai."

Western investors also often comment that Shanghai authorities follow the rules compared with Chinese officials in the provinces, particularly in southern China. Whereas officials in Guangdong and the Shenzhen special economic zone, for instance, often interpret regulations flexibly, their Shanghai counterparts are less likely to let firms cut corners. As a result, companies hoping for a concession or an informal arrangement are best off locating elsewhere. While some managers complain that this inflexibility makes life more difficult, most executives at multinationals say they prefer it to the alternative because it makes their operating environment more predictable. They also find Shanghai to be a relatively ethical place to do business, particularly compared with southern China. Paul Stepanek, the general manager of Jason Precision Components, a Nasdaq-listed American firm, spoke about his company's experiences in Shenzhen and Shanghai. In 1999, he recounted:

We started making components for videocassettes in Shenzhen in 1994. In Shenzhen, there's much more of a cowboy mentality. Everything is negotiable, from taxes to customs clearance. We officially registered our Shanghai factory, which makes starters for gasoline engines, in September 1998. The whole regulatory process, including building up the business and getting documents in line, was very much more by the book. In Shenzhen, for example, the authorities, to make their area more competitive, let you do this thing called *zhuan chang* or factory transfer, which allows a company to import a material duty-free, process it, then sell it to another company for assembly and export. However, according to Chinese law this is not allowed and, in Shanghai, you can't do it. You can only import duty-free if you import the material, process it, and export it yourself. In Shenzhen, the authorities are very pragmatic when applying laws and try to get away with as much as they can. In Shanghai, they enforce the laws more to the letter. Being able to do "factory transfer" in Shenzhen is great for us and the price of manufacturing is more in Shanghai than in Shenzhen at present. But the Shenzhen authorities have been talking about actually implementing the law for five years, and one of these years the directive is going to stick. So we're living with more uncertainty in Shenzhen than Shanghai. Also as a businessman, it doesn't matter if they charge 1000% duty as long as all my competitors all pay tax at the same rate. They key question is whether the referees are applying the rules to everyone in the same manner. In Shenzhen, a few areas are enforcing the law, but others aren't.

Western executives also find some of the tedious aspects of doing business in China, such as paying taxes, easier in Shanghai, mostly because the bureaucracy has more experience dealing with foreign firms than in less-popular investment spots. They also praise the Shanghai authorities for implementing directives aimed at streamlining bureaucratic procedures for things like project approvals and annual business license renewals. Xavier Naville, a Shanghai-based French executive at international food caterer Creative Food Technologies, for instance, finds the annual license renewal process in Shanghai much easier than in Beijing. In 1999, he commented:

When you want to get your business license renewed in Beijing, you have to go to each individual ministry: fire, environment, customs, etc., to get their approval. That means we have to hire consultants with the right contacts to visit each ministry for us. Some companies have hired people specifically dedicated to doing this. In Shanghai, we give all our documents ourselves to a government coordination center, which handles everything with the different bureaus. In our experience, the Shanghai government's administration is excellent compared to Beijing.

This is not to say that dealing with the Shanghai bureaucracy is seamless, particularly at the middle and lower levels where officials are less educated. Like anywhere in China, the city's personnel department appoints bureaucrats for their loyalty more than for their strong functional background. Also, the country's education system does not train people in reflective thought but instead in memorizing and following the leader. Once in the system, a bureaucrat can be severely sanctioned for taking initiative that leads to "mistakes." As a result, when bureaucrats confront problems that they do not fully comprehend, their natural instinct is to take a conservative approach. Freshfields' Givant, for instance, regularly runs into problems registering mortgages for loans for financial service clients because officials in the bureaus still do not understand the underlying function of mortgages and are afraid of taking actions that might subject them to criticism from their superiors.

Also, a complicated apparatus remains in place in Shanghai, and all around China, to control and monitor foreign investment. Projects still need multiple approvals, even though the Shanghai Foreign Investment Commission, the "one-chop shop," coordinates the approval process so that firms officially do not have to interface with as many government bureaus. The project vetting process within the bureaucracy is as elaborate and thorough as ever. As a result, foreign investors hoping to move their project's approval smoothly through the bureaucracy are well advised to meet with various bureau officials to ensure their cooperation. And it still normally takes a long time to get that final chop. "The project approval process has gotten somewhat easier," said Freshfields' Givant, who has worked in Shanghai since the mid-1980s. "But 15 years down the road, the speed of getting projects approved has improved just marginally."

Connections still count for a lot in Shanghai, and Shanghainese working for foreign companies often find themselves pulling strings and relying on personal relationships within the city's bureaucracy to expedite matters for their company. "In Shanghai, you have to find friends in the bureaucracy who will tell you the short way to get what you want. If you don't have friends, people will give you a hard time and you'll have to achieve your objective the regular way, which can take a long time," commented a middle-aged Shanghainese manager with a European multinational. And some foreign executives have run into corruption. The 35-year-old American general manager of a German distribution company, for instance, vividly recalled a 1996 meeting in one of the majestic neoclassical buildings along the Bund, during which a department manager at a Chinese state-owned trading corporation offered to smuggle in the German firm's wares. At the meeting, the Chinese manager calculated for the American how much it would cost the company to import certain computer products into Shanghai at the official 33% tariff. Noticing the look of dismay on the American's face, the official invited the executive to follow him to the building's lobby. Once there, he explained *sotto voce* that there was a way to pay less than half the official tariff. Should regulators audit the German company's Shanghai office, the trading corporation official could provide fake documentation. The American did not take him up on the offer, but feels that it is impossible to succeed in China without partaking in illegal arrangements from time to time.

Still, when asked to compare Shanghai with other investment sites in China, foreign executives find the city to be a less corrupt, more predictable, and in many cases, more cosmopolitan place to conduct business. They are also generally pleased with the quality of personnel they have hired there compared with most elsewhere in China. Although foreign firms endure the same problems finding seasoned financial controllers, marketing managers, and experienced executive secretaries, they are impressed with residents' technical skills. "Give them the tools and they are as good as anyone," said Ashley Steinhausen, the Shanghai-based director of Allied Professional Services, which recruits talent for high-tech multinationals. Western executives find Shanghai's young people eager to learn, ambitious, and pragmatic, making Shanghai a relatively good place to build a team in China. According to Troy Shortell, the Hong-Kong based regional marketing manager for Danish logistics company East Asiatic Co., whose company has offices in Shanghai, Guangzhou, and Beijing, young Shanghainese are more trainable than their Beijing counterparts, who tend to be stubborn and less motivated. At the same time they are more dependable than their colleagues in southern China, who, though highly trainable, are notorious for job-hopping.

What foreign managers do not find often is an entrepreneurial streak—despite Shanghai's reputation, dating from the pre-1949 period, for producing China's greatest entrepreneurs. Creative Food Technologies, for instance, wanted to set up a franchise-type agreement with a Chinese company in Shanghai. The Chinese firm would be expected to build a catering business to a certain size, at which point Creative Food Technologies would offer the entrepreneur a compensation fee for his efforts based on the value of the company he had created. The firm advertised for the position in Shanghai, but when candidates saw the contract they said it was too risky. "We got much more response in other places. We found that even people in Beijing are more entrepreneurial. In Shanghai, we ended up having to buy out some existing caterers instead of going ahead with our original plan," said Naville. Multinational executives also run into problems when posting their Shanghai staff elsewhere in China. Most Shanghainese believe Shanghai is far superior to other Chinese cities and their haughty behavior towards non-Shanghainese has earned them a reputation for arrogance. Naville commented: "Shanghainese don't want to leave Shanghai. They don't like to travel to other places in China. They don't look at it as an adventure. They get homesick. If I send them to Beijing, they piss everyone off."

Part of the reason that Shanghainese generally prefer not to live elsewhere in China is that living conditions in their city are better. Foreign managers in China are also coming to that conclusion. This was not always the case. Through the 1970s, 1980s, and much of the 1990s, Beijing had more infrastructure in place for foreign expatriates. Not only was it the home of China's largest diplomatic community, but many multinational corporations set up there first offices there, particularly if good relations with central government authorities were crucial to their business. Although Beijing is still home to the mainland's largest population of foreigners, Shanghai has in many ways become a nicer place for Western expatriates to live. Even before the central government decided to rebuild Shanghai in the early 1990s, the city had a certain allure for Westerners because of its pre-1949 colonial history and its European-style streets and architecture. Many Westerners automatically feel more at home in this environment compared with Beijing's imperial, Soviet, and traditional Chinese atmosphere. This allure has since magnified thanks to the better job that the Shanghai government has done managing the city's urban environment than the local Beijing government. Although air pollution is still a serious problem for Shanghai, it has improved somewhat as a result of the municipal government's efforts to shut down or move out polluting factories. Air pollution in Beijing, on the other hand, is as bad as ever or worse, thanks to a combination of coal soot, auto exhaust, factory emissions, and construction dust. Likewise, Western executives regularly complain about horrendous traffic in Beijing, whereas Shanghai's Herculean efforts to construct elevated highways, tunnels, and other transportation infrastructure during the 1990s has resulted in much smoother traffic flows. A deluge of foreign investment in apartments, shops, malls, restaurants, bars, cafes, nightclubs, and golf courses in Shanghai have made expatriate social life much more varied than it was earlier in the decade. Although Beijing's arts scene is more lively than Shanghai's, cultural life in Shanghai has improved. For instance, big international troupes that used to bypass Shanghai during China tours for lack of an appropriate performance venue now regularly include a stop at the city's newly constructed Grand Theater. Shanghai is not an oasis of Chinese or Western culture, but it is no longer a desert either.

China Headquarters?

Multinationals tend to view Shanghai as a good sales and marketing base in China. In 1998, Michael Enright, a former Harvard Business School professor now at Hong Kong University, conducted a survey that queried multinationals on how Shanghai fit into multinational corporations' Asia-Pacific operations. Enright sent a detailed set of questions about Shanghai to executives posted in Shanghai and a somewhat less-detailed questionnaire to executives elsewhere. The 80 respondents to this section of the survey were multinationals across industries, employing some 25,000 people in Shanghai. A third of the firms manufacture in Shanghai, while most have set up service operations, a sales office for a manufacturing company, or a representative office for a financial services company. Roughly 85% of the multinationals queried in 1998 said that their Shanghai operations are important to their corporation for sales and marketing purposes to the exclusion of everything else. While some of these companies set up in Shanghai to penetrate China as a whole, most use it to sell to Shanghai or the Yangtze River Delta and east China. They have offices in other parts of the country to manage sales and marketing for other regions. That said, they all expect their Shanghai office to be significantly more important to their corporation in five to seven years.

For multinationals, Shanghai today is more often a center for east China than a headquarters driving all of their China operations. However, the city's huge market, strategic location, large talent pool, infrastructure improvements, growing sophistication, and privileged status in China will inevitably lead more multinationals in the future to locate their China or Greater China headquarters there, moving those operations out of their home office, Hong Kong, or even Beijing. Consumer product companies such as Mary Kay, Carrefour, and Henkel, as well as financial service firms like Standard Chartered Bank are among the multinationals that have chosen to put their China headquarters in Shanghai. Companies in industries like telecommunications, information systems, and infrastructure still gravitate toward Beijing, however, since strong relationships with the central government are paramount to success in those industries in China. As China's economy becomes more market-oriented in the 21st century and Shanghai outpaces Beijing in creating a better environment for multinationals and expatriates, Shanghai should attract the largest proportion of multinationals setting up China or Greater China headquarters.

Asia-Pacific Headquarters?

If Shanghai's reemergence as China's most important center for foreign business seems predestined, its future as the most popular place for multinational corporations to locate their Asia-Pacific headquarters is less clear. Some multinationals do foresee locating their Asia hub in China, and Shanghai will undoubtedly lure some of that business. According to a 1999 poll conducted by the Hong Kong Chamber of Commerce, 12 out of 295 respondents with headquarters in Hong Kong chose China as their first choice for a regional command center. In January 2000, French telecommunications giant Alcatel announced it was moving its Asia-Pacific headquarters from Paris to Shanghai to be close to its largest pool of customers in the region. However, the results of Enright's 1998 survey, called "City Centers of Asia/Pacific," suggest that the trend is at best a trickle. The survey's results, based on roughly 1,000 responses from executives as well as one-on-one interviews, reveal scant interest among multinationals in moving their Asia headquarters to Shanghai. The reasons are manifold, having to do more with general China issues than Shanghai-specific problems. Companies cite China's unstable political system, half-open economy, myriad restrictions on doing business, and lack of free-flowing information. They also feel uneasy about locating sensitive documents in a city with an immature legal system and a national government hypersensitive to national security risks. Indeed, they wonder if they will have total control of their records or if the authorities will do things with them without their consent. The lack of free and easy access to Shanghai for some employees based in the region is also a hindrance. If a corporate emergency occurs, for instance, and headquarters want employees from around the region to arrive in Shanghai immediately, it might not be able to get people there from Taiwan and the Philippines quickly enough for political reasons. The Philippines and China could be in conflict at the time over the Spratly Islands, or China might once again be threatening to bomb Taiwan. Shanghai, moreover, still lacks the high-quality local management and support staff necessary to run regional operations. Multinational managers often find themselves spending significant time supporting their secretary in Shanghai—not the other way around. The immaturity of China's banking system, meanwhile, makes it unsafe to close large international deals in Shanghai—a key requirement for an international business center. Howard Chao, the Shanghai-based lawyer with O'Melveny & Myers, commented:

How many really big closings have I had in Shanghai? Zilch. The concept of a closing is alien to China except where you have to have it—like if you buy a house here, you have to have a closing here. But if you have your druthers, you always have your closings in New York or Hong Kong, because at a closing you have to transfer large sums of money, usually U.S. or Hong Kong dollars, effectively, quickly, and reliably. You need to time these things so that they can happen simultaneously, but none of these things can happen in China. You can't call the Shanghai Branch of the Bank of Communications and ask them to immediately wire dollars to the Bank of China branch because foreign exchange is highly regulated here. To do a closing, you often need an escrow agreement, but Chinese banks don't have escrow departments yet. Also, many things, like transferring equity in a joint venture, are contingent on government approval here. So basically lots of tools used in a closing are not available in Shanghai. The reliability of the banking system is crucial because we're talking about a lot of money. If you lose US$200 million for two days in the banking system then you've lost a lot of interest. During a corporate closing in Hong Kong money is transferred instantly. Can Shanghai match Hong Kong? Anyone who asks that doesn't really understand what Hong Kong does and what Shanghai is like today. Shanghai is not yet a good place to do business for matters that do not involve China. In terms of being a true regional center, it's not enough to spend money on hardware, like new bridges, fiberoptics, phone systems, and great office buildings. That's not how it works.

Although not as critical for Shanghai to achieve its regional aspirations, quality-of-life issues also still hold the city back. Despite the progress made, Shanghai on a number of lifestyle fronts still has a long way to go to catch up with Hong Kong and Singapore, its most serious rivals at the end of the 1990s. For instance, although Shanghai hospitals offer some of the best healthcare available in the country and the local government has allowed a few clinics catering to foreigners to set up in Shanghai, the level of care is still inadequate. Most Western expatriates opt to have serious ailments treated outside of China. If they do not return to their home country for treatment, they often choose Hong Kong or Singapore. The government has been reluctant to open up China's heavily subsidized hospital industry to foreign investment and, as a result, the sector has been slow to reform and improve. Another lifestyle drawback for Western expatriates is limited access to nature—a day on a golf course is the closest one gets within an hour's drive to a large open green space. My husband and I remember well what a liberating feeling it was just to step onto a fairway after living in Shanghai for almost a year—so used had we become to spending our life surrounded by buildings. Of course, the city has some parks, but they tend to be small, crowded plots of land made up of concrete walkways surrounded by trees rather than expansive lawns. Walks in the woods, sailing on the sea, and cycling through scenic, uncongested vistas are not part of weekend life in Shanghai, where urban sprawl stretches far beyond the city limits. A cruise down the Huangpu River, the body of water that flows past Shanghai's famous Bund into the mighty Yangtze River, brings views of one grimy factory after another. Sporty outdoor leisure activities generally are not available without hopping on a plane or driving for more than an hour. Few expatriate residents dare jog outdoors due to the city's poor air quality, exercising instead in indoor gyms. Both Hong Kong, with its miles of mountain hiking trails and ocean, and Singapore, with its huge rolling parks for cycling and jogging, offer far more outdoor sporting and nature activities.

This is not to say that situation is not improving in Shanghai. Thanks to government spending on new highways in and out of Shanghai, escaping the city for greener climes has become easier. The municipal government has constructed a new park, known as Central Park, on the Pudong side of the Huangpu River and has spruced up older parks, in part by replacing the high concrete walls surrounding them with iron grating. It has also encouraged property developers to turn undeveloped plots temporarily into green space. But while these and other measures make the city feel more green, it does not resolve residents' isolation from nature. Having grown up without it, most Shanghainese do not seem to notice, but most Western expatriates do. Simon Lichtenberg, a Danish entrepreneur with a Shanghainese wife, for instance, has few regrets about spending most of his future life in Shanghai except for the city's lack of nature. "Now I was not born in the countryside, but I always walk in the forest in Denmark. I like to watch birds. Nature is what I miss most in Shanghai. To get to it, you have to go far away," he explained. While quality of life does not determine whether a city becomes a company's Asia-Pacific command center, regional managers who have to move their families there do consider the issue after more important criteria have been fulfilled.

China's embrace of market economics—no matter how plodding at times—makes most foreign executives optimistic that Shanghai will eventually achieve a level of regulatory openness, rule of law, banking system maturity, information exchange, staff capability, and quality of life comparable with Hong Kong or Singapore. They differ, however, on how long that will take, with the most starry-eyed predicting five to 10 years and others forecasting 20, 30, 40, or 50. The question of timing is an extremely tricky one. In some ways, the pace of change in Shanghai has met or exceeded expectations, particularly when it comes to erecting new infrastructure. Few foreign executives, for instance, would have imagined in the early years of the decade that they would be able to travel in 1999 from Pudong to the Hongqiao airport on the opposite end of town in less than 30 minutes, but that is exactly what they are able to do. In other ways, the pace of change has disappointed or is not as much as meets the eye. While China has made progress reforming its civil and commercial legal systems during the decade, foreign businesses still face tremendous obstacles resolving commercial disputes. The Communist Party continues to see law as a tool for maintaining power and achieving its ends, rather than as an arbiter of impartial justice. Dawdling deregulation in the securities industry means that foreign securities firms do far less business in Shanghai than they expected in the first half of the 1990s. Builders in Shanghai might put up a three-bedroom house with a swimming pool for expatriates, but the quality is often far below international standards and Western expectations. "What's not there yet is the software—an understanding of the expectations of Western companies and how business operates internationally. If the service doesn't match the hardware, then it can't work," said the Shanghai-based managing director of an international property consultant in late 1999. "I can't see Shanghai becoming a regional headquarters for 20–30 years." (Like many foreign executives in Shanghai, he spoke only on condition of anonymity for fear of offending Shanghai officialdom and causing problems for his company.)

China's entry into the World Trade Organization is undoubtedly a step in the right direction for Shanghai's aspirations as an Asian headquarters since it will accelerate the opening of new markets, force state enterprises to compete and reform, increase transparency in the regulatory system, and encourage other improvements in the city's software. Still, there are indications after China signed a WTO accession agreement with the United States in November 1999 that the Chinese will drag their feet in implementing some of the changes and try to erect various non-tariff barriers similar to those erected in Japan.[6] As a result, gauging the impact of China's entry into the trade body on the city is not straightforward. Without political reform in China, Shanghai's ability to catch up with Hong Kong in terms of rule of law, free information flows, and decision-making autonomy is also problematic. At the start of the 21st century, highly controversial political reform is on the back burner while an insecure central leadership does all it can to quell dissent and ward off threats to its power. Only a soothsayer can predict when the climate will become more favorable. Still, many foreign executives anticipate that the changes needed in Shanghai will eventually occur, which is why they are optimistic for Shanghai's resurgence to the level of a Hong Kong or Singapore, if not in the near term, at least in the long term.

Some observers contend that Shanghai ultimately has a huge advantage over Hong Kong and Singapore in the competition to attract headquarters for multinationals in the Asia-Pacific region. The reason: lower costs combined with the potential size of the China market. As China becomes a significant percentage of multinationals' Asia-Pacific revenues, the argument goes, companies will move their regional headquarters to China, and as the government's role in business recedes, they'll increasingly choose Shanghai over Beijing. But while the argument holds for China headquarters and even Greater China headquarters, the size of China's market ironically could prove a reason why many multinationals do not move their regional headquarters to Shanghai. The companies queried in Enright's 1998 survey, "City Centers of Asia/Pacific," are concerned that a regional executive posted in Shanghai will inadvertently dedicate his or her time to China rather than to the region because China itself is such a time-consuming market. According to Enright, Shanghai is more likely to go the way of Tokyo rather than the way of Hong Kong or Singapore. He said:

Marketing and sales operations, manufacturing operations, and a certain amount of logistics will occur in Shanghai, but it's unlikely that Asia/Pacific management and coordination activities, which now take place in Hong Kong and Singapore, will move to Shanghai. For political reasons, to show support for the mainland, a few companies have moved a regional manager to Shanghai, but if you look at the staff functions for regional activities, they have not moved. The only companies that can move from Hong Kong to Shanghai are those for whom the mainland is their primary business in Asia and Hong Kong and Taiwan are add-ons.

What Return on Investment?

Despite Shanghai's progress in making itself attractive to multinationals, making money in the China market has come no more easily for firms based there than for those located elsewhere in the country. Multinationals' expectations of how quickly they can make their operations break even on an annual operating basis and earn a return on their total investment have often been disappointed. In Shanghai and around China, foreign investors have been hurt by severe competition, ineffectual or uncooperative joint-venture partners, troublesome and anticompetitive regulations, and their own overoptimistic assessments of the size of the market. In many cases, the joint ventures they scrambled to set up with Chinese partners in the late 1980s and early 1990s have cost more than anticipated and carved out a smaller-than-expected market share. Profitability has been elusive. According to the official news agency Xinhua, almost 50% of all foreign ventures in Shanghai lost money in 1998, with their losses totaling 3.9 billion yuan (US$470 million). The figures mirror nationwide trends. When A.T. Kearney/Economist Intelligence Unit (EIU) surveyed 70 managers at multinational companies operating in China in 1998, only 40% said they were profitable. The rest were either just breaking even or losing money. More than a third did not expect results through 2001 to meet their original expectations.[7]

Many investors have only themselves to blame. Delirious with visions of China's immense potential, they rushed into Shanghai and other cities without always knowing their market or their partners. Wilfried Vanhonacker, a professor at China Europe International Business School (CEIBS) in Shanghai, commented in late 1997: "People are not very happy. Foreign companies were a little naïve about China." This is not to say that things have not worked out as planned for some companies or that many are not building businesses that will ultimately be successful. Moreover, some companies planned not to make money for an extended period, say five years, as part of a strategy of grabbing market share. But the story of the 1990s for foreign investors in Shanghai and around China has been one of unforeseen troubles that have made it difficult to meet goals laid out in their original feasibility studies. Said Billy Hsieh, a tax partner at Price Waterhouse in Shanghai, in 1997: "Compared to people intentionally making losses to get market share, we've seen more people push back breakeven because the market turned out to be more difficult than anticipated." A Shanghai-based lawyer with a British law firm added: "People are realizing that they are not making enough money in China. I'm seeing clients that after 10 years are not making a profit on some or all of their joint ventures." As a result, many multinationals in Shanghai and around China started reassessing and reorganizing their China operations in the late 1990s. John Hutton, a Shanghai-based audit partner at PricewaterhouseCoopers, commented in November 1999: "Multinationals still look at China as an opportunity, but not as the gold mine or easy pickings they thought it was going to be."

What happened? For one, during the 1990s Shanghai, and China in general, became one of the most competitive markets in the world. In 1992, after Deng Xiaoping signaled an end to the tight credit policies hobbling the Chinese economy, both foreign and domestic investors streamed into a wide array of industries. Shanghai, with its preferential government policies, educated workforce, large market, and strategic location, was a particularly strong draw. The result of all this investment: overcapacities and fierce competition across many industries. By the mid-1990s, for instance, China boasted roughly 1,500 foreign pharmaceutical joint ventures and an even greater number of domestic drug-makers. Said Vanhonacker: "There is no market in the world that is more competitive than China. Over a very short time span, companies looked at an opportunity and did not realize how many others were looking at the same opportunity. Multinational corporations had a short window to seize an opportunity. As soon as others saw you were doing well, they jumped in." This situation led Cecilia Yang, the Mary Kay cosmetics official, to comment: "Shanghai is a tough place to be in a glamor business because every other foreign company is thinking the same way. Name one brand that you know that is not in Shanghai."

The Retail Rush

Shanghai's retail sector illustrates the point particularly well. Because of Shanghai's reputation for setting fashion trends in China as well as the preferential policies that made Shanghai one of the earliest cities in China to open its retail sector to foreign investors, retailers started flocking to the city in the mid-1990s. The conventional wisdom was that if a brand could make it in Shanghai, it could make it anywhere in China. Moreover, Shanghai, with its 14-million-plus population, already boasted one of the highest per-capita annual incomes in China—7,196 yuan (US$869) in 1995. Its retail sales, which ranked first in the country, were surging more than 20% a year. That was bait enough for foreign and domestic investors, who built more than 70 large shopping centers and plowed 40 billion yuan (US$4.8 billion) into retail space by the beginning of 1998. Beauty salons, wedding shops, supermarkets, brand-name boutiques, and upscale department stores soon crowded the city's major thoroughfares. When Hong Kong businessman Richard Lai set up one of Shanghai's first upscale beauty salons on fashionable Maoming Road in 1991, he raked in 100,000 yuan (US$12,000) in sales a month and experienced annual sales growth of 20% a year. By 1996, however, sales were flat or declining—a situation that he attributed to excessive competition. He said:

Since I arrived, between 100 and 200 sizable salons offering good service have set up. Maybe 20% of my competitors are from Hong Kong and Taiwan but the rest are from southern China. The market is becoming really saturated and yet people are still coming in. No one thought the market would develop so quickly. This is not an easy market—not at all.

Or take department stores. They popped up in the city at a rate of one a month between 1994 and 1996, including 15 new foreign joint ventures. Most of the foreign-invested projects have been vying for the same top 5%–10% of the city's consumers, often offering the same mid-high to high-priced designer dresses, shoes, and imported perfumes. Japanese retailer Isetan, for instance, did a booming business when it first opened its store on Shanghai's fashionable Huaihai Road in 1993, pulling in more than 250 million yuan (US$30 million) in sales annually. But by the second half of the decade, sales growth had slowed to single digits and the company's second and much larger store on Nanjing Road, which opened its doors in 1997, was looking forward to lean years. At the end of 1997, Akiyoshi Ikeda, the general manager of Isetan's flagship Huaihai Road store, admitted that consumers in Shanghai had a hard time differentiating one foreign-invested department store from the next and lamented the oversupply in his sector. "About 5% of 14 million people can afford the prices at our department store. Now there are 22 department stores going after this market. According to international standards, one department store should serve 200,000 people. But here you have 22 stores chasing only 700,000 people!" he exclaimed.

At the same time, retailers have overestimated the actual size of the market and its rate of growth. They did not anticipate the slump in consumer demand that occurred during the last few years of the decade as the Chinese economy slowed, layoffs picked up, and government policies forced citizens to pay more for big-ticket items like housing, schooling, and medical care. In some cases, the location retailers chose for their store did not turn into a popular shopping district as quickly as expected. Raymond Ngoh, a manager at Shanghai Shui Hing, a Hong Kong-invested department store, talked to me in 1996 about the difficulties the department store was facing. He said:

People's spending power is not up to our expectations. There's big gap between our projected sales and the present situation. We based those projections on population statistics and income per family. Now sales are off by more than half of what we predicted in our feasibility study. We don't understand how the Chinese collect statistics. And there's just been too much competition over a short time frame. Now the economy is slowing down. Consumer spending habits are changing. They're spending less on consumer products and more on other sectors, like insurance and housing—things that they didn't have to worry about before. Stores are offering very aggressive promotions to attract customers. Expenses for the store are up because wages are growing 10% a year. Margins are being squeezed.

Under such conditions, only the retailers with the strongest strategies, best locations, lowest overheads, or deepest pockets have survived and prospered. Shui Hing is not one of them. It pulled out of the market a year or two after my discussion with Ngoh. Other losers in the retail shakeout gripping the city include Dutch supermarket operator Royal Ahold, the Hong Kong supermarket chain Park N' Shop owned by Hutchison-Whampoa, and the bankrupted Yaohan Group, which opened a glitzy, multi-floor 108,000-square-meter store in 1996 in Pudong. Hong Kong department store operator Sincere closed its second store in Shanghai Square. The French-inspired Shanghai Printemps, despite its impressive neoclassical architecture and prime location on Huaihai Road, is another well-known loss maker,[8] seen by retail analysts as selling the wrong merchandise to the wrong customer. Instead of up-market shops, the luxury mall at the Kerry Center on Nanjing Road offered mostly store windows covered with brown paper at the end of 1999. Some retailers that did their homework, like British retailer Marks & Spencer, have decided not to enter the market at all after posting an executive to Shanghai in the mid-1990s to study the sector. Others, like Hong Kong's Hang Lung Group, have decided to change their strategy. Talking about the retail mix at the Grand Gateway mall in Xujiahui that opened at the end of 1999, Hang Lung's Shanghai-based deputy general manager, T.B. Seow, said: "If you see someone committing suicide, you don't follow. We originally expected to fill the mall with shops offering mid, mid-high and high-priced merchandise. But now I've filled it with low, mid-low, and mid-priced retailers."

The most successful foreign retailers in Shanghai ultimately have tended to be those that are able to establish themselves as a market leader, like Hong Kong's Gold Lion in menswear, or companies that take a "pile them high, sell them cheap" approach to sales. The Taiwanese-managed Pacific Department store has gained a following, for instance, by relying heavily on discounting. Huge discount hypermarkets opened by operators such as Carrefour of France and Metro of Germany have also proved popular.

Not only do they offer cleanliness, Western management, and one-stop shopping, they also provide something that most other foreign retailers do not—low prices. Ni Qian, a 26-year-old freight manager, for instance, became a convert to Carrefour after she found her favorite shampoo selling there for 15% less than what she normally paid for it. Except for clothes, vegetables, and meat, she said she bought most items there. Of course, the trick in the hypermarket business is to expand the number of outlets and increase sales fast enough to support back office and warehousing costs. Carrefour, which in 1995 announced plans for more than 30 hypermarkets in China, had by 2000 opened more than 20 stores in 14 Chinese cities.

Shanghainese cost-consciousness stemmed both from necessity and habit. The Shanghainese are known throughout China for their calculation skills and their determination to get the most value for their money. Dashiell Qian, a Shanghainese manager for Sears Buying Services, expounded to me on this aspect of the Shanghai psyche, which in general makes local residents both fierce negotiators during contract talks and smart shoppers who value cost-savings over convenience. Over coffee in the old Park Hotel, he said:

Shanghainese children are taught from an early age to evaluate the real value of things. Now my family was quite a bit better off than most of my friends, but I remember my parents teaching me like this:

Let's say I want to go to Maoming Road from my home, but the bus only stops before Maoming Road at Chengdu Road and after it at Shimen Road. Now Shimen Road is closer to Maoming Road than Chengdu Road, but the fare to the Shimen Road stop is seven mao (US$.008) whereas the fare to Chengdu Road is only four mao (US$.005). I remember my family instructing me to pay four mao to Chengdu Road and walk a little more, instead of paying seven mao to Shimen Road and walking a little less.

This thinking goes deeper than just saving money—going all the way to Chengdu Rd for four mao is getting the full worth of my four mao since the earlier stops also cost four mao. But paying seven mao to get to Shimen Road is bad value for money because I can go much further on the bus than Shimen Road for seven mao. So if I get off at Shimen Road I will feel ashamed for not making the most of the seven mao.

The MNC Experience

Many foreign investors, not just retailers, have overestimated potential sales, underestimated the amount of competition they would face, and misjudged Chinese buying behavior. For some projects, the market has not progressed as quickly as anticipated. Take the diesel engine market. Among other projects in China, American heavy equipment maker Caterpillar signed a joint venture agreement in 1994 with state-run Shanghai Diesel, an important Shanghai state enterprise, to make diesel engines. The two companies were not completely new to each other at that time. They had first started working together seven years earlier, when Caterpillar licensed some of its engine technology to Shanghai Diesel. Shanghai Diesel, however, was never able to assimilate the technology. According to John Airola, the general manager at Caterpillar Shanghai Engine Co., Caterpillar believed that by entering into an equity joint venture it could reduce costs enough to make its engine competitive in the marketplace. "We felt we would be able to meet the needs of discerning customers for our world-class product," he said. Between 1992 and 1994 when Caterpillar and Shanghai Diesel were negotiating the joint venture, China's economy was racing ahead at a double-digit clip, encouraging the partners to make aggressive projections about the venture's engine sales. Their projections were sorely disappointed and losses piled up, causing Caterpillar to pull out of the venture in 1997. In the fall of that year, I talked to Airola about the project's problems. A good-natured American from the Midwestern United States, he had moved with his family to Shanghai a few years earlier. He was also the president of the American Chamber of Commerce in Shanghai at the time. Walking through the venture's headquarters on the grounds of Shanghai Diesel, I passed one empty cubicle after another—testimony to the project's demise. Airola explained:

The marketplace was not what we expected for mid-range diesel engines. We brought in a world-class product, but customers want to buy Chinese-class products and the marketplace did not migrate to Caterpillar's product. We assumed there would be this migration. Our product was basically double the price. Eventually we would be able to bring the cost down by localizing components. We were working with customers to make them understand that it was not just the initial cost, but the life cycle cost of the product that was important. The higher price included service, durability, and better fuel efficiency. When you look at the life of our diesel engine, it is cheaper in the long term. However, in today's marketplace, customers are buying on initial price. In the life of the joint venture the discerning customer was not happening and your guess is as good as mine when it will happen. We felt that the product did not have a future in the short term, but also in the short term we were not meeting the targets set in our feasibility study. The gap was significant.

In some cases, the market situation changed significantly by the time foreign investors finished negotiating their ventures and built their factories. Reeling from inflation rates exceeding 20% at the end of 1994, for instance, the central government launched an austerity program that unexpectedly crimped local firms' spending power and slowed project approvals. Also, domestic players in some industries have become competitive more quickly than anticipated. In the electrical appliance industry, for instance, multinationals did not expect low-cost local producers like Sichuan Changhong, Qingdao Haier, and Guangdong Kelon to upgrade quality, service, and marketing in such a short time. They also did not expect China to experience a glut in television sets, refrigerators, and other home appliances in the second half of the decade, but that was what happened when domestic and foreign investors rushed in at the same time to satisfy pent-up consumer demand. Shanghainese and other city dwellers soon had their fill. By the end of 1998, more than 80% of urban households had bought a refrigerator, washing machine, and at least one television set, according the State Council's Development Research Center.[9] To make matters worse, changes in government welfare policy also bit into consumer demand. Instead of spending their money on home appliances in the late 1990s, urbanites started saving for healthcare, housing, and education.

For Whirlpool of the United States, these trends would have proved challenging under any circumstances, but flaws in its China strategy made them overwhelming. In the mid-1990s it negotiated and started operations at four different joint ventures in China with four different Chinese partners to produce four different appliances. For instance, it began manufacturing refrigerators in Beijing, air conditioners in Shenzhen, and washing machines in Shanghai. Like quite a number of multinationals, including Siemens Group with 40 ventures in China by 1997,[10] it tried to do too much too quickly. Robert Hall, the Hong Kong-based president of Whirlpool Asia, explained:

Managing four joint ventures with four different partners was a real challenge given the intensity of the competition. It makes it difficult to focus your efforts. It generated too high a cost situation. It was part of our strategy to do the four at the same time as quickly as we could. With 20/20 hindsight, there are many things we would have done differently.

Unable to focus its resources and weighed down by the high costs generated by four new joint ventures, Whirlpool by the late 1990s had sold its shares in two ventures and looked for new ways to make its remaining two work. Its Shanghai washing-machine joint venture, for instance, is manufacturing for Chinese home appliance maker Guangdong Kelon under the Chinese company's brand name—a rather ignominious arrangement for a multinational bent on capturing the China market for its own brand.

The intensity of the local and foreign competition has also put downward pressure on prices across many industries. It has often left multinationals in those industries producing below capacity and unable to obtain sufficient production volumes to bring production costs down. At the same time, companies have watched their fixed costs, particularly salary and benefits, follow an ascending arc. The result: pinched profit margins. The market for private telecom switching equipment is a prime example. During a conversation with Northern Telecom's Jackson Wu in 1997, he described the market situation as 'lean and mean" and commented how most foreign players' factories stood half idle. He added:

I've been is this market about 20 months. My impression is that every company believes it is a huge market and wants some part of the pie. This has led to severe competition and price erosion faster than any place in the world. Prices have been falling 10% a year. Then if you look at fixed costs, they're getting higher and higher. Because there's a lack of middle management experience, headhunters charge excessive fees and we have to pay a premium for people. The cost of providing a welfare safety net for workers is also rising, so compensation costs are getting higher. Office rents are also high. As a result, margins are squeezed. Everyone is just trying to keep sustaining power—to wait it out for the next couple of years until China joins the WTO [World Trade Organization]. Then the telecom market will be revitalized.

According to Siemens' China president Ernst Behrens, demand turned out to be less than expected for these switching systems, which was why the German company's joint venture making them in Shanghai was not working out well. "Generally, when things go wrong, it's a market problem," he said.

Regulatory restrictions have stymied foreign investors in Shanghai and elsewhere in China, often preventing them from entering potentially lucrative lines of business and making it impossible for them to do business as they would in market economies. For instance, navigating China's multitiered and immature distribution system has been one of the trickiest problems that foreign firms face, but regulations restricting joint ventures to marketing and distributing only the products that they produce have been especially onerous. Among other things, multinationals with more than one manufacturing venture were not able to consolidate all those products under one sales team in the 1990s. Instead, each subsidiary had to invest in its own marketing, sales, and distribution systems and deal individually with each distributor.

Foreign investors must contend with sudden rule changes as well. Sometimes a shift has affected all foreign investors. Confident about its ability to woo multinationals with its domestic market, for instance, in 1994 the central government started to rescind foreign investment incentives and hit foreign investors with new tariff, tax, and administrative rules. Sometimes the changes are industry-specific. Take China's efforts to rein in ballooning healthcare costs. They led to a host of new regulations that, by the middle of the decade, dramatically changed the profitability equation for multinational pharmaceutical makers. These include stringent rules governing the drugs eligible for insurance reimbursement—rules that Shanghai enforces particularly rigorously. Manufacturers have subsequently been operating far off their sales and profit targets. Ronald McPhearson, the Shanghai-based marketing director for Eli Lilly Asia, explained in 1997:

People are beginning to realize that in the near term the streets in China are not paved with gold. As late as three years ago companies may have been more bullish about near-term prospects. Their expectations were based on the approval of new compounds, which was much easier than now. Once the compound gets approved, the problem then is getting it reimbursed. The capacity at a lot of folks' manufacturing joint ventures is now significantly underutilized with only a few exceptions to the rule. Now companies are having difficulties meeting corporate expectations. They're asking themselves tough questions about profitability and if they need to be here and maintain a presence. Everyone agrees that 20 years from now China will be among the top three markets in the world for pharmaceuticals— if not the top. That said, here people are struggling to remind the people at corporate headquarters of China's strategic importance and to manage corporate expectations.

One Bed, Two Dreams

On top of market and regulatory woes, multinationals in Shanghai and elsewhere have often found themselves in unhappy or unfulfilling marriages with the Chinese partners. Most foreign investors entering China in the 1980s and 1990s did so in an equity joint venture with one or more Chinese entities—either because Chinese law did not allow wholly foreign-owned subsidiaries in their industry or because conventional wisdom said multinationals needed a Chinese partner's connections to be successful in China. Local governments, particularly in a city like Shanghai with a large state-owned sector, encouraged foreign firms to hook up with local firms as a way of pushing the reform of these enterprises, injecting them with fresh capital, and transferring foreign technology. Making alliances work between corporations in advanced market economies is never easy. But in China, where large gaps exist between understanding of local and international business practices and the needs of Chinese and multinational firms, creating happy marriages has proved particularly challenging. These differences have often led partners toward different goals and disagreements over strategy. For instance, many multinationals went to China in the 1990s to make long-term strategic investments. If they had to lose money for a while to gain market share, so be it—they had deep pockets to cover those outlays. Instead of repatriating profits, they wanted to reinvest earnings in the venture for its expansion. Chinese companies were far less flush, often suffering from bloated workforces and poor business results. Most Chinese partners did not contribute cash to the joint venture in the first place, putting in land and other assets instead. They preferred to take profit from the venture and distribute dividends. They sometimes did not have enough money for the next stage of the venture's expansion or to cover investment overruns, but were reluctant to let the foreign partner inject more money unilaterally and dilute their equity stake. A senior official at the American Chamber of Commerce in Shanghai commented: "Lots of people rushed into a joint venture so that they could be in China, but they did not understand what their partner needed and wanted."

Foreign firms often complain that their Chinese partners in Shanghai and elsewhere are less helpful than expected. "Our partner did nothing for us—not when we needed assistance going through the bureaucracy and not with marketing and sales," said the American general manager of the European toolmaking joint venture in Shanghai. Chinese partners often make promises during contract negotiations that they are unable to keep, like getting the venture preferential tax treatment or helping it to market products and navigate the bureaucracy. In some cases, the Chinese side simply exaggerates its abilities. In other cases, it has turned out to be the joint venture's competitor and has curbed its helpfulness. Competition between partners has led to friction over which brand to promote—the joint venture's or a parent company's—and which markets those brands can enter. For instance, in 1986 when Bayer AG of Germany wanted to make premium-quality false teeth in China, it teamed up with state-owned

Shanghai Dental Materials Factory, the country's largest maker of artificial choppers. Shanghai Dental made porcelain teeth and one-layer plastic teeth, but it did not make the cutting-edge three-layer plastic variety that Bayer wanted to introduce to China. The first hint of competition came early in the venture's life when Shanghai Dental reneged on its obligation to sell a quarter of the joint venture's production. So as not to compete with its Chinese parent in the low end of the false tooth market, the venture also verbally agreed to only sell its premium three-layer teeth in China—a promise Bayer came to regret. By the mid-1990s, it was clear that the market for two-layer plastic teeth was potentially much bigger than the three-layer tooth business. Two-layer teeth cost less to produce and retailed for half the price of the venture's product. Not surprisingly, the Chinese partner hotly pursued the new two-layer business, which was off-limits to the joint venture. Ned Imbrie, the venture's American general manager, advised: "Don't form a joint venture with a competitor. It closes off all sorts of avenues. They have access to all your development plans, your financial plans. They know how much money you have and need. They know your profits. They know your pricing. They know it all."

Chinese partners have bones to pick with multinationals as well, particularly when the joint venture is not performing as well as anticipated. Misunderstandings and differences in approach that Chinese partners might overlook if the venture is on track can turn into major points of contention. At the end of 1997, I interviewed the vice president of Shanghai Jiabao Group, which had a joint venture to produce lightbulbs with a subsidiary of General Electric. The U.S. diversified conglomerate had more than 20 ventures in China at the time. Shanghai Jiabao Group, a township enterprise founded in 1970, had been China's biggest lighting maker when it listed on the Shanghai Stock Exchange in 1992. It signed an agreement with GE Lighting in 1993, taking a 35% stake in the venture. It contributed its entire lighting division, including employees, land, and factories, which then accounted for some 80% of the Chinese group's business. Besides cash and technology, GE Lighting supplied management know-how.

From Shanghai Jiabao's perspective, its cooperation with the American company proved an utter failure owing primarily to the poor management decisions, excessive spending habits, and cultural insensitivity of its American partner. Usually when a joint venture goes sour, both partners agree not to air their grievances against each other in public—the foreign partner especially does not want to do any further damage to relationships in China or attract bad publicity. But in my rather long history of researching and writing about joint ventures, I have never run into such an upset, angry partner as Shanghai Jiabao. Upon arriving at the Chinese company's headquarters in a Shanghai suburb, I was ushered into a conference room with a long table. Across the table sat a number of Shanghai Jiabao officials, with Vice President Shen Jinlin sitting in the middle wearing a dark gray suit. As Shen gave me Shanghai Jiabao's take on the troubled alliance, his initial measured tones slowly gave way to impassioned outbursts. He said:

GE Lighting was wholly responsible for management after the joint venture was established. They began with technical reform and imported six production lines from Hungary, of which two produced lamps and the rest lightbulbs. Those production lines were very detrimental to the joint venture. Now it was quite reasonable for GE to import production lines because it wanted to improve product quality. The problem was that after installing the lines, they discovered that locally made components, like sockets, filaments, and lampshades, were of inferior quality. So they started importing them from other countries, like India, although under the original plan, they were supposed to buy these components domestically. Many of those imported products proved to be useless, even inferior to the Chinese-made goods. This caused production to slow down. The foreign partner just did as it liked, which was different from the original plan. It did not want to hear what the Chinese partner had to say.

Another reason why the venture is losing money is that management costs soared to the sky. The senior managers are all from the United States, except for one Chinese. There are more than 10 expatriates. Their salaries are set according to American standards. Several managers' salaries amount to half of the total employee wage bill. Besides salaries, they leased a pile of cars, which cost a lot of money as well. For them, they're just maintaining the same standard as they would for managers in America. But for a Chinese company whose products sell for a much lower price, which have a much lower profit, such standards are a luxury. These management costs have put pressure on the joint venture.

Six Hungarians came to install the production lines and stayed in a hotel a month. They spent 12 million yuan (US$1.4 million) in a single month. There was no limitation on food and telephone calls. They were buying bags of things for personal use.

What's worse is that the venture's managers do not have lighting equipment experience so they are not familiar with the field and as a result they had to hire other experts to come help. When one sort of problem occurs they hire experts in that field. The foreign experts kept coming.

Because of their lack of good understanding of the China market, the foreign managers were quite slow in deciding the appropriate pricing strategy of how much to raise prices and when. We lost good opportunities. If you raise prices at an inappropriate time, the result is a sudden increase in inventory and the production stops. This happened a few times over the last two to three years. Who can afford to have this happen several times? The problem was that there was no stable pricing strategy. Sometimes lower, sometimes higher.

GE policy when adopted in China should be localized to some extent. They should try hard to avoid using foreign managers. If an interpreter is always needed between managers and employees, it makes things harder. Because of cultural differences, maybe one single problem will not solve in a normal way, and that one single problem will lead to more problems. You can solve this problem by finding an appropriate candidate in the China market and training him well. These people are familiar with China's situation and after training will be familiar with GE's situation. His creativity and motivation will increase rather than just having to passively adopt what foreign managers say. There's a lot of talent in Shanghai.

GE does enjoy very sophisticated policies but the managers did not practice them. We meant to learn good things from GE—management and technology. But the real situation is disappointing.

According to feasibility study's projections, the profits were supposed to cover all previous losses in year four. The venture was supposed to lose money during the first three years. I believe the losses were more than 100% greater than expected. Last year they were 40 million yuan (US$4.8 million) and this year they will be even worse! Production was a lot lower too. We were prepared to lose money, but did not expect to lose that much money! This joint venture was established on the base of a very good Chinese factory—not a loss-making state enterprise. We are quite bitter: to change a profitable company into a loss-maker!

I talked to David Wang, the chairman of GE China, over the telephone shortly after my visit to Shanghai Jiabao Group to get the American multinational's view on the joint venture and its partnership with the Chinese company. While I expected the GE China head to put his best spin on a bad situation, I was rather surprised when he labeled the project a "huge success." The two sides' outlook could not have been further apart, underscoring just how differently Western multinationals and Chinese companies, even nonstate-owned ones, approach business. It was also clear, from Wang's comments, that GE had no doubts about whose approach was the better one.

According to Wang, GE needed to reform a factory of several thousand people in the shortest time possible. He said:

At Jiabao we did a joint venture with an existing operation. We didn't build the joint venture from scratch so we had to fix old processes and bring in new technology. We needed to change the mindset of a lot of people. For instance, it was a lot just to convince the factory manager to put more lights in the factory and keep them turned on. This required a change of mindset. Don't scrimp on every penny. Spend money where it matters. This was effort-intensive.

While he admitted GE was extravagant by its own standard with expatriates at the joint venture, he contended that the cost was a drop in

the bucket compared to the urgency of the task. He did not agree with
Shen that the joint venture's pricing strategy was flawed, commenting:

Raising the price—they didn't agree with this strategy. Marketing is not normally
a strong point of Chinese companies. We dumped money into quality. When we
felt we had better quality, we raised the price. They did not agree with either
policy—of spending money to raise quality or raising the price. By raising prices,
many customers who they used to have went elsewhere. But these weren't the
customers we go after. At the end of the day we have higher volume and are
getting the customer to pay a higher price. We're getting premium prices for
both the GE brand and Jiabao's original Hu brand. When Chinese pay higher
prices it means they like it. We have introduced the GE brand.

However, Wang conceded that Jaibao's original Hu brand was no
longer as prominent in the market as it once was. "They probably see it
as taken over by a foreign brand," he said. "We want GE to be a Chinese
brand." He disagreed that the imported components were inferior to
domestically produced parts. "The Chinese partner looks at pennies, not
at the future. If the imported components were not any better than the
local ones, then we wouldn't buy them," he said. He added that the
venture was exporting lamps, mostly to Korea, indicating its improved
quality. As for the production stoppages that incensed Shen so, Wang
commented: "We introduced a broad line of products. We're learning
about the market, which one sells well, which doesn't. If you look at a
certain segment there may be more inventories than desirable, but if you
look at others there are less." He admitted that the venture lost more
money than expected during its first three years of operation, but insisted
that the venture would break even in year four. "The task took a little
longer than anticipated," he said. "In reality, we're meeting our final
objective in breaking even after three years and at the same time producing
at world-class quality. This partner was frustrated because it had to go
through money-losing years, even though it planned to do that. It's hard."
Left to its own devices, Shanghai Jiabao, he claimed, "Would have made
money by milking the thing dry until one day it dies. They were not
investing to create a higher-quality product and would have had to
compete by lowering their price." Ultimately, the multinational had no
regrets about how it managed the venture even though its actions caused
tremendous ill will with its Chinese partner. Wang said:

Communication was not good. We did not want to argue points ad infinitum.
We had a burning sense of urgency. You can argue that they did not feel their

views were listened to. Sure there were a lot of those kinds of feelings. Given what we were facing, it was better to do it the way we did it. Life is short.

Fed up with the venture's results and lacking confidence in the GE's management style, Shanghai Jiabao Group's general manager and founder, Yang Jianqiang, offered to take over the venture's management and guarantee a fixed annual profit. GE declined and the Chinese company sold most of its stake in the venture back to its American partner in 1997. Shanghai Jiabao vice president Shen said:

Our general manager had a severe quarrel with them. He said: 'If you're not competent, I will take responsibility. I will guarantee an annual 20 million yuan (US$2.4 million) pretax profit. Otherwise, we will just transfer our holding to you.' They did not accept our offer and we just wanted to return it quickly. Our general manager is very upset. He just watched the joint venture go down and down.

When I asked Wang what GE thought of Yang's offer, he commented that 20 million yuan in pretax profit was peanuts for a company like GE that earned US$7.3 billion after tax. "We want a business for the long term, that is number one in China. Without quality and technical leadership, we're not going to get there," he said. So the American multinational gladly bought most of Shanghai Jiabao's shares in the joint venture—a route that many multinationals started taking in the last half of the decade.

This is not to say that all multinationals have ended up in disappointing relationships with Chinese partners, or that all joint ventures got off to a bad start, have not met expectations, or failed to capture significant market share. Volkswagen's carmaking joint venture in Shanghai, established in the 1980s, had a 48% share of China's car market in 1998 and did 25.2 billion yuan (US$3 billion) in sales.[11] While results at Siemens' joint venture making high-end private telephone switching equipment in Shanghai have disappointed, the German conglomerate considers its power transmission joint venture in the city a success. Siemens China president Behrens explained why the latter venture has done well:

It is in a good industry and offered a good product range. Coincidentally, both sides are pulling the rope in the same direction instead of pulling in different directions. Also, the general manager is skillful. The right person was chosen to run things. When he started he did not know a word of Chinese. But he tried to be part of the community. So now he understands the culture and speaks Shanghainese. He's very well accepted. He's a technical expert, so he knows what he's talking about. He's not just a manager. He knows his product.

Ingersoll Rand's air compressor joint venture in Shanghai—one of seven ventures in China—is also a success, making a profit from the first full year of operations and meeting its annual sales goal in just three years. This particular venture has done well for a number of reasons, but clearly the most important is that market conditions have been favorable to the venture's products (stationary compressors for industrial use and mobile compressors for use on construction sites). The venture's customers, both state enterprises and other joint ventures, were ready to buy the more-advanced technology that Ingersoll Rand offered when it first entered the market in the late 1980s. Moreover, its compressors are used in many different industries, so if one market segment becomes oversupplied, goes into decline, or shrinks because of Beijing's austerity policies, the venture can refocus on other segments that are still vibrant. "I'm lucky. There's no cyclical nature to the business. We have the market. All I have to do is recognize the trends," laughed the venture's long-serving managing director, Douglas Dawson. Also, the venture experienced little competition for the first five years of operation. "Now this is not the case. Now we basically deal in China with all the competitors worldwide," he said, "so we had a head start." It helped as well that the initial investment was small, only US$5 million. As a result, the venture did not have to sell all that many machines initially to break even, but could slowly build up its reputation. It started off with one expatriate—Dawson—and only added a technical expert four years later and a financial controller a year after that. "We followed the rule of one expat per 100 people. A high number of expats just makes it difficult to get the financial results needed," he said. By the end of 1997 the venture had roughly 350 employees, up from 11 initially.

Ingersoll Rand's relationship with the Chinese partner in the venture has also been consistently supportive—a situation undoubtedly helped by the venture's early profitability. The project has another advantage as well. Instead of setting up in a corner of its Chinese parent's lot, like many unhappy joint ventures, it was built from scratch on the opposite side of town from the Chinese parent, thereby avoiding overstaffing problems, jealousies over the venture's higher salaries, and myriad other picayune problems. It is also highly unusual for a foreign manager like Dawson to remain at the same joint venture for so long. He admitted the continuity probably has helped the venture, but felt that a five-year posting probably would have been sufficient. On the other hand, the three-year commitments that many expatriates make are too short—a common complaint heard from Chinese partners. Said Dawson: "The first year you spend figuring out how to do business. By the time you start making a contribution your second year, you're starting to think about the next phase. You need five years to build knowledge and relationships. You need to build a track record to gain people's trust."

Some companies do better in their later China ventures after learning lessons the hard way. Take the experience of a large American building materials multinational in Shanghai. According to the general manager of the company's second joint venture, who was also involved in the earlier effort, the first attempt failed for the same reason that many companies fared poorly in China in the 1990s: They did a poor job researching the market. Requesting that I not attribute our conversation to him or his company, the affable American executive said:

In our case, we were in the wrong place at the wrong time, with the wrong product. The market wasn't there and soon sales were not as good as anticipated. Sales were at least 50% lower than expected in the feasibility study. There was no profit. We thought it would be profitable after two to three years. The partner was okay, but didn't contribute much. For the first JV [started in 1991], it was an emotional decision. We thought China was the largest market in the world. But this is misleading. We really didn't do much homework. After two years we knew there was very little chance to make any money ever, so we dissolved it.

Its second joint venture has fared far better, with sales and profit exceeding forecasts. Again, the reason: "We did our homework really well," he said. He went on to explain how the multinational visited many places in China to scout out options and used internal and outside consultants to conduct numerous market surveys. It also helped that by then the executive had already spent a lot of time living in China. "We were in China already and knew what was going on," he said. "Before we just spent one week learning and then returned home. This time, it took two years to form the joint venture."

Return of the Adventurers

No discussion of foreign business in Shanghai is complete without mentioning the experience of Western entrepreneurs seeking their fortune in Shanghai. Mostly men in their twenties or thirties, they usually have a taste for adventure and an interest in China that predated their desire to set up a business in Shanghai. As a result, they usually speak Mandarin.

They are attracted to Shanghai for a wide variety of reasons, including its relatively high living standards for China, its pre-1949 mystique as a haven for foreign business, and its potential market. Some have set up restaurants, bars, and other small retail establishments in the city. Others have established consulting and computer-related firms catering to foreign multinationals. Yet others have tried their hand at manufacturing for export or the domestic market. As in many parts of Asia, Internet-related endeavors have recently become the rage. But no matter what their business, these entrepreneurs, like multinationals, arrive with great hopes and enthusiasm. Some have already left the city, beaten by the market and the system. Others have left it running from the law, after learning the hard way that Shanghai is not a city where foreigners can break the rules for long. Some pray that a larger company will buy them once they finally build the business to a decent size. A handful have actually accomplished what many dream of: They have made their fortunes—albeit rather modest ones.

They will never say that their success has come easily. Bob Adelski, founder of Hutchen Ltd., which in 1999 exported roughly US$20 million a year in power tools and other electrical equipment, recalled how "No" was the most common reply he heard from Chinese factories when he started his export business in Shanghai in 1988. He also recounted how every day brought another long negotiation with a stubborn state-run company that had no idea about quality control. The biggest problem of all, however, was physically getting to manufacturers, which were often located in other provinces. Surrounded by power tools in his modern office on Yanan Road, Adelski, a congenial 46-year-old American with a marine's haircut, said in late 1999:

Today Ningbo is only a four-hour drive away thanks to all the new infrastructure development in China. Before it used to take 10 hours. Roads were two lanes. Life was a series of long traffic jams and trucks spewing exhaust. It was slow, slow, slow. Today everything is much easier. You can get flights everywhere. There are freeways everywhere. Now we get e-mailed photos of products from Chinese factories, half of which are private, not state-owned.

Not that doing business has become a piece of cake for Adelski. China's quick development in the 1990s brought a whole new set of problems, including cutthroat competition. "We compete with guys who sell for 2% profit. Our overheads alone are 30%. But we survive with better service, quality, and integrity," he said, adding pensively: "It's not realistic to get into the import–export business now because the local private trading companies are getting so good. The Hong Kong and Taiwanese guys are also already there. The Asians have gone up the learning curve. I was in early and able to do all my learning before that happened."

For Simon Lichtenberg, a Dane in his early thirties, his first business forays were not just difficult, they were downright perilous. A Chinese language student at Shanghai's Fudan University in the 1980s, Lichtenberg returned to Shanghai with a German friend in July 1993 with big plans to start a timber trading business. He found it difficult to break in, however, and soon was trying to trade shoes to Europe, shrimp to the United States, and Danish furniture to China. Nothing came through and eight months after his arrival he had yet to earn a single cent. Instead, he and his partner had spent their entire US$30,000 in seed capital. They owed a Danish company nearly US$2,000 and were three months behind in rent and telephone bill payments. That was when crisis hit. Lichtenberg, a slight man with reddish-brown hair who looks anything but a wheeler-dealer, had agreed to sell 10,000 tons of steel from a large Russian supplier for US$2.5 million to a large state-owned company in Shanghai. There was a lot of speculation in steel at the time in China and Lichtenberg's Chinese client resold the order to a well-connected customer in Zhejiang province, promising to pay high penalties in the event of late delivery. Unfortunately, the steel never arrived. "It became obvious to us that the steel was not there. We were stupid. The big Russian supplier turned out to be a Polish guy with a company in Austria. He was a small-time broker who thought he could buy steel but actually couldn't. When he realized he couldn't get the steel, he disappeared," Lichtenberg recounted. Representatives from the Chinese state enterprise and its well-connected Ningbo client subsequently called the Dane and his partner to a meeting in an office along the Bund. There, they threatened to beat the pair up and confiscate their passports unless they paid US$200,000. Finally, after eight hours of sweaty negotiations, during which the entrepreneurs were not allowed to leave the room, the Chinese businessmen agreed to accept US$50,000 in compensation at a future date. A month later, Lichtenberg's first timber deal went through as did some other transactions, allowing him to pay off his debts and get his business underway. By the second half of the decade, Lichtenberg's Trayton Timbers was doing a booming business exporting various types of wood from Africa and Malaysia to China, India, and Europe, making him one of the most successful Western entrepreneurs in the city.

But there is more to Lichtenberg's story than just timber trading. He also built a business retailing imported Scandinavian-style furniture from Denmark. His experience, however, highlights a common problem bedeviling foreign investors and small-scale foreign entrepreneurs in particular: Lower-cost Chinese outfits copied his designs and stole his business. In 1995 Lichtenberg became the franchiser in China for a subsidiary of Denka Holdings, Denmark's second-largest furniture group. His timing was perfect: Urban Chinese were just starting to buy new apartments and refurbish old ones as part of the central government's housing reforms. Using the Bo Concept brand name, he set up Bo Concept outlets in Shanghai and other cities in China, netting an after-tax profit of almost US$500,000 in 1996. Trouble soon followed. Besides foreign and domestic manufacturers pouring into the furniture market, lower-cost Chinese producers started making exact copies of Lichtenberg's furniture. In 1997, 12 factories specializing in Bo Concept furniture, but having nothing to do with Lichtenberg or Denka Holdings, started operations. Some used Bo Concept's Chinese logo. Others kept copies of Bo Concept's catalogues in their showrooms and made replicas for customers. Lichtenberg subsequently spent much of 1998 and 1999 trying to get the factories to stop selling furniture under the Bo Concept brand. He also sued the most egregious offender. When I talked to Lichtenberg at the end of 1999, he had, with the help of lawyers and two Shanghai government bureaus, finally made headway stopping some of the fake production, although the lawsuit dragged on. In the meantime, Lichtenberg had to lower prices significantly to stay competitive. Add it all together, and 1998 and 1999 were very tough years for the entrepreneur's furniture operation. Although it did not run a loss in 1999, profits dropped drastically. On the bright side, his timber business consistently did well—so much so that he invested US$2 million profit from it into a sofa factory to supply Swedish furniture maker Ikea and other retailers. The venture started making an operating profit in 1999 after only four months of production. All in all, Lichtenberg is pleased with his group's progress, even if the road to riches in Shanghai has not always been an easy one. "I came here to create something. It wasn't really about money. I felt there was an opportunity," he explained.

Adelski expressed similar sentiments. Although he admitted that his efforts had turned him into a multimillionaire, he also pointed out that he does not live in a grand mansion with an army of servants like success-ful foreign entrepreneurs in Shanghai before 1949. Instead he lives in a

120-square-meter flat with his Shanghainese wife and six-month-old daughter. He said:

I put in my time. It took me 10 years after I started my own company. I've been out in Asia for 21 years. I consider myself pretty successful because I can think of only two other guys with white faces who have come in and built substantial businesses in Shanghai. I'm one of the most successful and this is pretty modest. If your only objective is to make money, you're a fool to come to Asia and to come to Shanghai. Foreigners are not coming here and making money fast. Your chances of making money are much smaller than in the United States.

Upon hearing Adelski's comment, I couldn't help but think of a conversation I had over dinner a few days earlier with one of Shanghai's wealthy "princeling entrepreneurs"—high-ranking officials' offspring who run private businesses often off the back of their stellar connections. Requesting anonymity, he boasted how he did not even need to hire a sales force for his handful of businesses—all he needed were "friends" to direct deals his way. Oozing a mixture of bravado and sincerity, he said: "Shanghai is the best city in the world to do business and I have evidence. It's easy to make money. The market is big. If you invest one cent you can get one dollar back. In foreign countries, making one cent become 10 cents is difficult." Indeed, there are people getting rich quickly and easily in Shanghai. It just is not usually the foreigners.

Soul Searching

Whatever the reason—overly optimistic initial projections, heated competition, greater-than-anticipated losses, culture clashes, broke Chinese partners, or some combination of the above—many foreign investors in Shanghai and around China have been reexamining their China strategies and making changes. In the late 1990s, foreign law firms in Shanghai regularly received calls from clients asking to restructure, downsize, or dismantle existing operations—a trend that accelerated as the Chinese economy slowed and Asia's economic downturn intensified. The goal for multinationals is to better control their future. Some have pulled out of hopeless loss-making joint ventures, like Caterpillar and Whirlpool. American management consulting group A.T. Kearney reported in 1999 that almost 25% of multinationals in its survey had decided to withdraw from at least one China venture. Foreign investors are also taking advantage of a more amenable regulatory environment to merge multiple joint ventures; turn joint ventures into wholly foreign-owned companies; or increase equity stakes in existing operations. They are also exploring the possibility of transforming their ventures into joint stock companies. This structure potentially allows them to remove Chinese partners from day-to-day management, a source of tension in many joint ventures, without losing insider status like wholly foreign-owned firms. To cut costs, companies across many industries in the late 1990s began sending expatriate staff home before their contracts expired and replacing them more quickly than initially intended with local staff. Vanhonacker, the professor at CEIBS in Shanghai, commented in November 1999:

Companies have changed their outlook. The longer road to profits is no longer acceptable. There's lots of pressure to do well from headquarters. Patience has run out. The attitude is that it's not enough to talk about profits in the long term—they have to do it now. So they're cutting costs and getting operational control.

A few days later, John Hutton, the Shanghai-based partner at PricewaterhouseCoopers, added: "The perception of what China is has changed. People thought it was high-cost, but also high return. Now the market is not as big as people thought. It's quite segmented and takes quite a bit of effort. Companies are adopting a lower profile and a lower-cost strategy."

What does the future hold? Barring large-scale political turmoil, the outlook for multinationals and Shanghai looks reasonably bright. For one, China's entry into the World Trade Organization will mean new market opportunities and the breakdown of some of the vexing regulatory obstacles hindering them from doing business. Leading up to its WTO accession agreement with the United States in November 1999, for instance, China in July of that year lifted its ban against foreign firms involvement in wholesaling, clearing the way for multinationals with more than one joint venture to consolidate and distribute those products themselves. Likewise, after China joins the global trade body, the central government will gradually allow foreign companies to distribute and provide after-sales service for their own imported products. While some firms already manufacturing in Shanghai and other places in China worry that a flood of imports might hurt their competitiveness, most look forward to easier market access. As China's anointed commercial hub, offering some of the best infrastructure in the country to multinationals, Shanghai stands to gain much from the renewed foreign interest in China that will come with the country's WTO entry.

But while stars once again fill some investors' eyes, Shanghai-based foreign executives are generally more measured. They welcome China's entry into the trade body, but are concerned that China, which has a patchy record on implementing trade agreements, might not fully deliver on its WTO promises—either due to resistance at the local level or because a particular WTO commitment and government policy do not mesh. Speaking in late 1999, Hutton, the PricewaterhouseCoopers' partner, commented: "Foreign investor interest in Shanghai has not picked up over the last two years and is slower than it was four years ago. There will probably be an investment spurt because of WTO, but really people want to wait and see how the agreement is carried out. The Chinese will have to implement the WTO changes and that will take time."

Such realism is refreshing and is another factor brightening the outlook for multinationals in Shanghai and around China. Foreign investors have gained practical experience and are taking as much control of their China operations as regulations allow. So after the dust settles on the restructuring, reassessment, and cost-cutting activity gripping foreign firms, there should be an increasing number of success stories like that of the American building-material firm's second joint venture in Shanghai. Companies that have learned the lessons of the past will spend more time understanding the market and their partners, rather than rushing into China with a bottomless budget in a quixotic quest for its mega-market.

Notes

[1] Given that the general manager threatened to find me in my home and shoot me if I printed his or his company's name, both will remain anonymous.

[2] Shanghai has roughly 14 million permanent residents and three million migrant laborers who are not counted as official residents.

[3] *See* Don Rimmington, "History and Culture" in *Shanghai and The Yangtze Delta: A City Reborn*; edited by Brian Hook, Oxford University Press, Hong Kong.

[4] *Business China*, Jun. 25, 1990.

[5] "China Statistics Yearbook," 1999.

[6] The Dec. 8, 1999, issue of the *International Herald Tribune*, for instance, reported that China was refusing to implement the agricultural protocol it finalized with the United States in April 1999 until it joined the World Trade Organization. On Jan. 8, 2000, the *South China Morning Post* published an AFX-Asia article quoting the comments of Long Yongtu, China's chief WTO negotiator, to the *Guangzhou Daily*. Long contended that China's concession to allow 6,000 US meat factories to sell to China was purely semantic and would not result in more imports of US meat. He said: "Diplomatic negotiations involve finding new expressions. If you find a new expression that means you have achieved a diplomatic result. In terms of meat imports, we have not actually made any material concessions." The March 2, 2000, issue of *The Asian Wall Street Journal* reported that the central

government was considering placing new restrictions on the amount of domestic currency that foreign banks can lend in China.

[7] There's no question that penetrating the China market proved a tougher slog for many foreign investors than anticipated and that it has taken them longer to make money than expected. However, drawing firm conclusions about company profitability is a complicated issue. According to statistics, many foreign firms operating in Shanghai and China in general were not profitable.

However, the official numbers released by Xinhua are somewhat misleading. For one, they did not take into account that many foreign-invested ventures in China were still in the start-up phase, which often required large one-off expenses and costly expatriate personnel. And they did not reflect firms' strategies of reinvesting earnings, spending heavily on advertising, and keeping prices low to build market share. Moreover, the reason that foreign firms report earnings to the Chinese authorities is for tax rather than performance-rating purposes. Since all companies want to pay as little tax as possible, they naturally report their earnings in the most "tax-efficient" manner possible. From the Chinese government's perspective, the statistics also overstated losses because they do not include the tidy sums secreted out of China in the form of high salaries for expatriate employees, entertainment expenses, and purchases by affiliated companies.

That said, the official figures also do not consider the vast sums of money multinationals have showered on China, which joint ventures do not include in their profitability reports. Such expenses included the cost of expatriate housing and multimillion-dollar training programs. As a result, while a joint venture may book an operating profit, the mother company is experiencing a loss. Dennis Simon, the director of China Strategy at Andersen Consulting, said only half-jokingly: "If you ante up their total investment in China, no company will be profitable to 2050."

[8] The *South China Morning Post* reported on Mar. 27, 1997, that Shanghai Printemps incurred losses of HK$4.2 million (US$540,000) in 1995 and HK$6 million (US$770,000) in 1996.

[9] *Shanghai Star*, Dec. 7, 1999.

[10] In the Nov. 6, 1997 edition of the German newspaper *Handlesblatt*, Siemens Group China analyst Kleo Freese-Holzmann commented: "We have overestimated the tempo. The China engagement has cost us a lot of money. More than we had planned." He also commented that by German accounting standards most of the German conglomerate's joint ventures in China were not profitable and had not met expectations.

[11] *Shanghai Star*, Feb. 9, 1999.

8

Made in Shanghai

In 1997, my editor asked me to write an article on technology in China. I knew from previous research that some of China's top consumer appliance companies, like Qingdao Haier in Shandong province, Guangdong Kelon in Guangdong province, and Wuxi Little Swan in Jiangsu province, had started channeling resources into research and development, including setting up R&D centers overseas. I also knew that Wuxi Little Swan had just launched a new washing machine series based on innovations made to imported technology. I decided to focus my article on the state of technical innovation—to what extent China's homegrown companies were innovating and why.

Shanghai seemed like a good place to start my research. After all, it housed some of China's finest universities, boasted a skilled workforce, and was an important manufacturing base. The city's newspapers regularly carried articles about how high-tech industry accounted for a growing percentage of industrial output and how information technology, bio-pharmaceuticals, and new industrial materials had become Shanghai's "new development focus" in the 1990s.

My first inkling that Shanghai might not provide many success stories came when I had my news assistant call the administrative office of Zhangjiang High-Tech Park in Pudong to ask to set up interviews with domestic companies located there that had successfully developed, manufactured, and marketed innovative products. The voice on the other end of the line replied that there were none. Of course, Shanghai's story is not as sorry as that, but in further conversations with foreign venture capitalists, Shanghai officials, and businesspeople, it has become clear that Shanghai companies are not leading the country in developing new products or becoming the Chinese version of

Silicon Valley. Instead, Beijing, the political capital in the north, and Shenzhen, the freewheeling special economic zone in the south, have emerged as more vibrant centers of innovation and high-technology in China.

The question is why. There are many reasons, but the most alarming one is this: The Shanghai government, after 20 years of reform, still tightly controls its companies and in the process is suffocating them. This is also a reason that "Made in Shanghai" no longer signifies the best domestically made goods in Chinese consumers' minds and that private entrepreneurs have not made much of a mark on Shanghai industry. The Shanghai government's determination to use state-planning methods to advance its manufacturing prospects in China's budding market economy provides yet another example of how the city's software lags far behind its hardware and how Shanghai is not as modern on the inside as it looks on the outside.

Manufacturing Colossus

For more than 100 years, manufacturing has been central to Shanghai's wealth. When the Chinese Communists marched into Shanghai in 1949, they not only captured China's financial and commercial heart, they also took control of the country's largest industrial base. Shanghai's factories had been built by Western and Chinese industrialists, most of whom fled Shanghai prior to the takeover. In 1949, those factories accounted for one-fifth of China's entire industrial output.[1] Although the Communist Party quashed Shanghai's financial and commercial vibrancy, it needed the city's factories, technology, skilled labor, and managerial know-how to build socialism.

Shanghai before 1949 chiefly churned out textiles and other consumer goods. In subsequent years, the city's new masters started developing heavy industries dear to Communist hearts: steel, machinery, petro-chemicals, and electronics. They also needed to transform the ownership of Shanghai's factories, four-fifths of which were in private hands at the time of the Communist takeover.[2] The Party soon brought them under state control, appointing their leaders and integrating them into the state plan.

Meeting the government's output plan became manufacturers' primary objective and by all accounts Shanghai companies soon excelled at this task, turning the former capitalist bastion into a paragon of state-planned production. Shanghai's industrial output surged 11.3% a year on average between 1950 and 1980.[3] Its per-capita industrial productivity in 1979 was China's highest. At the same time, the city maintained its reputation for producing the highest-quality products in the country. Its consumer goods, which usually won nationwide quality competitions, led the market in sales. For instance, the Tianjin Quanye Department store in the northern city of Tianjin in 1978 carried 30,000 types of products from all around China. Shanghai-made products accounted for a quarter of the department store's sales.[4]

The central government's emphasis on building heavier, more capital-intensive industries in Shanghai also bore fruit. Their output soon matched light goods production and, by the 1970s, Shanghai's steel industry, which had accounted for only 4% of the country's steel output in 1957, made up 22% in 1973, and was the second largest in the country. Shanghai also became a force in oil refining, petrochemicals, and machinery for the oil industry and emerged as a dominant electronics supplier, boasting more electronic instrument factories than any other city.[5]

In the 1980s, Shanghai's manufacturing dominance began to ebb. Paramount leader Deng Xiaoping did not pick Shanghai to lead China's reforms, but instead opted to experiment first in Guangdong and other areas along China's southern coast. He had a number of reasons for treating Shanghai more conservatively, but important among them was the central government's financial dependence on the city's manufacturing revenues. Meanwhile, the central government allowed Guangdong and Fujian to offer preferential policies to foreign investors and remit a much smaller percentage of profits to Beijing. Shanghai's efforts to attract foreign investment and enter a more favorable revenue-sharing scheme with the central government proceeded far more slowly. At the same time, the central government encouraged raw material suppliers in inland provinces to set up their own low-value-added processing and allowed rural township enterprises and private entrepreneurs to establish operations. Suddenly state enterprises in Shanghai and elsewhere faced competition for both markets and materials. A decade after Deng's historic policy shift, Shanghai's percentage of the national industrial output had declined from one-eighth in 1979 to one-fourteenth in 1991.[6] Beijing's undernourished golden goose could no longer produce as many eggs relative to more-flourishing parts of the country. The central government did, however, bestow a number of projects on

Shanghai that improved it capital-intensive manufacturing capabilities: the Baoshan Steel Mill, the Jinshan Petrochemical Complex (now known as Shanghai Petrochemical), and a passenger car joint venture with Volkswagen of Germany.

It was not until the early 1990s that the central government had second thoughts about concentrating Shanghai's resources solely on manufacturing. At the 14th National Congress of the Chinese Communist Party in October 1992, President Jiang Zemin confirmed China's plans to "establish Shanghai as an international economic, financial, and trading center as soon as possible," and make Shanghai the spearhead of the country's development strategy. Today Shanghai's service sector is well on its way toward overtaking manufacturing as the city's dominant growth engine. Whereas services only made up 31% of the city's economic output in 1991, by the end of 1998 they contributed 47.8%.[7]

This trend, however, does not mean that Shanghai intends to give up its status as a leading manufacturing center in China. The central government approved the creation of the vast Pudong New Area to help the city expand its indigenous manufacturing capabilities and attract foreign manufacturers. In the 1990s it also allocated to the zone a number of major manufacturing and research projects to support key industries. These include a US$1.5-billion carmaking venture with America's General Motors, a US$1.2-billion semiconductor foundry slated to form the backbone of China's electronic industry, and a national center for biotechnology and pharmaceutical development. Chinese leaders worry that without strong manufacturing industries, Shanghai will not be able to employ all of its 14 million permanent residents (not including its three-million-strong migrant worker population). Shanghai authorities also fear that other provinces will, over time, develop their own trade and financial sectors to service manufacturers and will subsequently pump less business through the port city. Shanghai does not want to make the mistake of "hallowing out" like Hong Kong and other major international cities and is, therefore, determined to have its own manufacturing to support its service sector in the future. Moreover, the central and Shanghai governments have invested large sums of state money into Shanghai industry—capital that they do not want to evaporate. Rather than depend on private and other alternative forms of indigenous investment, the Shanghai authorities in the 1990s generally sought to achieve their manufacturing dreams by reforming and fortifying the city's state enterprises and attracting foreign investment.

The central government's preferential policies, a loose credit environment, and a foreign investment stampede helped Shanghai's industrial growth rebound sharply during the decade. The turnaround, however, disguised an alarming trend: The city's indigenous consumer product makers generally fared poorly in market competition. Numerous famous Shanghai brands, including Jinxing, Kaige, and Feiyue television sets, Shangling and Shuanglu refrigerators, Baromen suits, and Nie'er and Strauss pianos, lost their following to better domestic companies and foreign firms. White Cat detergent, Three Gun underwear, and Jahwa cosmetics are among the few that have maintained their appeal. In 1998, consumer goods produced by the city's state-owned enterprises held only a 10% share of Shanghai's market, causing Shanghai Commerce Commission official Chen Yuxian to comment: "The city is being challenged by products from other parts of the country."[8] Echoing the analysis of observers both in Shanghai and out, Pan Ming, a Shanghainese economist with Prudential-Bache Securities in Hong Kong, commented: "Shanghai companies used to dominate the national market, but have not done well in most consumer product areas. Although there are still some good companies, it's nothing like it used to be. I can see the decline of Shanghai's indigenous industries." Indeed, their performance to date suggests that the city will not have the manufacturing future it craves based on the accomplishments of its homegrown enterprises, but rather on the achievements of joint ventures and wholly foreign-owned companies managed by foreign multinationals. Jonathan Woetzel, a Shanghai-based principal at McKinsey and Co., in late 1999 explained:

When I think about a vibrant economy, it's an economy with strong companies from Shanghai, located in Shanghai, and dedicated to Shanghai. Those companies don't really exist. The government can make it attractive to foreigners to invest in a zone and multinational corporations can use Shanghai as a convenient manufacturing location, but that's a different strategy than trying to develop local companies.

Goodbye to Textiles

The declining competitiveness of Shanghai's labor-intensive, light industries is in some ways to be expected. Brisk demand for property and for skilled workers in Shanghai in the 1990s has made the city a relatively expensive place to manufacture compared to neighboring provinces. A typical example of the forces buffeting Shanghai's producers in the 1990s is Shanghai Wool & Jute, a large state-owned textile manufacturer in Shanghai. According to business development manager Xuan Weiming, it paid workers an average wage of 9,200 yuan (US$1,108) a year in 1995, twice as much as it competitors paid in nearby Jiangsu and Zhejiang provinces, and three times more than rivals located deeper in China's interior.

Shanghai's faltering competitiveness, however, goes much deeper than high land and wage costs. In the 1990s, state-run enterprises dominated Shanghai's indigenous industry. In provinces like Guangdong, Fujian, Zhejiang, and Sichuan, homegrown, nonstate companies—rural enterprises and private businesses—developed more quickly. When these nonstate firms first entered the market, they normally went into labor-intensive manufacturing of low-value-added goods that did not require large capital infusions. State-run firms around the country have had trouble competing with these new homegrown players as well as with foreign-invested ventures, and Shanghai's companies have been no different.

The problems of Shanghai's and China's state enterprises are manifold. Under socialism, public-sector companies had twin goals: to produce and to take care of workers. That latter goal became a major disadvantage in the reform era. Although state-owned enterprises in Shanghai and around China started laying off workers in the 1990s, they often labored during the decade with aging workforces that were far larger than needed for the job. Shanghai Wool & Jute, for instance, was responsible for 50,000 workers and 28,000 retirees before 1995. It not only paid their wages, it also took care of housing, medical needs, and pensions, which together added 70% to its compensation costs. Meanwhile, rural township enterprises and private companies not only had young, smaller workforces, they often did not provide benefits. "Our enterprise is not just responsible for producing, it is also responsible for employees' lives," complained Xuan, the business development manager. "The pressure is too great. The burden makes us less competitive." At the same time, rural enterprises often were able to negotiate preferential tax policies with their local governments, exacerbating state-run firms' higher cost structure. They could easily beat state enterprises on price. Shanghai Wool & Jute's biggest competitor, a rural enterprise in Jiangsu province called Jiangsu Sunshine Group, for instance, could sell cloth at 120 yuan (US$14.5) per meter and make a profit, whereas

Shanghai Wool & Jute would make a loss selling at 150 yuan (US$18) per meter.

Initially, state firms had a number of important advantages over new homegrown competitors. For instance, they had a monopoly on overseas connections with foreign buyers as well as raw material and technology suppliers. That meant that Shanghai Wool & Jute could purchase advanced imported equipment while a start-up like Jiangsu Sunshine had to buy equipment second-hand from state-owned companies. State firms also had more experienced workers. As a result, even if the state enterprise could not match its competitors' low prices, it could always beat them on quality. But by the early to mid-1990s, the upstarts had often caught up.

Low employee motivation at state firms compared with that of their competitors also hindered Shanghai manufacturers. At Jiangsu Sunshine, for instance, the base wage was a low 150 yuan (US$18) a month in the mid-1990s. But management had implemented incentive pay and so a worker's monthly bonus might reach 850 yuan (US$102) depending on his and the company's performance. Jiangsu Sunshine salesmen also earned attractive commissions on sales made. Monthly bonuses at state enterprises, on the other hand, varied little since managers were reluctant to implement incentive schemes for fear of angering workers and managers habituated to equal treatment. Yan Yushan, a frustrated mid-ranking employee at Shanghai Wool & Jute, explained in 1996:

Management is not aggressive in attracting customers. All they do is read newspapers and sip tea all day. They're not flexible. They don't want to do small orders or change to meet customers' requirements because it's too much trouble. All they want to do is fill big orders. I had an Italian customer that wanted to reduce the thickness of a merino wool fabric, but when I brought the order back to headquarters, management refused. Even though they could make some profit it was still too much trouble. What does it matter? Managers just get the same salary, whether they sell more or not! Maybe your bonus rises a little—50 yuan (US$6) max—but it doesn't make an impact.

The 48-year-old Yan, who I met while interviewing managers at Shanghai Wool & Jute in 1996, invited me in early 1997 to drive a few hours to Jiangsu Sunshine to have a look at the rural enterprise that had steadily eroded Shanghai Wool & Jute's market share. We first stopped at the rural enterprise's sales office in Shanghai, where Yan introduced me to a number of former Shanghai Wool & Jute employees. One of them was a slight, balding, middle-aged man surnamed Tao who had been a low-level office clerk at Shanghai Wool & Jute before becoming

Jiangsu Sunshine's chief marketing agent. Yan looked admiringly at his former colleague and said:

I've known two Taos. Before he left Wool & Jute in 1992, he was your average white-collar man, drinking tea, reading newspapers, and killing time. He was a nobody. Everyone shouted at him. They handed him odd jobs and he never complained. But he developed a good relationship with a manager at Sunshine who offered him at least four times more money than he made at Wool & Jute. Now he's busy. He's become somebody.

Tao, a slight, balding man, agreed. He said:

My job is not easy. I'm very busy. It's not like all Shanghainese want to work for Sunshine because they have to work hard. Shanghainese are spoiled. Here you need your own initiative. It's worthwhile for me. Sunshine values my talent.

Hearing Yan wax lyrical about his friend's transformation and knowing how unhappy he was at Shanghai Wool & Jute, I could not help but ask him why he stayed there. He seemed both energetic and intelligent. That's when he announced he planned to quit. His voice packed with emotion, he said:

I'm going to retire early. At my age, nobody usually quits his job. But I want to use my skill. I want a challenge. I want to do something. If I go to a technical seminar and know more than my boss, he doesn't like it. If I show some motivation without my boss's approval, he'll be angry. Good people are not promoted. I don't want to be a yes-man anymore—always drinking tea and reading newspapers. It makes me sick.

When I called Yan several months later, he had already found a new job acting as the Shanghai representative for a Canadian textile machinery supplier. He was ecstatic to be using his skills. Meanwhile, his old employer, like many other state enterprises in Shanghai, was busy laying off workers, merging or bankrupting factories, and selling land to pay employees and cover debts.

Goodbye to Electrical Appliances

Given Shanghai's high land and labor costs, the rise of new low-cost producers, and the problems dogging old state enterprises like Shanghai

Wool & Jute, Shanghai's moves to dismantle its textile and other labor-intensive industries make sense. The world is populated with former towns that lost industries to lower-cost locations and Shanghai is now one of them. Shanghai has instead decided to concentrate resources on more capital- and technology-intensive sectors. The government has designated six "pillar" industries: steel, power, petrochemicals, tele-communications, home appliances, and automobiles. In 1996, the city spent 29.5 billion yuan (US$3.6 billion) on the six pillars, representing some 59% of total industrial investment.[9] Shanghai is also moving into high-tech, knowledge-based industries where it expects to have a comparative advantage within China because of its relatively well-educated populace.

By the second half of the 1990s, Shanghai's pillar industries accounted for more than half the city's industrial output. Among the firms boosting this performance has been Baoshan Steel, China's most modern and most efficient steel producer. Shanghai Petrochemical, another highly capital-intensive project, is also an industry leader. The Shanghai authorities, meanwhile, expect Shanghai Automotive Industry Corp., which has carmaking joint ventures with both Volkswagen and GM, to be the first Shanghai company to make *Fortune Magazine*'s list of the world's 500 largest companies. But behind these success stories lie disturbing developments in the most competitive and unprotected sector among Shanghai's pillar industries: household electrical appliances.

During the decade, a string of Chinese companies that mastered skills needed to succeed in a market economy emerged in the house-hold electrical appliance sector. Leading manufacturers by the mid-1990s made high-quality products, regularly churned out new models, and offered good after-sales service. They created strong brand names and effective national marketing and distribution networks. They spotted industry trends and adapted their strategies accordingly. Today they export and manufacture overseas, conduct research and develop-ment, and in some cases develop proprietary technology. Unlike foreign makers of soda, shampoo, and other fast-moving consumer products, which overwhelmed Chinese companies with their marketing prowess in the first half of the 1990s, foreign multinationals in the home appliance sector have had a much harder time capturing market share. Indeed, U.S. white-goods maker Whirlpool scaled back its operations in China in part because local competition proved fiercer than expected.

But while Chinese companies like Qingdao Haier, Guangdong Kelon, Sichuan Changhong, Wuxi Little Swan, Shenzhen-based Konka, Guangdong-based TCL, and Jiangsu Chunlan flourished, Shanghai's premier household appliance makers foundered. During the last half of the 1990s, refrigerator makers Shanghai Shangling and Shanghai Shuanglu watched their sales drop dramatically and profits disappear, while sales and profits surged at China's leading refrigerator makers, Qingdao Haier and Guangdong Kelon. Likewise, washing machine maker Wuxi Little Swan made a profit of 227.7 million yuan (US$27.4 million) in 1998; its Shanghai rival, Shanghai Narcissus, lost 64 million yuan (US$7.7 million). While Sichuan Changhong expanded its national market share from 22% to 27% and increased after-tax profit by 24% in 1996, sales of Shanghai Video & Audio's Jinxing brand television sets sagged 50%. Sales of Jinxing television sets have since rebounded, but the company is still weak compared with Sichuan Changhong and Konka. Pan Ming, the Shanghainese economist at Prudential-Bache Securities, recalled in 1999 helping his mother buy a color television set in Shanghai. Perusing the Sichuan Changhong models, Pan noticed that they were similar in quality to his Japanese set, but cheaper in price. "Then I compared the quality of Jinxing TVs with Changhong TVs. I thought Changhong was much better. I felt disappointed. I next turned to air conditioners and refrigerators and found they were all made by other provinces," he said glumly.

Considered the best in the land in the 1980s, Shanghai electrical appliances by the mid-1990s had failed to capture market share nationwide and had started to forfeit their home market.[10] These firms made little effort to market or advertise their products or develop nationwide distribution. They also did little to improve their technology and product quality, rarely coming out with new models. Unlike at Wuxi Little Swan, Qingdao Haier, and Sichuan Changhong, which had long-serving and even visionary executives at their helm, the Shanghai government rotated the heads of its companies often. So when the supply of televisions, refrigerators, and air conditioners suddenly exceeded consumer demand in the middle of the decade, Shanghai companies were ill-prepared to compete with the country's strongest domestic players.

Shanghai's failure in this case cannot simply be chalked up to higher costs and the intractable troubles of old, large state enterprises. Although Shanghai's companies in this sector are still state-owned, they are often relatively new and relatively small, and therefore not overwhelmed with thousands of redundant workers. They have had access to the same imported technology as other domestic players. Moreover, a number of the firms that have excelled in this sector, such as Wuxi Little Swan in Jiangsu province, Sichuan Changhong in Sichuan province, and Qingdao Haier in Shandong province, are basically state enterprises too.

The case of Shanghai Shangling, Shanghai's leading refrigerator maker, is illustrative. Established by the Shanghai government in 1985, Shangling got off to a roaring start. It imported advanced technology and equipment from Japan and, in 1988, the central government gave it and Qingdao Haier awards for quality. "Shangling was the first fridge company in the history of China to win a gold prize," company Vice General Manager Lu Moquan told me proudly during an interview in 1997. With demand for refrigerators raging in China in the early to mid-1990s, companies making refrigerators could sell everything they produced. Trucks from department stores would wait in line outside Shanghai Shangling's factory. The company was even able to fob off its refrigerators at retail prices to suppliers, who could easily sell them for a 20%–25% markup. Shanghai Shangling's output in those days increased 30%–50% a year. In 1993, its sales reached 1.2 billion yuan (US$142 million), well ahead of Qingdao Haier's 766 million yuan (US$92 million) in sales.

In the meantime, the Shanghai government had big plans for Shanghai Shangling, hoping to create a Shangling group of companies. This initiative was part of China's plans to create large enterprise groups, or conglomerates, to fend off foreign competition and to reform the state enterprise sector by merging "good" companies with loss-makers. The central and Shanghai governments hoped to create economies of scale, spread management expertise, and pool resources. They also wanted profitable companies to absorb the debts of loss-makers so that China's state banks would not have to write off bad loans. To avoid politically unsavory layoffs, the profitable companies also absorbed most of the struggling company's workforce. Shangling's general manager, Jiang Shilong, however, did not like the idea of assuming the burden of several loss-making companies. The Shanghai government subsequently replaced him in 1994 with a more pliant administrator—a 58-year old executive named Ge Wenbin, who had a strong manufacturing background.

In 1996, the Shanghai municipal government also told Shanghai Shangling to increase production to 1.2 million units. The timing, however, could not have been worse. During the early to mid-1990s, factories manufacturing refrigerators and other "hot" consumer products had sprouted around the country. And players like Qingdao Haier were aggressively trying to break into the Shanghai market. Also, some 70% of urban families in China already owned refrigerators by the end of 1995. Soon there were far more refrigerators for sale than consumers willing to buy them and Shanghai Shangling's sales at the end of 1995 started falling for the first time.

How did Shanghai Shangling react? At first it did nothing—nothing apart from following the strategy already laid out by the Shanghai government, which was to produce 1.2 million refrigerators in 1996. "They kept producing until the end of the third quarter," explained Jason Yin, a Shanghai-based industry analyst at a foreign brokerage. "Already, 800,000 had been produced when they finally realized they had no chance of selling 1.2 million units. In the end, they produced 800,000 units and sold only 600,000." In 1996, Shanghai Shangling's refrigerator sales plummeted 30% to 1.4 billion yuan (US$169 million), while Qingdao Haier's sales surged 73% to 2.6 billion yuan (US$313 million). At the end of that year, the Shanghai government replaced 58-year-old general manger Ge with a 42-year-old named Cheng Junming. Cheng had previously run a state-owned investment firm and, according to company managers, was one of the "best entrepreneurs in China."

In 1997, I spoke with Vice General Manager Lu and company executive Liu Huiqun about the company's precipitous fall from grace and its plans for turning the situation around. Their comments show to what extent Shanghai Shangling, Shanghai's best refrigerator maker, had neglected the "software" of a market economy—software that its major competitors in other provinces did not ignore. The company typifies the behavior of Shanghai's indigenous consumer product makers during the reform era. For one, Shanghai companies were notorious for their complacency and arrogance well into the 1990s. Even Shanghai Mayor Xu Kuangdi hinted at this problem in 1995 when he commented on television that although Shanghai faced growing competition from other parts of the country, it still maintained a sense of superiority.[11] Shanghai Shangling's Liu confirmed that complacency reigned at her employer. Recently transferred to the company's new marketing department, the middle-aged manager said,

Before our refrigerators just sold too well. We were like the daughter of the empress who has no fear of never marrying. Our previous general manger came from the manufacturing department. He had conservative ideas. He didn't understand that the market had changed. He just thought the market would be soft for a while. So he just sent refrigerators to the storeroom, saying that we would sell them once the market returned. We kept manufacturing old models with old colors. The company did not know what was going on in the market— no survey, no nothing.

Liu's comments alluded to another problem besetting Shanghai's homegrown companies: a failure to recognize the importance of marketing strategy and product innovation. Shanghai Shangling, for instance, only had 20 people on its sales team until 1995 and did not have a functioning marketing department until 1996, even though Guangdong Kelon and Qingdao Haier were already aggressively promoting their products. While they set up sections dedicated exclusively to their brands in major department stores, Shanghai Shangling was happy to let department store management promote its brand for it. Shangling launched only three new products in 1995 and, according to Liu, the products were new only in the sense that the company had slightly modified their appearance. Management made little effort to improve product function, strictly control quality, and cut manufacturing costs. For example, Shanghai Shangling's purchasing department did not bother to compare vendors when ordering supplies. The company advertised very little. "We thought our products were good. We didn't need to advertise," Liu explained. "Other successful refrigerator makers paid a lot of attention to advertising and marketing when the market was still good."

Moreover, the company did not expand much outside of Shanghai, a common mistake made by Shanghai's homegrown consumer product makers. Its sales and distribution network did not reach beyond eastern China in the mid-1990s and consumers could buy its refrigerators in only 200 sales outlets. Shanghai managers generally assumed that Shanghai's market was sufficiently large to buoy sales, neglecting to realize that rivals from other provinces planned to feed on it too. Traditional Shanghainese attitudes toward the provinces have also impeded Shanghai companies' expansion into the hinterland. Shanghainese are often not willing to move to places they consider more backward than Shanghai, but they often do not have enough confidence in non-Shanghainese in those places to hire them to run their business there. Woetzel, the McKinsey consultant, commented in 1999: "Shanghainese don't want to travel and they don't want to let people in. Shanghai consumer product companies can't imagine being a national company. They're stuck in this place and can't grow." Although some Shanghai consumer product companies aggressively sought nationwide market share in the 1990s—the Shanghai press, for instance, regularly ran stories praising White Cat Detergent Company for establishing a sales network in 29 provinces by 1998[12]— they were the exceptions.

At the start of 1997, Shanghai Shangling's new government-appointed "entrepreneur" initiated a series of changes aimed at making the refrigerator maker more market-oriented. He sent mid-level managers and engineers into the field to talk to Shangling users about product quality, beefed up the company's after-sales service program, linked salespeople's income to their performance, and expanded the company's distribution network. Both Liu and Lu were excited by the prospect of becoming a more market-oriented company. I asked Liu, who had worked for many years in administration at Shanghai Shangling, if she liked her new job in the company's new marketing department. Nodding her head, the matronly manager said:

I like it very much. It's a kind of art to sell products to people in different ways. Now I understand what they like. In Sichuan, people prefer the color yellow. Shanghainese prefer milky white. In the countryside, especially in the north, people like a picture of a fat baby on their refrigerator. Shanghainese really hate that. I need to understand culture, habits, and psychology. My job is much more interesting.

Unfortunately, Shangling's initiatives proved too little too late. Its competitors had already grown too strong. In 1998, Qingdao Haier Refrigerator did 3.8 billion yuan (US$458 million) in sales and made a 274-million-yuan (US$33 million) profit. Guangdong Kelon did 3.8 billion yuan (US$458 million) in sales and earned profits of 667 million yuan (US$80 million). Shanghai Shangling, meanwhile, only sold 440 million yuan (US$53 million) worth of refrigerators to eke out a profit of 10 million yuan (US$1.2 million).

Apart from management complacency, poor marketing strategies, and other internal problems, Shanghai's consumer product companies also complained that they suffered from a relative lack of municipal government support. According to Shanghai Shangling's Lu, for instance, the refrigerator maker could not spend as much money on advertising or R&D as rivals elsewhere because the Shanghai government owned many more companies than other cities and, as a result, its support was scattered rather than focused on a handful of firms. Moreover, the Shanghai government preferred to support new and more prestigious industries like telecommunications and cars. Lu explained:

Shanghai companies can't put as much money into advertising as Haier [partly owned by the Qingdao government] and Kelon [a rural enterprise] because conditions in Shanghai are different. Shanghai has six pillar industries and electrical appliances are just one of them. Qingdao, on the other hand, does not have much industry and the Qingdao government can invest a lot of money to help Haier. And Kelon can get money from within its own company.

In 1997, I asked Shanghai Vice Mayor Zhao Qizheng why he thought Shanghai's household appliance sector had fared so poorly. Zhao was considered one of Shanghai's most sophisticated officials. That's why I was a little surprised when he spouted Lu's argument of lack of government support as the primary reason. Relaxed and polished-looking, Zhao commented:

Yes, Shanghai is behind in this area [household electrical appliance]. Maybe Shanghai has ignored this area. We led it 20 years ago. So probably we thought it's fine and that we can develop other industries like cars, computers, and so on. Now other places [in China] are better in this sector.

Stressing the government's role in improving these firms, he went on to describe how the Shanghai government planned to invest more money in the electrical appliance sector and merge faltering enterprises to form group companies. These were the sole solutions to the sectors' woes that he mentioned, as if they would be enough to buttress Shanghai firms facing stiff competition from more market-oriented rivals. Also, both Lu and Vice Mayor Zhao failed to mention the favoritism that the Shanghai government has traditionally shown its companies on their home turf. Hu Xiongfei, deputy director of the Shanghai Economic Commission, gave an example in 1998:

When Sichuan Changhong, a state enterprise owned by the central government, wants to sell its TV sets in Shanghai to compete with our Shanghai Jinxing brand, obviously we give priority to Jinxing. The Shanghai Economic Commission would likely contact the Shanghai Commerce Commission to reach an agreement to support Jinxing in terms of sales channels and distribution of profits. In this way, we provide a cushion not just against products made by central government companies but against all non-local products.

As part of ongoing efforts to separate government functions from state enterprise management, the Shanghai government implemented reforms in 1996 to transform the Shanghai Economic Commission from a municipal government entity with direct ownership of city's state enterprises into a regulatory body that would indirectly guide enterprise development. However, the intended impact of the reform has not yet been fully felt. "This is a complicated reform that can't be carried out overnight," Hu said. "Obviously there are still relationships between the Shanghai Economic Commission and Shanghai's state companies. I think it will take eight to 10 years to achieve this."

Between this local protectionism and the head start Shanghai's companies had in winning Shanghai residents' hearts, the city's home appliance firms had little excuse for not at least dominating their home market. The Shanghainese, who traditionally have enjoyed a reputation for being the best managers in China, simply did not manage their businesses well.

Unfortunately, the household electrical appliance sector was not the only pillar industry to suffer from inertia in the 1990s. Consultants working in other important industries in the city—telecommunications, automobiles, steel, and energy—noticed similar attitudes and behavior. Take telecommunications. Chinese companies have proven highly competitive in the programmed switching market, a relatively new and high-tech business for China. The country's top five homegrown manufacturers[13] together accounted for at least 50% of sales in the sector in 1998, and have been dubbed the "five golden flowers" of China's telecommunications industry. None of them are from Shanghai. Shanghai's claim to fame in the programmed switching market is Shanghai Bell— a joint venture with European switching giant Alcatel. Or consider automotive components. Shanghai wants to be the Detroit of China and will probably get there thanks to car manufacturing ventures with Volkswagen and General Motors that the central government allocated to the city. Foreign auto component manufacturers have also set up joint ventures in Shanghai, which started coming on-line in the last few years of the decade. But Shanghai's own state-owned component suppliers, enjoying little competition for most of the 1990s, failed to impress. They were unable to improve design and quality sufficiently to produce parts that consistently met international standards. Jonathan Woetzel, the Shanghai-based principal at McKinsey & Co., commented in 1997:

There's been complacency in this industry as well. Auto component companies are sitting on real estate downtown waiting to sell. They see they have a cash cow. You see it in their mindset when it comes to concepts of customer service and quality levels. They don't think it has to be better than good enough. This is common in other industrial sectors in Shanghai like steel and energy. It's just more obvious in the auto industry because automobiles are a consumer good.

Baoshan Iron & Steel Co. generally gets high marks from analysts as the mainland's most profitable and efficient steel manufacturer. However, it is by no means a typical Shanghai indigenous state enterprise. Established by the central government in a Shanghai suburb in the early 1980s with modern imported equipment, it has not suffered from overstaffing and other traditional state enterprise ailments. Moreover, it reports directly to the central government rather than to Shanghai authorities. The steel mills that the Shanghai government administered itself (until their government-mandated merger with Baoshan Iron & Steel in late 1997) were inefficient, overstaffed producers, losing money in 1995 and making only a small profit in 1996.

State Enterprise Reform—Not Far Enough

In many ways the failure of Shanghai's homegrown firms to adapt well to China's burgeoning market economy reflects the limited success and slow pace of state enterprise reform in Shanghai and China in general. To its credit, the Shanghai government has managed the difficult problem of downsizing hundreds of thousands of surplus state workers well. It has organized job training programs, employment agencies, and—most importantly—a new welfare system that provides workers some benefits without bankrupting the city. Although life is tough in Shanghai for laid-off workers and finding a decent job is not easy, they are not starving and there has not been as much labor unrest as in some other parts of the country. Throughout the 1990s the Shanghai government has also methodically implemented other popular reforms at its state enterprises. It has given managers more autonomy, introduced boards of directors and other corporate management structures, turned industrial bureaus into holding companies, merged enterprises, brought in new investors, and so on. The problem is that the most popular reforms of the day did not go far enough for most of the 1990s. They did not eradicate government interference or provide managers effective incentives. As a result, they did not significantly transform and improve enterprise management. "Basically there has been no fundamental change," admitted the head of a quasi independent think tank in Shanghai in late 1999.

In 1998, I visited a number of state enterprises in Shanghai to learn how state enterprise reform was faring. One of them was machinery-maker Pacific Mechtronic Group, a Shanghai-based holding company that has been at the forefront of state enterprise reform in Shanghai. Pacific Mechtronic was formed in 1994 by the merger of Shanghai's machinery and textile equipment bureaus, as part of Shanghai's holding company reforms, which aimed to separate government and enterprise functions by turning government bureaus into corporations. The new holding company subsequently merged the 33 factories under the two former bureaus into 13 companies. Besides consolidating factories and forming holding companies, the group has tried to improve management at its subsidiaries with a slew of other reforms. A number of managers at Pacific Mechtronic Group and its subsidiaries talked to me in 1998 about the results of those reforms. Because they were at the time taking new initiatives that they expected to improve management, they were not afraid to discuss past failures. The contract responsibility system, which was popular in China in the late 1980s and early 1990s, for instance, led factory managers to use their new limited autonomy to maximize personal gain rather than invest for the company's long-term success. Group research head Tan Wenhui, a stocky middle-aged man with a round face and disarming laugh, explained: "It resulted in short-term behavior. Since the factory leader didn't own the assets, but just had the right to use them, he would overuse the assets to get as much benefit as possible before the contract was finished. He was likely to put the profits into his pockets rather than reinvest."

Pacific Mechtronic also merged factories to achieve economies of scale and make better use of resources and personnel. But management problems persisted. Discussing the merger of three of the group's factories in the first half of the decade, Tan commented:

The merger was only a merger in form. It did not create a new system of management. All the workers went to one factory. The holding company appointed the new general manager from among the former factory leaders. He was the one who was the strongest, but we found that we were wrong. He worked very hard, but didn't understand a market economy. He just listened to administrative instructions from the holding company. Also, conflicts occurred between the personnel in the three different factories.

This is not to say that the government's policy of merging enterprises cannot improve competitiveness. Following the downturn in Shanghai's household appliance sector in the mid-1990s, the Shanghai government merged its four television makers together. Afterward, Shanghai Jinxing was able use the three other companies' sales network to extend its reach. It was also able to increase production to 800,000 units a year, which allowed it to cut prices and increase bargaining clout with department stores. "We put all the management together and improved it," said the Shanghai Economic Commission's Hu Xiongfei in 1998. "It's better than before although not as competitive as Sichuan Changhong, which produces 6.8 million sets annually."

But while government-orchestrated mergers under the right conditions have raised efficiency, they have not proved a panacea since they have not generally led to a fundamental change in how these companies are run. Moreover, the city's efforts to turn its bureaus into holding companies, though a first step toward breaking the link between government and state-owned companies, was a change in form but not in substance. The holding companies were staffed with the same bureaucrats, who were responsible to the same organs above and dealt with the companies under them in the same bureaucratic ways. In the mid-1990s, the Shanghai government tried to improve management at its new holding companies (former bureaus) and their subsidiaries by introducing a variety of shareholding reforms. These included turning holding companies like Pacific Mechtronic and their underlings into limited liability companies, selling shares to a small number of outside investors, and listing shares on China's stock markets. Although these reforms clarified ownership, the performance of Pacific Mechtronic's companies continued to disappoint. A public stock offering, for instance, provided its subsidiary Shanghai Erfangji Co. with new capital, but as of 1998 the company had reported losses for four straight years. Although the textile industry's retrenchment as a whole explained some of its woes, Tan, Pacific Mechtronic's head of research, pinned the blame mostly on "unscientific" management resulting from the Shanghai government's continuing majority ownership of the company. "Nothing changed because the state-owned portion remained more than 50%. The minority shareholders did not have enough power to make a difference in decision-making," Tan said. "At board meetings, there was usually a discussion. The general manager would first talk briefly about the company's performance and prospects. The whole meeting would last about an hour, without letting minority investors examine the enterprise in detail—let alone give their point of view."

As majority owner, Pacific Mechtronic continued to intervene heavily in its subsidiaries' operations, giving orders to its government-appointed general managers. Tan and the other managers at Pacific Mechtronic described the situation as *laoban shuole suan*—or "whatever the boss says goes." General managers have not traditionally had much voice in decision-making. They, for instance, have not had the power to choose their own senior executives and have needed the holding company's approval to make investment decisions above a fixed amount, export, and develop new products. According to Wu Lingling, the general manager of Pacific Mechtronic subsidiary Aton Electric:

In the past, it was administrative instruction that counted. If a factory leader had different ideas, he would not be strong enough to fight against his boss. For example, if Pacific Mechtronic's finance department wanted to borrow money, the company had to lend the money. And you had to do that without any specific interest rate.

The holding company was not the only entity to meddle in the subsidiaries' operations. The subsidiaries also had to respond to various local administrative bureaus in charge of managing state assets, setting economic strategy, collecting taxes, overseeing foreign trade, and so on. Tan explained:

There's been too much interference from administrative bodies, which are eager to control and have a finger in the pie. If some of these organizations want to inspect the enterprise, you need to have someone there to receive them. Also, you frequently have to give them statistics and reports. And you need their approval for this or that. At present there are too many mothers-in-law.

Meanwhile, the government's system of appointing "entrepreneurs" to run the city's enterprises and rotating them from one company or bureau to another has perverted behavior. State enterprise general managers have tended to care only about the current market situation rather than the future. They know that by the time the future has arrived they will have been promoted to another enterprise or position in the bureaucracy or even to a plum sinecure in the central government. According to Tan, being a manager in the state enterprise system has been "a way of social climbing." Shanghai's undeclared status as a training ground for central government leaders has exacerbated this tendency since a posting in the nation's capital is more possible than for bureaucrats from other provinces. Li Bo, a Shanghai-based consultant involved in state enterprise restructuring in China, explained: "If you've been successful in Shanghai, you will be quickly promoted to the central government. It's possible that Shanghai's success in politics hurts the city's success in economics."

But even if the enterprise did not perform well during the manager's tenure, the manager would usually be transferred to another position without suffering any adverse consequences. "It has really only been up to the factory leaders' decency. If he happened to be a decent or responsible person, then things went better for the enterprise. If he was not a decent person and things didn't go well, that was okay too," Tan commented. The system has also encouraged a "yes-man" culture as current and future job prospects depend on how well managers follow their superiors' orders. It has led good managers to be replaced for resisting their superiors' desires, and has even caused managers who build a profitable business to be transferred in order for an official to place his own man at the helm of a prosperous company. There's no guarantee that the replacement will be as capable as the original and, in the end, the enterprise and its employees are the ones to suffer.

Since the 15th Communist Party Congress in September 1997, state enterprise reform has taken a promising tack. President Jiang Zemin decreed at the congress that the state would "release" from its ownership small and medium-sized state enterprises. The policy has freed state firms like Pacific Mechtronic to lease and sell majority stakes in their smaller companies to employees, private entrepreneurs, foreigners, and others. Previously, such moves would have been criticized as privatization, which the Party viewed as ideologically unacceptable. The Shanghai government has also been experimenting with new market-oriented ways to motivate executives, including firing them and giving them stock options. The reforms, depending on how and to what extent they're carried out, raise for the first time the possibility of fundamental management change.

Pacific Mechtronic's Tan took me to visit Aton Electric and another small company where new shareholding reforms had advanced the farthest. Wu Lingling, the 45-year-old general manager at Aton Electric, for instance, described to me in 1998 how she was purchasing 1.1 million yuan (US$132,530) worth of the company's shares in installments, which she said encouraged her to manage the company to the best of her ability. Although Pacific Mechtronic is still the company's largest shareholder and the state-owned textile holding company continues to control 20%, Pacific Mechtronic has sold half of the company's shares to employees and outside investors. As a result, she said, she no longer felt compelled to acquiesce to Pacific Mechtronic's demands to the same extent as previously. Wu, who had been a factory leader at another group subsidiary before the government transferred her to Aton Electric in 1994, proudly told me about her refusal in 1998 to agree to the holding company's request for a large loan, unless it signed a promissory note to pay annual interest. When Pacific Mechtronic refused her terms, she ignored its objections by including the interest payment in Aton Electric's annual budget, which went before Aton's board of directors for approval. In the end, Pacific Mechtronic paid back the loan with the interest. Of course, Aton still had to loan Pacific Mechtronic money, suggesting that the holding company still has some influence over the company's management. I asked if she worried about continued government interference given that the state still owned half of the company's shares. Reveling in her small budget victory, Wu commented:

This is a problem, but there always has to be a dominant shareholder. It's already very bold for Pacific Mechtronic to transfer so many shares to other parties. Since these reforms, Pacific Mechtronic has not put its finger in the pie in terms of company management. It's true that if I make Pacific Mechtronic mad, they could give me a hard time since they are still the largest shareholder, but I don't worry about that now because we have the same common interest to manage the company's assets well. Before the purpose was not so clear.

Wu's experience was encouraging. But it was also clear that Pacific Mechtronic was showing me its most promising example of reform. Aton, which makes electrical components for textile machinery, enjoyed a number of advantages that other small and medium-sized state enterprises would be lucky to replicate. For one, in 1996 the Shanghai government gave the former loss-maker permission to do what many struggling state enterprises wait in line for years to do: It was allowed to declare bankruptcy. The central government in the 1990s limited the number of bankruptcies each year to control the number of laid-off workers annually and protect its banks from intentional debt avoidance. Wu explained.

For us bankruptcy was very important because we could not survive with a debt-to-equity ratio of 150%. Each year we had to pay seven million yuan

(US$843,373) to service our debt, but in 1995 our annual sales were less than 10 million yuan (US$1.2 million). Before that our sales had been 30–40 million yuan (US$3.6–US$4.8 million) a year, but they dropped because our products couldn't meet the needs of the market. If our quality had been good, there would have been a lot of demand.

Aton subsequently let go 900 employees, retaining only 70 people from the old company. It no longer has a heavy debt burden to service or an army of retirees on its payroll. It has also signed a licensing agreement with U.S.-based Rockwell Automation to assemble machine components based on Rockwell technology and receives training and technical support from the American company. As a result, Aton sales have grown and the restructured company is once again profitable.

Unfortunately, not all small and medium-sized state enterprises are as well-positioned as Aton to profit from these reforms. Some of the loss-making subsidiaries in Pacific Mechtronic's stable were still waiting for permission to go bankrupt in 1998. Laden down with debts and excess employees, they were hard pressed to attract a foreign partner. "For small state enterprises, the more beautiful girls get married first," quipped Tan. Pacific Mechtronic's "less beautiful girls" meanwhile did what they could to survive. A subsidiary that manufactures spare parts for textile weaving machinery, for instance, was selling land-use rights of its properties, going into real estate development, and renting out workers. Also, the Shanghai government in some cases is selling only minority stakes of subsidiaries to employees and outside investors, particularly if it believes the company shows promise. Unfortunately, it is hard to imagine that these companies, despite their status as shareholding companies with multiple investors, will not continue to experience government interference. And there's no guarantee that once small and medium-sized firms are "released," their managers will be skilled enough to beat the competition and turn losses into profits. Still, some of them will, which will be an improvement from the past.

But if the Shanghai government is "releasing" troubled small and mid-sized state enterprises, it has no intention of giving up majority control of its most important companies. Mirroring central government efforts at the national level to equip its largest enterprises to compete at home and abroad against multinational corporations, the Shanghai government is turning 54 of its 270 group companies into conglomerates (nine of them are also on the central government's list of favored group companies). Of those 54 "conglomerates," 31 are involved in manufacturing industries, including automobiles, steel, chemicals, computers, electronics, household electrical appliances, and garments. They are expected to develop new products and power Shanghai's manufacturing sector through the 21st century. Like provincial governments around China, Shanghai's has been busy bulking up its budding conglomerates through mergers and offering them preferential policies. Special privileges vary from province to province depending on the local government's level of prosperity. The Shanghai government can afford to be quite generous, offering more than 20 perks, including 100% tax refunds, forgiveness of debts incurred from municipal government-driven investments, and priority in obtaining loans. Explaining the thinking behind the conglomerate policy, the Shanghai Economic Commission's Hu Xiongfei commented:

The goal is to resolve historic problems. Now it may seem that offering special treatment to key local companies flies in the face of China's bid to enter the World Trade Organization [which requires equal treatment of domestic and foreign companies], but the fact is that the government wants to relieve these companies of their historic burdens to help them develop quickly so that they can compete equally with foreign companies in the open market. So these are preparations for China's entry into the World Trade Organization.

Although Korea's economic woes during the Asian Financial Crisis of 1997–1999 are often blamed on the coddling of that country's big business groups, Shanghai's and China's policy of creating conglomerates through state-orchestrated mergers and preferential policies continues to barrel ahead. Sitting in a modern conference room at the Shanghai Municipal Government's headquarters, Hu explained why I should not worry that Shanghai's conglomerates will face the same fate as Korea's. He said:

Conglomerates in Korea played an important role changing Korea from an agricultural to an industrial country. Their failure was not because conglomerate policy was wrong but because Korean politics were so corrupt and its legal system was not sophisticated enough. Preferential policies did not cause Korean conglomerates problems, the corruption of government officials did. Korean law says loans should not exceed 20% of assets, but loans exceeded more than 200% of assets! It's illegal! So the policy of conglomerates in China is not changing. We just need to pay attention to the financial and legal system to monitor how these financial institutions help out conglomerates. If we Chinese learn the lesson of Korea's conglomerates I believe we can do well.

I would like to be as optimistic as Hu, but China at the start of the 21st century does not have a sophisticated legal or financial system either, and corruption continues to be a problem for China too. More importantly, the policy has come along just as China's banks are trying to overcome their long history of making loans according to government fiat. It may slow that trend since these "pet" groups will need loans to grow and banks will inevitably feel pressure to lend to them. Also, given how important these conglomerates are to the Shanghai government's strategy, it seems unlikely that Shanghai bureaucrats (including holding company executives) will not continue to interfere in their affairs. That would not be worrisome if local authorities had a track record of nurturing market-oriented firms capable of competing successfully in fierce competition without protection, but that has simply not been the case.

When I first seriously started looking into the problems of Shanghai's indigenous manufacturing industries in 1996 and 1997, many thoughtful observers saw government meddling in companies business operations as a major obstacle to their development. For instance, Li Bo, the Shanghai-based consultant involved in state enterprise restructuring in China, remarked:

There's been too much interference. Shanghai 'entrepreneurs' are too controlled and too conformist. In the 1980s, the city had good products. "Made in Shanghai" was a brand name. But the success of the past created a kind of arrogance, which when combined with strong regulation from different government bodies, made companies slow to react.

Indeed, observers saw government interference in Shanghai as even greater than in other parts of China. Commenting on Shanghai's economic bureaucracy, Woetzel, the Shanghai-based principal at McKinsey, noted: "It's more control-oriented and less change-oriented than in southern China and even in some northern cities like Tianjin. In Shanghai they say: 'We've always done it this way. We're the center of China.'"

Unfortunately, the Shanghai government shows no sign of changing its ways as the city enters the new century, auguring poorly for the future of Shanghai's homegrown manufacturing effort. A tight team of people at the top—including vice mayors Chen Liangyu and Jiang Yiren—control the city's economic bureaucracy. Although managers these days no longer feel complacent and are more likely to recognize what they need to do to improve their businesses, they feel powerless to force change within the current power structure. Woetzel explained in November 1999:

Senior managers of Shanghai state enterprises can't say 'boo' without getting these guys' approval. These guys have authority over approving major investments and personnel decisions. If you ask them why they do it, they say 'My money, my companies.' Shanghai government officials are reasonably competent. They're good a building bridges, but they're not good at managing companies. Their interest comes down to not rocking the boat, not firing large numbers of people in an unmanaged way. They have to be in charge to manage layoffs. In the midst of all this management, companies have to grow to have markets and make profits. The bureaucrats have not made the connection between entrepreneurs and loosening of the city's control. They think they can have state-sponsored entrepreneurs in Shanghai. They haven't realized that they are slowly killing their companies.

Stifled Innovation

The Shanghai government's control tendencies have also hampered its goals of fostering innovation and high-tech development. The trend is alarming given that Shanghai manufacturers, who can no longer beat their rivals on price, need to offer more technologically advanced products to compete. It also calls into question the ultimate success of the city's drive to develop three new high-tech industries: information technology, biotechnology, and new industrial materials.

The Shanghai government is well aware that the city so far has failed to emerge as the country's technological leader. At the Municipal Government Work Conference on December 6, 1999, Mayor Xu Kuangdi conveyed his disappointment that Shanghai is "lagging behind Shenzhen and Beijing in technological innovation."[14] The question is whether the city's officials will realize before it's too late that their determination to use state-planning means to achieve their goals is a big part of the problem.

In the summer of 1997, I discussed the state of innovation in Shanghai with a government official at Shanghai's Science and Technology Commission. We met in the air-conditioned comfort of a Western fast-food restaurant not far from the government's new headquarters near People's Park. The official, who looked to be in his late thirties, was not sure at the time exactly why cities like Shenzhen and Beijing seemed to be progressing faster on the high-tech front. However, he did patiently explain that Shanghai's innovation problems, like so many of its manufacturing problems, are rooted in China's state-planning history and Shanghai's status as a stronghold of state enterprise.

Under the traditional state-planning system, companies relied on the government for everything, including research. Instead of enterprises having their own research and development staff, the government would assign R&D projects to state-run research institutes and university labs. It would then allocate the technology developed in these labs to its state enterprises. The research institutes, the official explained, worked to satisfy the government rather than the market.

Although good basic research often took place in Shanghai's research institutes and university labs, the state-dominated system hindered that research from generating commercially viable products. Gui Aizhen, a 53-year-old entrepreneur and a member of the Shanghai Enterprises Association for Science and Technology, recounted to me how she spent part of her career in the 1980s conducting research on metals in a state-run lab. When she eventually made a breakthrough, she had to get her innovation certified by the government. The officials in charge criticized her work so heavily that she broke into tears. The second time she applied for certification, she obsequiously told the officials she changed her report according to their suggestions, even though she really only changed it a little. They liked the innovation more, they said, but not enough to certify it. When she applied for approval a third time, she again told the officials she had modified her work significantly, although in reality she had not changed it at all. They lauded her achievement and awarded her an official certificate of innovation. They then stuffed her report into a file and forgot about it. "When I asked why no one was using a good innovation they told me it was none of my business. The government wasted their money and time," she said, shaking her head. She subsequently left the institute to start her own company, which by the end of the 1990s was considered one of Shanghai's only successful private manufacturing companies in heavy industry. Unfortunately, Gui was arrested in July 1999 on embezzlement charges. Meanwhile, her former research institute during the same period made little progress transforming its innovations into marketable products. Blaming the situation mostly on government intervention and the Communist Party's personnel appointment system, Gui said in early 1999: "In my view, the key problem is that the government appoints the directors of the research institutes. The position is not market-oriented. They're bureaucrats. All they care about is their position. They are very conservative."

Research institutes' dependence on the government for work and poor incentive structures, moreover, has stifled researchers' drive to achieve. The comments of a scientist at a research center under Shanghai's chemical bureau in 1997 were particularly telling. Surnamed Li, his job was to develop new industrial materials. Li, a thin, talkative man in his early thirties, said:

Most research institutes get money from the government—not from companies—so their research does not have much of a goal. It also doesn't have a time limit so there's no time pressure. If they get a result, the researchers may be able to ask for a bonus, but it's a very small amount of money. If the government gives them a project, they have to take it whether they think they can do it or not. Also, the institutes apply to get government projects, even when they don't think they can succeed—it's just good for the reputation of the research institute to get the project. If they actually succeed, of course it's good. But if you don't succeed, no one blames you. The bureaucrats that award the projects and issue the money don't understand the technology anyway, but they understand that it's difficult to succeed.

Meanwhile, state-owned companies in Shanghai and around the country in the 1980s and 1990s found another channel for obtaining technology: foreign companies. But while they could use the imported technology, even Shanghai's largest and most successful companies usually were unable to improve it, said the Shanghai science commission's official. Most domestic companies did not have their own scientific talent. The official estimated in 1997 that only one-fifth to one-quarter of Shanghai's scientists were employed in enterprises—the rest worked for institutes, universities, or the government. Chinese companies also had to attend to other pressing matters, like setting up distribution channels and downsizing their workforces. Most Chinese enterprises saw little need for innovation since demand for goods in China always exceeded supply up until the second half of the decade. Manufacturers could pretty much sell whatever they produced without concern for cutting costs, upgrading quality, or releasing new products. As long as state enterprises obtained money, either from the government or foreign investors, they could buy the materials, equipment, and land they needed. Obsessed with short-term profits, they were less interested in strengthening their core business than investing in the latest "hot" sector—whether it be shopping malls, television sets, or health tonics. Investing in R&D seemed both expensive and risky compared with channeling funds into something tangible like real estate.

Another obstacle preventing the commercialization of research was funding. Innovators like Gui who were unable to finance their projects through state research institutes had only one other way to obtain money—hitting up family and friends. China's state banks normally lent money to state enterprises, not to young companies with no assets and no track record. The situation improved somewhat in the last part of the 1990s as the central and Shanghai governments started recognizing the value of innovation and private enterprise. The Shanghai government, for instance, set up venture capital companies and technology incubators aimed at helping start-up companies develop. Foreign venture capital companies have also started investing in promising technology projects, as have local companies such as Shanghai Fortune High-Tech (Group) Co. China's nascent venture capital industry, however, has been fraught with even greater risks than in most markets due to regulatory hurdles. Normally, venture capitalists earn their money by helping make start-ups attractive for other companies to buy or by taking the new company public. But both acquisitions and public listings in China require government approvals. In the 1990s, the central and Shanghai governments by and large only approved big state-owned companies to list shares, thus depriving innovators, venture capitalists, and even prospective employees of a major incentive for involving themselves in risky start-ups. In June 1998, Shanghai Fortune Hi-Tech Group was, in fact, the first nonstate enterprise in Shanghai to win approval to go public in the city. Recognizing this problem and hoping to resolve the country's unemployment crisis, the central government took a step in the right direction when it announced plans in 1999 to make it easier for small and high-tech companies to list shares.

Starting an innovation-based firm has been risky in other ways. Innovators have had to worry about other companies copying their idea or product since enforcement of intellectual property rights is poor in China. Then there are the other "special characteristics" of doing business that create additional market risk. Before taking the job at the research institute under Shanghai's chemical bureau, Li, the Shanghai-based researcher, actually developed a cable product that was innovative for China and was trying to make a business out of it. His biggest challenge, however, was getting payment from state-owned factories to maintain enough floating capital to keep the business going. "If you do not have a close relationship with the customer, then they won't give you money after they buy your products," he said, explaining that the close relationship was needed so that the procurement manager felt safe accepting his bribe. "Offering a cheaper, higher-quality product is not what makes you their preferred supplier," he concluded.

Given these and other obstacles, it is hardly surprising that Shanghai and China in general did not churn out many innovative or high-tech products in the 1980s and 1990s. That said, as competitive pressures started to mount in the Chinese economy, some Chinese homegrown companies in the electrical appliance and telecommunications fields started moving up the technology curve and even innovating off of imported technologies. Shanghai's indigenous companies, however, have generally been slower off the mark for the same reason that many have lost market share: too much government control. The Shanghai government may tell its electronics companies to produce DVDs and wide access phones or some other hot high-tech consumer product, but they do not have the proper systems in place—the organization, the people, or the approval authority—to seize the opportunity. If the general manager of a Shanghai state enterprise wants to hire 15 engineers in the United States to work for him, it will take countless approvals, by which time rivals will have already established their brand.

During the last half of the 1990s, information technology was probably the best business opportunity in China. The Shanghai government named it one of the city's three key high-tech industries. Municipal authorities subsequently put considerable effort into developing the city's computer industry, extending low-interest loans to support indigenous computer brands like Changjiang and Huadong. But in 1999, the three top computer makers in China in terms of sales and brand recognition were Legend, Founder, and Great Wall—all Beijing-based companies. Legend, which has proven particularly adept at sales, marketing, and product development, captured nearly 30% of China's personal computer market by late 1999.[15] A good indicator of where activity is concentrated in China's information technology industry is the investment portfolio of IDG Technology Venture Investment. Since 1996, the subsidiary of Boston-based International Data Group has invested more than US$100 million in software, telecom, Internet, and other high-tech companies in China and is considered the most aggressive foreign player in the field. At the end of 1999, it had invested in 30 companies in Beijing, more than 10 in Shenzhen, and seven in Shanghai. Another indicator is the whereabouts during any given week of my husband, who is a Hong Kong-based investment banker focusing on technology companies. He regularly travels to Shenzhen and Beijing to work on technology deals, but rarely to Shanghai. This is not to say that Shanghai has not been gripped by Internet fever like Shenzhen, Beijing, and many other cities in Asia. It has been. The level of activity, however, has not as significant as in China's capital city or in the southern special economic zone bordering Hong Kong.

In late 1999, I paid another visit to the Shanghai Science and Technology Commission official to get an update on the city's efforts to foster innovation and promote high-tech industries. I asked him why Shanghai's home-grown companies did not appear to be emerging as key domestic players in the information-technology sector, given its supposed importance to the city's future. Whereas when I first met him in 1997, he could not tell me why Shanghai lagged, this time around he had the answer. With an air of resignation, he replied: "It's a systemic problem. Most information technology companies in Shanghai are backed by the government and are not successful."

Of Shanghai's three high-tech industries, the city's biotech/pharmaceutical sector holds the most promise. Its labs do international-caliber basic research, including developing advanced cloning technology. The city also faces very little domestic competition. However, its biotech companies are still small, involved mainly in R&D. That is partly because the local market is not yet prosperous enough to support the industry, but also because firms are short of funds to develop into large, internationally competitive companies. Indeed, Shanghai's pharmaceutical industry as a whole pulled in total revenues of less than two billion yuan annually (US$240 million) at the end of the decade and could not boast a nationally known brand name. Just as in the information technology industry, government ownership was holding the city's homegrown biotechnology and pharmaceutical companies back. The official explained:

It's not a problem of the pharmaceutical industry, it's a problem of enterprises in Shanghai in general. An enterprise can only grow big when the government invests money. In Shanghai the government has only invested in the automobile industry and other big industries. Except for government investment, there's really not much private investment. So it's hard for biotechnology and pharmaceutical companies to grow big. There are instead many small companies.

The city's plan for developing its three key high-tech industries in the future, unfortunately, does not leave much room for hope. Although it will make it easier for small companies to obtain funds, it is indicative of the city's control fetish and continued use of state-planning methods to succeed in a market economy.

The official patiently explained the plan to me. In 1998, the Shanghai government set up an innovation center to identify high-tech innovations for commercialization. The center has already pinpointed more than 600 projects, offering them preferential policies like tax breaks, land, and help obtaining funding. To facilitate financing, the municipal government established a venture capital fund in August 1999. It supplied most of the capital, some 600 million yuan (US$72.3 million), while the city's listed arm in Hong Kong, Shanghai Industrial Holdings, contributed 200 million yuan (US$24.1 million). True to form, the government appointed a bureaucrat—a former director of the Shanghai Science and Technology Commission—to head the fund. Underneath the foundation, the Shanghai government has set up a number of venture capital management companies to choose and manage the city's promising high-tech projects. Five of the venture capital firms are government companies, one is a shareholding company, and a seventh company is foreign-invested.

At this point in our conversation I had to ask the official if he thought the scheme would succeed. To me it sounded heavy on government involvement, auguring a repeat of past management problems. Instead of evading the question or reciting a pat response like most bureaucrats, the official said earnestly, "It will be very hard for this plan to work. It's all government. The five management companies are government companies so they will choose government projects which will have difficulty succeeding." Meanwhile, Guangdong province, which has been taking a more hands-off approach, is already far ahead of Shanghai in developing private high-tech enterprises. The cautious optimism that the official exuded when I first interviewed him in 1997 had disappeared completely. His brow furrowed, he then told me he planned to quit the science commission to work in the private sector. He said: "I want to be a real man. I want to do something."

Private versus Public

The official, who I have not named for fear that his comments will get him into political trouble, hopes to start his own venture capital fund. He would like to attract foreign investment since in his view the greatest obstacles holding back Shanghai's indigenous companies are their dependence on the Shanghai government for funds and the Shanghai government's half-hearted embrace of private enterprise. Five years earlier the official had written a report for the Shanghai government advocating it develop the city's private sector more aggressively. But, according to the official, city leaders at the time did not agree. Indeed, despite the city's reputation for producing China's greatest entrepreneurs before 1949,

Shanghai in the reform era has been slow compared with provinces like Guangdong, Fujian, Sichuan, and Yunnan to embrace private industry. The absence of private companies is particularly noticeable in Shanghai's manufacturing sectors. As of early 1998, some 98% of the city's private enterprises were involved in commercial and service industries.[16]

Although developing a significant private business has not been easy in China in general, it has been harder in Shanghai than in these other regions. One of the reasons is that the Shanghai government, by all accounts, has over the years implemented the central government's discriminatory policies against private entrepreneurs more strictly. In the 1980s, those policies were particularly draconian. Private enterprises in China, for instance, were subject to an 80% tax rate, much higher than the tax rate levied on state and collective enterprises. Although budding private entrepreneurs often avoided the private rate by registering illicitly as a collective, they risked going to jail for tax evasion during periodic government campaigns against "bourgeois liberalization." Chen Rong, a former peasant in a rural Shanghai suburb, for instance, closed down his successful garment factory at a huge loss during a crackdown in 1989 after watching another entrepreneur on his street who registered as a collective receive a 1.5-year jail sentence. During the same crackdown, the four Liu brothers in Sichuan province asked the Communist Party Secretary in their county if they should return the 10 million yuan (US$1.2 million) in factories and other assets they had accumulated from chicken farming and supplying animal feed. The Party Secretary refused their offer. According to Liu Yongxing, one of the brothers: "The Party Secretary told us to keep them because that way we would make more contribution to the country. He told us not to worry and that the government would protect us. He told us to develop just as we wanted." The Liu brothers subsequently built their business into China's largest private company—the Hope Group. Meanwhile, the irrepressible Chen Rong decided to take a less high-profile tack in Shanghai. In the early 1990s he started playing China's newly opened stock markets and by the middle of the decade reemerged with his earnings to build a profitable bowling alley equipment business. Still, had he not felt it necessary to shut down his operations in 1989, his company would undoubtedly be much larger today.

After China's paramount leader Deng Xiaoping set off an economic boom in China in 1992, the central government relaxed somewhat its policies toward private enterprise and, following the central government's lead, so did Shanghai. Tax rates became more reasonable, private enterprise zones sprang up in the city's rural suburbs, and by 1997 the number of private enterprises in China's most populous city increased 30 times its 1991 level to reach 68,200.[17] However, the Communist Party still maintained that private enterprise was only a "supplementary part" of the Chinese economy rather than an "important constituent." As a result, discrimination continued, particularly when it came to obtaining bank loans, listing on China's stock exchanges, and importing and exporting. Once again, Shanghai implemented these restrictions well. In 1997 when Vantone Group, a private development and investment company with operations around China, tried to get a loan from a state bank in Shanghai, the bank official told company executives that it was not permitted to give loans to private companies. According to Gao Peng, an urbane, smartly dressed Vantone executive based in Shanghai:

In our own experience, it was much easier to get a loan in Hainan. We got a loan there from a state-run bank. It would also be easier to get a loan in Guangdong. These places are more market-oriented. Shanghai is more conservative than any other place in China in terms of how to differentiate state property from private property.

The only reason Shanghai Just Huahai Metal Products Co. was able to grow into a company with sales of US$150 million by 1998 was that Gui, the metal materials innovator, managed to register it as a foreign joint venture in 1990—even though she funded the firm with private money. The maneuver made Shanghai Just Huahai eligible for tax holidays, import-export rights, bank loans, and other preferential treatment denied private companies. A few months before her arrest on embezzlement charges in July 1999, Gui explained:

The government only gave private enterprises the right to import and export this year. That's eight years after we started importing and exporting. So even today I do not believe it would be possible to have such a large-scale private enterprise as this in Shanghai, although you could probably have it somewhere else in China.

At the 15th Party Congress in Beijing in September 1997, the Communist Party officially upgraded the private sector's official status to a "significant constituent" of China's economy and later amended the country's constitution to reflect the upgrade. China's swelling legions of laid-off workers accounted for the change in semantics. The Party realized that the only way it could create enough jobs to prevent social upheaval was to unshackle its private sector. More bank loans, approval to list shares on China's stock markets, import-export rights, and greater representation in rule-making bodies have been some of the privileges promised. Since the Party Congress, private entrepreneurs in Shanghai have noticed a marked improvement in attitudes. In April 1998, for instance, Shanghai Mayor Xu Kuangdi held a meeting with 12 local private entrepreneurs to hear their concerns. Local newspapers have been full of stories about private enterprise and laid-off workers-turned-private entrepreneurs. Restrictions and fees that made it too costly for private businessmen to enter certain sectors have been eased. State banks, under pressure to shape up their debt-ridden balance sheets, started courting successful entrepreneurs like the 39-year-old Chen Rong. "I feel there's been a big change since the 15th Party Congress," said Chen, who had the honor of attending the April 1998 meeting with the mayor. He was looking forward to even more improvement in the future.

That said, the central government's and hence Shanghai's embrace of the private sector at the onset of the 21st century is still arm's length. Discrimination against private firms in Shanghai, although reduced, has by no means disappeared. They still are prohibited from entering certain fields like financial services and while state banks now want to lend to them, they are far less generous than with comparable state enterprises. Driving into Shanghai in a black sedan from his company headquarters, Chen explained:

Banks started coming after me once they realized my financial status, but they would only give me a small loan. They'd give a state enterprise more. So to obtain enough financing, I have to borrow from several banks. I just thought it was too much trouble to do that. I want to borrow 30 million yuan (US$3.6 million). A state enterprise with my situation in Shanghai could get 100–200 million yuan (US$12–US$24 million) easily. If I were in Guangdong or Sichuan, I probably could get the 100–200 million yuan.

Why have Shanghai authorities been stricter in implementing central government's policies toward private firms? Their behavior may stem from the central government's closer scrutiny of Shanghai as a result of the city's importance to the Chinese economy. Shanghai's status as a stepping stone for officials to posts in the central government also tends to make city leaders more careful. Whatever the issue, Shanghai tends to toe the Party line more closely than most other provinces. But behavior of Shanghai bureaucrats probably has had more to do with Shanghai's position as a bastion of state enterprise in China and the importance of state enterprises to the city's GDP. In 1997, I interviewed Yuan Enzhen, a distinguished professor at the Shanghai Academy of Social Science, about state enterprise reform in Shanghai. In the context of explaining to me why it was critical that Shanghai reform its state enterprises successfully, he commented: "It is very important that Shanghai carry out these reforms because Shanghai is a very important state enterprise base in China. Whenever [President] Jiang Zemin comes to Shanghai, he mentions that Shanghai is the center of state-owned enterprise. So Shanghai has to provide a good example for the entire country." An important part of the Shanghai government's job ultimately has been to protect and improve the value of the state's assets, which the authorities have tried to do by implementing reforms and providing bank loans and other support to state enterprises. They have been reluctant to privatize the city's most important state enterprises and have preferred not to invest government money in private companies. Their attitude is: "Why should we use government money to make you [the private entrepreneur] rich," the official at Shanghai's science commission explained.

Moreover, Shanghai has not needed to develop its private sector to augment its coffers and provide jobs to the same extent as regions that enjoy less government investment, like Guangdong, or that have attracted less foreign investment, like Yunnan. Without money to invest, they encouraged whatever kinds of financing were available. Once private enterprises started accounting for a large proportion of local government tax revenues, local authorities tended to give them support. In Shanghai, private enterprises only made up for 4.2% of the city's fiscal revenue in 1997.[18] In neighboring Zhejiang province, they accounted for 43% of GDP in 1998 (although many of those are probably former rural enterprises).[19] Wang Guoming, the vice secretary general of the Shanghai Private Enterprise Association, a state-affiliated liaison office for the government and private companies, commented:

There are many private enterprises in Shanghai, but the dominant part of the Shanghai economy is state enterprises. The city's pillar industries in particular are still dominated by state enterprises. Private companies can go into sectors that state enterprise can't do or are reluctant to do.

So while private entrepreneurs have opened plenty of restaurants and shops in Shanghai, they have not done much in manufacturing industries.

Shen Hanyao, the president of the Shanghai Institute for Economic Development, added:

In Shanghai, the scale of private enterprises is relatively small because there was strong competition from both state enterprises and foreign-invested enterprises in every field. So private companies in Shanghai have found it harder to compete. If a private investor takes one million yuan (US$12 million) or 10 million yuan (US$1.2 million) to Hainan, where there are few state enterprises and foreign-invested companies, the local government thinks highly of him and gives him support. But in Shanghai one million yuan is almost nothing. It's natural because many multinational corporations invest in Shanghai. If I must make a choice, I want to do business with the multinational corporation because it is bigger, has more money, and can pay more.

Apart from a large state sector and strong foreign investment hindering private sector development, Shanghainese themselves have shown less of an entrepreneurial streak than businessmen in some other parts of China.[20] Repeating oft-heard comments from Shanghainese and non-Shanghainese alike, Zhou Quan, an IDG Technology Venture Investment executive heavily involved in technology projects in China, said:

The Shanghainese make very good workers, managers, and representatives for multinational corporations. They are extremely capable. They follow rules and regulations. But trying to find people who take risks to do something different is difficult in Shanghai. The culture of the city is deeply against it.

I found such remarks surprising at first. After all, before 1949 Shanghai produced some of China's most successful and innovative entrepreneurs.[21] But then again, Shanghai today is no longer a city of immigrants bent on survival, which explains in part residents' relative lack of entrepreneurial drive. Of the more than 600,000 Chinese living in the foreign-run International Settlement in Shanghai in 1915, more than three-quarters of them came from Jiangsu, Zhejiang, Guangdong, and Anhui provinces.[22] Shanghai was the promised land, offering laissez-faire capitalism and refuge from famine and political upheaval in the hinterland. Ningbo natives soon dominated finance, Cantonese excelled in retail, and former Wuxi residents did well in textiles. Shanghai was a melting pot of talent from around China and private entrepreneurship flourished. The Communists, however, restricted migration after the 1949 takeover. Although systems for controlling people's movements have broken down in the reform era and the Shanghai government has set up programs to attract talented Chinese from other parts of the country, it is still not easy for people from other provinces to become permanent Shanghai residents or move to Shanghai without first having an employment contract. Shenzhen, which was no more than farmland 20 years ago, is by all accounts the most entrepreneurial place in China, in part because it is populated with Chinese from all around the country who left their homes in search of opportunity. "Shenzhen has a lot of people who are trying to do something new, like in San Francisco. Shenzhen is extreme," says Zhou. He and other business people I've interviewed have also found people in Beijing to be more willing to take risks than the Shanghainese, which helps explain why IDG has 30 investments in the capital and only seven in Shanghai. Beijing also enjoys some characteristics of an immigrant culture, as the central government throughout the history of the People's Republic has recruited talented people from the provinces. The chief executive officers of IDG's 30 high-tech investments in Beijing, for instance, are generally in their early thirties and second-generation immigrants. "These are not real Beijing people," Zhou commented.

In some ways, the same lack of desperation that has deterred the Shanghai government from embracing private enterprise seems also to have stifled risk-taking passion in the city's residents. Shanghai is well-off compared with most other Chinese provinces and salaries are relatively high. When state enterprises were strong, there were always plenty of stable jobs available. In the 1990s, young Shanghainese could find high-paying white-collar jobs at multinational corporations. Taking risks tends to be easier for people who have little to lose, like Chen Rong, the Shanghainese entrepreneur who started out life as a poor peasant in the city's rural suburbs. Since the Shanghainese have generally felt that they have something to lose, their capacity for taking risks has been lower. Moreover, Shanghainese are known throughout China for their pragmatism and ability to calculate the bottom line in every situation. Given what they would have to give up to strike out on their own, they tend to decide the risk is not worth it. Interestingly, the recent Internet craze in Asia has kindled an entrepreneurial spark among educated Shanghainese, probably because they can see a clear upside. (Internet entrepreneurs generally do not have to invest much themselves and are targeted for financing by venture capital firms like IDG. All that Internet entrepreneurs really stand to lose is a bit of time.) Talented Shanghainese who have a good job, but would like to start their own company, report receiving heavy pressure from family members not to jeopardize their future. And although Shanghainese are money-oriented, it doesn't mean they are obsessed with becoming rich. Pan Ming, the Shanghainese economist, explained:

People say that they can still fill their stomachs, so that's good enough. I haven't seen the mentality of being hungry to make it big. This is something the Shanghainese lack. Shanghainese families are concerned with having a comfortable lifestyle. They like to make their home very delicate and beautiful.

Chen Rong, the successful private entrepreneur, added: "The Shanghainese people tend to be satisfied with a little wealth. Once they earn one to two million yuan (US$120,000–US$240,000) they think it's enough."

Who's the Boss?

In early April 2000, Huang Qifan, the chairman of the Shanghai Economic Commission, reported at a press conference in Shanghai that the city had basically completed efforts to restructure its state enterprises. He reeled off a list of impressive statistics indicating that Shanghai was in sight of meeting the central government's deadline for turning around loss-making state enterprises by the end of 2000. For instance, the state sector's asset-liability ratio fell to 52% in 1999 from 84% in 1994. Only 20% of the city's 546 large and mid-sized state companies in 1999 incurred losses.[23] How did Shanghai achieve these feats? According to Huang, the city did it by transforming the shareholding structure of its large and medium state enterprises. "Ninety percent of Shanghai's state-owned enterprises have been transformed into companies of which 80% now have multiple investors."[24] It also accomplished the task by "releasing" its small state enterprises and its unprofitable ones, thereby shrinking the city's state sector. He said: "Shanghai industrial enterprises have achieved a breakthrough. An exit strategy for loss-making enterprises has been established and we're operating under the rule of survival of the fittest." The Shanghai government, like governments around China, has been busy merging, closing, selling, and listing companies; downsizing workers; selling enterprise property to relieve debts; and extending privileges to pet conglomerates to meet Premier Zhu Rongji's deadline.

Unfortunately, unless these companies have overcome their management problems—starting with government interference—these improved results may just be temporary. Jonathan Woetzel, the Shanghai-based principal at McKinsey & Co., offered a telling anecdote. The firm, whose consulting contracts are a good indicator of enterprise restructuring activity in China, employed 35 people in its Shanghai office and 35 people in its Beijing office at the end of 1999. However, 60 of those people worked in Beijing and only 10 in Shanghai; in other words 25 employees in the Shanghai office traveled to Beijing for work on a regular basis. The firm was also doing a lot of business in Shenzhen, the special economic zone bordering Hong Kong. The reason: many more companies in Beijing and Shenzhen than in Shanghai had hired the consulting firm to help them restructure their operations, which Woetzel attributed to the Shanghai economic bureaucracy's conservative, control-oriented attitudes. And if more companies in Beijing and Shenzhen are seriously restructuring now, rather than simply turning themselves into shareholding companies, they probably will do better than Shanghai companies in the future. "They will come down here and buy Shanghai companies," Woetzel predicted, adding, "Our guy is missing the boat."

Shanghai, with its competitive advantage in capital intensive projects and ability to attract foreign investment in pillar industries, will have something of a car, steel, and chemical industry in the future—and even some pharmaceuticals and electronics companies. But Shanghai will have few internationally competitive homegrown brands, like Legend or Haier. The software of a market economy has not moved into place quickly enough and the moment of opportunity has in many cases already passed.

In the end, manufacturing in the city will likely be built more on the efforts of foreign multinationals rather than on the city's indigenous manufacturers. Foreign-invested firms contributed almost 40% of the city's industrial output in 1998 and, they accounted for almost two-thirds of all exports during the first half of 1999. So rather than resembling Taiwan, which derives its economic energy mainly from homegrown entrepreneurs, Shanghai in the future will probably look more like Singapore, drawing much of its vitality from multinational corporations.

Although the Shanghai government embraced foreign investment in the 1990s, foreign company dominance and the virtual extinction of the pure Shanghai brand were not the intended outcomes of the municipal authorities' strategy. Shanghai was also supposed to be a center of state enterprise, which is why city authorities have spent so much effort during the decade implementing reforms aimed at improving company performance. But the dominance of multinational management is happening by default partly because of the Shanghai government's heavy handedness with its own companies.

That said, at the start of the 21st century the Shanghai authorities do not appear to bemoan their dependence on foreign management for manufacturing vibrancy. At the April 4, 2000, press conference in Shanghai, the economic commission's Huang told reporters that China's entry into the World Trade Organization did not concern him much. Shanghai, after all, had joint ventures with two of the world's largest automobile manufacturers, Volkswagen and General Motors, which were producing the most competitive cars in the domestic market. By teaming up with the largest chemical companies in the world, he said, Shanghai will beat the competition in the domestic chemical industry.

Where does this leave the Shanghainese? It leaves them with a prosperous city that derives most of its wealth from its service industries and foreign investment. Not a bad place to be. Indeed, in terms of material comfort and pleasant physical environment, there are far worse fates than resembling Singapore. But unless the Shanghai government can stand back and let indigenous private enterprise flourish, the trend also leaves Shanghainese mostly in the employ of others. Ironically, history stands to repeat itself. Just as before 1949, Shanghainese will owe their livelihood to foreigners.

Notes

[1] Christopher Howe, "Industrialization under Conditions of Long-Run Population Stability: Shanghai's Achievement and Prospect," in *Shanghai: Revolution & Development in an Asian Metropolis*; ed. Christopher Howe; Cambridge University Press; p. 157.

[2] Ibid., p. 167.

[3] Yang Dongping, *City Monsoon: The Cultural Spirit of Beijing and Shanghai* (Chengshi Jifeng: Beijing he Shanghai de Wenhua Jingshen), Oriental Press (Dongfang Chuban Shi), 1994, p. 314.

[4] Ibid., p. 318.

[5] *See* Christopher Howe, op. cit., pp. 180–184.

[6] Ibid., p. 316.

[7] *Shanghai Star*, Mar. 12, 1999.

[8] Ibid., Oct. 2, 1998.

[9] *Shanghai Today*, Vol. 1 Issue No. 4, Aug. 1998, p. 21.

[10] According to a survey of 80 department stores and shopping malls in Shanghai in the first quarter of 1997, Shanghai-made color televisions and microwave ovens had a 17% market share, air conditioners had 37%, and refrigerators had 41%. *See Shanghai Star*, May 13, 1997.

[11] *South China Morning Post*, Mar. 1, 1995.

[12] *Shanghai Star*, Jul. 7, 1998.

[13] The five companies are Huawei, Zhongxing, Datang, Julong, and Jinpeng. Of them, Shenzhen-based Huawei and Zhongxing are the leaders, doing well both in traditional switchboard business and their diversification into higher-margin telecom products.

[14] *Shanghai Star*, Dec. 7, 1999.

[15] *The Asian Wall Street Journal*, Nov. 15, 1999.

[16] *Liberation Daily*, Jan. 3, 1998.

[17] *Liberation Daily*, Jan. 3, 1998.

[18] Ibid.

[19] *Shanghai Star*, July 23, 1999.

[20] *See* Wong Siu-lin, "The Entrepreneurial Spirit: Shanghai and Hong Kong Compared," *Shanghai: Transformation and Modernization under China's Open Policy*, ed. Y.M. Yeung and Sung Yun-Wing, The Chinese University Press, Hong Kong, pp. 26–43.

[21] *See* Marie-Claire Bergere, *The Golden Age of the Chinese Bourgeoisie 1911–1937*, Cambridge University Press, 1989, pp. 99–139.

[22] Betty Peh-T'I Wei, *Shanghai: Crucible of Modern China Hong Kong*, Oxford University Press, 1987, pp. 123–124.

[23] *South China Morning Post*, Apr. 5, 2000.

[24] Ibid.

9

Conclusion: Waiting for Shanghai

S hanghai in the year 2000 reminds me of a body that has been revived from a deep freeze and displays great outward signs of vitality. Upon closer examination, however, it is clear that the blood still does not pump fast enough to certain key organs. The medicine so far administered—favorable treatment from Beijing, competent top local level management, and plenty of foreign investment—has made the heart pump again, but it has yet to eradicate some serious clotting leftover from the city's Communist past.

China's biggest city has done well at building the hardware of a thriving, modern metropolis. Few cities in the world can boast of cutting traffic snarls in half while spurring nearly a decade's worth of double-digit growth. Few cities in Asia, and in China in particular, can point to an improving pollution record. Few have laid off so many workers over a short period without serious social unrest. Most Shanghai residents today enjoy more opportunity than ever before and are working hard to take advantage of it.

The Shanghai government deserves credit for its role in managing the city's spectacular urban renewal. Granted, the city in the 1990s has enjoyed more favorable conditions than any other in China, including preferential government policies and an avalanche of foreign investment. But rather than squandering the opportunity presented by the central government's call to make Shanghai the "Dragon Head" of China's economic development, Shanghai leaders seized the moment. Had the

Shanghai government been more corrupt than honest or more incompetent than capable, Shanghai would not win generally favorable reviews from foreign investors who do business around China.

However, the lesson of Shanghai in the 1990s is that heavy government intervention works for some things, but not for others. It works for quickly erecting highways, digging sewer systems, building convention centers, hosting high-profile events, streamlining bureaucracy, laying off workers in an orderly fashion, and even enforcing laws when there is a will to do so. They city's deep state-planning background combined with the detail-oriented and conscientious nature of many Shanghainese makes the Shanghai government well suited for implementing big projects and achieving tangible objectives, normally on deadline. But the Shanghai experience also shows that heavy government intervention does not work well for building strong indigenous brands, encouraging entre-preneurship, nourishing innovation, and unleashing creativity in a market economy. As global competition grows, it is these latter skills that will be critically important for success. Roads and other infrastructure in Silicon Valley illicit numerous complaints from users, but the area is still a mecca for research and development and a cradle of the New Economy in the United States. What matters increasingly for Shanghai is this softer side of city-building.

The challenge for Shanghai in the 21st century will be to put a modern city's software into place—things like the rule of law; free-flowing economic and business information; greater transparency and account-ability in the public and private sectors; vibrant and well-regulated capital markets populated by good companies and strong intermediaries; intellectual and artistic freedom; greater political responsiveness to local constituents; and decision-making autonomy from Beijing. Many of these tasks have been stymied by the Communist Party's desire to maintain its monopoly on power.

This is not to say that Shanghai has not made headway in building some of the softer components of a world-class business center. Take respect for intellectual property rights, the lack of which has been a long-standing problem for foreign investors in China. The experience of Danish entrepreneur Simon Lichtenberg, who owns the China franchise for Denmark's second largest furniture group,[1] shows both how far Shanghai has come and how far it has to go. In 1997 Lichtenberg discovered that 12 factories in Shanghai were copying the Danish company's "Bo Concept" designs. He sought redress with various government agencies in Shanghai that have jurisdiction over intellectual property matters—the State Administration for Industry and Commerce at both municipal and district levels, the Shanghai Patent & Trademark Bureau, and the courts. With the help of these agencies he eventually succeeded in curbing the copying. But it has been a long, hard slog requiring numerous visits to the bureaus, help from the Danish Embassy, letters to Shanghai's mayor, and dogged persistence. "It took an abnormal amount of effort," says Lichtenberg. Bo Concept's lawsuit against a particularly damaging copycat, started in June 1999, has been stuck in Shanghai Intermediate court for over a year (as of August 2000). Because so few precedents exist in China, the judge has felt it necessary to seek the advice of experts in Beijing. On one hand, the situation shows how seriously courts in Shanghai take cases involving foreigners. On the other, it demonstrates the paucity of legal expertise plaguing municipal court systems in China.

Some people may be disappointed to learn that Shanghai's reemergence is not leading to the return of Old Shanghai. Certainly, some phenomena from before 1949 have reappeared: There are more foreigners, more businesses, more opportunities, more pleasure, more prostitutes, more drugs in Shanghai than 10 years ago. These are by-products of the freer, more market-oriented society that Shanghai has become. But Old Shanghai's excessive debauchery, acute inequality, and overwhelming commercial and cultural dominance are unlikely to be repeated. Old Shanghai was a product of a unique time in history when Britain, France, Japan and the United States controlled its territory and ignored Chinese law. Businessmen and gangsters ran the International Settlement, taking a hands-off approach to regulation and putting their own profit and pleasure above all else. Workers, including children, often toiled seven days a week, 12–16 hours a day. So exploited, impoverished and diseased were they that Chinese in Shanghai lived only to an average age of 27 in the 1920s—the life expectancy of Europe in the Middle Ages.[2] But with warlords ravaging the rest of China during the first quarter of the 1900s, Old Shanghai was the freest, safest, and most prosperous city in the country. It became the promised land for China's dislocated peasants and intellectuals, fostering conditions conducive to creativity and entrepreneurship. Similarly, foreign refugees and adventurers landed in droves on Shanghai's shores since the city was the only one in the world that did not require passports or other papers.

Shanghai at the beginning of the 21st century was governed much differently. It is run by an interventionist, control-oriented bureaucracy that is tightly linked to the central government in Beijing. One of its primary functions is to ensure social stability, which means both stifling political dissent, limiting domestic and international immigration, and providing at least a modicum of economic assistance to its citizenry. Most residents do not live in squalor and they are not dying in the city's streets. (Today average life expectancy in Shanghai is well over 70 years.) At the same time, intellectuals and artists do not enjoy greater freedom from government censors than artists and intellectuals in other parts of the country—and in some cases they enjoy even less. Vice is back, but Shanghai is not once again turning into the "Whore of the Orient"— illegal licentious behavior is far more flagrant and less controlled in other cities in China and Asia. Foreign business has also made a comeback, but foreigners generally abide by Chinese government regulations and do not run the city for their own profit as they once did. And unlike in China's pre-Communist days, the city is not an oasis of stability in a desert of chaos. Urban centers around China, such as Shenzhen, Guangzhou, and Beijing, are also modernizing and competing with Shanghai to lure China's best students, artists, and entrepreneurs. Likewise, when Old Shanghai reigned supreme in Asia, other metropolises in the region, like Hong Kong and Singapore, were villages by comparison. But at the start of the 21st century, Shanghai is the one trying to catch up to fierce competitors. In short, Old Shanghai was an aberration of history, never to be repeated.

And yet the world has an unending fascination with Old Shanghai— a curiosity that has spawned over the past decade a cottage industry of books, movies, paintings, restaurants, clubs, and even retail outlets that aim to capitalize on people's desire to experience that "golden" era. Just look at the commercial success of Shanghai artist Chen Yifei's series of paintings depicting scenes from Old Shanghai, which have sold for hundreds of thousands of dollars. Foreign expatriate groups in Shanghai try to recapture the ambiance by holding balls and parties with pre-1949 themes on the grounds of magnificent art-deco establishments. Donning a tuxedo and gown, my husband and I on several occasions joined hundreds of other expatriates and a scattering of Chinese to sip champagne and twirl the night away in elegant ballrooms—just as kindred spirits might have done 50 years earlier.

It is easy for foreigners to get caught up in pre-1949 nostalgia, which can lead them to attribute qualities to Shanghai and its residents that often do not jibe with current reality. The city may have nurtured many of

China's most prominent private entrepreneurs before 1949, but it has yet to do the same in the reform era. Today the Shanghainese are not known in China for their entrepreneurial, risk-taking flair. Other cities, such as Shenzhen, offer a more welcoming environment to private businessmen. Despite the Shanghainese reputation for business savvy, Shanghai's local consumer brands failed to capitalize on their early head start and have fared poorly during the intense market competition of the 1990s. When I think of great indigenous Chinese brands today, names like Legend, Haier, Kelon, Hope and Huawei spring quickly to mind. None of them originated in Shanghai. Old Shanghai in its heyday was China's most active and innovative cultural center, but in 2000, Beijing wins that title hands down. Old Shanghai is renowned for being China's financial heart and Asia's financial hub in the 1920s. But with so many of China's important financial institutions and decision-makers currently headquartered in Beijing and with so little international business conducted in the city, it clearly can't claim the same today. The city's illustrious past has helped heighten excitement about its reemergence, but such nostalgia combined with exaggerated government, corporate and, media rhetoric has skewed perceptions, creating expectations of a speedier recovery for Shanghai than is possible. Although clearly a city on the ascendance, Shanghai still has a ways to go before it can be considered the New York of China—let alone of Asia and the world.

The biggest breakthrough in recent years toward knocking down the barriers holding back Shanghai is China's pending ascension to the World Trade Organization (WTO) and the U.S. Congress's vote in May 2000 to grant China "permanent normal trading relations (PNTR)." Had the United States balked at China's WTO entry or voted against extending normal trading rights to China, it would have dealt a severe blow to reform efforts in Shanghai and China in general. Rejecting China's bid would have strengthened the position of inward-looking, xenophobic conservatives within the Chinese leadership who believe that the United States is trying to contain China. Reform-minded leaders who fought hard for China's entry into the WTO would have lost credibility and political power. The momentum for reform, which sagging economic growth and sporadic social unrest in the late 1990s had already slowed, would have faltered further. Rebuffing China's bid might have also made President Jiang Zemin more susceptible to hard-liners advocating the use of force to reunify Taiwan with China. War with Taiwan and China's ensuing pariah status in the international community would certainly have set back Shanghai's goal of becoming an important international financial, business, and cultural center.

Luckily, trends today look more favorable. While China will unlikely be a perfect citizen in the WTO, the momentum in China is clearly gaining for greater economic openness and fairer market competition. China's pending WTO ascension and permanent normal trading relations with the United States have strengthened the hand of reformers, which will help them push through difficult reforms in the future. As for Shanghai specifically, the city stands to benefit more than most from China's WTO membership. WTO entry will slowly open China's services sector to foreign investors. It stands to reason that Shanghai, as China's anointed services center, will attract a significant portion of new foreign investment in the sector. China's entry into the trading organization will reinforce Shanghai's cosmopolitan, outward-looking impulses. Moreover, given Shanghai's symbiotic relationship with the central government, the more change-oriented and daring the leadership in Beijing, the greater the chance of implementing reforms needed for Shanghai to develop into a world-class city. The quicker national and city leaders push through reform, the shorter our wait for Shanghai.

Notes

[1] *See* Chapter 7, p. 32.
[2] Harriet Sargeant, *Shanghai*, Jonathan Cape, London, p. 151.